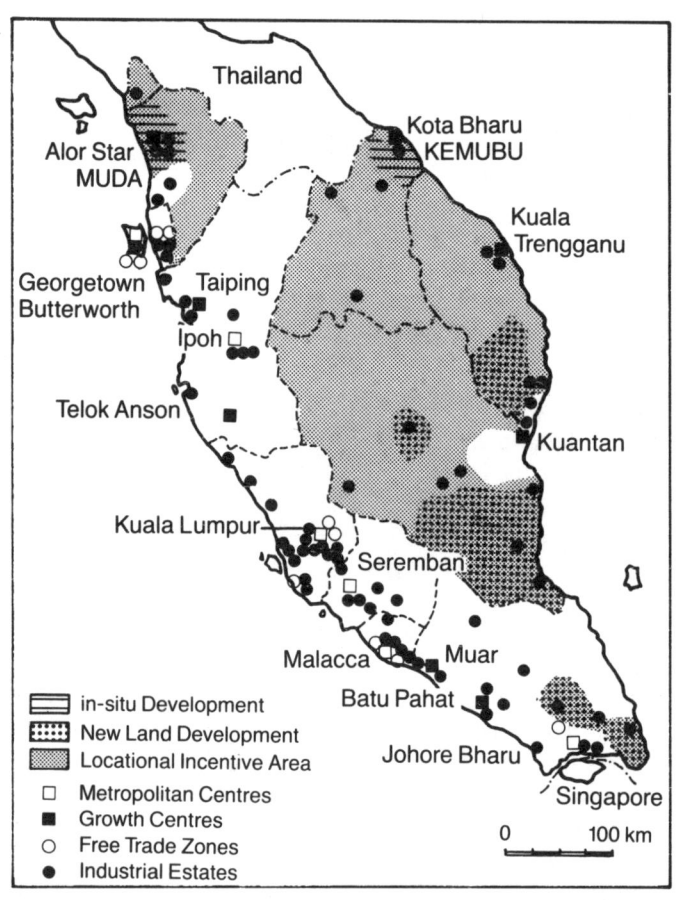
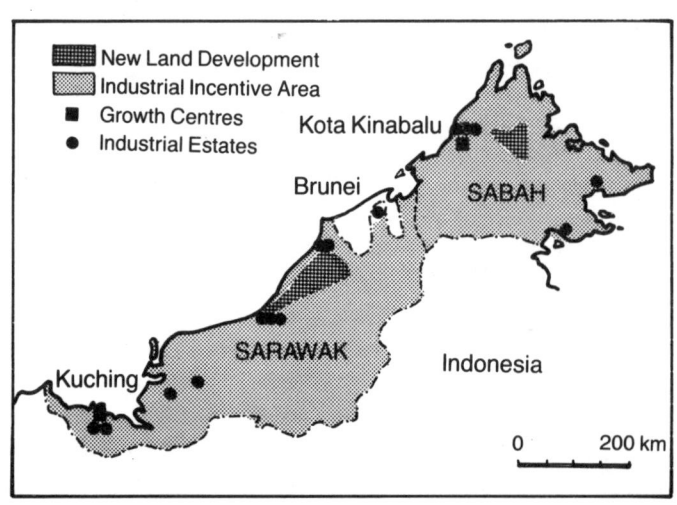

INDUSTRIALISING MALAYSIA

Despite growing concern over environmental issues and the sustainability of economic growth, industrialisation is still generally associated with progress and development. This is particularly true in Third World countries where industrialisation is often the nation's top priority.

Industrialising Malaysia presents a critical analysis of the experience of industrialisation in Malaysia, examining the role, impact and efficacy of post-independence industrialisation policies. The volume seeks to refocus attention on some major intended as well as unintended implications and consequences of policies and performance. A wide range of issues is covered: in addition to general historical commentaries and sectoral studies, there are analyses of Direct Foreign Investment, technology, linkages, Free Trade Zones, Industrial Estates and rural development. In discussing these issues the authors also examine the duality in Malaysian industrialisation between the import-substituting sector and export-oriented industries. Throughout, arguments and analyses are clearly presented and in many instances are supported by case studies while the final chapter offers advice for future policy options.

The editor, Jomo K.S., is professor of economics at the University of Malaysia. The book has a wide range of international contributors with half drawn from Malaysia and the other half from India, the USA, the United Kingdom and Australia.

INDUSTRIALISING MALAYSIA

Policy, performance, prospects

Edited by
Jomo K.S.

London and New York

First published 1993
by Routledge
11 New Fetter Lane, London EC4P 4EE

Simultaneously published in the USA and Canada
by Routledge
29 West 35th Street, New York, NY 10001

© 1993 Jomo K.S.

Typeset in 10/12pt Garamond by
Ponting–Green Publishing Services, Chesham, Bucks
Printed in Great Britain by
Mackays of Chatham PLC, Chatham, Kent

All rights reserved. No part of this book may be reprinted or reproduced or utilized in any form or by any electronic, mechanical, or other means, now known or hereafter invented, including photocopying and recording, or in any storage or information retrieval system, without permission in writing from the publishers.

British Library Cataloguing in Publication Data
A catalogue record for this book is available from
the British Library

ISBN 0–415–09647–2

Library of Congress Cataloging in Publication Data
has been applied for

ISBN 0–415–09647–2

CONTENTS

List of Figures vii
List of Tables viii
Notes on Contributors xii
Acknowledgements xiv
List of Abbreviations xv

INTRODUCTION 1
Jomo K.S.

1 MALAYSIAN INDUSTRIALISATION IN HISTORICAL PERSPECTIVE 14
Jomo K.S. and Chris Edwards

2 LABOUR FLEXIBILITY IN THE MALAYSIAN MANUFACTURING SECTOR 40
Guy Standing

3 DIRECT FOREIGN INVESTMENT IN THE MALAYSIAN INDUSTRIAL SECTOR 77
Anuwar Ali and Wong Poh Kam

4 FREE TRADE ZONES AND INDUSTRIAL DEVELOPMENT IN MALAYSIA 118
Rajah Rasiah

5 MALAYSIAN MANUFACTURING SECTOR LINKAGES 147
Leslie O'Brien

6 MALAYSIAN RURAL INDUSTRIALISATION STRATEGIES IN NATIONAL PERSPECTIVE 163
Ashwani Saith

7 TECHNOLOGY TRANSFER IN THE MALAYSIAN MANUFACTURING SECTOR: BASIC ISSUES AND FUTURE DIRECTIONS 190
Anuwar Ali

8	ELECTRONICS AND INDUSTRIALISATION: APPROACHING THE 21ST CENTURY *David O'Connor*	210
9	TEXTILES AND CLOTHING: SUNRISE OR SUNSET INDUSTRY? *David O'Connor*	234
10	MADE-IN-MALAYSIA: THE PROTON PROJECT *S. Jayasankaran*	272
11	PROSPECTS FOR MALAYSIAN INDUSTRIALISATION IN LIGHT OF EAST ASIAN NIC EXPERIENCES *Jomo K.S.*	286
12	STATE INTERVENTION AND INDUSTRIALISATION IN SOUTH KOREA: LESSONS FOR MALAYSIA *Chris Edwards*	302
13	POLICY OPTIONS FOR MALAYSIAN INDUSTRIALISATION *Chris Edwards and Jomo K.S.*	316
	Statistical Appendix	335
	Bibliography of unpublished official sources	341
	Index	343

FIGURES

Figure 1.1 Relationship between GDP per capita and the share of manufacturing value added in GDP in selected economies, 1984   17
Figure 1.2 Malaysia: real effective exchange rates, 1960–88   31
Figure 3.1 Approved equity investment trend in the Malaysian manufacturing sector, 1971–87   78
Figure 3.2 Proposed called-up capital, 1984 and 1987   80
Figure 4.1 Free Trade Zones in Peninsular Malaysia, 1989   120
Figure 12.1 Price distortions and growth in the 1970s   304
Figure S.1 Manufacturing sector: contribution to GDP, 1960–2000   336

TABLES

1.1	Manufacturing's share of gross domestic product and employment, 1947–91	14
1.2	Average annual growth rates of manufacturing value added and manufacturing exports, 1971–89	15
1.3	Exports of manufactured goods, 1970–91	16
1.4	Gross domestic product by sector, 1960–89 (%)	18
1.5	Protectionism in Malaysia, 1962–82	19
1.6	Manufacturing protection and the subsidy equivalent, 1969 and 1979	20
1.7	Manufacturing sector effective rates of protection on profits, 1970 and 1979 (M$bn)	21
1.8	Effective rates of protection by manufacturing sub-sector, Peninsular Malaysia, 1962–72	23
1.9	EPZs in Malaysia, 1972–82 (M$m)	27
1.10	Wages in manufacturing, 1963–83	27
1.11	Economic gains to Malaysia from EPZs and LMWs, 1972–97	28
1.12	Public sector investment and foreign debt, 1980s	30
1.13	Balance of payments, 1970–87 (US$bn)	30
1.14	Terms of trade, 1965–87	31
1.15	Gross domestic product (GDP) and net output in manufacturing (NOM), 1971–89	33
1.16	Gender distribution of manufacturing employment by sector, 1957–85	35
1.17	Malaysian manufacturing, 1987	37
2.1	Change in manufacturing employment by industry, 1985–8 (% of establishments)	55
2.2	Change in employment by ownership, 1985–8 (% of establishments)	55
2.3	Expected/planned employment change in next two years, by industry, 1988 (%)	56
2.4	Main factor besides demand affecting employment, by industry, 1986–8 (%)	58

TABLES

2.5	Main factor besides demand expected to affect employment in next two years, by industry, 1988 (%)	59
2.6	Change in employment, by state, 1985–8 (%)	60
2.7	Expected/planned employment change in next two years, by state, 1988 (%)	61
2.8	Change in employment, by establishment size in 1985, 1985–8 (%)	62
2.9	Expected/planned employment change in next two years, by establishment size, 1988 (%)	62
2.10	Change in value of sales in past two years and the perceived impact on employment, 1988 (%)	64
2.11	Establishments whose increased sales had 'increased employment', by establishment size, 1988 (%)	64
2.12	Establishments whose reduced sales had 'decreased employment', by establishment size, 1988 (%)	65
2.13	Main form of temporary work arrangement, by establishment size, 1988 (%)	66
2.14	Whether or not temporary workers given new contracts, by establishment size, 1988 (%)	67
3.1	Trend of DFI flows in industrial projects granted approval, 1971–88	78
3.2	Distribution of approved projects by degree of foreign participation, 1984–7	79
3.3	DFI stock in manufacturing firms in actual production, 1981–6	81
3.4	Equity capital stock ownership structure in the manufacturing sector, 1978 and 1985 (%)	82
3.5	Ownership and paid-up capital of companies in production, by race, industry and size of company, 1983	82
3.6	Share of manufacturing industries by foreign majority-controlled firms, 1974–85	83
3.7	Distribution of employment and capital structure by industry of companies in production as at 31 December 1986	85
3.8	Sources of foreign equity in industrial companies in production, 1986 and in approved projects, 1980–7	86
3.9	The top five countries in terms of paid-up capital by industrial sector as at 31 December 1986	88
3.10	Before-tax probability estimates of manufacturing firms, by ownership, 1970–85	92
3.11	After-tax probability estimates of manufacturing firms, by ownership, 1970–85	93
3.12	Export and import propensity of manufacturing firms, by ownership, 1970–85	94
3.13	Investment propensity of manufacturing firms, by ownership, 1970–85	95

TABLES

3.14	Tax as a percentage of total profit of manufacturing firms, by ownership, 1970–85	97
3.15	Profile of parent TNCs	100
3.16	Profile of TNC operations in Malaysia	104
3.17	Forms of transnational corporate involvement in selected industries in developing countries	106
4.1	Free Trade Zones in Malaysia, 1987	121
4.2	Paid-up capital in Free Trade Zone firms, 1987	128
4.3	Ownership of Free Trade Zone firms, 1982	129
4.4	Free Trade Zone firms and employment, 1972–87	134
4.5	FTZ employment characteristics by industry, 1987	136
4.6	FTZ and non-FTZ manufactured exports, 1972–82	137
4.7	Raw materials, capital equipment and sales of Free Trade Zone firms, 1972–82 (M$m)	141
5.1	Type of goods produced, by industry, 1985	149
5.2	Source of production equipment and instrumentation	156
5.3	Source of inputs, by industry	157
5.4	Destination of outputs (market), by industry	158
7.1	Types of technology transfer agreements, 1970–87	196
7.2	Technology transfer agreements, by country of origin, 1975–87	197
7.3	Technology transfer agreements, by industry groups, 1975–87	198
7.4	Receipts and payments of rent and royalties, 1980–8	199
7.5	Interest and royalty payment outflows from Malaysia, 1982–7	200
7.6	Estimated total royalties for approved agreements, by year, 1985–7	200
8.1	Output shares of major sectors of the electronics industry, 1982 (%)	212
8.2	Growth trends in the electronics industry, 1986–8	222
9.1	Share of manufacturing value added and merchandising exports contributed by textiles and clothing	236
9.2	Exports, imports and import/export ratios for textiles and garments, 1984–8 (M$m)	237
9.3	OECD imports of textiles and clothing, by region/country of origin, 1987	237
9.4	Comparison of average hourly labour costs in spinning and weaving, 1990	241
9.5	Selected characteristics of the textile and clothing sectors, 1984	242
9.6	Distribution of spinning capacity, by country, 1985	243
9.7	Distribution of weaving capacity, by country, 1987	244
9.8	Exports of textiles and clothing, 1963–90 (US$bn)	246
9.9	Textile yarn, fabrics and related products: imports into OECD from selected countries, 1975–87 (US$m)	247
9.10	Apparel and clothing accessories: imports into OECD from selected countries, 1975–87 (US$m)	248

TABLES

9.11	Net trade balances with developing countries in textiles and clothing, 1973–88 (US$bn)	252
9A.1	Hong Kong: exports, imports and trade balance for textile products, 1978–86 (US$m)	261
9A.2	Republic of Korea: exports, imports and trade balance for textiles, 1981–5 (US$'000)	262
9A.3	Taiwan: exports, imports and trade balance for textiles, 1979–86 (US$'000)	264
9A.4	Thailand: exports, imports and trade balance for textile products, 1984–7 (US$'000)	265
9A.5	Indonesia: exports, imports and trade balance for textile products, 1983–8 (US$'000 and kg '000)	266
11.1	Manufacturing sector growth indices, 1970 and 1990 (%)	287
11.2	Average growth rates in East Asian NICs and Malaysia, 1965–88 (%)	288
11.3	Contribution of manufacturing to GDP in East Asian NICs and Malaysia, 1965–88 (%)	288
11.4	Contribution to exports and imports in East Asian NICs and Malaysia, 1965–88 (%)	289
11.5	Literacy rates and real wages in East Asian NICs and Malaysia	293
12.1	Education: South Korea, Malaysia and the LDCs, 1965 and 1985	309
12.2	GDP, population and manufacturing industry: South Korea and Malaysia, 1965 and 1987	313
13.1	Studies of industrial policy in Malaysia in the 1980s	318
S.1	Gross domestic product, by industry of origin, 1970–2000 (M$m in 1978 prices)	335
S.2	Unemployment and employment, 1985–2000	336
S.3	Foreign participation by selected countries in approved projects, 1985–91	337
S.4	Investments approved by MIDA in manufacturing projects, 1987–91	337
S.5	Approved projects by ownership, 1987–91	338
S.6	Distribution of industrial estates by state, as at 1 January 1992	339
S.7	Free Trade Zones by state, as at 1 January 1992	340

NOTES ON CONTRIBUTORS

Anuwar Ali (PhD, Canterbury, 1983) is Associate Professor in the Faculty of Economics, National University of Malaysia, Bangi, Selangor. He has written extensively on Malaysian industrialisation and technology issues.

Chris Edwards (PhD, East Anglia, 1975) is Senior Lecturer in the School of Development Studies, University of East Anglia, Norwich, UK, author of *The Fragmented World* and co-author of *Why Economists Disagree?* He has worked on Malaysian industrialisation since the late 1960s, wrote his PhD thesis on the subject and was recently UNIDO technical adviser to the Malaysian government.

S. Jayasankaran (BSc, Malaya, 1977) is a senior journalist with *Malaysian Business* and has written extensively on Malaysian political economy.

Jomo K.S. (PhD, Harvard, 1978) is Professor in the Faculty of Economics and Administration, University of Malaya, Kuala Lumpur, Malaysia. He is author of *A Question of Class: Capital, the State and Uneven Development in Malaya* and *Growth and Structural Change in the Malaysian Economy*, and editor of *Islamic Economic Alternatives*, among others.

Leslie O'Brien (PhD, Monash, 1979) is with the Economic Development Division of the ACT Chief Minister's Department, Canberra. She previously held an appointment to the Industrialisation in Southeast Asia Program in the Research School of Pacific Studies at the Australian National University. Since 1973 she has worked on industrialisation and development in Singapore and Malaysia.

David C. O'Connor (MA, Stanford, 1978) is at the OECD (Organization for Economic Co-operation and Development) Development Centre, Paris, and has written extensively on development issues in Southeast Asia.

Rajah Rasiah (PhD, Cambridge, 1992) is a Lecturer in the Faculty of Economics, National University of Malaysia. He has written a great deal on industrialisation in Malaysia.

NOTES ON CONTRIBUTORS

Ashwani Saith (PhD, Cambridge, 1975) is Professor of Rural Economics at the Institute of Social Studies, The Hague, and has published a great deal on rural development issues.

Guy Standing (PhD, Cambridge, 1975) is in the Labour Market Research Department, International Labour Office, Geneva, and has worked on Malaysia since the early 1980s. He has published extensively on labour issues.

Wong Poh Kam (PhD, MIT, 1979) is Senior Lecturer in the Faculty of Business Management, National University of Singapore, and has written extensively on Malaysian industrial and urban development issues.

ACKNOWLEDGEMENTS

This volume was originally conceived in 1987 as I was preparing an article on Malaysian industrialisation for publication in a special issue of *Political Economy* (Vol. 3, No. 2) edited by Amiya Bagchi. I was encouraged by Chris Edwards in early 1988 while on sabbatical in Cambridge, England. Later, several former colleagues, especially Anuwar Ali, supported the effort. Ashwani Saith, Guy Standing, Rajah Rasiah and especially David O'Connor all willingly contributed. Later, Leslie O'Brien and Jayasankaran helped to fill in some gaps. Chris Edwards, David O'Connor and Paul Lubeck also gave me some useful critical feedback on the earlier drafts of the papers in this book.

Although their proposed contributions did not quite fit into this volume, I also appreciate the willingness of two former colleagues, Chee Peng Lim and H. Osman-Rani, to contribute to this effort. An unplanned by-product of this book is another one entitled *Promotion of Small-Scale Industries and Strategies for Rural Industrialisation: The Malaysian Experience*, published by the Friedrich Ebert Stiftung in Kuala Lumpur in cooperation with the Institute of Strategic and International Studies (ISIS). This includes Chee's paper and the longer original version of Saith's article in this volume. I am especially appreciative of all the support I received because I had no material incentives to offer in return – no research funds, no honoraria, no conference travel.

All this selfless endeavour attests to the sincere commitment of the various contributing authors to this volume regarding the urgent necessity for industrial policy reform in Malaysia to achieve more dynamic, innovative, sustainable, integrated, balanced and equitable manufacturing sector growth. While not endorsing the role of government in the past, we all believe that progressive state intervention is not only desirable, but necessary to achieve such ends.

The support I received from my colleagues – especially Ooi May Lee, Tan Kock Wah and Loke Chee Fong – has been crucial for completing this work. At home, my children, mother and grandmother made it possible for me to finish preparing this volume, despite all odds.

To all, my sincere thanks.

JOMO K.S.

ABBREVIATIONS

ADB	Asian Development Bank
AFL–CIO	American Federation of Labor and Congress of Industrial Organizations
APO	Asian Productivity Organisation
ASEAN	Association of South East Asian Nations
CAD	computer-aided design
DFI	direct foreign investment
EC	European Commission
EEC	European Economic Community
EOI	export-oriented industrialisation
EPR	effective protection rate
EPU	Economic Planning Unit (Prime Minister's Department)
EPZ	export processing zone
FDI	foreign direct investment
FELDA	Federal Land Development Authority
FIDA	Federal Industrial Development Authority
FTZ	Free Trade Zone
GATT	General Agreement on Tariffs and Trade
GDP	gross domestic product
GSP	Generalised System of Preferences
HICOM	Heavy Industries Corporation of Malaysia
ICA	Industrial Coordination Act
ILO	International Labour Organisation
IMF	International Monetary Fund
IMP	Industrial Master Plan
IPU	Industrial Policy Unit
ISI	import-substituting industrialisation
JETRO	Japan External Trade Organisation
JICA	Japan International Co-operation Agency
JIT	just-in-time
LDC	less developed country
LMW	licensed manufacturing warehouse

ABBREVIATIONS

MAEI	Malaysian-American Electronics Industry
MFA	Multi-Fibre Arrangement
MICCI	Malaysian International Chamber of Commerce and Industry
MIDA	Malaysian Industrial Development Authority
MIMOS	Malaysian Institute of Microelectronic Systems
MIPS	Malaysian Industrial Policy Study
MITI	Ministry of International Trade and Industry
MNC	multinational corporation
MTI	Ministry of Trade and Industry
NEP	New Economic Policy
NIC	newly industrialising country
NIE	newly industrialising economy
OECD	Organization for Economic Co-operation and Development
OPP	Outline Perspective Plan (1971–90)
PDC	Penang Development Corporation
Proton	Perusahaan Otomobil Nasional (National Automobile Enterprise)
R&D	research and development
RDA	Regional Development Authority
RIE	rural industrial estate
SIE	semi-urban industrial estate
SMIs	small and medium industries
TNC	transnational corporation
TTU	Technology Transfer Unit
UIE	urban industrial estate
UNCTC	United Nations Centre for Transnational Corporations
UNDP	United Nations Development Programme
UNIDO	United Nations Industrial Development Organization

INTRODUCTION

Jomo K.S.

Ever since the Industrial Revolution from the late eighteenth century, economic progress and development have been closely identified with industrialisation. Although this association has come under increasing challenge in the last decade – partly owing to the environment and resource crises raising fundamental questions about the sustainability of economic growth – it continues to influence economic policymakers, especially in the Third World. Politicians and technocrats all over the world still appear to share this vision, and this is no less true in Malaysia. In fact, most influential Malaysians view industrialisation as the nation's greatest priority and ticket to progress in the future.

While there are varied views about the industries to be prioritised in this process, there seems to be a consensus that industrialisation is the key to future development. Nevertheless, old debates – e.g. between import substitution and export orientation, or the balance between heavy and light industries, or the role of foreign capital or Chinese industrialists – continue to animate Malaysian discussions of industrialisation. There is also growing concern over issues which did not receive quite the same attention in the past (e.g. the environment, resources or even technology dilemmas), while some other issues (e.g. regional, spatial and other distributional considerations) appear to have receded in significance in recent years.

The story of Malaysian industrialisation really begins after Independence since there was not much manufacturing activity to speak of before 1957 owing to British policies consistent with a typical colonial division of labour. Colonies like Malaya were expected to supply raw materials and provide the market for manufactured imports from Britain, excet where transport and other considerations necessitated local processing. Furthermore, Singapore was the regional centre for the British Empire, and hence where most industries for Malaya were concentrated (Puthucheary, 1960; Wheelwright, 1963a, 1963b). When Malaya – or what is now known as Peninsular Malaysia – achieved Independence in 1957 without Singapore, the newly independent hinterland lost much of its modest industrial sector. The formation of Malaysia, including Singapore, in 1963 briefly revived the possibility of building on the colonial inheritance until the island's secession less than two years later.

In the meantime, however, import-substituting industrialisation had been promoted from the late 1950s, attracting foreign (mainly British) capital-intensive industries to relocate behind the tariff walls erected by the newly independent government. As the limitations of this strategy became more pronounced in the mid-1960s, the government was easily persuaded to switch to labour-intensive export-oriented industrial growth to inject fresh dynamism and mop up the growing ranks of the unemployed. Tax concessions, new labour policies and other incentives from the late 1960s provided an attractive environment for such investments, which only really took off in the early 1970s.

This coincided with the beginning of the New Economic Policy (NEP). The NEP was introduced by the Malaysian government after the May 1969 post-election race riots, ostensibly to create the socioeconomic conditions for improved inter-ethnic relations – and 'national unity', it was presumed – by reducing poverty and inter-ethnic occupational and wealth 'restructuring' through government intervention. The NEP involved greater state intervention and public sector expansion, including regulation of manufacturing sector investments. Recognising the basic incoherence and lopsidedness of such industrialisation, the then new Mahathir government promoted heavy industries in the early 1980s in an ill-conceived effort to ensure more balanced industrial growth. This brief effort at a second round of import-substitution was doomed from the outset because it was weighed down by the domestically oriented heavy industrialisation programme. However, state intervention generally has been undermined by economic liberalisation and structural adjustments since the mid-1980s. Although export-oriented manufacturing growth has recovered since 1987 after the Industrial Master Plan (IMP) was announced in early 1986, few would claim that the recent industrial resurgence has been due to the implementation of the South Korean-style 'pro-active' market-augmenting state intervention recommended by the IMP. A brief review of Malaysian industrialisation is provided in the first paper in this volume to offer a historical backdrop to the more detailed subsequent discussion (the most recently available data are given in the Statistical Appendix at the end of the book).

This volume is primarily concerned with critically analysing Malaysian industrialisation experience and the role, impact and efficacy of industrialisation policies. Such critical evaluation is deemed necessary to learn from Malaysia's own experience as well as from other more relevant experiences. Only by correctly assessing the implications of existing constraints can policymakers make the most of currently available opportunities. The papers in this volume are mainly concerned with the dynamism and coherence of the manufacturing sector. Most of the authors are concerned about the nature of Malaysia's manufacturing sector growth, its internal linkages and its ability to sustain growth in the light of its already heavy, but still growing, reliance on foreign investment, technology and markets. Some of the imbalances considered include the distributional implications of foreign dominance, control of technology, industrial relations, wage policy and spatial dispersal, which has been marginalised as a matter of policy concern since the mid-1980s.

By international standards, Malaysia's relatively low level of industrialisation contrasts sharply with its relatively high per capita income, in terms of the manufacturing sector's contribution to both GDP (gross domestic product) as well as employment. The consequences of this for Malaysia's export and import profiles are still quite pronounced in the early 1990s despite rapid economic growth as well as considerable diversification and industrialisation. Malaysian export-led growth has resulted in agricultural, mining as well as manufacturing enclaves. An important consequence of this legacy has been relatively high wage rates in contrast with the relative underdevelopment of Malaysian industrial skills and productivity.

The relationship between employment and wages in the manufacturing sector has been the subject of much debate and discussion. The evidence for Peninsular Malaysia from the 1960s to the 1980s suggests that there is no simple relationship between industrialisation and labour employment or wage levels (see Jomo and Osman-Rani, 1984). Rather, the evidence seems to suggest that the capital intensity of import-substituting industries allowed wage levels to rise for the relatively few workers employed, since wage costs comprise only a relatively small proportion of their total production costs. With the switch, after the post-1985 depreciation of the ringgit, to internationally competitive export-oriented production – where the relatively low production costs, especially of labour, in Malaysia have been an important factor in foreign manufacturing capital's location in the country – wage levels declined, especially in the new labour-intensive factories. However, as industrialisation, public sector expansion and the growth of other services reduced unemployment, wage levels began to rise again in the late 1970s and early 1980s. Although the evidence for the 1980s is less conclusive, it seems likely that the two recessions in the early and mid-1980s and rising unemployment between 1983 and 1987 weakened labour's bargaining position once again, adversely affecting wages in most sectors. In any case, while difficult to demonstrate conclusively, the evidence suggests that real wage rates have not kept up with increases in labour productivity in the manufacturing sector.

With the weakening position of labour and changing government policy in favour of employers, especially in the 1980s, labour flexibility appears to be on the increase in Malaysian manufacturing. Increased labour flexibility has been part and parcel of the liberalised investment climate for manufacturing actively promoted by the government from the mid-1980s. With manufacturing employment expansion slowing down sharply in the mid-1980s, rising unemployment levels were exacerbated by some retrenchments. The current policy obsession with 'international competitiveness' has resulted in various efforts to reduce labour costs further, e.g. amendments to the labour laws, official hostility towards trade unions, official tolerance of illegal labour immigration and other recent labour policy changes. However, since labour costs generally comprise a small proportion of total production costs, not much can be gained through such policies. Instead, an improved regulatory framework should couple labour security with labour flexibility, to ensure better skill utilisation, development and replenishment in the transition from an export-oriented economy based on low-cost labour to one based on higher technology, more value-added production as well as more complex and dynamic production and work processes.

Guy Standing (Chapter 2) confirms many of the earlier general observations about trends in the direction of greater labour flexibility using evidence from a large comprehensive survey of manufacturing firms in 1988. He notes the apparent stability in firm employment size between 1985 and 1988, arguing that small firms rarely expand and have a greater tendency to perish; hence, manufacturing employment growth is more likely to come from larger firms. Coming soon after a severe recession, the survey found that increased sales had not resulted in a corresponding increase in employment. Instead, many firms have been shedding labour, reducing the fixed core of their workforces. Many firms have retrenched workers, only to rehire them at lower wage rates and with less security of employment. Thus, and in many other ways, firms have bypassed official regulations in order to lower wage and non-wage labour costs. The casualisation of employment contracts has been complemented by the growth of job and labour contracting, while more new workers are being put on probation for longer periods of time. Hence, at the lower end of the labour market, there seems to be a significant shift away from regular full-time direct wage employment. Standing also notes that the increase in internal labour market flexibility, involving matters such as recruitment, training, retraining, mobility and retrenchment, supports other findings of greater inequality in remuneration within the manufacturing sector, especially between lower-paid blue-collar workers on the one hand and white-collar workers and management on the other. With the feminisation of the manufacturing workforce, the urgency of reducing gender inequality in the labour market cannot be overemphasised. Interestingly, the survey found that overall demand, business uncertainty and technological changes, rather than wage costs and other labour-related factors, were most often cited as factors influencing firms' employment policy.

The significance of direct foreign investment (DFI) in the development of Malaysia's manufacturing sector is examined more closely by Anuwar Ali and Wong Poh Kam (Chapter 3). Their survey of the period 1970–87 clearly shows that both DFI and domestic investments have grown unevenly. DFI contribution is analysed by output, employment creation, sectoral distribution, country of origin, performance, profitability, export propensity, import propensity, investment income flows as well as tax-revenue contributions. Their findings – from case studies of twenty-five transnational corporations (TNCs) operating in Malaysia – survey employment creation, equity structures, NEP ownership restructuring, inter-industry linkages, TNC decision-making processes, and negotiation processes between TNCs and the relevant government agencies.

There are important differences between export-oriented and domestic-oriented TNCs, with the former tending to be mostly fully foreign owned, while the latter have a considerably higher degree of local equity participation. While the former have been largely exempted from NEP ownership restructuring requirements, many of the latter have accommodated themselves to this requirement to their own advantage. With few exceptions, management control remains mainly in expatriate hands and does not necessarily reflect ownership. Except for resource-based industries, domestic linkages have not been well developed, though there has been greater upstream and downstream integration in recent years. As for decision making, there appears to be room for considerable local autonomy within constraints defined by the TNCs' global interests, particularly in investment decision making, acquisition of input supplies and domestic marketing, in contrast to greater, more centralised foreign control of technology sourcing and international marketing.

Export-oriented TNCs have generally been more profitable and dynamic, though their domestically oriented counterparts have generally also been quite profitable with the protection they generally enjoy. Since 1986, domestic investments have barely kept pace with the upsurge of DFI, which has already resulted in a dramatic increase in foreign-controlled ventures encouraged by the new relaxed investment conditions. Since both foreign and Bumiputera equity participation are positively related to firm size, this has been invoked to justify government preference for foreign as well as larger firms. Not surprisingly then, the foreign firms seem quite satisfied with the role of the Malaysian government agencies they deal with, recognising that the investment climate improved in their favour in the 1980s.

Industrial policy in Malaysia is widely acknowledged to have favoured large-scale industries over their small-scale counterparts. Despite a great deal of rhetoric and the adoption of policies ostensibly favouring the development of small and medium-sized industries, efforts to promote small industries in Malaysia have been weak, uncoordinated, unsustained and uneven. Even definitionally, there is little consensus among the relevant government agencies over what small industries are. The main problems faced by small industries seem to involve poor access to credit institutions, technology, management training, marketing, sub-contracting opportunities, suitable sites and premises as well as discriminatory government policies and practices (Chee, 1990). Notwithstanding such evidence of discrimination against small industries, various papers in this volume suggest that national industrialisation policy should not be built primarily around the promotion of such industries.

Industrial estates were first promoted in Malaysia in the 1950s as part of the Malayan import-substitution industrial development strategy. By the early 1990s, more than three decades after the establishment of the first industrial estate, Malaysia has over a hundred spread all over the country. The Malaysian industrial estate programme has been praised by the United Nations Industrial Development Organization (UNIDO) for its efficient subsidised provision of industrial sites and supporting infrastructure, as well as its generous package of fiscal incentives, particularly tariff protection. However, while they have promoted manufacturing growth, their record as far as spatial distribution is concerned leaves much to be desired. The uneven success of industrial estates – e.g. as measured by occupancy rates – reflects the failure of government efforts at spatial dispersal of the manufacturing sector. This record prompted the IMP planners virtually to abandon the government's previous commitment to industrial dispersal in favour of a West Coast manufacturing corridor.

Four phases in the development of industrial estates may be distinguished. In the 1950s, the sole industrial estate in Petaling Jaya sought to develop manufacturing in Malaya away from the traditional centre, Singapore. During the 1960s, new estates near the major state capitals represented the first efforts at industrial dispersal. In the 1970s, the strategy was more rural in orientation, and even sought to develop previously neglected and underdeveloped areas, before the general manufacturing slowdown in the early and mid-1980s prompted the IMP's abandonment of industrial dispersal policy.

The failure of the industrial estate policy to achieve more balanced dispersal has been attributed to three factors:

1 industrialisation policy – both import substitution and export promotion – has favoured estates with locational advantages;
2 the advantages offered by peripheral industrial estates have been insufficient to offset their disadvantages;
3 industrial estates have often merely encouraged the relocation of some industries within the same region, rather than attracting new manufacturing investments, thus not adding to regional growth and employment.

There is also considerable unproductive rivalry between the various authorities involved. Regional imbalances thus seem inevitable as the location of manufacturing firms results from decisions guided primarily by profit considerations. Hence, it is uncertain that more centralised planning and coordination to ensure more balanced industrial dispersal will succeed.

The development of Free Trade Zones (FTZs) has been a crucial component of the export-oriented development strategy adopted in the late 1960s. The Free Trade Zones Act of 1971 paved the way for new industrial estates exempt from customs regulations, developed by state development corporations and catering to firms manufacturing for export. FTZ firms now dominate Malaysian manufactured exports, although the actual value of their contribution is probably significantly distorted by transfer pricing to maximise firm profits globally. Together with the package of new incentives, labour law amendments and government industrial promotion efforts through the then Federal (now Malaysian) Industrial Development Authority (FIDA), the creation of these FTZs – also known elsewhere by various other names, such as export processing zones – is widely believed to have been crucial to the early success of export-led industrialisation. The subsequent development of licensed manufacturing warehouses (LMWs) was also inspired by the FTZ concept, without being constrained by the FTZs' spatial requirements. FTZs have been particularly successful in attracting transnational industrial capital seeking to relocate abroad to minimise production – especially wage-costs, tax payments and other obstacles to profit maximisation.

FTZ exports, like Malaysian manufactured exports in general, have been dominated by electronic and electrical components and products as well as textile and garment manufacturing, which involves mainly female workers. Technological changes have slightly reduced the significance of labour costs, allowing wages to go up with skills and productivity. However, international competition has encouraged greater management flexibility, particularly with regard to labour, resulting in greater subcontracting and labour flexibility in general.

Technology control and market access have ensured foreign capital's clear domination of FTZ manufacturing activity even when engaged in joint ventures with domestic investors. However, pragmatic transnationals increasingly utilise the experience and expertise of Malaysian personnel, not only in activities located in Malaysia, but also in international firm operations. The FTZ record on technological transfer and industrial linkages has hardly been impressive, although developments since the late 1980s have begun to change the picture as transnational firms find it in their interest to transfer technology, to make greater use of more skilled labour, and to develop greater local linkages to enhance production flexibility and reduce inventories in line with the growing popularity of just-in-time (JIT) production systems.

Rajah Rasiah's contribution on the FTZs (Chapter 4) provides a concise account of their development in Malaysia. He contrasts the nature of manufacturing activity in the FTZs during the 1970s and early 1980s with more recent developments, which involve greater capital intensity, since the mid-1980s. By 1987, Penang had the lion's share of FTZ development, in terms of number of firms, employment, developed area and firms' fixed assets. Selangor accounted for much of the remainder, with Malacca taking up the balance. Rajah's paper considers various influences on FTZ employment and wages, taking into consideration the implications of recent developments. Leslie O'Brien's survey of linkages (Chapter 5) affirms evidence from input–output tables and other macroeconomic sources of a poorly integrated Malaysian manufacturing sector. Her findings strengthen the arguments made in earlier chapters about the basic structural weaknesses of Malaysian industrialisation.

Ashwani Saith (Chapter 6) uses a review of Malaysian rural development strategies as an opportunity to examine a wide range of issues relevant to balanced development. He critically examines the notion of rural industrialisation, contrasting the locational definition and a linkage approach, with the latter encouraging migration to work in local urban centres. Saith then examines Malaysia's rural industrialisation experience and strategies for income and employment generation, particularly among poorer rural communities, using the linkage approach. He reviews the limited empirical evidence on rural non-farm activities (NFA), ranging from household production to large-scale industrial plants. He focuses on rural labour force characteristics and non-farm occupations, relating them to poverty and inequality. According to Saith, NFA were primarily initiated by rural entrepreneurs and encouraged by the state, but often failed to develop very much for sociological reasons. Lastly, Saith examines important aspects – including industrial location, linkages, leakages and migration – of the new rural industrialisation development strategy, as initiated in the Fifth Malaysia Plan for 1986–90.

With the accelerating pace of technological change, the dilemmas of technology transfer to developing countries have become more acute. The notion of catching up industrially implies the development of a sufficiently dynamic domestic technological capacity in a highly competitive economic environment. The number of technology transfer agreements has increased in recent years with the shift away from technologically packaged foreign investments. Japan, the United Kingdom and the United States lead the number of agreements by country, while electronic and electrical products, followed by chemicals, fabricated metals and transport equipment, lead by industry type. Royalty payments have increased considerably as a consequence.

Anuwar Ali's contribution to this volume (Chapter 7) argues that technology has not been effectively transferred or acquired in Malaysia, thus undermining the national capacity for industrial dynamism. He reviews basic problems in efforts to transfer technology to developing countries, including the limited range of technology available owing to supply controls, exacerbated by intense competition among potential recipients, the use of technology pricing for transfer pricing purposes, restrictive terms and conditions, technology recipients' poor absorptive and adaptive capacities as well as poor research and development, and the rapid pace of technological change, ensuring continued dependence on suppliers. Of the officially registered technology transfer contracts, more than half involved technical assistance and know-how, and almost a quarter involved management services and joint ventures. Anuwar also reviews the existing policy framework and approval mechanism for royalty payments, focusing on existing policies for remuneration of technology transfer. The author argues that important reforms in manpower training and R&D policy, and technology policy more generally, could significantly enhance Malaysia's industrial capacity.

INTRODUCTION

The electronics industry has accounted for much of export-oriented industrialisation since the 1970s, contributing more than half of manufactured exports for many years. Semiconductor assembly has dominated electronics production in Malaysia. Industrialisation was originally seen in Malaysia as providing an opportunity to reduce vulnerability to the volatile world market for Malaysia's primary commodity exports. However, the highly cyclical global market for computer chips and other electronic exports and fear of the implications of growing automation have forced a reconsideration of the role of electronics in Malaysia's future industrialisation.

The future of the electronics industry needs to be more closely linked to the growth of Malaysia's industrial sector and economy as a whole, e.g. by applying electronics technologies to enhance efficiency in industrial production generally. The manufacture of hardware should be only the start of more advanced and widespread development of microelectronics and the new information technologies. The production of consumer electronics could also reduce current dependence on semiconductor assembly while creating greater opportunities for forging backward linkages to component suppliers and supporting industries. The recent post-1985 international currency realignment has favoured Malaysia in this regard, though more policy initiatives may be necessary to take greater advantage of the new opportunities arising from the globalisation of high-technology production.

Although Malaysian textiles and garments were long written off as a declining industry and less technologically dynamic than electronics, their resurgence in recent years suggests that the sun has risen again on that industry. While electronics is often seen as the largest industry in terms of employment, with about 100,000 employees, it has been estimated that twice that number are involved in textiles and garments, though a great number are not employed in time-rated factory work. Import quotas under the Multi-Fibre Arrangement (MFA) have also been an important consideration in transnational textile firms locating in Malaysia.

In view of their significance in terms of employment, value added, export earnings and, belatedly, linkages to the domestic economy, David O'Connor addresses a range of difficult questions about the future role for electronics, textiles and garments in the Malaysian economy (Chapters 8 and 9). The third and final industry case study in this volume examines the officially much-touted made-in-Malaysia Proton car project. Jayasankaran (Chapter 10) reviews the development of the project from its original conception – as part and parcel of the early 1980s' heavy industrialisation efforts – until the late 1980s, when management control was given by the Malaysian Government to its Japanese partner, Mitsubishi.

Under the premiership of Mahathir Mohamad since mid-1981, there has undoubtedly been a stronger commitment to accelerating the pace of industrialisation. His 'Look East Policy' – to emulate Japan, South Korea and now Taiwan – has been widely seen as an exhortation to accelerate the pace of industrialisation, although it is now currently interpreted to refer mainly to the development of work ethics believed by Mahathir to be crucial to rapid industrialisation (e.g. see Jomo, 1983). In the early 1980s, UNIDO sponsored studies which went into the formulation of the Industrial Master Plan (IMP), announced in early 1986. Its useful critique of Malaysia's manufacturing sector has since been selectively translated into a renewed emphasis on export-led industrial growth largely under foreign auspices. Other economic policy reforms in the mid-1980s, which might be seen as part of the government's voluntary 'structural adjustment' liberalisation package, clearly also prioritised industrial investment, especially from abroad. The acceleration of manufacturing investment, output and exports since 1987 appears to have provided eloquent testimony to the success of these recent initiatives.

However, it is also clear that most recent foreign investments in manufacturing have come from the East Asian region, notably Japan, Taiwan, Hong Kong and Singapore, though of course Singapore investments are also likely to be offshore in origin but channelled through regional headquarters in the island republic. This new wave of East Asian investment has several distinctive characteristics. Many have been motivated by the significant appreciation of their respective currencies, especially against the Malaysian ringgit, which even declined against the US dollar after the September 1985 Plaza II international currency realignments agreement. Rapid growth, full employment and the expansion of domestic markets have raised living standards and wage levels in the East Asian NICs.

In contrast, ringgit depreciation, structural adjustments, economic liberalisation, deflationary fiscal policies, rising unemployment as well as hostile labour laws and policies lowered real wage levels in Malaysia in the mid-1980s. With encouragement from the Japanese Ministry of International Trade and Industry (MITI), even Japanese small and medium industries (SMIs) relocated abroad, especially in Thailand and Malaysia. The growing adoption of just-in-time (JIT) production arrangements, with much reduced inventory requirements, further encouraged industrial relocation in economies like Malaysia, which also offered relatively good infrastructure and political stability.

After the US administration withdrew trade privileges under the Generalised System of Preferences (GSP) from East Asian newly industrialising countries (NICs) in 1988, and the AFL-CIO (American Federation of Labor and Congress of Industrial Organizations) petitioned the US Congress to do the same to Malaysia for violating labour rights – by not allowing electronic industry workers to unionise – the Malaysian prime minister ordered Malaysian politicians, civil servants, academics and the media to avoid mention of Malaysia achieving NIC status. This instruction – ostensibly to ensure Malaysian retention of GSP privileges for its exports – introduced an unusually modest tone to talk of Malaysian industrialisation. In early 1991, however, Mahathir announced that Malaysia would aim to achieve developed (industrialised) country status by the year 2020, bypassing NIC status in the process. This announcement – as part of an important position paper (Mahathir, 1991) – clearly reiterated industrialisation as the unquestioned developmental priority for the decades ahead. This is expected to set the tone for post-1990 economic policy, which has been the subject of much debate and concern as the 1971–90 Outline Perspective Plan (OPP) period for implementation of Malaysia's New Economic Policy (NEP) drew to a close.

Despite Malaysia's high growth rates since the 1960s, the contribution of its manufacturing sector still lags behind. Moreover, the structure and composition of Malaysia's manufacturing sector remain quite different, especially from the economies of South Korea and Taiwan – which are far more relevant for comparative purposes than either Hong Kong or Singapore, both of which have long been profitable city entrepôts and regional centres and are not suitable for emulation.

Another important difference has been in the role of domestic capital in the industrialisation processes. Domestic capital has led the industrialisation process in South Korea, Taiwan and even Hong Kong, whereas in both Singapore and Malaysia the governments have favoured foreign capital. In contrast to the economic and industrial nationalism of South Korea and Taiwan, the Malaysian government's preference for transnational capital appears to be influenced by its concerns about Chinese wealth accumulation in the nation.

One other significant factor may be the more favourable international environment obtaining in the 1960s and 1970s, when the Asian NICs took off. In contrast, the 1980s proved to be more difficult internationally, while there are fears that the situation may deteriorate further in the 1990s with a further slowdown in the growth of international trade, the strengthening of regional blocs and greater restrictions on technology transfer. The crucial role of the state, even in Hong Kong, also needs to be emphasised, in contrast to the ideological explanations of NIC success by free market conservatives. In contrast, while the Malaysian state has also been dirigiste and developmentalist, it has been less efficiently and less effectively so, with inter-ethnic redistribution its main priority. Structural adjustments and other recent initiatives have begun to compensate, but doubts persist as to whether this may be too little too late. Other similarities and differences are also considered in an effort to assess the prospects for 'catching up' through comparative analysis of industrialisation policies and experiences.

Although the Malaysian Government has officially eschewed seeking NIC status, the earlier discussion has underscored the value of considering Malaysian development in comparative perspective with the four East Asian 'tigers', especially South Korea and Taiwan. Mahathir's efforts to accelerate Malaysia's industrialisation by invoking the Northeast Asian examples of Japan, South Korea and Taiwan underscore the relevance of comparative studies of industrialisation. Malaysia is widely considered to be on the brink of 'NICdom', though there is still considerable controversy over what this implies. My paper (Chapter 11) compares and contrasts Malaysia's potential and experience with those of South Korea, Taiwan, Hong Kong and Singapore – the four generally acknowledged Asian NICs. It focuses particularly on conjunctural issues (history, regional considerations, international economic conditions, etc.) as well as on the role and nature of state intervention promoting industrialisation.

The following paper by Chris Edwards (Chapter 12) emphasises the crucial role of pro-active, market-augmenting state intervention in explaining South Korean industrialisation over the last three decades. In the process, he tries to identify important lessons for emulation by the Malaysian Government in trying to achieve more rapid, balanced and integrated industrial development. The preceding papers, especially the last two, have made the case that judicious state intervention has been essential for the late industrialisation project. The concluding contribution (Chapter 13) by Edwards and myself attempts to spell out policy options for the 1990s in the light of Malaysian and East Asian NIC experiences in the preceding decades.

Hence, as Malaysia approached the middle of the IMP period and the end of the NEP's Outline Perspective Plan period (1971–90), this volume was being prepared to contribute to the continuing discussions on the future of industrialisation in Malaysia by critically reflecting on past experiences and policies.

There remain significant gaps in this volume, important for fuller consideration of questions of industrial coherence and balance. For instance, it would be useful to have a good overview of the politics of industrial policymaking, as well as an overview of problems relating to the industrial work environment and occupational hazards (see Nicholas and Wangel, 1990). The environmental consequences of industrialisation in Malaysia have also not been given adequate attention (e.g. see Shiode, 1989). Work on the labour process in the Malaysian manufacturing sector is still in its infancy (e.g. see Rajah, 1987), while other crucial industrial labour issues are only beginning to be examined.

While not challenging the desirability of industrialisation in itself, this volume seeks to refocus attention on some major intended as well as unintended implications and consequences of industrialisation policies and performance. By renewing the focus on questions of integration and distribution, it is hoped that attention will shift away from the current obsession with quantitative growth aggregates to the more subtle, but nevertheless crucial issues involving the quality and nature of industrialisation.

When the IMP was first announced in early 1986, during Malaysia's most severe recession in recent times and after years of poor manufacturing growth, its targets seemed unrealistically ambitious to many. Five years later, after the manufacturing boom since 1987, many of these same targets have already been exceeded and in retrospect seem to have been too modest.

INTRODUCTION

However, far less attention is given to the no less important qualitative aspects of Malaysia's industrialisation. Perhaps even more importantly, there is only a vague understanding and appreciation of the complex relationship between industrialisation and other aspects of development in Malaysia, which this volume also tries to address.

REFERENCES

Chee, P.L. (1990) 'Promotion of Small Industries: The Malaysian Experience', in *Promotion of Small-Scale Industries and Strategies for Rural Industrialisation – The Malaysian Experience*, Friedrich Ebert Stiftung, Kuala Lumpur.

Jomo K.S. (ed.) (1983) *The Sun Also Sets: Lessons in Looking East*, INSAN, Kuala Lumpur.

Jomo K.S. and H. Osman-Rani (1984) 'Wage Trends in Peninsular Malaysia Manufacturing', *Kajian Ekonomi Malaysia*, 21, 1 (June): 18–38.

Mahathir Mohamad (1991) 'Malaysia – The Way Forward', *ISIS Focus*, 72 (March).

Nicholas, C. and Arne Wangel (eds) (1990) *Safety at Work in Malaysia*, Institute for Advanced Studies, University of Malaya, Kuala Lumpur.

Puthucheary, J.J. (1960) *Ownership and Control in the Malayan Economy*, Eastern Universities Press, Singapore.

Rajah Rasiah (1987) 'Pengantarabangsaan Pengeluaran dan Pembahagian Buruh Antarabangsa: Kajian Kes Industri Separa Konduktor di Pulau Pinang', M.Soc.Sc Dissertation, Universiti Sains Malaysia, Penang.

Shiode Hirokazu (1989) *Japanese Investment in Southeast Asia: Three Malaysian Case Studies*, Centre for the Progress of Peoples, Hong Kong.

Wheelwright, E.L. (1963a) 'Industrialization in Malaya', in T.H. Silcock and E.K. Fisk (eds), *The Political Economy of Independent Malaya: A Case Study in Development*, University of California Press, Berkeley.

Wheelwright, E.L. (1963b) 'Reflections on Some Problems of Industrial Development in Malaya', *Malayan Economic Review*, 8, 1 (April).

1

MALAYSIAN INDUSTRIALISATION IN HISTORICAL PERSPECTIVE

Jomo K.S. and Chris Edwards

In 1989, the net output of the manufacturing sector accounted for just over a quarter of the gross domestic product of Malaysia, and manufacturing employment accounted for 17 per cent of total employment (see Table 1.1). Since independence in 1957,[1] the rate of growth in manufacturing output has been rapid, with the share of manufacturing in total gross domestic product

Table 1.1 Manufacturing's share of gross domestic product and employment, 1947–91

Year	Manufacturing value added as % of total GDP	Manufacturing employment ('000)	Manufacturing employment as % of total employment
1947[a]	5.7	126	6.7
1957[a]	6.3	136	6.4
1960[a]	8.7	n.a.	n.a.
1965[a]	10.4	217	8.4
1970	13.1	448	11.4
1975	16.4	n.a.	n.a.
1980	19.6	802	15.8
1985	19.7	836	15.1
1986	20.9	818	14.7
1987	22.5	921	15.7
1988	24.4	1,013	16.6
1989	25.5	1,171	18.4
1990	26.9	1,290	19.5
1991	28.2	1,374	20.1

Note: [a] 1947–65 figures refer to Peninsular Malaysia only.
Sources: L. Hoffman and S.E. Tan, *Industrial Growth, Employment and Foreign Investment in Malaysia*, Oxford University Press, Kuala Lumpur, 1980, Appendix AII.1; Malaysia, *Fourth Malaysia Plan, 1981-85*, Kuala Lumpur, Table 4-6; Malaysia, *Fifth Malaysia Plan, 1986-90*, Kuala Lumpur, Table 3-5; Bank Negara Malaysia, *Annual Report*, Kuala Lumpur, various years; Ministry of Finance, *Economic Report*, Kuala Lumpur, various years; and Malaysian Industrial Development Authority, *MIDA Report 1987*, MIDA, Kuala Lumpur.

Table 1.2 Average annual growth rates of manufacturing value added and manufacturing exports, 1971–89

Year	Growth (% pa) of	
	Manufacturing value added	Manufacturing exports
1971–75[a]	11.6	27.5
1976–80	13.5	24.9
1981–85	4.9	14.3
1986	7.5	23.0
1987	13.4	32.5
1988	17.6	32.1
1989[b]	13.0	36.5

Notes:
[a] Average annual growth rates before 1970 are not shown because the system of calculating National Accounts was changed from 1969.
[b] Preliminary.
Sources: MIDA, *MIDA Report 1987*, Kuala Lumpur; Bank Negara Malaysia, *Annual Report*, Kuala Lumpur, various years.

rising from less than 10 per cent in the late 1950s to 26 per cent thirty years later. The average annual growth rate of manufacturing output consistently exceeded 10 per cent in the decade 1970–80, averaging 11.6 per cent during 1971–5 and 13.5 per cent during 1976–80, before declining to an average of 4.9 per cent during 1981–5, and then rising to 12.6 per cent during 1986–9 (see Table 1.2).

Manufacturing has come to play a bigger role as a foreign exchange earner in line with the government's intention of reducing Malaysia's dependence on primary exports (see Table 1.3). Manufacturing's share of Malaysia's gross commodity exports rose rapidly from just 12 per cent in 1970 to more than 20 per cent in 1980 to more than half in 1988, although, of course, these figures are somewhat misleading because of the relatively high import content of manufactured exports.

Nevertheless, the average annual growth rate of manufactured exports has been impressive, averaging 26 per cent during the 1970s, declining to 15 per cent from 1980 to 1985 before rising again to 31 per cent from 1985 to 1988. The decline in the growth rate in the early 1980s can be attributed partly to Malaysia's rising real effective exchange rate over that period and partly to the recession in the international economy.

Besides manufacturing's growing contribution to total GDP and to export earnings, it has also accounted for an expanding share of employment. Prior to Independence, manufacturing was a minor source of employment, accounting for under 7 per cent of the country's labour force in both 1947 and 1957. Even by 1965, the manufacturing sector was employing only a little over 8 per cent of the workforce. With the advent of more labour-intensive industries in the late 1960s and in the 1970s, manufacturing employed more than 15 per

Table 1.3 Exports of manufactured goods, 1970–91

	1970		1980		1985		1988		1989		1990		1991	
	M$m.	% share	M$m.	% share	M$m.	% share	M$m.	% share	M$m.	% share	M$m.	% share	M$m.	% share
Food, beverage and tobacco	112	18	475	8	594	5	1,043	4	1,788	5	2,061	4	2,243	4
Textiles, clothing and footwear	40	7	806	13	1,289	11	2,958	11	3,198	9	3,983	8	4,805	8
Wood products	88	14	467	8	363	3	918	3	1,184	3	1,535	3	2,063	3
Rubber products	17	3	84	1	133	1	326	1	1,143	3	1,356	3	1,749	3
Chemicals and petroleum products	197	32	361	6	1,412	12	1,912	7	2,698	7	3,192	7	3,539	6
Non-metallic mineral products	20	3	61	1	150	1	444	2	658	2	771	2	888	1
Iron and steel and metal manufactures	26	4	161	3	300	2	1,000	4	1,469	4	1,629	4	1,883	3
Electrical and electronic machinery and appliances	17	3	2,832	46	6,028	50	14,039	52	20,743	57	26,496	56	35,602	58
Other machinery and transport equipment	68	11	407	7	1,031	8	1,625	6	1,244	3	2,234	5	3,292	5
Other manufactures[a]	27	5	447	7	831	7	2,820	10	2,467	7	3,886	8	5,363	9
Total manufactured exports	612	100	6,101	100	12,111	100	27,085	100	36,592	100	47,143	100	61,427	100
Total exports (fob)	5,200		28,013		37,576		54,596		67,824		79,646		94,497	
Manufactured exports as % of total exports	12		22		32		50		54		60		65	

Note: [a] Includes paper and pulp products, scientific instruments, etc.
Source: Ministry of Finance, *Economic Report*, various years.

cent of the total labour force by 1980, but the share remained the same in 1985, before rising again to more than 17 per cent in 1989 (see Table 1.1). The average annual manufacturing employment growth rate of 7.6 per cent during the decade 1970–80 was considerably higher than the 4.1 per cent recorded for the economy as a whole.

In spite of its rapid rate of growth since Independence, the Malaysian manufacturing sector in the 1980s was still considered marginally underdeveloped, given the level of its national income (or more precisely its gross domestic product) per capita. This is shown in Figure 1.1, from which it can be seen that the proportion of Malaysia's GDP contributed by manufacturing was slightly under 20 per cent, whereas it 'should' have been over 20 per cent to accord with a supposedly 'normal' pattern of development. Malaysia's less-than-20 per cent of GDP in manufacturing is in sharp contrast with the 30 per cent of South Korea – a country with roughly the same level of GDP per capita (but with a bigger population).

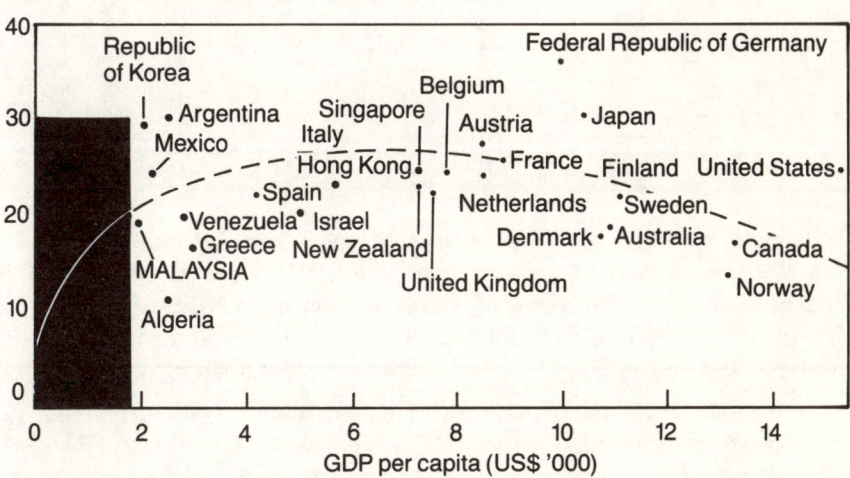

Figure 1.1 Relationship between GDP per capita and the share of manufacturing value added in GDP in selected economies, 1984
Source: World Bank (1987: 51).

This 'backwardness' of industry is in spite of considerable incentives granted to the manufacturing sector in post-colonial Malaysia. But Malaysia was a late starter. The encouragement since Independence in the late 1950s has contrasted sharply with the lack of encouragement under British colonial rule. The British were reluctant, for two reasons, to give any preference to domestically produced manufactured goods. Not only would the substitution of imported manufactures by protected domestic production reduce the import duty revenue to the government, but it was also likely to raise the prices of some of the goods consumed by plantation workers on the (mostly) British-owned rubber estates, thereby adding to the upward pressure on wages, and reduction of profits, on the estates (see Edwards, 1975: 288, 315).

Thus, manufacturing was not very significant in the Malaysian economy during the colonial era, when plantation rubber agriculture and tin mining dominated. British colonial economic policies shaped much of the nature and extent of industrial development in the colonies. With emphasis given to export-oriented raw materials production and British manufactured imports, local industry was largely confined to processing raw materials for export and producing certain items for local consumption, especially if favoured by preservation and transport cost considerations.

Table 1.4 Gross domestic product by sector, 1960–89 (%)

Sector	1960[a]	1970	1980	1989
Agriculture	40	31	23	20
Mining	6	6	10	10
Manufacturing	9	13	20	26
Others	45	50	47	44
Total	100	100	100	100

Note: [a] Peninsular Malaysia only
Sources: Alavi (1987: 14); Ministry of Finance (1989: xii, xiii).

Thus, at the time of Independence, Malaysia was an economy heavily geared to the export of primary commodities. In 1960 (three years after Independence), two-fifths of the GDP came from agriculture, compared with less than 10 per cent from manufacturing (see Table 1.4). Industrialisation in Malaysia since the late 1950s can be divided into four phases as follows:

1 a first phase of import-substituting industrialisation (ISI) from the late 1950s to the 1960s,
2 a period of export-oriented industrialisation (EOI) beginning from the late 1960s,
3 an attempted push for a second phase of ISI, involving heavy industrialisation, in the first half of the 1980s,
4 a renewed commitment to and growth of EOI from the second half of the 1980s.

IMPORT-SUBSTITUTING INDUSTRIALISATION

In contrast to colonial policy, post-colonial Malayan and Malaysian governments have actively sought to promote industrialisation. While these early industrialisation efforts were sometimes erratic and haphazard, government policies from the late 1950s clearly favoured import-substitution industrialisation, with government intervention largely limited to the provision of infrastructure facilities and other incentives. The strategy sought to encourage foreign investors to set up production, assembly and packaging plants in the country to supply finished goods previously imported from abroad. To promote such import-substituting industries, the government directly and indirectly subsidised the establishment of new factories and protected the domestic market.

Industrial investments were quite responsive to these government efforts. During the 1960s, net output in the manufacturing sector in Malaysia grew rapidly from 9 per cent of total GDP in 1960 to 13 per cent in 1970 (see Table 1.1). Tax incentives had been offered to pioneer industries since 1958 but from the beginning of the 1960s, with the establishment of the Tariff Advisory Board, import-substituting industries were encouraged by providing protection through import duties and quotas (see Edwards, 1975: 288). In spite of the tax holidays (extended in 1968 by the Investment Incentives Act), the greatest incentive to the growth of the manufacturing sector was provided by protection. Without the profits made possible by the protection, the tax holidays or other concessions on profits, taxes would not have been of any use (for more details, see Edwards, 1975: 289, 298). The tax concessions merely made the protection even more valuable.[2]

Thus it is incorrect to claim that: 'Protective tariffs were not used as a major instrument of industrial development in the period 1959–68' (see Lim, 1973: 255). In a very detailed examination of protection in the Malaysian manufacturing sector, Edwards calculated that the (weighted) average effective rate of protection (EPR) rose from 25 per cent in 1962 to more than 65 per cent by the end of the decade (see Table 1.5). These EPRs were calculated making extensive use of direct price comparisons,[3] to eliminate 'tariff redundancy' as far as possible. Thus, Edwards' estimates represented the actual, and not merely potential, effective protection.

Table 1.5 Protectionism in Malaysia, 1962–82

Year	Effective rate of protection in manufacturing (% on value added)
1962	25
1966	50
1969	65
1972	70
1979	24
1982	23

Sources: 1962-72, Edwards (1975: 98); 1979 and 1982, MIPS (1984: 26) and World Bank (1989: 64) – the ERPs for these years are probably understated.

Although David Lim was wrong about the significance of protection as a policy instrument in the 1960s, he was right in noting that the nominal rates of protection in Malaysia were not very high in the same period. But many of the industries established were merely packaging and assembling imported components for sale in the protected domestic market. The low ratio of value added to sales meant that a low nominal rate of protection actually resulted in a high effective rate. For example, in 1970, protection on cars pushed up the price to the consumer by about 20 per cent, but this nominal protection was equivalent to an effective rate of protection (on value added) of about 325 per cent (see Edwards, 1975: 45, 115).

The effective rates of protection were small in comparison with the rates estimated for some other developing countries (see Edwards, 1985: 213), but they were equivalent to very large subsidies, as shown in Table 1.6. Based on Edwards' study, the subsidy equivalent of protection for 1969 was about M$300 million, equivalent to just under 4 per cent of GDP, or about 14 per cent of total government operating expenditure. For 1979, according to the Malaysian Industrial Policy Study (MIPS), the subsidy equivalent was M$1,400 million, more than 3 per cent of GDP and 13 per cent of total government operating expenditure.

Thus, since the 1960s, the subsidies given by the structure of protection to manufacturing companies in Malaysia have been substantial. And it is not surprising that the rate of protection, when calculated on profits, has also been very large.

Table 1.6 Manufacturing protection and the subsidy equivalent, 1969 and 1979

	1969	1979
Sample results:		
1. Subsidy equivalent (SE) of protection (M$bn)	0.3	1.4
2. SE as % of value added at domestic prices	31	18
For all Malaysia:		
3. Total value added in Malaysian manufacturing at domestic prices (M$bn)	1.2	8.3
4. SE for all manufacturing (M$bn)	0.4	1.5
5. GDP (M$bn)	9.6	45.1
6. Public sector current expenditure (PSCE) (M$bn)	2.1	11.5
7. SE as % of GDP	4.2	3.3
8. SE as % of PSCE	19	13

Sources: 1969, rows 1 and 2, from Edwards (1975: 97); 1979, rows 1 and 2, calculated from MIPS (1984: 105, 106); row 3 from Ministry of Finance, *Economic Report*, various issues; row 4 calculated by multiplying row 3 by row 2; rows 5 and 6 from Ministry of Finance, *Economic Report*, various issues; row 7 calculated from rows 4 and 5; row 8 calculated from rows 4 and 6.

The calculations by Edwards suggest that the EPR on value added (of about 70 per cent in 1970) was equivalent to an EPR when calculated on profits of more than 1,000 per cent (see Table 1.7). Similarly, in 1979, whereas the EPR on value added was estimated at about 20 per cent, this was equivalent to an EPR on profits of more than 500 per cent.

Table 1.7 Manufacturing sector effective rates of protection on profits, 1970 and 1979 (M$bn)

	At 'domestic prices'	At 'world prices'
1970:		
Value added	0.79	0.47
Wages, depreciation and other costs	——— 0.45 ———	
Profits	0.35	0.02
Therefore, whereas the EPR calculated on value added was (0.79-0.47)/0.47 i.e. approximately 70 per cent, the EPR calculated on profits was (0.35-0.02)/0.02, i.e. more than 1,000 per cent!		
1979		
Value added	7.8	6.45
Wages	——— 1.6 ———	
Depreciation and other costs	——— 4.6 ———	
Profits	1.6	0.25
Therefore, whereas the EPR calculated on value added was (7.8-6.45)/6.45, i.e. just over 20 per cent, the EPR calculated on profits was (1.6-0.25)/0.25, i.e. more than 500 per cent!		

Sources: 1970: from Edwards (1975: 108); 1979: from MIPS (1984: 84–6, 105, 106).

Given such a potential gearing-up of profits through protection, it is hardly surprising that companies were prepared to lobby Malaysian politicians so assiduously and to offer them directorships on the boards of subsidiary companies in Malaysia. What Anne Krueger has called 'rent-seeking' (the expenditure of resources to get such government-endowed rents) became widespread in Malaysia (see Edwards, 1975: 295) and almost certainly continues to be.

But rent-seeking was not the only problem to stem from this import-substituting industrialisation phase. There were four other problems, as follows:

1 There was no pressure on the companies to seek out exports. In 1970, exported manufactures (excluding tinned pineapples and sawn timber) were only 4 per cent of all exports (Edwards, 1975: 298, 299). This meant that, for industries subject to economies of scale, production was limited to a small domestic market and was therefore high cost. An example of such an industry was motor vehicle assembly. By 1983, the domestic

market for cars was about 118,000 (IMP, 1985, Executive Highlights: 58) compared with a typical annual output for a motor car assembly plant in the USA or Western Europe of about 250,000. Yet in Malaysia the domestic market was being supplied not by one plant, but by a dozen (see Osman-Rani, in Jomo, 1985: 32).

2 The import-substitution tended to be limited to final consumer goods, with the protection being higher on those goods than on intermediate manufactures. In 1969, the EPR on consumer goods was 85 per cent, compared with an EPR on intermediate goods of 45 per cent (see Edwards, 1975: 293). The protection given to consumer goods set up a lobby against protection being given to intermediate industries. For, if the latter were given protection, this would automatically reduce the effective protection on the final stage industries, unless the protection was raised on the consumer goods. But if that were done, not only would inflation be boosted, but the domestic market would shrink even further.

3 The majority of the import-substituting industries were set up by foreign-owned companies. By 1970, more than three-fifths of all manufacturing and mining output in Malaysia was under the control of foreign companies, and the EPR was higher on average for those industries dominated by foreign capital (Edwards, 1975: 298, 331). Not only did protection give rise, in many cases, to high profits at the expense of domestic consumers, but these profits, which accrued mostly to foreign companies, were more likely to be remitted out of the country.

4 There was a regional concentration of industry. The bias in favour of consumer goods and the domestic market, together with the lobby effect, meant that production in large-size plants tended to be set up near the large towns on the west coast of the Peninsula. Small-scale plants tended to be pushed out and regional dispersion was unprofitable. This meant that after 1963, when East Malaysia (Sabah and Sarawak) was incorporated into the Federation, the East Malaysians paid higher prices for the protected manufactured goods while getting few of the industrialisation benefits. As a result, parallels were drawn between the 'exploitation' of East Pakistan (now Bangladesh) by West Pakistan and the relationship between East and West Malaysia.

There was considerable variation among industries in terms of the level of protection (see Table 1.8). Private profitability gave little indication of 'social efficiency' (as measured by the domestic resource costs of earning foreign exchange savings). In Edwards' study, in 1970, of thirty-nine 'industries' (defined by 4 and 5 digit classifications) analysed, twenty-three were highly profitable for the companies involved and sixteen were only marginally profitable or unprofitable. Industries with a domestic resource cost (DRC) to foreign exchange ratio above 1.25 were defined as 'socially inefficient' (see Edwards, 1975: 172). With this definition, four of the twenty-three highly

Table 1.8 Effective rates of protection by manufacturing sub-sector, Peninsular Malaysia, 1962–72

Sub-sector		Effective rate of protection (%)			
MIC group	Description	1962	1966	1969	1972
112	Rubber processing	−25	−15	−20	−10
1331	Coconut processing	200	nva	nva	nva
30	Food processing	5	55	65	80
31	Beverages	15	40	40	15
32	Tobacco products	60	110	125	115
33	Textiles	55	110	95	95
34	Clothing	25	40	400	400
35	Sawmilling/plymilling	10	40	55	70
36	Furniture	50	50	40	230
37	Paper and paper products	40	95	140	95
41	Chemical products	20	20	50	50
42	Petroleum products	0	0	0	0
43	NMMP (Cement, etc.) products	10	25	25	25
44	Basic metals	−10	40	130	105
45	Metal products	15	40	30	35
47	Electrical m/c and products	35	155	410	440
48	Transport equipment	–	–	135	140
49	Plastic products	15	65	265	415
1–49	All sub-sectors	15	45	45	55
30–49	All sub-sectors (excl. Group 1)	25	50	65	70
Value added at domestic prices (M$m)		1963	1967	1969	1970
Sub-sectors for which EPR calculated		281	523	842	908
Total in census/survey		420	644	992	1,182
% 'coverage'		67	81	85	76

Source: Edwards (1975: 98).

profitable industries were inefficient, and ten were borderline. Where high profits were made, they generally accrued to foreign-owned companies; if it is assumed that these profits were remitted, then the ten borderline industries would also be 'inefficient' (as defined). Of the sixteen less profitable industries, seven were 'efficient' (Edwards, 1975: 174–5). Thus, for example, ply-milling was efficient but not particularly profitable, whereas the soap and rubber-product industries were inefficient but highly profitable. Motor assembly was not only inefficient but also less profitable than most other manufacturing industries. In 1970, rates of profit were high in Malaysian manufacturing: the average rate of profit was more than 30 per cent per annum (see Edwards, 1975: 122). And for 1979, the MIPS estimated that the rate of profit was 26 per cent (MIPS, 1984: Table 5.14).

The net result of this first phase of industrialisation was that the mass of the population in Malaysia was being charged (as consumers) above world prices and receiving little or no benefits from the industrialisation. On average in 1970 the domestic prices of goods manufactured in Malaysia were about 25 per cent above world prices. This surcharge to consumers in the form of protection amounted to as much as M$500 million (see Edwards 1975: 171), or about M$50 per Malaysian. In 1979, the surcharge was still about 25 per cent of world prices, and equal to about $4.5 billion (calculated from MIPS, 1984: 82), or more than $300 per Malaysian. These 'infant' industries were not being forced or induced to grow up. There was little pressure to transfer technology or skills. There was admittedly some growth in manufacturing employment between 1957 and 1970, but it was small.

The real output growth rate of industries qualifying for pioneer status tax incentives from the government in fact dropped quite dramatically, reflecting the inherent limitations of import-substituting industrialisation in a small open capitalist economy. Not only did the small domestic market reflect the country's relatively small population and its relatively low average income level, but, perhaps more importantly, its skewed distribution of income, and hence expenditure pattern, shaped the nature of effective demand, i.e. the nature of the domestic market for any particular good. Without a more equitable development strategy that might transform the pattern of effective demand, domestic industrial production for mass consumption needs could not expand very much.

In addition, the sector's labour absorptive capacity was still relatively low in the 1960s. The number of workers employed in the manufacturing sector in 1965 was still only about a third of the number in agriculture. With the growth of big industry outpacing small-scale enterprise, and with capital-intensive industries expanding much faster than labour-intensive ones, employment creation lagged considerably behind investment growth during the period of import substitution.

By the mid-1960s, the inherent contradictions of the Malaysian import-substitution strategy were becoming clear. The Raja Mohar Committee was established to recommend measures to accelerate industrial growth. It proposed several measures, including diversification into new industries. Its proposals resulted in the 1968 Investment Incentives Act to encourage the expansion of manufactured exports. Hence, the 1968 legislation reflected a strategic switch in emphasis from import-substitution to export-oriented industrialisation. Meanwhile, the Federal Industrial Development Authority (FIDA), established in 1965, had been activated from 1967 to attract and develop such industries.

By the late 1960s, the 'easy stage' (IMP, 1985: 8) of ISI had run its course, but the industrial development had done nothing to prevent the build-up of racial tensions, which exploded in the post-election riots of May 1969. Income distribution at the end of this period was more unequal than it had been a decade earlier (see Jomo and Ishak, 1986). At the beginning of the 1970s, the declaration of the New Economic Policy (NEP) by the new government under the leadership of Tun Razak coincided with the new phase of export-oriented industrialisation (EOI). The labour laws were also amended in late 1969, after the declaration of a state of emergency in the aftermath of these riots, to use and control labour more effectively in the new, mainly labour-intensive export-oriented industries, e.g. by strengthening the Registrar of Trade Unions' powers to prevent electronic factory workers from forming a union, by allowing shift work for women, by restricting the right to strike, and by otherwise limiting trade union activities and rights.

EXPORT-ORIENTED INDUSTRIALISATION

The NEP set out two broad objectives:

1 to eradicate poverty irrespective of race:
2 to eliminate the identification of occupation with race.

The introduction of the NEP coincided with a change in direction in industrial policy from the ISI policy, which had exhausted its first 'easy stage' by the end of the 1960s. A policy of promoting export-oriented industries had been launched from the late 1960s, but only got going in the early 1970s.

The switch to an export-oriented industrialisation strategy gave fresh impetus to industrial growth. The new emphasis was supported by the New Economic Policy's commitment to modernising Malaysia's open capitalist economy. Increasing local (including state) ownership of productive assets, especially in primary production, and even reduced foreign ownership of industry (with actual foreign control ensured through technology and marketing) were soon no longer considered incompatible with further integration and profitable participation in the world economy. By the early 1970s, government efforts to attract and encourage export-oriented industries were in full swing. Various new measures – notably the establishment of Free Trade Zones from the early 1970s – were introduced to facilitate and encourage Malaysian manufacturing production for export mainly using imported equipment and material. Such export-oriented industrialisation was certainly consistent with the emerging new international division of labour, with transnational enterprises globally relocating various production, assembly and testing processes to secure locations offering reduced wage and other production costs.

The development of export processing industries in Malaysia was rapid. A recent study of export processing zones (EPZs) in Malaysia stated that: The importance of EPZs in Malaysia . . . is unique among the developing countries establishing these zones. Nowhere else is their role as significant, either in absolute terms or as a proportion of overall manufacturing activity (Warr, 1987: 30).

Two main types of export-oriented industries have developed. Resource-based industries have involved the increased processing of older (e.g. rubber, tin) and newer (e.g. palm oil, timber) primary commodities for export. Processing of these natural resource-based exports has continued to grow for some time. By 1981, off-estate processing and wood products together still accounted for 22 per cent of manufacturing output. Scope for further expansion in this area is constrained by growth in production costs of the raw materials concerned, as well as tariff, transport and other trade barriers in the more industrially developed economies, whose governments generally continue to favour the import of raw materials rather than finished products. In the case of the wood industry, for example, the problem is further exacerbated by vested interests (timber concessionaires, logging contractors and their foreign financiers), tax structures and policies favouring the export of sawn logs or sawn timber rather than manufactured wood products (INSAN, 1989).

Thus although the processing of rubber, palm oil and wood products has continued to expand, non-resource-based export industries have been far more important since the 1970s, in terms of growth and employment generation. Most have mainly involved the relocation of certain labour-intensive aspects of manufacturing processes in stable low-wage environments, such as those offered by export processing or Free Trade Zones and licensed manufacturing warehouses (LMWs). The most dramatic growth has involved electrical and electronic components, which have accounted for slightly more than half of total manufactured exports since the mid-1980s (see Table 1.3).

Three important effects of the EOI can be highlighted as follows:

1 There was little net foreign exchange saving. A major criticism of the ISI phase had been that there was little foreign exchange saving. In the import-competing sector in 1970, gross foreign exchange savings of M$600 million were about one-fifth of gross domestic sales of M$3 billion (see Edwards, 1975: 97, 171); in 1979, gross sales totalled M$22.6 billion while gross foreign exchange savings, at about M$6.3 billion (MIPS, 1984: 84, 86, 105), were about 28 per cent of sales. Thus, the import-competing sector was import substituting, but, once capital goods imports and profit remittances were taken into account, the net foreign exchange saving as a percentage of domestic sales was small. At least, it was expected that the export-oriented industries would show greater net foreign exchange earnings. This, however is not the case, judging from the period 1972–82, for which the figures were set out in the MIPS *Final Report*. As can be seen from Table 1.9, even though sales (the large majority of which were exports) totalled M$23,057 million over the eleven-year period 1972–82, net exports totalled only M$6,853 million after deducting the material inputs (the large majority of which were imported) of M$16,204 million. Thus, material inputs averaged 70 per cent of gross sales. Furthermore,

Table 1.9 EPZs in Malaysia, 1972–82 (M$m)

	Sales	Materials	Wages	Electricity	Taxes	Profits	Capital expenditure	Net cash flow
1972	7	4	3	–	–	–	2	–2
1973	224	159	23	2	–	40	69	–29
1974	482	395	57	5	–	25	235	–210
1975	769	571	69	17	–	112	176	–64
1976	1,277	865	103	23	–	286	65	221
1977	1,313	885	141	24	1	262	81	181
1978	2,379	1,702	204	29	1	443	93	350
1979	3,933	2,066	250	42	3	572	263	309
1980	4,294	3,003	355	62	1	873	200	673
1981	4,523	3,027	423	94	4	975	286	689
1982	4,856	3,527	446	99	8	776	273	503
Total	23,057	16,204	2,074	397	18	4,364	1,743	2,621

Profits as a percentage of sales = 19
Discounted rate of profit (internal rate of return calculated from the net cash flow) equals more than 50% per annum.

Source: MIPS (1984: 120, 122).

most of the companies producing in the export processing zones were still foreign owned (in terms of employment, about 90 per cent of the FTZ activity in Malaysia is controlled by foreign companies; Ariff and Semudram, 1987: 40), so that most of the profits will have been remitted. Thus, once the profits of M$4,364 million are deducted, the net foreign exchange earnings are reduced to M$2,489 million, only a little over 10 per cent of gross sales.

2 Although manufacturing employment increased faster in the 1970s than it had in the 1960s – the total employed in manufacturing rose by more than 400,000 in the 1970s (see Table 1.1) – wages in the EPZs have been very low. With the increase in low-wage EPZ employment, by 1978 the average real wage in the manufacturing sector was below that of 1968 (see Table 1.10).

Table 1.10 Wages in manufacturing, 1963–83

Year	Average full-time factory worker's wage (M$ per month in 1968 prices)
1963	125
1968	132
1973	111
1978	124
1983	177

Source: Jomo (1986: Table 6.2).

3 There was little technological transfer or development of skills in the industries established in the EPZs and few linkages with the rest of the economy. As Warr put it: 'The degree of linkage between FTZ firms and the domestic economy, through the purchase of domestically produced raw material and capital equipment, has been disappointing' (Warr, 1987: 53).

In his cost-benefit analysis of the Malaysian EPZs, Warr calculated that, despite the lack of linkages with the rest of the economy, there was a net benefit, albeit small, to the economy from these industries (see Table 1.11). The net benefit in present value terms over the twenty-five year period 1972–97 would be M$2.3 billion (measured in 1982 prices). This estimated gain over twenty-five years is less than 4 per cent of the M$60 billion GDP for the one year of 1982.

Table 1.11 Economic gains to Malaysia from EPZs and LMWs, 1972–97

	Net benefit[a] (M$m)	'Shadow prices' used
Foreign exchange	1,000	1.11
Employment	1,222	0.825
Local raw materials	232	0.90
Local capital equipment	95	0.91
Electricity	113	0.93
Taxes	90	1.00
Administrative costs	−60	1.00
Land subsidy	−435	1.00
Total	2,257	

Note: [a] Net benefit is the benefit from 1972 to 1997 (at 1982 prices) discounted at 7.5% per annum. Warr used actual figures for the period 1972–82 and projected figures for the period 1982–97.
Source: Warr (1987: 48, 50–2).

HEAVY INDUSTRIALISATION: A SECOND ROUND OF IMPORT SUBSTITUTION?

By the beginning of the 1980s, a substantial EOI sector had developed in Malaysia, superimposed on the ISI sector, which had been promoted through the 1960s. This was the context for the launching of a heavy industrialisation programme – a second phase of industrialisation – in the 1980s. In the early 1980s, there was a major push for heavy industries by the Malaysian government. The model for this attempted second stage of import-substituting industrialisation was South Korea, which had vigorously promoted heavy industries from 1972 to 1979. The modelling in South Korea was consistent with the 'Look East' strategy which the Malaysian government adopted, under the leadership of the Prime Minister, Mahathir Mohamad, from the early

1980s (see Jomo, 1985). The heavy industrialisation programme was to be carried out through a public sector agency, namely the Heavy Industries Corporation of Malaysia (HICOM). In the Malaysian context, 'heavy industrialisation' meant the setting up of a hot briquetted iron and steel billet plant, an additional cement plant, the national car project and small engine plants. According to Khor Kok Peng, the investment costs of these (and of an industrial estate in Selangor) to HICOM totalled M$3.8 billion (Khor, 1987: 147). A number of other major projects were approved for HICOM in the early 1980s (see Jomo, 1985: 377).

Considering the nature of Malaysia's manufacturing sector in the early 1980s, it may have been desirable to support certain heavy industries to develop a more balanced, integrated and coherent national economy and industrial sector. Unfortunately, the output of some of the heavy industries developed by the Malaysian government soon faced especially stiff international competition (owing to excessive global production capacity) and required heavy protection, with little likelihood of viability otherwise, e.g. steel, cement, petrochemicals, shipbuilding and repairs (see Pura, 1985). Most of these heavy industries – including the Malaysian car project, three motor-cycle engine plants, a petroleum refining and petrochemical project, a sponge iron and steel billet plant, two new cement factories and a pulp and paper mill – faced major gluts on the world market from the outset (see Bowie, 1988). The significant protection required has raised the production costs and consumer prices for other parts of the Malaysian economy. Thus, heavy industrialisation has involved massive government borrowings from abroad for investment in these projects, which, with their heavy imports of capital goods and long gestation periods, would seem to have been socially unprofitable.

As a result of these investments in heavy industrialisation, the annual public sector investment in commerce and industry rose from M$0.3 billion in 1978–80 to M$0.9 billion in 1982 and M$1.5 billion in 1984. Most of the investments were financed by external borrowing. As the World Bank has pointed out: 'In 1981 and 1982, net public foreign borrowing amounted to 7.5 per cent and 9.6 per cent of GNP respectively. Over the period of forced expansion, 1981–1984, foreign savings on average financed 28 per cent of total investment compared to the Plan forecast of 0.2 per cent' (World Bank, 1989: 14). The World Bank further indicated that: 'This recourse to external funds helped these agencies [public enterprises] escape the surveillance and discipline that could have been imposed by the Federal government had there been a greater reliance on the Treasury as a source of funds' (World Bank, 1989: 14).

Thus, in the first half of the 1980s, as public investment rose, so did long-term external debt. As Table 1.12 shows, the federal overnment's external debt more than doubled in the two years from 1980 to 1982, from just under M$5 billion in 1980 to M$12.5 billion in 1982. As a percentage of GDP at market prices, this debt doubled from 10 per cent in 1980 to 20 per cent in 1982. The percentage continued to rise to more than 38 per cent in 1986.

Table 1.12 Public sector investment and foreign debt, 1980s

Year	GDP M$bn	Public sector investment M$bn	Public sector investment % of GDP	Long-term capital flows M$bn	Federal government external debt M$bn	Federal government external debt % of GDP
1980	51.4	8.9	17	0.2	4.9	10
1981	58.5	11.6	20	3.0	7.8	13
1982	62.6	11.4	18	5.2	12.5	20
1983	69.9	12.5	18	6.3	20.8	30
1984	80.0	12.0	15	4.7	23.1	29
1985	77.5	10.9	14	2.5	28.1	36
1986	71.7	7.5	10	2.1	27.6	38
1987	79.7	8.9	11	-2.6	25.9	32
1988	90.8	10.7	12	-5.0	25.3	28

Note: Long-term capital flows are official flows only and exclude flows on the 'corporate investment' account.
Sources: Ministry of Finance, *Economic Report* (1981: x, xi; 1983: xiii; and 1989: x, xi, xiv, xv, xii).

Table 1.13 Balance of payments, 1970–87 (US$bn)

Year	Goods and non-factor services			Net factor payments and transfer	Current balance	Net long term
	Exports	Imports	Balance			
1970	1.8	1.6	0.2	−0.2	–	–
1975	4.2	4.4	−0.2	−0.3	−0.5	0.8
1980	14.1	13.5	0.6	−0.9	−0.3	1.1
1981	13.1	14.7	−1.6	−0.9	−2.5	2.3
1982	13.7	16.1	−2.4	−1.2	−3.6	3.9
1983	15.6	17.3	−1.7	−1.8	−3.5	3.2
1984	18.4	17.8	0.6	−2.3	−1.7	2.4
1985	17.2	15.6	1.6	−2.3	−0.7	0.7
1986	15.8	14.1	1.7	−1.7	–	0.4
1987	20.1	15.9	4.2	−2.0	2.2	−0.7

Source: World Bank (1989: 144).

But, as a result of net foreign inflows (see Table 1.13), in 1981 and 1982 the central bank's foreign exchange reserves increased and 'pressure to depreciate the exchange rate was temporarily diverted' (World Bank, 1989: 14). Thus, the external financing gave support to Malaysia's real effective exchange rate so that it appreciated through the first half of the 1980s, as can be seen from Figure 1.2.

Thus, through the first half of the 1980s, in spite of a deficit on the external current account, Malaysia's effective exchange rate rose in real terms – and, as it did, the export-oriented manufacturing sector became less and less competitive. This was reflected in an increase in the trade deficit on manufactures

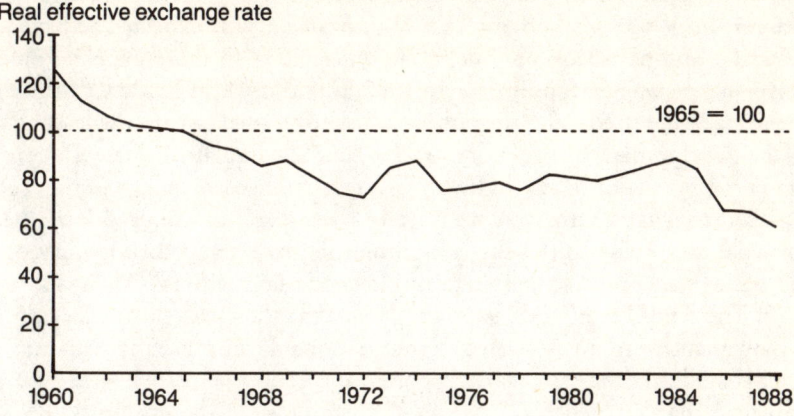

Figure 1.2   Malaysia: real effective exchange rates, 1960–88
Source: Wood (1988: 106, 127); World Bank (1987: 13).

from US$5.3 billion in 1980 to US$6.8 billion in 1982. Manufactured exports more or less stood still over this period, while manufactured imports increased substantially (see World Bank, 1989: 144). It is important to re-emphasise that this appreciation of the real exchange rate was not due to a surge in primary commodity prices forcing up the exchange rate and making the manufacturing sector less competitive internationally. In fact, as Table 1.14 shows, Malaysia's barter terms of trade declined significantly from 1980 to 1982.

As foreign financing helped sustain the real exchange rate, thus rendering Malaysian manufacturing less competitive, manufacturing growth slowed.

Table 1.14   Terms of trade, 1965–87

Year	Term of trade (P_x/P_m) (1978 = 100)
1965	107
1970	94
1975	82
1980	111
1981	101
1982	99
1983	102
1984	109
1985	104
1986	88
1987	94

Source: World Bank (1989: 143).

But at the same time, the performance of the heavy industrialisation programme itself was weak. Being capital-intensive, it was expected to have long gestation and pay-back periods, but even relative to these expectations, its performance was disappointing. In 1989, the Mid-Term Review of the Fifth Malaysia Plan stated that: 'the public sector continued to play the leading role in the development of heavy industries', but it complained that: 'In general, the performance of heavy industry projects sponsored by the public sector was far from satisfactory. A number of these projects suffered from heavy financial losses due to the sluggish domestic market and the inability of the industries concerned to compete in international markets' (Malaysia, 1989: 196). The Mid-Term Review pointed out that the costs of production and management were high relative to international levels, that the situation was exacerbated by the low capacity utilisation of the plants, and that the industries had created few linkages with the rest of the economy (see also Ariff and Semudram, 1987: 46, 47).

Thus, Malaysian industrial policy in the early 1980s started with a big push for heavy industrialisation, but by the middle of the decade there was little prospect of that programme succeeding, at least within the 1980s, and when, in the mid-1980s, Malaysia's terms of trade fell sharply, the economy was in crisis.

For example, Malaysia's cement production capacity of 7.2 million metric tonnes annually was double domestic consumption in the mid-1980s. Surcharges on imported cement to protect the domestic market now exceed 50 per cent. After government agencies invested over M$1.2 billion in the Perwaja steel plant in Terengganu, it was found that the prototype 'direct reduction' industrial process used was not viable, for which the supplier agreed to pay only M$467 million in compensation. Since the value of the ringgit halved against the yen after September 1985, the actual compensation in yen terms is considerably lower than what it may appear to be in ringgit terms, especially if interest charges in the interim are also considered.

Similarly, the economic burden of the Proton car project in the first decade of its existence has been estimated to be at least M$1.6 billion (Chee, 1985). The project was originally based on estimates of annual car sales rising by 8 per cent annually from 110,000 in 1982. Instead, total sales dropped to only about 30,000 in 1987 as a result of the recession and increased car prices due to the depreciation of the ringgit (especially against the yen and Deutschmark) and higher import tariffs to protect the Malaysian car.

On the whole, rising real international interest rates, quick and lucrative returns from property investments, rising wages as unemployment declined, and a recession in international markets for Malaysia's manufactured exports all adversely affected new manufacturing investments in the first half of the 1980s. By the middle of the decade, Malaysian heavy industrialisation showed little prospect of succeeding, at least within the decade. As the Industrial Master Plan (IMP) later recognised, the debate on heavy industrialisation

HISTORICAL PERSPECTIVE

should not have been about whether or not to develop such industries, but rather, which industries to develop (Shiode, 1989).

CRISIS AND RECOVERY

The middle of the 1980s was a period of crisis for Malaysia, with the government, led by Mahathir, being enmeshed in a series of controversies. Underlying the political crises was an economic one. In 1986, real gross domestic product was at about the same level as it had been in 1984 (see Table 1.15). And, as about '60,000 Malaysians returned home in 1986 after losing their jobs in Singapore ... according to the latest reliable estimates, the number of unemployed [was] around 450,000, yielding an unemployment rate of 8.2 per cent' (Ariff and Semudram, 1987: 25). There was a particularly severe recession in manufacturing in 1985. Real manufacturing output in that year dropped by over 3 per cent (see Table 1.15). Manufactured exports were lower in 1985 than in 1984. A 1989 World Bank report on Malaysia attributed this partly to a recession in the global semiconductor industry and partly to a loss in Malaysia's competitiveness (World Bank, 1989: 17).

Table 1.15 Gross domestic product (GDP) and net output in manufacturing (NOM), 1971–89

Year	GDP		Population	GDP per capita	NOM	
	Total (M$bn)	Year-to year (%)	(million)	(M$ '000)	Total (M$bn)	Year-to year (%)
1971	22.2	–	10.7	2.1	3.1	–
1972	24.3	9.5	11.0	2.2	3.6	11.6
1973	27.2	11.9	11.3	2.4	4.1	13.9
1974	29.4	8.1	11.6	2.5	5.1	24.4
1975	29.6	0.7	11.9	2.5	5.2	2.0
1976	33.1	11.8	12.2	2.7	6.2	19.2
1977	35.6	7.6	12.5	2.8	6.8	9.7
1978	38.0	6.7	12.8	3.0	7.4	8.8
1979	41.5	9.2	13.4	3.1	8.2	10.8
1980	44.7	7.7	13.8	3.2	8.9	8.5
1981	47.9	7.2	14.1	3.4	9.3	4.5
1982	50.4	5.2	14.5	3.5	9.7	4.3
1983	53.6	6.8	14.9	3.6	10.4	7.2
1984	57.7	7.6	15.3	3.8	11.7	12.5
1985	57.2	-0.9	15.7	3.6	11.3	-3.2
1986	57.9	1.2	16.1	3.6	12.1	7.1
1987	60.9	5.2	16.5	3.7	13.7	13.2
1988	66.3	8.9	16.9	3.9	16.2	18.2
1989	71.3	7.5	17.4	4.1	18.3	13.0

Note: The GDP and NOM are based on 1978 prices. In 1989 prices, the GDP and GDP per capita figures for 1989 are 100.7 and 5.8 respectively.
Sources: Ministry of Finance, *Economic Report* (1974: vi, vii; 1981: xii, xiii; 1983: xiv, xv; and 1989: vi, xi, xii, xiii); *Malaysian Management Review* (1989: 19, 27).

The recession was accompanied by an outflow of capital. Under these circumstances, the exchange rate either had to be protected by further overseas borrowing or by exchange controls, or it had to fall. It fell, and fell sharply. In 1986, the exchange rate of the ringgit to the US dollar fell by a little over 7 per cent, but in terms of the IMF's Special Drawing Rights (a basket of currencies), the ringgit fell by 20 per cent (see Ministry of Finance, 1989: li), and the real effective exchange rate fell by about the same percentage (see Figure 1.2).

This depreciation in effect of the ringgit lowered production costs in Malaysia as real wage costs declined over the mid-1980s with the rise in unemployment as well as new labour policies and laws weakening organised labour's bargaining position and enhancing labour flexibility. In addition, the sharp decline in Malaysia's real effective exchange rate coincided in 1986 with a relaxation of the guidelines imposed under the Investment Coordination Act (for example, the requirements for local shareholdings were relaxed) and a reinforcement of tax concessions under the Promotion of Investments Act. The real depreciation, the relaxation of the Investment Coordination Act and the Promotion of Investments Act made Malaysia a very attractive place for investment, and these factors, combined with favourable external market conditions, have resulted in a resurgence of export-oriented manufacturing, largely under the auspices of foreign capital.

In terms of US dollars, manufactured exports in 1987 were 15 per cent higher than in 1985, while manufactured imports (again in terms of US$) had risen by only 6 per cent over the same two-year period (World Bank, 1989: 144). As a result, there was a transformation in the balance of payments: whereas in 1982 there had been a deficit on the current account of about 14 per cent of GNP, in 1987 this had been transformed into a surplus of 8 per cent (World Bank, 1989: 1).

RESTRUCTURING AND REAPPRAISAL

Thus, by the end of the 1980s, the manufacturing sector in Malaysia was once more expanding at a rapid rate. In general, over the past three decades, this has been the pattern for the manufacturing sector – namely one of rapid growth. As Table 1.1 showed, manufacturing employment grew eightfold between 1957 and 1989 and employment in manufacturing in 1989 was more than 17 per cent of the labour force. This growth of manufacturing employment has been accompanied by rapid increases in both Malay employment and female employment in manufacturing.

Malay participation in manufacturing employment has grown rapidly from 20 per cent in 1957 to 29 per cent in 1970 and to 54 per cent in 1980 (McGee *et al.*, 1986: Table 2.5). This is not surprising in view of the limited new employment opportunities in peasant agriculture, where Malays have historically been concentrated, relatively faster Malay population and labour force growth rates, and government efforts to raise Malay employment in the 'modern capitalist' sector generally. Since manufacturing and services have been heavily concentrated in major urban centres on the West Coast, despite some weak government efforts to disperse new industries (Spinanger, 1986), and with high Malay participation in the rapidly expanding government sector, Malay urbanisation has risen considerably, especially since the 1970s. The proportion of Malays living in urban areas grew from 21 per cent in 1957 to 38 per cent in 1980 (McGee et al., 1986). Hence, the growth of industry and services, coupled with NEP restructuring stipulations, has somewhat reduced the identification of ethnicity with economic function and urban–rural location.

The tremendous rise in manufacturing employment has not only led to rising Malay participation in manufacturing; there has also been a fast rise in female participation in manufacturing employment (see Table 1.16), particularly as a result of the size of employment in the electronics industry (see Grace, 1990). Female labour constituted almost two-thirds of the increase in the Malay manufacturing labour force between 1970 and 1980 (McGee et al., 1986); as a result, then, the manufacturing labour force has been feminised, especially in the 1970s. As Table 1.16 shows, the proportion of female labour in manufacturing increased substantially from only 11 per cent in 1957 to 29 per cent in 1970 and 41 per cent in 1980. The expansion in female employment in manufacturing was substantially due to the rapid expansion of the female-dominated textiles, clothing and electronics industries. By 1983, almost half (46.7 per cent) of all female workers in the manufacturing sector were in these sub-sectors, compared with only 7 per cent of male workers. This phenomenon of female preponderance in certain jobs is related to employer preferences and 'job discrimination'. Women are presumed to be more proficient in routine tasks requiring finger dexterity and patience (qualities desired by management for electronic assembly work and garment-making), and tend to be disproportionately employed in industries in which workers are unorganised or poorly organised and 'willing' to accept low wages and inferior working conditions. Thus, in 1984, although women formed about a third of Malaysia's total workforce, they accounted for only about a quarter of trade union membership.

Table 1.16 Gender distribution of manufacturing employment by sector, 1957–85

	1957		1970		1980		1985	
	Male	Female	Male	Female	Male	Female	Male	Female
All manufacturing	89	11	71	29	59	41	55	45
Textiles and clothing	59	41	39	61	27	73	n.a.	n.a.
Electronics	99	1	85	15	27	73	8	92

Sources: McGee et al. (1986); Ministry of Labour, *Labour and Manpower Report, 1985-86*, Kuala Lumpur.

Thus, over the past three decades, there has been rapid growth in Malaysian manufacturing net output (value added) and employment, and there have been considerable changes in the composition of the manufacturing labour force. Nevertheless, the manufacturing sector in Malaysia remains a highly segmented one. It is a tripartite structure, with a resource-based export-oriented sector quite separate from import-substituting industries, which are in turn quite separate from the export-oriented clothing and electronic industries in the EPZs. Table 1.17 summarises the manufacturing sector in 1987 in these terms.

Import substitution in Malaysia has generally involved the assembly, packaging and final processing of finished goods – previously imported from abroad – by domestic labour, using machines and material largely imported from abroad. The goods have been produced almost entirely for the domestic market behind high protective barriers. The employment-generating capacity of such industrialisation has been limited by the typically capital-intensive foreign technology utilised, the weak linkages of these industries with the rest of the national economy, and the small domestic market. Being relatively capital-intensive industries, however, the employers have generally been more capable of conceding real wage increases to labour since their wage bills account for a relatively small proportion of production costs.

In contrast, the success of export-oriented industrialisation has been contingent on the government's ability to attract foreign investors seeking to lower production costs (especially labour costs) to be more competitive in the international market. Precisely because of their use of labour-intensive production techniques, these industries tend to generate more employment directly, while being more sensitive to changes in wage costs. Since many such industries are considered to be 'footloose' – i.e. easily capable of relocating if sufficiently attracted by circumstances elsewhere – the government tries to ensure that the investment climate remains attractive to the investors concerned for fear of losing them to competing host governments. As noted earlier, these industries are almost entirely locked into the international economy.

By contrast with the ISI and EPZ sectors, the resource-based industries are producing for export on the basis of domestic materials. But, for a variety of reasons, these industries have faced considerable obstacles to the upgrading of their value added. Thus tyres are the major rubber products in the world market, but escalating tariffs and transport costs, combined with the lack of a local source of synthetic rubber, have meant that the Malaysian production of tyres has been limited. Palm oil refining has been more successful in Malaysia, but the development of the wood products industry has been slow. One of the major obstacles to the development of the wood products industry has been the way in which logging concessions have been granted. The issue of licences has not been subject to composition but, at the same time, the way in which logging concessions have been issued has not encouraged long-term investment in the industry.

Table 1.17 Malaysian manufacturing, 1987

MIC Code	Industry descriptions	Gross output (M$m)	Exports (M$m)	% of gross output exported	Value added (M$m)	Value added as % of gross output
	Resource-based industries:					
31152/3	Palm oil refining	6,081	4,046	67	671	11
35591	Rubber remilling (off-estate)	2,733	2,596	95	382	14
33	Wood products – sawmilling	1,431	1,652	115	457	32
	– others	1,389	937	67	500	36
355	Rubber products (excl. 35591)	1,629	330	20	517	32
	Subtotals	13,263	9,561	72	2,527	19
	Import-substituting industries:					
31	Food, bev, tobacco (excl.31152/3)	7,068	1,004	14	1,975	28
34	Paper and paperboard	1,484	201	14	608	41
351–4/356	Chemicals and petroleum products and plastics	8,117	1,749	22	2,526	31
36	Non-metallic mineral products	1,612	302	19	790	49
37/381	Iron/steel, metal products	3,567	782	22	874	25
384	Transport equipment	1,338	97	7	380	28
	Subtotals	23,186	4,135	18	7,153	31
	Export-oriented industries:					
32	Textiles/garments	2,943	2,208	75	928	32
382	Machinery	1,151	555	48	330	29
383	Electric and electric m/c	9,512	10,291	108	2,147	23
	Subtotals	13,606	13,054	96	3,405	25
	Others (specify):					
385	Professional and scientific equipment	320	385	60	107	33
390	Others	321			125	39
	Subtotals	641	385		232	36
	Total	50,696	27,135		13,317	26

Sources: Department of Statistics, *Malaysia Industrial Survey, 1987*; Department of Statistics, *Malaysia External Trade Statistics, Exports (Parts I–IV) and Imports (Parts I–III), 1987*, Kuala Lumpur; Bank Negara Malaysia, *Quarterly Bulletin*, 5, 1, June 1990.

Ignoring for the moment the resource-based industries, the Malaysian manufacturing sector is a 'dual' one, with an ISI sector producing for the domestic market almost entirely separate from the export-oriented industries in the EPZs. Although this dualism was acknowledged in a World Bank study on Malaysia published in 1980 (see Young, Bussink and Hassan, 1980: 189), it was not recognised by the World Bank in its 1987 *World Development Report* (World Bank, 1987). In that report, the World Bank categorised Malaysia as being 'moderately outward-oriented' for the 1963–73 and 1973–85 periods (see World Bank 1987: 83). But averaging the ISI and EOI sub-sectors of Malaysian manufacturing in this way makes little sense. Indeed it makes as much sense to say that a person with one foot in boiling water and one foot in ice cold water is 'moderately comfortable'.

This dualism is a major problem facing the Malaysian economy. The major questions raised are: How can the EPZ sector be integrated with the domestic sector? How can the ISI sector be integrated into the export markets? Should Malaysian industrial policy in the 1990s be market oriented or plan oriented, or is a combination of the two feasible and desirable? These are the fundamental questions which provide the framework for the following chapters and to which we return in more detail in the final chapter.

NOTES

1 Malaysia (or at least Peninsular Malaysia) gained its political independence in 1957. In 1963, the North Borneo states of Sarawak and Sabah joined the Federation, as did Singapore. Two years later, Singapore left the Federation to become a separate republic and since then, Malaysia has consisted of the eleven states of Peninsular Malaysia and the two East Malaysian states of Sabah and Sarawak.
2 This was also true in the 1970s. According to the MIPS, the subsidy equivalent of tax and credit subsidies in Malaysia in 1979 was M$505 million (see MIPS, 1984: Table 5.11). The MIPS stated that this was a potential or maximum figure, but was, even so, only about a third of the subsidy-equivalent of protection.
3 'Since the Edwards study draws extensively on price comparisons, it might have minimised any errors from using tariff rates as proxies for NPRs.' (Rhee, 1980: 2–17).

REFERENCES

Alavi, R. (1987) 'The Phases of Industrialisation in Malaysia, 1957–1980s', MA dissertation, UEA, Norwich, UK, September.

Ariff, M. and Semudram, M. (1987) *Trade and Financing Strategies: A Case Study of Malaysia*, Working Paper No. 21, Overseas Development Institute, London, July.

Bowie, Alasdair (1988) 'Industrial Aspirations in a Divided Society: Malaysian Heavy Industries, 1980–1988', paper for Association for Asian Studies annual meeting, San Francisco, 25–27 March.

Chee, P.L. (1985) 'The Proton Saga – No Reverse Gear! The Economic Burden of Malaysia's Car Project', in Jomo (ed.), *The Sun Also Sets: Lessons in Looking East*, 2nd edn, INSAN, Kuala Lumpur.

Edwards, C.B. (1975) 'Protection, Profits and Policy: An Analysis of Industrialisation in Malaysia', PhD Thesis, University of East Anglia, Norwich, UK.

Edwards, C.B. (1985) *The Fragmented World: Competing Perspectives on Trade, Money and Crisis*, Methuen, London.

Grace, E. (1990) *Shortcircuiting Labour: Unionising Electronic Workers in Malaysia*, INSAN, Kuala Lumpur.

IMP (1985) *Medium and Long Term Industrial Master Plan, Malaysia, 1986–1995*, UNIDO, Vienna, August.

INSAN (1989) *Logging against the Natives of Sarawak*, INSAN, Kuala Lumpur.

Jomo K.S. (ed.) (1985) *Malaysia's New Economic Policies*, Malaysian Economic Association, Kuala Lumpur.

Jomo K.S. (1986) *A Question of Class: Capital, the State and Uneven Development in Malaya*, Oxford University Press, Singapore.

Jomo K.S. and Ishak Shari (1986) *Development Policies and Income Inequality in Peninsular Malaysia*, Institute for Advanced Studies, University of Malaya, Kuala Lumpur.

Khor Kok Peng (1987) *Malaysia's Economy in Decline*, Consumers' Association of Penang, Penang.

Lim, D. (1973) *Economic Growth in West Malaysia, 1947–70*, Oxford University Press, Kuala Lumpur.

McGee, T.G. et al. (1986) *Industrialisation and Labour Force Processes: A Case Study of Peninsular Malaysia*, Australian National University, Canberra.

Malaysia (1989) *Mid-Term Review of the Fifth Malaysia Plan, 1986–1990*, Government Printer, Kuala Lumpur.

Malaysian Management Review (1989) Special Issue on the New Economic Policy, 24, 2, August.

Ministry of Finance (1989), *Economic Report 1989/1990*, Kuala Lumpur.

MIPS (1984) *Final Report of the Malaysian Industrial Policies Studies Project*, IMG Consultants Pty Ltd, Sydney.

Pura, R. (1985) 'Doubts over Heavy Industrialisation Strategy', in Jomo (ed.), *The Sun Also Sets*, INSAN, Kuala Lumpur.

Rhee, Y. (1980) 'Incentive Systems and Policies for the Manufacturing Industries in Malaysia', World Bank, December.

Shiode, H. (1989) *Japanese Investment in South East Asia: Three Malaysian Case Studies*, Centre for the Progress of People, Hong Kong.

Spinanger, D. (1986) *Industrialisation Policies and Regional Economic Development in Malaysia*, Oxford University Press, Singapore.

Warr, P.G. (1987) 'Malaysia's Industrial Enclaves: Benefits and Costs', *The Developing Economies*, 25, 3, March.

Wood, A. (1988) 'Global Trends in Real Exchange Rates, 1960–84', World Bank Discussion Paper No. 35, World Bank, Washington, DC.

World Bank (1987) *World Development Report 1987*, The World Bank, Washington, DC.

World Bank (1989) *Malaysia: Matching Risks and Rewards in a Mixed Economy*, The World Bank, Washington, DC.

Young, K., Bussink, W. and Hassan, P. (1980) *Malaysia: Growth and Equity in a Multiracial Society*, Johns Hopkins University Press, Washington, DC.

2

LABOUR FLEXIBILITY IN THE MALAYSIAN MANUFACTURING SECTOR

Guy Standing

Malaysia may be one of those countries in which there is successful industrialisation without there ever being a period in which manufacturing accounted for anything like a majority of total employment. Policymakers and social scientists in the 1990s may also look back on the growth of labour flexibility in the manufacturing labour market of the late 1980s as not just a response to the international economic crisis of the early and mid-1980s but a critical phase in the emergence of a modern society and economic structure.

This is not to suggest that the phase is desirable in itself, or even necessary. It does, however, pose considerable dilemmas for those who will have to shape labour market policy in the era following the end of the New Economic Policy (NEP) in 1990. As will be suggested in this chapter – albeit tentatively and partially – a more flexible labour market will place a far greater onus on labour policy to provide protection against abuse and insecurity and to provide an environment in which the interests of equity and efficiency are jointly served.

This chapter is based in part on the analysis of a survey of over 2,600 manufacturing establishments across Peninsular Malaysia carried out in 1988 (see Appendix 1). The context of the study was particularly intriguing, for the 1988 Manufacturing Labour Flexibility Survey (MLFS) came at the mid-point between the end of the crisis that hit the economy in the early 1980s and the beginning of the post-NEP era. In a sense, the survey was designed to tell a story about what had happened, was happening and was likely to happen between 1985 and 1990. The story may be deficient in details and unclear in some respects, but it had been hoped that it would establish a national benchmark for economists and policymakers inside and outside Malaysia to examine subsequent labour market changes in an era of structural adjustment and accelerated industrialisation. As a detailed analysis has been presented to the Economic Planning Unit (EPU) in the Prime Minister's Department, this chapter will only review the principal findings.

Any study of the manufacturing labour market in Malaysia has to be placed very firmly in the historical context of the objectives and evolution of the NEP and the underlying development goals of successive governments since Independence in 1957. To put the story in context, it is worth reminding ourselves of the main macro-policy changes influencing Malaysian industrialisation.

Malaysian industrial policy has passed through four distinctive phases. The first was one of import substitution, which lasted from Independence in 1957 until 1968; the second was what might be called selective export-led industrialisation, from 1968 until the early 1980s; the third was a phase of crisis and retrenchment, from 1983 until 1986; and the fourth could be described as liberalised export-led industrialisation, which began in late 1986.

From 1958 until 1968 the most symbolic policy instrument for manufacturing investment and employment was the Pioneer Industries Ordinance, which provided fiscal incentives to production rather than tariff protection; this was supplemented by the Tariff Advisory Board, set up to promote 'infant industries' through the granting of selective protection. It was a decade in which capital-intensive industries flourished, partly because tax exemptions were linked to capital expenditure. Total manufacturing employment grew, but only slowly.

In 1968 there was a marked shift to export-led industrialisation with the introduction of the Investment Incentives Act, drafted in the face of chronically high unemployment and growing racial tensions. The latter were associated with the labour market stagnation and growing inequalities that had accompanied the pattern of economic development. The Investment Incentives Act boosted export-oriented industrialisation by providing tax relief for export-oriented firms, investment tax credits, accelerated depreciation allowances, export incentives, tariff protection for new manufacturing establishments and exemption from import duty and surtax. These were complemented by the establishment in July 1971 of the Labour Utilisation Relief, which granted tax relief to companies based on the number of workers employed, and by the abolition of the 2 per cent payroll tax so as to encourage labour-intensive industries. But this second phase of export-led industrialisation was also marked by the strong direct involvement of government, in that industrial growth was made dependent on the restructuring objectives of the NEP. Public enterprises spread, as did public investment in private industrial enterprises, while government regulations played an important role in shaping the emerging pattern of employment.

From then until the early 1980s the growth of manufacturing output, exports and employment was spectacular, far faster than the equivalent for the whole economy. Between 1970 and 1980 the value of manufacturing exports almost doubled in real terms, and as a share of total exports rose from under 12 per cent to 22 per cent (see Table 1.3 above). The manufacturing employment growth rate was double that of the whole economy, while its share of total employment rose from 11.4 per cent in 1970 to 15.8 per cent in 1980 (see Table 1.1 above). Most of that growth came in export-oriented sectors and most of that in the free trade zones. Most spectacular of all was the expansion of the electrical components and electronics sector, mainly through electronic component assembly.[1] Overall, manufacturing employment more than quadrupled between 1968 and 1980, reaching 802,000 in 1980 (Department of Statistics, various years). By the early 1980s it was not just the estate and construction industries that were complaining of labour shortage, for by then there was a tight labour market in many parts of the country.

In 1983 the international recession and the collapse of commodity prices began to bite. For a while total manufacturing employment stabilised, with falls in key export sectors such as textiles and rubber products. Then in 1985–6 a severe recession – the worst since Independence – shook manufacturing, obliging managements to focus on their labour policy and resulting in widespread retrenchments in wood products, electrical goods, electronics, textiles and many other industries. To a certain extent it was the responses to this upheaval – which in later times may be seen as a hiccough in the country's industrialisation – that formed the context of the MLFS.

One can identify 1986 as the beginning of a fourth distinctive phase, that of liberalised export-led industrialisation. Its key features have been a relaxation of the NEP in the interest of boosting industrial investment, exports and employment, with the intention of attracting more foreign investment, coupled with a reversal of the longstanding policy of promoting industrialisation through investment in publicly owned enterprises.[2] In particular, there has been a drive to create 'Malaysia Inc.' via privatisation. There has been the much-discussed *Industrial Master Plan 1986–95*, which *inter alia* identified twelve industrial sectors for special expansionary treatment in the early 1990s. More immediately, the 30 per cent foreign equity restriction on foreign investment was dropped; since 1986 foreign investors have been able to hold up to 100 per cent of the equity as long as the company exported at least 80 per cent of its production, and could hold up to 51 per cent if more than 51 per cent of its production was exported or if the output consisted of high-technology products. New investment applications received from October 1986 until 1990 were allowed to have any level of foreign equity as long as the company agreed to export more than 50 per cent of its product or if it employed more than 350 Malaysians.

This fourth phase has involved a macroeconomic policy shift within the NEP away from restructuring towards boosting economic growth, primarily through its focus on market liberalisation. This is not to suggest that policymakers abandoned the one, or had formerly given the other no attention, merely that there has been a perceptible reorientation. It seems, for example, that there has been a shift from income redistribution, via the expansion of public non-financial enterprises, the public sector and tax-financed subsidies to Bumiputra interests, to capital redistribution, via privatisation and a more concerted policy of subsidising export-oriented enterprises. Probably, a policy of market liberalisation means that micro-level policies will have to bear more responsibility for social restructuring, not just in the conventional Malaysian sense but in terms of protecting all vulnerable groups in the labour market.

Although unemployment rose to over 10 per cent in 1987 and 1988, by then industrial expansion was once again impressive. The ideas of supply-side structural adjustment were being promoted in an international atmosphere favouring labour and capital market 'deregulation', including the wholesale privatisation of economic and social activities. Industrial policy has shifted towards a more market-oriented, outward-oriented strategy that favours multinational capital and more management control of their establishments. By 1988, with privatisation in full swing, the industrial structure seemed set for a period of profound change.

That reorientation made it important to take stock of how manufacturing firms had responded to the shocks of the mid-1980s and to obtain an impression of how the further influx of foreign and export-oriented firms could be expected to tilt subsequent labour market developments.

Our core hypotheses can be stated quite clearly. In the second half of the 1980s a more sharply defined industrial dualism had been emerging: large establishments had been growing and strengthening their position relative to small ones, while within establishments of almost all sizes and in all industries a labour flexibilisation process had been gaining strength, involving a shift away from employment security and a shift of employment risk from companies to workers.

If these trends were supported by the data, then policymakers might be advised to address both questions with some urgency in the post-NEP era, particularly as the most disadvantaged groups tend to be crowded into more precarious forms of employment. It would be in nobody's interest for industrial fragmentation to undermine the considerable social achievements of the past two decades. Yet it will be argued that certain long-term trends in the labour market that were expected to accompany industrialisation, including the 'formalisation' of employment, have been checked if not reversed. This partly reflects adoption of trends from highly industrialised economies and partly arises because manufacturing enterprises in Malaysia have realised the advantages of alternative employment relations.

SUPPLY-SIDE VERSUS SOCIAL ADJUSTMENT LABOUR MARKET POLICIES

At this point it might be useful to step out of the Malaysian scene to consider the swirl of international debate surrounding the two vogue notions of 'structural adjustment' and 'labour market flexibility', the latter being seen by many as a necessity for the former, which in turn is seen as necessary for successful industrialisation and development.

For a long period the dominant mode of economic thinking about the medium and long term was what might be called 'social adjustment'. In essence, its underlying model is Keynesian, with a social-democratic ethos and a belief that markets could and should be circumvented or moderated by institutional and other regulatory devices in the interest of both equity and long-run economic growth.

For well-known reasons, this model was put on the defensive by the economic upheavals of the 1970s and 1980s and the pressure for rapid and extensive adjustments to internationally transmitted economic shocks and instability. The pursuit of outward-oriented development became a global panacea, with earnest economists everywhere diligently searching for 'rigidities' – particularly associated with trade unions and labour regulations – that were alleged to be raising production costs and undermining the international competitiveness of country X or Y. There re-emerged an overwhelming faith in markets untramelled by regulations, collective organisations or other institutional interventions. This supply-side critique has been pervasively influential during the past decade, becoming the conventional wisdom of the era. In Malaysia, as elsewhere, it can be predicted that the next few years will witness a critical debate between this supply-side model of structural adjustment and a re-emerging social adjustment model that is more concerned with distributional issues.

One can juxtapose, necessarily rather crudely in the interest of brevity, the two perspectives as they relate to labour market policy and the pursuit of labour flexibility. In doing so, we may be able to highlight some of the critical dilemmas facing economists and planners considering the next phase of Malaysia's economic development. As for the notion of labour flexibility, it has been used as a euphemism for many changes but ultimately refers to the responsiveness of the labour market, the ease and cost with which labour mobility of various types can be achieved, and the ease with which the workforce can be adjusted to achieve rapid productivity growth. For unions and workers, flexibility has suggested insecurity; for employers, it has suggested efficiency and adaptability. In a sense, both sides are correct.

In recent years the pressure for adjustment to external shocks and the belief in outward-oriented development have led to a sustained 'supply-side' critique of many labour market policies that had been perceived as desirable attributes of socioeconomic development. One is therefore obliged to consider this critique, and the appeal of alternatives that they wish to put in its place, dwelling rather more on those that might have resonances to Malaysian debates.

LABOUR FLEXIBILITY
Price versus social distortions

The essence of a social adjustment strategy is 'growth with social protection'. Among its elements are the following labour-related aspects. First, to ameliorate poverty of the most basic kind, there are usually food subsidies and price support systems to encourage the production of domestically consumed food. Critics say this is a 'market distortion'. Second, there is usually some minimum wage protection machinery, designed ostensibly to reduce exploitation and alleviate poverty. Critics say that this amounts to a market distortion, raising wages above the market-clearing, equilibrium level, deterring employment by favouring capital–labour substitution and increasing 'inequalities between the formal and informal sectors'. Third, there are institutional forms of labour security protection – safety-and-health standards, employment security regulations (preventing arbitrary dismissal, for example), limits on working time, overtime, etc. These are also intended to protect workers from exploitation and, by ameliorating working conditions, enhance productivity. Critics say these amount to market distortions since they represent non-wage labour costs and rigidities that impede labour mobility and thus the efficient allocation of resources.

Fourth, the social adjustment school believes in promoting freedom of association and that participatory collective organisations, notably trade unions, should be given an active role, to encourage dynamic efficiency, to strengthen democratic tendencies, to ensure more equitable income distribution and to restrict discrimination. Again, critics see such organisations as market distortions in that they limit the ability of firms to react to market forces and limit the realisation of high profits that could boost investment. Fifth, the social adjustment school sees public expenditure as complementing private expenditure, as potentially productive and as a means of mobilising and retaining resources for national development. Critics say this too is a market distortion, arguing that it results in 'financial crowding out' of private investment and growth, while being unproductive, unresponsive to market forces and an inappropriate standard-setter for wages and conditions of employment.

By contrast, the labour-related policies that characterise the supply-side strategy focus on price mechanisms and overcoming price distortions. Its approach to structural adjustment combines a 'stabilisation' policy and a development policy, for which a set of microeconomic reforms are perceived as necessary for macroeconomic success. Stabilisation essentially means a deflationary monetary policy to hold down domestic demand – so limiting imports – and combat inflation. That means temporarily lowering consumption and employment. This is complemented by an 'outward-looking' development strategy, involving 'trade liberalisation', nominal and real exchange rate devaluation and a shift in relative prices between tradable and non-tradable goods and services. Governments should cut subsidies to basic consumption goods, thereby raising the relative return to investment in tradable goods and services. The social adjustment school might say that this results in 'social distortion' and that subsidies on non-tradables promote productivity of the current and future workforce while lowering the efficiency wage in the sectors. The evidence is far from conclusive that cutting such subsidies is unequivocably beneficial for development.

Minimum wages and relative wages

The supply-side strategy puts overwhelming emphasis on 'competitiveness', which *inter alia* means reducing labour costs and making them more flexible. Statutory minimum wages are opposed on the grounds that they price goods out of the market that would be produced by low-paid, low-productivity workers, thus causing unemployment. Critics of that view refer to the multiple functions of minimum wages. They note that very low wages encourage low productivity and favour unscrupulous employers over those more concerned for long-term stability and community development. Perhaps most importantly, although minimum wages may be above the average or marginal income of those outside modern, export-oriented industrial enterprises, or above the 'aspiration wage' of unemployed job-seekers, it cannot be presumed that they exceed the optimum 'efficiency wage', the wage at which the average worker works with optimal effort. Finally, critics of a policy of wage reduction claim that lowering unit labour costs can be achieved either by lowering wages with constant productivity (or with a lower decline in the latter) or by raising productivity with constant wages (or with a a rise in the latter, if they rise less than productivity).

Those advocating a supply-side approach also press for relative wage changes or adjustment in the 'equilibrium' structure of wages. Supposedly, wages of skilled workers in consumer goods industries have to decline, to encourage them to shift to export industries, while wages in the latter should stabilise, or rise *if* inter-sectoral labour mobility is slow or limited. They also contend that reducing wage differentials by minimum wage regulations or other mechanisms reduces the return to education and training to the point that the incentive to invest in them is insufficient. This is further reason, in their view, to avoid minimum wage machinery.

This too is not clearcut. At the micro-level, real wages may fall below the efficiency wage level, so resulting in poor or stagnant productivity. At the macro-level, it is too easy to assert that high unemployment (in whatever form) is 'classical', due to excessive real wages. It may be more 'Keynesian' in nature, even in low-income countries and even where there is high inflation. In that case, the critics would say, if real wages rose, not only would there be efficiency gains in tradable industries, but demand for wage goods produced outside the export-oriented sectors would grow. Structural adjustment could be aided because the demand for such goods would stimulate small-scale, informal businesses. If so, higher real wages would not 'crowd out' investment in tradable sectors, but could create a virtuous process of accumulation in low-income sectors.

As for securing labour mobility into the tradable sectors, the supply-side school, recognising that relative wages are 'sticky', argues that, as most governments have little control over private sector wages, they should concentrate on reducing public sector wages. They should also restrict wage indexation, and wage subsidies designed to limit unemployment resulting from structural changes are opposed on the grounds that they would slow the shift of resources into export industries from those supposedly with low to those with high social marginal product.

However, do wages in non-tradable sectors have to fall? The social adjustment side would argue that labour market policies, notably those associated with (re-)training and mobility, could avoid the need for wider wage differentials. Some argue that by *reducing* wage differentials, labour mobility from low- to high-productivity sectors would be accelerated, rather than slowed, if only because that would raise the relative and absolute return to high-productivity sector investment, while high costs in low-productivity industries would squeeze firms out of business. They also argue that it is too facile to claim that, by narrowing wage differentials, minimum wages deter skill acquisition by reducing the return to education. There are many non-wage benefits of education, and as in any case schooling is a job screening device, it is the enhanced access to job opportunities that maintains high individual economic returns to education and training. In sum, low wages plus wider differentials are not a panacea for labour market adjustment.

Public versus private sector employment

As for reducing public sector wages, this may or may not make sense. In many countries, just as it has been too easily presumed that the public sector is 'bloated' and that it is socially unproductive, it has become almost an article of faith that public sector wages and fringe benefits are excessive. It may be that wages should be reduced; or it may be that they should be maintained while public employment is cut to raise efficiency; or it may be that wages and employment should be cut relative to expenditure on other inputs involved in social service provision. All these responses are possible. But the necessary analysis rarely precedes the action taken.

Similarly, one should be wary about justifying wage cuts by reference to higher productivity in the private sector. That might be valid. But *if* high profits in some private sectors were the result of wages and working conditions that were so poor that workers could be productive only for a while before having to leave or before reaching the point where employers sought their replacement, then a policy of cutting public sector wages could compound an overall problem of stagnant labour productivity. Again, one cannot presume that if relative prices are in imbalance the higher one should be lowered.

Another aspect of public sector wage and employment policy is that, while salaries, benefits and employment security of a core of public sector employees may be advantaged in many countries, there are many whose wages are low by comparison with many private sector workers and whose security of employment is minimal. In the face of public expenditure cuts those workers are the first to suffer. Yet they are often the least skilled and thus the least able to transfer from non-tradable to tradable sectors. In short, the role of the public sector in labour market adjustment is a major unresolved issue.

Unemployment policies for structural adjustment

The structural adjustment model expects a period of resource reallocation – through trade liberalisation, market deregulation, etc. – to lead to a transitional period of high unemployment. Advocates and critics alike agree that this should be minimised. But supply-side economists would leave that largely to market forces, and would explain prolonged high unemployment as due to 'market failure' or even 'voluntary unemployment', whereas social adjustment proponents call for institutional mechanisms to secure labour reallocation, and thus would attribute high unemployment to inadequate labour market policies.

Conceptually there are four modes of labour (market) adjustment: (i) external (mid-career) labour market; (ii) inter-generational; (iii) internal labour market; (iv) redeployment.

The first can be painful, since it means existing workers being retrenched in some sectors and competing for jobs in others, during which overall and relative wages are expected to adjust in response to labour market disequilibria. With the second, most of the existing workforce does not engage in mid-career job changes, but labour force entrants, mainly youth, are channelled into tradable rather than non-tradable sectors; in a period of structural adjustment, this mode can result in high youth unemployment, and possibly accelerated 'early retirement'. With the third mode, workers change jobs within enterprises, corresponding to product or technological changes or job restructuring. There is certainly scope for more resort to this form of adjustment, a point that we will take up later with regard to Malaysian developments. Finally, the redeployment mode relies more on the state or some institutional mechanism to direct labour mobility, perhaps on a subsidised basis or with retraining.

The more inter-sectoral and other labour mobility can be achieved by the third and fourth modes of adjustment, the less likely that structural change will result in high unemployment. As that would also mean less reliance on relative wage rate changes, the more policymakers can rely on modes (iii) and (iv), the less the need to widen wage differentials.

In discussing adjustment and employment, Streeten (1988: 27) recently concluded:

> There is one good aspect in conducting adjustment policies in the current environment of unemployment. It is easier to move unemployed workers into the right industries than to shift workers from one job to another. Redeployment and restructuring out of unemployment should be the programme for both developing and advanced countries.

No doubt that was drawing small comfort from adverse realities. But it is far from self-evidently true. Workers are rarely made more productive by experience of unemployment, especially if that is prolonged, while unemployed, impoverished workers are scarcely able to indulge in optimal labour market mobility in response to job restructuring. There is little evidence that high unemployment is either necessary for structural change or preferable to other forms of labour market adjustment, and a number of countries have shown that structural change can be achieved without any period of high unemployment.

Labour regulations and labour market fragmentation

Both the supply-side and social adjustment perspectives give a pivotal role to labour market 'dualism'. According to the former, excessive regulations and minimum wages are shown by the growth of the 'informal sector' and the non-growth of the 'formal', tradable sector. They advocate dismantling regulations so that more of the 'informal' can become 'formal' and so that employment can rise. The social adjustment school retorts that the long-term objective should be the extension of social protection to those currently uncovered and surviving in petty units of production or in other peripheral activities, whether productive or merely survival oriented. In particular, the social adjustment model would give high priority to anti-discrimination and protective regulations designed to reduce the marginalisation of socially vulnerable groups, notably women, children, migrants and ethnic minorities.

To be fair, the debate about the role and impact of labour regulations is unresolved. What we do know is that there has been an enormous growth in so-called informal economic activities all over the world. Part of that has been due to the international recession and so on, whereby the unemployed have taken up petty production and the like, or whereby those whose regular earnings have fallen have supplemented them with secondary activities. Partly it reflects a growth of sub-contracting by large enterprises to reduce costs, or as an aspect of privatisation or in response to the increased uncertainty and risk in times of recession and structural adjustment. And partly it reflects resort to more informal, unprotected types of worker to bypass regulations or reduce costs.

Considering such developments, statements about the supposedly adverse effects of labour market regulations on employment *levels* should be treated with reservation. This is important to stress, for a key theme of the supply-side perspective is that 'fewer labour market regulations ... would promote labour market flexibility and higher employment' in developing countries, and that 'rules on job security ... distort the labour market in ways that reduce employment and overall living standards' (World Bank, 1987: 32, 9). Yet labour regulations may have more impact on the *types* of employment rather than on the level and have positive effects on living standards by setting guidelines, which may not be met everywhere but which help to reduce the prevalence of poor working conditions, exploitation and oppression. Once again, these are empirical matters on which it is too easy to reach conclusions in the absence of real data.

The key theme is worker security, of which there are various forms. Unfortunately, some economists lump them together, thus blurring analysis and policy debates. One should distinguish between: (i) labour market security; (ii) employment security; (iii) job security; (iv) work security; and (v) income security. Labour market security is high when job changing involves only moderate personal costs and reasonable prospects of subsequent benefits, and is typically inversely related to the level of unemployment. Employment security is high when workers cannot be dismissed without either costs to employers or the satisfaction of pre-specified conditions. Job security is high when workers have rights to particular niches within enterprises, and where unions or other institutions safeguard craft barriers or skills. Work security is high when working conditions are safe and so on. Finally, income security is high when workers have their wages or earnings protected from income fluctuations, through indexation, collective bargaining or other forms of institutional protection.

All five forms of security have potential costs and potential benefits for enterprises. Because there has been overwhelming stress on their alleged costs in recent international debates, it may be appropriate to stress the potential benefits, bearing in mind that ultimately these too are empirical matters.

Take, for example, job security. Many firms have introduced job security arrangements precisely because they were perceived as conducive to productivity growth; this was the essence of Taylorist management, since narrowly defined job classifications were seen as enabling employers to have control over output, work input and labour costs. Accordingly, one should not presume that the erosion of job security is always desirable even on efficiency grounds. Moreover, job security surely encourages the development of technical skill within jobs, because workers can expect a return to training and informal learning. Against that, if job demarcation results in workers resisting technological change and redeployment, then regulations or union agreements protecting job security could hinder structural adjustment and thus impair economic growth.

However, it is employment security that most critics have in mind when castigating 'regulations', claiming that workers in secure employment have less incentive to be productive, are immobile in the face of a need for structural adjustment, or have to be compensated so much that the potential benefits of resource reallocation are lost. It is also argued that employment protection discourages firms from hiring and encourages them to opt for more capital-intensive techniques. Unfortunately, there is little evidence to support or refute such arguments. Moreover, employment security regulations also have potential benefits, as follows:

(a) they can improve workers' commitment to the enterprise and thus raise work motivation and productivity;
(b) they may reduce the 'transaction costs' of employment by reducing labour turnover, especially important where productivity rises with on-the-job learning;
(c) they may encourage worker acceptance of productivity-raising rationalisation and other modernisation measures;
(d) they may improve job and work flexibility, that is, improve the willingness of workers to accept occupational and work environment changes;
(e) they may induce greater acceptance of work disciplinary measures;
(f) they may improve 'dynamic efficiency', by obliging management to become more efficient and competitive by means other than by laying off workers;
(g) they may induce workers to accept lower wage rises in return for the employment security;
(h) they may reduce the probability of frictional unemployment by enabling workers to have adequate notice of impending job loss to seek out alternative employment.

In sum, the benefits of employment security may well offset the costs. But one should not stop there, for what is needed are forms of employment security that promote flexibility and productivity. That is the challenge that comes to the fore in the context of structural adjustment rather than stable development. Advocates of social adjustment would argue that only if workers could share in the decisions and in the benefits of investment could this issue be resolved.

Wage flexibility

As for income security, the supply-side view is that wages should be allowed to fluctuate and that, if they were tied more to economic performance and profits, not only would employment be stabilised cyclically, but it would do so at higher levels than with fixed wages. Critics of this view would argue that, as long as workers do not at least share in decisions over investment or productive strategy, it would be unjust for them to have to bear the risk. Moreover, if payment systems were made more flexible – as is happening in some countries where adjustment strategies are being implemented – then earnings differentials will grow between those in high-tech sectors and those outside them. This has been a feature of such systems. For some economists, that is perfectly acceptable, but from a social equity point of view it may be undesirable, leading to active discontent among those unable to share in the benefits. Furthermore, flexible payment systems may result in extremely low and uncertain earnings for low-productivity workers and may slow structural change rather than accelerate it, to the extent that capital could be tied up in inefficient, low-productivity production.

Again, there are pros and cons about more flexible payment systems. The challenge is to move towards systems that promote adjustment, productivity and flexibility while maintaining rather than disrupting progress towards social equity.

Education and training for adjustment

Both the social adjustment and supply-side models favour increased education and training to promote flexibility and adjustment. But there is a difference of emphasis. The supply-siders stress that schooling and training should be geared to the needs of export-oriented industries, and take an economic rate of return approach to investment in education and training. By contrast, the social adjustment adherents see education as more of a social end in itself, as well as a means of promoting development.

There is no space here for an extended discussion but, given the emphasis on education and training, a few words of caution are in order. It is conventional to argue that the economic rate of return to investment in schooling is higher than that in 'physical capital'. This is comforting. However, the utilisation of educated or trained workers may be very sub-optimal, since access to many jobs may require an excessive level of schooling, simply because schooling attainment is a convenient low-cost 'screening' device in recruitment. Far more attention should be given to the effective deployment of educated workers. The sub-employment of educated and technically proficient workers in large corporations, as well as in the public sector, is a phenomenon found in many countries.

We should be wary too about the potential abuse of the system for short-term efficiency purposes. It is no coincidence that the word 'schooling' means both taming and liberating. If used to produce docile, disciplined workers (as many stress as a primary objective; World Bank, 1987: 63), then it may actually hinder the workforce's mobility and relearning potential in future eras of adjustment. This is a reason for having reservations about policies based on short-term economic rates of return.

Similar problems arise in assessing the extent to which governments should invest in training, making it hard to accept that 'some developing country governments have tended to expand higher-level vocational training too fast'

(World Bank, 1987: 63). The difficulty is to identify appropriate criteria for reaching such conclusions.

Training policy can facilitate structural adjustment by raising the productivity of workers in existing jobs, by raising the overall productivity of the labour force, and by facilitating labour mobility as job structures change with technological and productive restructuring. Also, policy can be oriented towards either vocational (or craft) training or job training. The former puts emphasis on developing all-round capabilities, whether through prolonged apprenticeship or institutional courses. The latter means workers being trained solely for jobs they are required to perform in the immediate future. That is cheaper and has involved schemes that impart 'modules of employable skill'; as such, it may make fewer demands on trainee and trainer alike, requiring less formal schooling and work commitment. However, it probably also leaves the worker less adaptable and less equipped to shift jobs or work status in times of industrial restructuring. In effect, a low-cost option with a higher short-term return may yield a lower longer-term social return.

Similarly, training policy should not be divorced from job structures. If those are highly stratified, such that there is a limited internal labour market, the required amount of more costly off-the-job training will rise. To reduce the need for public investment in training schemes, policymakers could explore ways of promoting internal labour adjustment, through on-the-job learning, incentive structures, anti-discrimination regulations, etc.

Too often, a perceived shortage of skilled labour is *presumed* to mean that the appropriate policy is more schooling or training. It is conceivable that a more appropriate and cost-effective approach would be a policy to alter job structures rather than the attributes of people required to fill them. It is technologically deterministic to focus exclusively on training.

Finally, there is the form of training. Many economists favour government labour market training schemes as a way of easing labour force adjustments. Undoubtedly, such schemes have a role to play. But they do have drawbacks. If governments subsidise the training of the unemployed, firms may simply substitute those trainees for others already trained or partially trained, implying a 'substitution effect'. Or the subsidy may result in workers being trained who would have been trained anyway, resulting in a 'deadweight effect'. Or the trainees may be hired to do jobs for which their training is not really required, because the cost of the training is underpriced. Or, as a result of altering the effective 'price' of technically skilled workers, enterprises may alter job structures to increase the relative demand for workers with those skills, thereby contributing to a persistent 'shortage' of such workers. In sum, because labour market training schemes are very rarely evaluated, they tend to be overvalued as a means of promoting labour market adjustment. An alternative policy to facilitate labour mobility and adjustment is 'in-plant' training. If, as is common, this involves the use of subsidies, the same problems arise, perhaps in more acute form since employers receive the subsidy directly, even though the public cost of this form of training may be lower because part of it may be borne by employers.[3] Here, too, the challenge is to minimise substitution and deadweight effects.

These notes of caution should not be construed as dismissive of training policy per se. They do suggest that, in encouraging firms to train more extensively, other policies are worth more active consideration, such as anti-poaching regulations – preventing other enterprises attracting newly trained workers without bearing the costs of training – and statutory obligations on firms to train a stipulated percentage of their workforce, perhaps distributed across the range of skills normally required. Such proposals would have to be carefully considered so as to minimise costs and to maximise efficiency and dynamic flexibility. But they may be critical for successful labour force adjustment.

LABOUR FLEXIBILITY IN MALAYSIAN MANUFACTURING

The preceding may seem to have been a protracted theoretical discussion of little relevance to current developments in the Malaysian economy. It is hoped that is not the case, though by international standards the Malaysian labour market has been fairly deregulated in that there has been no minimum wage, no effective system of employment security, and so on. However, we turn now to a few aspects of the labour market that seem likely to emerge as more critical issues in the post-NEP era. The discussion will skirt the paramount issue of the NEP, if only because it is implicit in every labour market policy question and because others are much better equipped to deal with it. As the following highlights a few points from the 1988 MLFS, the focus is on manufacturing, which should not be taken to imply that this is seen as the only important sector. Indeed, the transition to a high-technology service-oriented economy will be a major challenge for Malaysia in the 1990s.

Labour absorption in manufacturing: recent trends and prospects

Overall changes, 1985–90

The manufacturing sector has long been regarded as a primary source of employment expansion in the country, especially considering the long-term labour displacement in agriculture and mining and the desired shift of the rural workforce into modern, urban-based industries. However, in the 1980s economists became less sanguine about the ability of manufacturing to provide large numbers of new jobs. Despite the unprecedented surge of manufacturing in 1989, a big question is whether or not the employment elasticity has shrunk to the point where reasonable output expansion could be achieved with little impact on employment. The cause could be technological or the result of a shift towards more capital-intensive industries and types of establishment or because companies are more inclined to pursue a labour-shedding and labour-avoiding policy in the wake of the recent recession.

Employment expansion in manufacturing slowed sharply in the mid-1980s when, as the MLFS shows, there were far more widespread labour surplus conditions than were implied by the level of retrenchments, conditions which persisted after 1985. Yet, according to retrospective data from the survey, between mid-1985 and mid-1988 a majority of manufacturing establishments in the country expanded employment. Export-oriented industries such as textiles and electronics, and to a lesser extent chemicals and wood products, recovered most robustly. But in such large employment-generating sectors as food, beverages and tobacco, non-metallic mineral products, basic metals and fabricated metals, machinery and equipment, only a minority of establishments expanded in the three years covered by the data (Table 2.1). Foreign establishments were far more likely to have expanded than were their Malaysian counterparts (Table 2.2).

Table 2.1 Change in manufacturing employment by industry, 1985–8 (percentage of establishments)

Industry	Fell		No change	Rose			Total
	>25%	0–25%		0–10%	10–25%	>25%	
Food	7.8	28.0	21.7	13.0	11.9	17.6	100
Textiles	10.5	21.0	8.8	9.7	15.5	34.4	100
Wood	8.7	22.6	12.6	13.7	12.6	29.9	100
Paper	6.7	27.9	8.5	9.1	12.1	35.8	100
Chemical	7.8	26.5	8.7	13.0	12.4	31.8	100
Non-metal	21.1	28.5	18.8	9.7	7.9	13.9	100
Basic metal	14.5	28.9	10.5	14.5	10.5	21.0	100
Fabricated metal	18.7	20.1	12.2	6.6	11.6	30.7	100
Electronic	17.2	19.0	3.4	8.6	13.8	37.9	100
Other manufacture	11.8	15.6	21.6	7.8	15.7	27.4	100

Source: MLFS, 1988.

Table 2.2 Change in employment, by ownership, 1985–8 (percentage of establishments)

Ownership	Fell			No change	Rose			Total
	>25%	10–25%	0–10%		0–10%	10–25%	>25%	
Foreign	9.1	14.9	11.7	6.4	13.9	10.7	33.3	100
Chinese Malaysians	10.7	12.2	8.5	17.2	9.5	13.6	28.3	100
Other Malaysians	14.6	15.6	15.7	10.0	12.1	10.3	21.6	100

Source: MLFS, 1988.

The MLFS also revealed that only a minority of employment establishments expected to expand employment in the following two years.[4] No doubt this partly reflected a lack of *planning* at the firm level, which is surely worth encouraging in the interest of promoting an orderly, efficient labour market and of helping planners formulate labour market policies. However, although the number of firms that expected to expand employment was much greater than the number that expected to cut it, the largest group by far consisted of those that expected no change (Table 2.3).

Table 2.3 Expected/planned employment change in next two years, by industry, 1988 (%)

Industry	Rise	Fall[a]	No change	Don't know	Total
Food, etc.	18.7	8.2	68.5	4.5	100
Textiles	47.3	7.0	41.9	3.7	100
Wood, etc.	30.5	6.9	57.7	4.9	100
Paper, etc.	39.9	8.3	49.4	2.4	100
Chemical, etc.	41.4	7.0	47.5	4.1	100
Non-metal	25.6	8.3	60.7	5.4	100
Basic metal	26.6	5.1	64.6	3.8	100
Fabricated metal	37.1	5.5	50.9	6.5	100
Electronics	51.7	13.8	34.5	–	100
Other manufacture	43.1	7.8	45.1	3.9	100

Note:
[a] Closing establishments and those under receivership included as expected 'falls'. 'Closing' includes those already closed, those not having any workers at the time of the survey and those planning to close or under receivership.
Source: MLFS, 1988.

A further substantial minority were uncertain. The net expected expansion corresponded to the bullish sentiments in mid-1988. Even so, only in the electronics industry did a majority expect to increase employment. If one excludes those without employees at the time and counts those under receivership or closing as expecting employment to fall, then over 7 per cent of all establishments were ready to admit that they expected employment to decline, whereas about a third expected it to grow. These figures have to be seen in the context of what was a booming economy when a strong expansionary sentiment could have been expected.

Establishments in export-oriented industries were most likely to be expecting to expand their employment. Even so, one can only be struck by the widespread caution, or pessimism, shown among firms manufacturing non-metallic mineral products, wood products and basic metal products.

One potential tool for employment planning policy is identification of what management perceive to be the main factors affecting their employment *change*. Normally, one would expect that the main factor would be the level of demand for their final product. But that cannot be presumed in any specific period. Accordingly, respondents were asked to identify the principal and second most important factors influencing their employment, and were asked separately about the past two years, the present (i.e. mid-1988) and the expected factors in the next two years.

Over the previous two years, from mid-1986 to mid-1988 (Table 2.4), the major factor besides overall demand was business uncertainty, which was scarcely surprising in the wake of the recession. This factor was particularly prominent in industries dealing with basic metals, non-metallic mineral products and wood products. It shows just how important the creation of an economic environment of stability and *steady* growth is to employment creation.

The second most cited factor was new technology, notably in electronics, followed by plant capacity, implying that a fairly large number of establishments could not expand employment without first expanding their productive investment. This raises questions about the extent to which financial and other encouragement is given to expansion of existing enterprises rather than new ones – a crucial policy issue for the 1990s.

A key point about Table 2.4 is the rarity with which labour-related factors were cited as having influenced employment, although some did report as their main or second most important consideration the desire for a *stable* workforce, presumably because either cutting or expanding the workforce could affect morale, productivity, training and supervision costs.

Wage costs were scarcely mentioned in any industry or size category of establishment, and nor were non-wage labour costs. As for the much-discussed labour shortage factor, a mere 1.5 per cent of all establishments mentioned a shortage of qualified labour as having had an adverse effect. Finally, at a time when some commentators were calling for reform of labour regulations to promote industrial employment, it is instructive that on the ground, as it were, employers did not see labour laws as having had any substantial effect. This is strong evidence from a large survey and should be recalled in the event of further calls for 'deregulation'.

As for what firms expected to be the major influences on employment in the next two years, much the same pattern emerged, with labour-related factors being remarkable for their insignificance, even as a secondary factor. Abstracting from the demand influence, Table 2.5 shows that new technology and business uncertainty were expected to be the main factors, followed by plant capacity and new products. Neither labour costs nor labour shortage nor labour laws were perceived as very significant at all. In sum, as employers saw it, it is market stability and technology that most influence plans and changes in employment.

Table 2.4 Main factor besides demand affecting employment, by industry, 1986–8 (%)

					Industry				
Factor	Food	Textiles	Wood	Paper	Chemicals	Non-Metal	Basic Metal	Fabricated Metal	Electrical
None	54.3	43.0	46.4	50.9	50.6	47.6	43.0	48.4	24.1
Work reorganisation	4.0	4.5	3.0	3.5	6.5	5.9	5.1	4.7	1.7
New technology	5.9	8.3	2.7	6.4	7.0	3.6	1.3	3.7	27.6
New products	1.8	3.3	3.8	2.9	5.5	2.4	6.3	5.5	8.6
Shortage of qualified labour	1.3	2.9	1.9	2.9	0.7	0.6	2.5	1.2	–
Firm restructuring	1.2	1.2	1.1	1.2	2.4	0.6	–	2.2	6.9
Wage rise	1.7	2.9	2.5	2.9	1.7	2.4	–	1.8	3.4
Export quota	0.3	4.5	1.1	1.2	0.2	–	–	0.6	1.7
Desire for stable workforce	3.7	3.3	3.8	4.1	5.1	3.0	5.1	3.5	3.4
Plant capacity	5.9	5.8	9.6	5.8	6.7	4.8	5.1	5.5	5.2
Non-wage labour costs	0.7	0.8	0.3	0.6	0.2	1.2	1.3	0.4	–
Business uncertainty	11.1	8.7	16.9	9.4	7.2	20.8	24.0	12.5	8.6
Labour laws	–	–	0.3	–	–	0.6	–	–	–
Other	8.1	10.7	6.6	8.2	6.0	6.5	6.3	10.0	8.6
Total	100	100	100	100	100	100	100	100	100

Source: MLFS, 1988.

Table 2.5 Main factor besides demand expected to affect employment in next two years, by industry, 1988 (%)

	Industry								
Factor	Food	Textiles	Wood	Paper	Chemicals	Non-metal	Basic metal	Fabricated metal	Electrical
None	42.3	35.1	29.5	40.9	36.9	39.3	35.4	40.0	27.6
Work reorganisation	2.0	1.6	6.0	8.2	4.6	5.4	2.5	3.9	1.7
New technology	11.6	8.7	6.6	11.1	10.6	8.3	7.6	6.5	19.0
New products	6.7	4.1	6.0	5.3	11.6	1.8	7.6	8.8	24.1
Shortage of qualified labour	0.7	2.9	1.6	1.7	0.7	–	2.5	0.8	–
Company restructuring	1.7	2.1	1.9	1.2	1.2	3.0	1.3	2.2	3.4
Rising wages	1.2	2.5	2.5	1.7	1.7	0.6	1.3	2.2	1.7
Export quota	0.2	6.6	4.4	0.6	1.4	–	–	2.3	1.7
Desire for stable labour force	2.3	2.5	3.8	1.2	2.2	3.6	3.8	2.7	–
Plant capacity	7.6	7.8	9.0	7.6	11.3	7.7	6.3	7.1	5.2
Rising non-wage labour costs	0.2	0.8	–	–	1.0	0.6	–	0.2	–
Business uncertainty	16.3	14.9	18.8	10.5	11.1	22.6	29.1	17.1	6.9
Labour laws	–	0.4	–	–	–	1.2	–	–	–
Other	6.5	9.5	8.2	9.4	5.5	4.8	2.5	5.7	8.6
Total	100	100	100	100	100	100	100	100	100

Source: MLFS, 1988

Industrial relocation and employment mobility: a new geographical divide?

Labour mobility and enterprise mobility may have a growing impact on restructuring in the 1990s. For years Penang and the Klang Valley have been the industrial hubs of the Malaysian economy, drawing capital and labour from the rest of the country and from abroad. In the late 1980s that began to change fairly dramatically, although it has probably been insufficiently absorbed into policy debates.

There has been a drift of manufacturing establishments and employment 'southwards', which other secondary evidence suggests has been a more general trend. Thus, as Table 2.6 shows, manufacturing establishments were far more likely to have expanded employment in southern states than elsewhere, except in Penang. For example, in Johore and Malacca nearly a third of all establishments had expanded their employment by more than 25 per cent between 1985 and 1988, and a further one in four had expanded by up to 25 per cent. By contrast, only a minority of establishments had expanded at all in Trengganu, Kelantan, Perak, Selangor and Kuala Lumpur, and hardly any in Perlis. Other states had modest expansion in net terms, though one should note the stronger growth in Kedah, as well as Penang, as moderating the 'southern' trend. There are various reasons for a southern drift, among which of course is the proximity of Singapore, with its tight labour market, rising labour costs and the desire of Singapore-based companies to set up factories close to where there is a more ample and lower-cost labour supply (Salem, 1988).

It is expected that Johore and Malacca will become the next industrial growth centres in the Malaysian economy, and these data lend support to that belief. Already Johore Bahru is closely linked to Singapore and the state government has made 'economic twinning' with Singapore one of the four components of its Development Strategy. But the drift southwards seems set

Table 2.6 Change in employment by state, 1985–8 (%)

State	Fell >25%	Fell 0–25%	No change	Rose 0–25%	Rose >25%	Total
Johore	10.5	22.2	11.0	23.4	32.8	100
Kedah	8.1	21.6	15.3	27.9	27.0	100
Kelantan	15.0	15.0	28.3	23.3	18.3	100
Malacca	11.8	15.3	16.5	25.9	30.6	100
N. Sembilan	5.7	25.3	17.2	27.6	24.1	100
Pahang	6.7	31.7	11.5	29.8	20.2	100
Penang	8.8	24.2	15.4	20.5	31.1	100
Perak	9.7	26.4	17.0	24.1	22.7	100
Selangor	14.0	28.2	8.0	22.8	27.0	100
Trengganu	14.5	34.5	20.0	18.2	12.7	100
Kuala Lumpur	15.4	21.1	15.2	21.4	26.9	100

Source: MLFS, 1988.

LABOUR FLEXIBILITY

Table 2.7 Expected/planned employment change in next two years, by state, 1988 (%)

State	Rise	Expected change Fall	No change	Don't know	Total
Johore	44.5	5.5	45.4	4.6	100
Kedah	42.7	6.8	47.0	3.4	100
Kelantan	21.3	3.3	73.8	1.6	100
Malacca	47.7	1.2	50.0	1.2	100
N. Sembilan	44.2	4.6	45.3	5.8	100
Pahang	26.5	2.9	68.6	2.0	100
Penang	40.2	2.6	53.6	3.7	100
Perak	27.7	3.7	63.4	5.2	100
Perlis	(40.0)	–	(40.0)	(20.0)	100
Selangor	32.0	7.4	55.0	5.3	100
Trengganu	12.7	1.8	78.2	7.3	100
Kuala Lumpur	23.9	5.4	64.3	6.4	100

Note: Figures in parentheses indicate that there were too few observations to justify confidence in the data.
Source: MLFS, 1988.

to continue (Table 2.7). Establishments in Malacca, Johore and Negri Sembilan were the most inclined to expect employment expansion. Conversely, the limited growth in the least-industrialised states should be a worry for those concerned with formulating post-NEP policies.

The intensification of establishment dualism?

Another crucial feature of recent changes in employment is that, while there was an overall stability in the size distribution of establishments, with a large majority remaining approximately the same size in 1988 as in 1985, only a very small proportion of establishments with less than five employees expanded. Employment growth was concentrated in establishments that were already large in 1985.

As Table 2.8 shows, a majority of very large firms with over 500 workers in 1985 had grown over the three years from 1985 to 1988, whereas only a minority of those with 1–4, 5–20 and 21–50 workers had grown. It appears that small firms were not a good source of new jobs in the late 1980s, which should be borne in mind in formulating policies for the post-NEP era.

Moreover, on balance only large firms with more than 250 workers expected to expand in the next two years; most other size groups tended to expect no change, although on average the smallest firms actually expected to shrink still further (Table 2.9). That surely is a signal of immense significance. It scarcely suggests that small is very beautiful, and probably partly reflects a realistic expectation among small-scale concerns that they may go out of business.

Table 2.8 Change in employment, by establishment size in 1985, 1985–8 (%)

Change in employment	Employment size in 1985						
	1–4	5–20	21–50	51–100	101–250	251–500	501+
Fell							
Over 25	3.6	10.0	12.1	10.5	12.6	15.6	17.0
10.1–25	–	12.6	13.5	10.5	16.2	20.8	18.9
0.1–10	–	4.0	10.2	13.3	16.8	7.8	7.5
No change	57.1	30.1	14.1	6.8	5.6	–	1.9
Rose							
0.1–10	–	3.8	10.1	16.4	13.3	7.8	18.9
10.1–25	3.6	11.0	10.2	14.1	13.8	16.9	7.5
25.1–50	10.7	9.8	12.7	13.1	10.1	13.0	15.1
Over 50	25.0	18.6	16.9	15.4	11.6	18.2	13.2
Total	100	100	100	100	100	100	100

Source: MLFS, 1988.

Table 2.9 Expected/planned employment change in next two years, by establishment size, 1988 (%)

Employment size	Rise	Fall[a]	Expected change No change	Don't know	Total
1–4	2.9	17.1	71.4	8.6	100
5–20	20.0	5.5	68.0	6.5	100
21–50	30.2	6.2	59.5	4.0	100
51–100	34.3	7.8	53.2	4.7	100
101–250	38.6	7.7	50.1	3.7	100
251–500	50.8	8.6	35.8	4.8	100
501–1000	54.6	10.5	33.7	1.2	100
1001+	56.2	10.9	29.7	3.1	100

Note:
[a] Includes closing concerns, etc.
Source: MLFS, 1988.

As many believe that small-scale enterprises have a great potential for generating employment, this point should be stressed. As research has shown elsewhere, the vast majority of small concerns begin and stay small and do not operate on the basis of expected expansion into corporate giants. They seek a niche of security. What this means is that those who push for deregulation and hefty subsidies, etc., for small-scale 'informal' firms, on the grounds that they could increase labour absorption, are effectively proposing an increase in the *number* of such concerns, not in their average size. The implications of that are not usually well articulated; one is inclined to believe that there is a distinct chance (to put it no stronger than that) that this strategy would merely force down average incomes and the 'survival probability' of any small-scale establishment – at least, of those not tightly linked to one or more larger-scale companies. That in turn would inhibit risk-taking investment, in-plant training, and so on.

Some economists have claimed that small firms in Malaysia are relatively efficient because they are subject to a higher degree of competition as a result of unrestricted entry into the industry. The only reason why they have not been able to hold their own is that the fiscal incentives are heavily biased against them. There would be widespread agreement that fiscal policy has favoured large, export-oriented companies, but there is little reason to suppose that an even more competitive environment, in which mere survival for small firms would have to be a very high priority objective, would be conducive to productive efficiency. In sum, manufacturing employment growth is likely to come from large firms rather more than from existing small-scale establishments.

The feeling that undue emphasis has been laid on the creation of new establishments is given added weight by the fact that most very small-scale firms could give no identifiable factor for not changing employment, further supporting the view that most small establishments do not actively contemplate expansion or, therefore, the constraints to it. They react, not plan – and they ought to be helped to do the latter. Scarcely any factor other than demand and business uncertainty was cited as influencing employment changes in small-scale establishments, whereas technological change and new products were the main factors in large firms. This pattern also applied to their future expectations. In an economic climate of more intense competition, such patterns suggest that small firms would be less inclined to expand employment than in more stable periods and be less able to take advantage of employment-enhancing technological change.

In the late 1980s, export-oriented firms expanded their employment, whereas import-substituting firms did not. As small firms scarcely export, whereas over half of all manufacturing establishments with over 500 workers export over three-quarters of all their output, this has been a major cause of the strengthening of large establishments and the weakening of small-scale units. Indeed, the close relationship between size, export orientation and employment expansion is an increasingly strong feature of the Malaysian economy.

There is little evidence that small-scale manufacturing firms could be the major source of labour absorption in the next few years. They are also relatively unlikely to be generators of new technology. Almost certainly, workers and others connected with such firms will also be subject to more income insecurity, as well as lower incomes. Such uncomfortable realities will need to be taken into account.

Sales and employment changes

Ignoring the (probably unsustainable) recent surge in manufacturing output, there is reason to be cautious about labour absorption. Nearly two-thirds of all firms increased the value of their sales in 1986–8. Yet only a little over half of those reported that they had increased employment as a result; for most of the remainder it had made no difference (Table 2.10).

Table 2.10 Change in value of sales in past two years and the perceived impact on employment, 1988 (%)

Employment effect	Value of sales	
	Risen	Fallen
Increased	52.2	2.9
Decreased	3.7	41.0
No change	43.6	54.6
Don't know	0.4	1.5

Source: MLFS, 1988.

This corresponds to the view that employers were reluctant to hire labour in the late 1980s, even when business was picking up, because of the lasting effect of the crisis of the mid-1980s. This leads one to ask whether manufacturing can be expected to be a major source of new jobs in the next few years. Will increased demand for the product be met by only limited labour absorption as firms either limit their output to 'plant capacity', introduce labour-saving technological change or turn to 'outsourcing'? These may become major questions for the post-NEP era and for industrial policy. And, although one should treat such qualitative data with due caution, Table 2.11 suggests that it was the larger firms that were relatively likely to expand employment in response to sales increases. So, a disturbing point for those who believe small-scale firms are the potential source of labour absorption is that the likelihood of increased sales leading to increased employment was positively related to the size of the establishment. The measure is crude, in that the scale of the rise in sales would have varied considerably. Nevertheless,

Table 2.11 Establishments whose increased sales had 'increased employment', by establishment size, 1988 (%)

Employment Size	%
1–20	25.3
21–50	42.1
51–100	54.5
101–250	54.6
251–500	73.5
501+	78.7

Source: MLFS, 1988.

the sample was large and the relationship quite strong. Moreover, of those whose sales had fallen, the larger the firm the less likely it was to have cut employment as a result (Table 2.12).

Table 2.12 Establishments whose reduced sales had 'decreased employment', by establishment size, 1988 (%)

Employment size	%
1–20	41.0
21–50	35.8
51–100	41.3
101–250	53.1
251–500	29.6
501+	36.4

Source: MLFS, 1988.

The growth of external labour flexibility

Industrial enterprises across the world have been responding to economic instability and international competition by making the level and structure of employment more flexible. In that regard Malaysian enterprises have been no exception.

In recent years, as noted above, there has been a fierce debate over the links between employment security and the level and growth of employment. Many economists argue that employment protection regulations and non-wage labour costs hinder employment growth. An alternative hypothesis that guided this study is that, faced with uncertainty and the need for labour flexibility, enterprises in Malaysia and elsewhere respond by trying to *bypass* (not evade) such regulations as well as social security contributions and other institutional 'rigidities' such as collective agreements. Firms find ways of containing wage and non-wage labour costs, while regulations and 'rigidities' act not so much on the level as on the nature of employment.

What seems to have happened is this. Nearly one in five manufacturing establishments suffered from surplus labour in the mid-1980s, and to increase their employment flexibility many reduced the fixed core of their workforces. Many retrenched only to rehire the same workers, often on lower wage rates and usually with less employment security. Very small-scale firms tended to replace wage workers with family, unpaid workers, or relied on them more exclusively. More importantly, very many firms resorted more to temporary or casual labour. In every manufacturing industry the number of firms resorting more to such workers relative to regular full-time workers increased, while firms that expanded total employment were the most likely to have expanded the proportion that were in temporary or casual work statuses.

In principle, there is no such category as temporary worker in Malaysian labour law. Its prevalence reflects labour market reality and the difficulty of enforcing the labour laws in circumstances where the major reason cited by respondents for hiring temporary and casual labour was either fluctuating demand or market uncertainty, followed by the ability to pay lower wages. The authorities would be concerned by widespread casualisation, and if it is accepted that casual workers need employment protection by enforcement of the labour laws, then it is important to know where in the country and in what types of establishment casual forms of employment have been spreading. This is particularly important given the limited number of labour law officers employed by the Ministry of Labour – some 200 in the whole country.

All this begs a number of questions. In what respects is temporary, casual employment precarious for the workers concerned, putting them in need of legislative and administrative protection? A lack of employment security is one major characteristic, but there one finds wide variation. Some temporary workers have the most precarious contractual relationship, that is, a casual work status involving an oral understanding that can be modified from day to day or week to week. Others have a written contract for some short-term period, such as three months or a month. In mid-1988 temporary workers in small-scale establishments tended to be in the most precarious, casual relationships (Tables 2.13 and 2.14), giving further cause for reflection about labour in small firms.

One feels that the Ministry of Labour should be enabled to ensure that temporary workers be given the minimal protection of written contracts of employment. Labour Inspectors could perhaps concentrate more on small-scale establishments, because it is there that temporary workers are most vulnerable to the absence of a protective contract. That conclusion follows unless, perhaps, those who favour labour market deregulation could show realistically that such protection would harm the employment prospects of the workers involved. That seems unlikely.

Casual workers also have little prospect of moving from temporary to regular or quasi-permanent status, particularly in smaller establishments. They are in effect used as a buffer or labour reserve, bearing the risks of

Table 2.13 Main form of temporary work arrangement, by establishment size, 1988 (%)

Work arrangement	Employment size						
	1–4	5–20	21–50	51–100	101–250	251–500	501+
Short-term, specific:							
written contract	–	10.5	23.5	40.2	66.4	81.0	72.1
oral contract	(66.7)	52.6	55.1	29.5	20.3	10.3	13.1
Continuing, casual	(11.1)	33.7	19.4	23.2	12.6	8.6	11.5
Other	(22.2)	3.2	2.0	3.6	0.7	–	3.3
Total	100	100	100	100	100	100	100

Source: MLFS, 1988.

Table 2.14 Whether or not temporary workers given new contracts, by employment size, 1988 (%)

Employment size	New, temporary contract	Regular contract	No new contract
1–4	(22.2)	–	(77.8)
5–20	30.9	9.6	59.6
21–50	38.1	13.4	48.5
51–100	47.7	17.8	34.6
101–250	47.9	18.7	33.3
251–500	46.6	25.9	27.6
501–1000	32.1	28.6	39.3
1001+	27.3	39.4	33.3

Source: MLFS, 1988.

cyclical fluctuations in demand. Is temporary employment a major form of labour stratification emerging in Malaysian industry, just as it is elsewhere? It was scarcely surprising that those employed as temporary workers were not compensated by higher wage rates, the reverse being the case, again most of all in small-scale firms. And they had much less access to fringe benefits than regular workers. In short, the lot of a temporary worker is not an enviable one. Moreover, not only had casualisation grown but overall firms expected to increase the share of total employment in temporary work statuses.

Contracting out employment has also been spreading, notably in larger companies and in Japanese companies most of all. But the trend has been fairly widespread. Again, this is symptomatic of a downloading of employment risk. However, in terms of employment flexibility the outstanding development has been a growth, or regrowth, of *contract labour*. In Malaysia this was a traditional feature of the wood products industry, but it grew between 1985 and 1988 in practically all industries. Firms also expected it to continue to grow relative to regular employment, particularly in the wood products, textiles and non-metallic mineral products industries.

In some respects contract workers are in a less precarious position than casual or temporary workers, and were less likely to be among the low paid. Often they have skills in demand. What they lack is employment security. Also, one suspects that a long-term cost of reliance on contract labour is that such workers have skills that do not evolve with technological change, if only because there may be a lack of pressure to innovate when production work is fragmented into contract labour. This need not be the case, but is a hypothesis that deserves to be pursued, especially given the spread of managerial models of decentralisation. Short-term expediency may have long-term costs in terms of lost dynamic efficiency, involving an atrophy of manual skills at a time when the need for higher-level skills is growing.

In sum, although there has been only a modest spread of part-time working, there has been a fairly substantial shift from regular, full-time wage and salaried employment to various forms of non-regular work status, particularly in the lower end of the labour market. This trend was widely expected to persist into the early 1990s, at least. It may have been started as a short-run response to the recession of the mid-1980s. That it was expected to continue suggests that it is a longer-term trend that will need to be addressed by policymakers in the post-NEP era. What sort of protection do such non-regular workers receive? For temporary and casual labour, the primary need is for income protection and contractual security, or at least knowledge of where they stand. For contract labour, the primary need is access to training and some mechanisms for reducing income fluctuations.

There is another type of employment flexibility that also needs to be monitored in the next few years. Many workers are put on probationary status for some months, during which they have no employment security and can be laid off at any time. Employers have good reasons for using this device. But there has been a tendency for the probation period to grow and for more workers to be in that insecure status. The most likely reasons are that such workers can be easily laid off and be paid lower wages and benefits. *If* probationary employment were abused, it could erode the already vulnerable position of those who have only a foothold on the labour market ladder. Tighter regulation of the probationary worker status seems desirable, so that it corresponds more closely to reasonable criteria, such as the time required to learn the skills required for the job.

As for the role of labour regulations on these trends, it is worth reiterating that they did not appear to have a negative effect on the level of employment. When asked whether the provisions of the Employment Act on termination of employment had affected their employment policy in any way, nearly 94 per cent of manufacturing firms said that it had not had any effect; only a little over 2 per cent said that it had affected the level of employment, and 1.6 per cent said that it had encouraged them to resort more to contract labour rather than direct labour. One must be wary about drawing too much from such figures, because the Act may have conditioned behaviour and was only one of various factors having an influence. Nevertheless, the responses do not indicate pressure or need for reform on employment grounds.

With the growing employment flexibility, there does not seem to be any need. It is not labour regulations that dictate employment levels but market influences such as cyclical fluctuations in demand, structures of production, technological options and the need for a flexible labour force. There is no evidence that labour regulations have affected those issues, so that one can conclude that there is no *prima facie* case for weakening existing regulations. Conversely, one might also be inclined to conclude that strengthening them or their implementation would have little effect on employment per se but may have a beneficial effect in encouraging good employment practices. In general, for both welfare and dynamic efficiency reasons, in the 1990s policymakers may be concerned to see that labour flexibility is achieved in a context of growing labour market and employment security, not the reverse.

Internal labour flexibility

We have been looking also at how firms have been adjusting 'internal labour market' practices, including many aspects of recruitment, training, retraining, mobility and retrenchment that may preoccupy policymakers in the next few years. Here there is only time to highlight one or two trends, which are elaborated elsewhere.

Preliminary analysis indicates that both labour turnover and internal labour mobility are low in manufacturing. The latter may be related to the growth of something like skill polarisation of employment, corresponding to what has been happening in some industrialised economies. This has implications for labour market and training policy. Technological and other changes have been increasing the demand for technicians and diminishing that for skilled manual workers. And large-scale establishments, which have been growing relative to smaller firms, have higher ratios of technical and semi-skilled workers to other categories than was found in small-scale firms. These combined shifts imply a reduced scope for internal labour markets, whereby workers who enter on lower rungs could expect to climb occupationally through on-the-job experience or training. If so, off-the-job training and qualifications will become more important for labour mobility and for overall labour efficiency. That will probably mean that government will have to assume a greater role in the provision or organisation of technical training. And if there is a further growth in demand for technicians, the fact that only larger and more profitable companies could afford to pay for training courses will surely mean that the government will have to strengthen 'anti-poaching' measures. Otherwise many firms will find that the prospective return to training such workers will be insufficient to justify the cost. Already small firms do little training and have faced difficulties in retaining those they have trained. The four modes of labour adjustment were discussed above. The data show that the least developed in Malaysia are the third and fourth modes, which happen to be the least painful for the workforce. In-the-job *retraining*, both to replace obsolescent skills and to augment those workers have absorbed, must play a greater role in the post-NEP era. And the Ministry of Labour will surely have to develop a more complex and multi-layered employment exchange service, to reduce frictional unemployment and help make the labour reallocation process more efficient.

The feminisation of labour

In many parts of the world, the growth of external and internal labour flexibility has led to a rapid growth in female employment (see, e.g. Standing,

1989). Of course, that was a feature of the second and third phases of Malaysia's industrialisation, involving an influx of young girls to carry out semi-skilled jobs in the main export industries. Some fears have been expressed about a reversal of that trend, through automation and declines in 'direct labour'. Yet in the late 1980s female employment grew across the board. A large number of establishments in the 1988 MLFS had increased their female employment share and reported that they expected to increase it further in the next two years. Moreover, the nature of the demand has been changing, since proportionately fewer women workers seem to be hired on the expectation that they would work for two or three years and then withdraw in their early twenties to have families. The Malaysian economy in the 1990s will have passed the stage when it could rely on low-paid, young female labour. Women have been gaining shares of skilled, technical and administrative employment.

The authorities may have to consider refining family policy to correspond to such changes in the labour market. More women should be enabled, if they choose, to remain in the labour force to pursue an uninterrupted 'career', which means that government and employers may have to give more attention to the provision of childcare facilities. Labour policy may have to shift from the point of labour market entry, since it is apparent that women have been gaining access to a broad range of jobs, towards measures to facilitate subsequent labour mobility. Other studies have found that women workers, unlike men, have had no discernible income return to labour market experience. In future, the discouragement of discrimination against women in the internal labour market of enterprises will be more important than at the enterprise entry point. This will have a triple purpose. It could reduce sex-related inequality in the labour market. It could reduce inter-household inequality – since almost certainly it is women from lower-income households who most suffer from discriminatory barriers, and it is they who provide a substantial share of their family income. And it could reduce ethnic inequality – since Malay women in particular will need to be assisted in obtaining upward occupational and income mobility. This issue will be made all the more critical if privatisation and cutbacks of the public sector continue, since the public sector has been a major source of upward labour mobility for Malay women under the NEP.

Wage flexibility and inequality

Income inequality has diminished in Malaysia according to official statistics. If so, whatever the causes, then the emergence of more flexible labour markets suggests that several specific forms of wage inequality may grow. Probably a growing proportion of the labour force in manufacturing is not having access to fringe benefits because of their work status; these nowadays have considerable financial value for many workers, and their exclusion from measures of earnings results in an understatement of earnings inequality, because it tends to be the lower-paid who do not have access to such benefits. There is also an international trend whereby management and white-collar workers are receiving larger shares of their incomes in the form of bonuses, shares and perks that lower-paid blue-collar workers do without. There is some evidence that this divergence has been growing in Malaysia too.

As for pay flexibility, efforts to promote 'profit-sharing pay' systems are in their early days in Malaysia, although of course traditional forms have characterised many small, family businesses. We found that only about 3 per cent of manufacturing establishments were operating a profit-related pay system, but various observers believe that this practice will spread as a means of imparting wage flexibility. If so, it can be predicted that it will contribute to income inequality, between those in large, profitable, export-oriented enterprises and those outside them, and between privileged insiders in such enterprises and others. Finally, if there is a skill polarisation of sorts in progress, that in itself could widen earnings inequality, enabling a small core of technicians and upper-level management to strengthen their position at the expense of middle-level supervision labour (which, quite clearly, has been shrinking) and skilled manual workers. This will pose policymakers with various dilemmas connected with tax policy and redistribution, in particular. It will also pose a challenge for trade unions, since bargaining only for 'insiders' may become increasingly difficult, especially if employers can effectively play off one group against another, if only by the threat of turning to more flexible worker categories. This is going to be a major dilemma for trade unions everywhere, and nowhere more so than in Malaysia where unions are facing a painful phase of adjustment.

Some concluding points: the danger of beggar-my-neighbour 'competitiveness'

The Malaysian economy has rebounded from the traumas of the mid-1980s, and industry surely faces the post-NEP era with justifiable confidence. The NEP has been a success by many yardsticks. But what we have called the fourth phase of the country's industrialisation strategy raises new types of challenge for policymakers.

One issue that must be reconsidered is the headlong pursuit of 'competitiveness' based on measures and pressures to lower labour costs, symbolised by amendments to the labour laws, hostility towards industrial trade unions, and so on. It is understandable that cost cutting should be a response to a recession, but already labour costs are only a small proportion of total production costs, while such a strategy is inherently unstable and inequitable. The call to pare labour costs usually means lowering the wages and benefits of low-wage production workers relative to those earning their income from profits or those in salaried employment whose incomes are tied to levels prevailing in other typically higher-income countries. That aside, the concern to cut labour costs in this way to match those of other economies is likely to be more than matched elsewhere, whether it be in Thailand or Indonesia tomorrow or some other countries shortly afterwards. 'Beggar-my-neighbour' wage cutting is simply not a realistic or desirable option. The emergence of a more flexible labour market may make wage and other labour cost cutting more feasible in the short run, but, as labour costs are probably only about 15 per cent of total production costs, there is not much to be gained by that route anyway.

It is the alternative strategy that deserves to be pursued more vigorously and single-mindedly, that of providing a regulatory framework coupling worker security with labour flexibility in which the overall utilisation, development and replenishment of skills can be ensured. A basic issue for Malaysia in the post-NEP era will be the awkward transition from an economy geared to exports based on low-cost, semi-skilled labour to one based on dynamic efficiency and technical skills. This in a sense is what lies behind many of the current traumas in the South Korean labour market. And this is what is meant by a Human Resource Development Strategy. As part of that strategy one could envisage a set of policies to promote the model of human-resource-oriented enterprises (HRE), firms that pursue active labour policies to upgrade their workforces through work design, training, retraining and negotiated flexibility.

Seeing the future labour policy framework in this way may not seem very novel. But being quite clear about it does alter one's sense of priorities and concerns. It implies a more systematic recognition that workers are more than factors of production. It will mean that very long workweeks of 60 hours or suchlike will be regarded as alien to dynamic efficiency, to be curtailed or discouraged as incompatible with the refinement of real technical skills. It will mean giving contractual security in which workers are encouraged to feel the dignity of work, which should not be seen as the right of a minority and which will be essential for effective labour utilisation in an era when 'flexible specialisation' of various kinds will be a key to long-term development success. It will mean creating a framework in which organisations genuinely representing the interests of workers will be integrated into the production process, where employers and government can recognise that this could be a vital source of pressure on industrial enterprises to achieve dynamic efficiency in the work process.

Such conclusions may seem to relate to some distant future. However, Malaysia's successful development owes a great deal to a correspondence between its industrial strategy and the character of its labour supply. The post-NEP era will see an evolution of that industrial strategy, to higher-technology, higher value-added production and more complex production and work processes. To be truly successful, the labour supply and the labour policies that shape it will have to evolve accordingly.

APPENDIX 1: THE 1988 MALAYSIAN MANUFACTURING LABOUR FLEXIBILITY SURVEY

This paper is based on a national establishment-level survey of manufacturing conducted in mid-1988, the methodological details of which are provided in the confidential final report to the Malaysian government. It is nevertheless appropriate to include a few methodological comments. Before doing so, it is nice to acknowledge the kindness and encouragement given by officials in the Human Resources Section of the Economic Planning Unit, in the Department of Statistics (DOS) – whose team of enumerators and supervisory staff entered the exercise with a professionalism and enthusiasm that should be more widely appreciated – and friends in the Ministry of Labour. None of them should be blamed for errors, but they know my gratitude. It was some of them who persuaded me to do this work and to return to Malaysia five years after having conducted two large surveys in the early 1980s, in the Federal Territory and PJ and in Kelantan. Therefore, I would like to take the opportunity to thank those who have helped and encouraged me during this survey, and to say that I will do so more formally when the full manuscript is finalised.

Briefly, it was decided at the end of 1987 to launch an establishment-level survey of labour market mechanisms. Initially we intended to select a few industries in three major urban-industrial areas, but it was then decided to make it a national, representative survey of the manufacturing sector as a whole, with a few minor omissions that had previously caused difficulty for the Department of Statistics' sampling frame. Clearly a national survey was preferable, although of course the increased scale and scope created a great deal of additional work. It was only feasible because we were able to mobilise a national team of experienced enumerators drawn from the Department of Statistics' staff. Ideally, it would have been better still to have included the construction and service sectors, but this was ruled out on practical grounds.

In the early months of 1988 the questionnaire design was finalised through a necessarily protracted process, which included numerous meetings, a seminar in the Bureau of Statistics in the ILO and a 'pre-pilot', in which we visited about fifty companies in Kuala Lumpur and Selangor, in each case using the draft questionnaires to structure interviews with senior personnel officers or senior management or the owner of the business. In March–April 1988 we organised two pilot surveys in and around the Free Trade Zone in Penang and Butterworth. In July there was a two-stage training process, the first week of which was devoted to the training of the supervisors and heads of local DOS offices, the second to training at the local level in all states of Peninsular Malaysia. The fieldwork was launched in the second half of July and lasted until the end of August. Data were checked at the local level and then validated in KL over the next few months. The real analysis of the data was started in early 1989 and completed late last year.

The contents of the survey could be described in various ways, none of which would be ideal. But, very approximately, the principal topics covered were as follows:

Employment structure 1985–88
Expected employment changes 1988–90
Wages, earnings, benefits, etc.
External labour flexibility – work statuses, etc.
Recruitment practices
Training and retraining
Internal labour flexibility – mobility, job structures, etc.
Labour turnover
Working practices
Technological change influencing employment
Labour regulations
Labour surplus, retrenchment, etc.
Labour shortages and responses.

Not all of these topics were covered in the same detail – or with the same degree of adequacy or success – but a considerable amount of information was gathered. The data were collected by means of a two-part questionnaire and a two-stage process. First, accompanied by a letter of introduction explaining the broad objectives of the survey, Section One of the questionnaire was delivered to the management of the establishment, with instructions that it should be completed and signed by a senior representative of management dealing with employment and personnel matters. Section One covered basic statistical data on employment, vacancies, working practices, earnings, payment system, working time, capital, sales, ownership, exports, etc. Then, a week or so later, the enumerator visited the establishment for a prearranged interview with the owner, manager or personnel officer. The interview itself was preceded by a check that Section One had been completed and correctly understood. The enumerator then proceeded with an oral interview based on Section Two of the questionnaire, which contained a mix of factual and attitudinal questions, most of which had sets of precoded responses.

One should stress these basic methodological issues, however dull they may be to the economist reader, because too many surveys are reported with unstated methodology. They can often be very slap-happy, undeserving of the seriousness with which the results and analysis are subsequently treated. Postal questionnaire surveys of the sort of issues covered by the MLFS are worth practically nothing unless one can guarantee a very high and representative response rate *and* that the respondent is senior enough and in an appropriate position to give valid, honest answers to questions that he or she has understood. I am not for a moment claiming that we overcame all such problems in this survey, far from it. But the pre-pilots, the pilots, the detailed training, the type of fieldwork and the validation procedures gave us a reasonable chance of obtaining reasonable data. It had been expected that we would attain a response rate of 50 per cent or less, given the sensitive nature of the issues, the type of respondents, the length of the questionnaires and the wide geographical coverage. It was a tribute to the team that we achieved a response rate of over 80 per cent; in only one state did we fail to secure a reasonable response rate, where fortunately there are very few manufacturing establishments. By any standards, with such a large sample and survey, the response rate was satisfactory.

In sum, the MLFS was both ambitious and fairly comprehensive – albeit intended to be only impressionistic on certain issues. It seems to have provided data of good quality for such a large establishment-level survey. When the analysis is completed, we hope that the information generated will provide a sound basis for policy debates and for follow-up work that will further the analysis of the Malaysian labour market and be a useful guide for policy formulation in the post-NEP era.

APPENDIX 2: EXPECTATIONS OF EMPLOYMENT CHANGES: A METHODOLOGICAL NOTE

Many methods have been devised for forecasting employment, but relatively few attempts have been made to ascertain company employment plans at the micro-level. As in all such exercises, three difficulties arise: first, unforeseen circumstances inevitably cause plans to be changed; second, many firms operate on very short-term planning horizons, essentially reacting to market and personal events; and, third, the limited reliability of necessarily subjective employment planning data will depend on the reference period set in the questions addressed to management.

Given those caveats, establishments were asked whether they expected or planned to increase or decrease employment or maintain the existing level during the next two years. Clearly, this is a short time horizon, but it was felt that extending it to, say, five years would have resulted in excessively unrealistic and 'soft' information. In any case, probably reflecting the lack of employment planning at the firm level as much as anything else, about half the sample reported that they expected or planned no change in their level of employment in the next two years.[5]

NOTES

1 One is tempted to call this phase assembly-led industrialisation, so prominent was this aspect of the process.
2 In an earlier survey done for the EPU in 1982, we showed how upward socioeconomic mobility in the labour market – a critical aspect of the NEP – had been achieved predominantly through public sector employment.

3 It is probably not uncommon for the 'subsidy' to exceed the cost of training.
4 See Appendix 2 for a brief methodological note on employment planning.
5 As a methodological and policy-relevant aside, while asking employers about their plans and expectations on employment is a useful means of helping planners and macroeconomic policy, one should not ask such questions through a postal questionnaire in which answers are obtained from junior employees. It is also recommended that in future separate questions should refer to *plans* and to *expectations*, with a specific question asking whether or not the company has formal plans for expanding or cutting employment. A potentially important aspect of such a process would be the encouragement given to firms to *plan* employment, which could only help to develop an orderly, efficient and more equitable labour market, which would be in everybody's interest.

REFERENCES

Department of Statistics (various years) *Industrial Survey*, Government of Malaysia, Kuala Lumpur.

Salem, E. (1988) 'Twinned Hinterlands', *Far Eastern Economic Review*, 18 August.

Standing, G. (1989) *Labour Flexibility and Global Feminisation*, ILO, Geneva.

Streeten, P. (1988) 'Employment and Macro-economic Policies', paper prepared for the UNDP, July, mimeo.

World Bank (1987), *World Development Report 1987*, The World Bank, Washington, DC.

3

DIRECT FOREIGN INVESTMENT IN THE MALAYSIAN INDUSTRIAL SECTOR

Anuwar Ali and Wong Poh Kam

OVERALL TREND OF DFI IN THE MANUFACTURING SECTOR, 1970–87

Before examining the Malaysian government's policies towards industrialisation and DFI, it is useful to have a broad overview of the macro trends and pattern of direct foreign investment in the industrial sector of Malaysia over the last twenty years or so.

The overall trend of direct foreign investment (DFI) approvals in the manufacturing sector of Malaysia is summarised in Tables 3.1 and 3.2 and Figures 3.1 and 3.2. Several interesting features can be highlighted. Firstly, the trend of DFI has been rather uneven over the years. After fairly rapid growth over 1970–4, a slump in DFI occurred in 1975 due largely to the promulgation of the Industrial Coordination Act (ICA) in that year. A period of depressed DFI ensued over the next two years while the ICA was being amended to reflect views from the private sector. The strong growth of the economy in 1978–9, however, helped revive foreign investors' confidence and DFI resumed a strong growth trend. Since 1981, however, there has been another rather drastic decline in DFI. It was not until the Investment Promotion Act was introduced in 1986 that DFI took off again.

Secondly, it should be observed that domestic investment in the manufacturing sector has also experienced uneven growth over the years. However, even though DFI recovered strongly in 1986, domestic investment remained depressed. Consequently, the share of DFI in total investments in 1987 exceeded 49 per cent for the first time in seventeen years (see Table 3.1). For the first five months of 1988, the DFI share in total approved investment increased further to 58.2 per cent.

Thirdly, not only was there an increase in overall DFI share in 1986–7, but this also has been manifested in a very dramatic increase in the number of wholly and majority foreign-owned ventures (see Table 3.2). While fully

INDUSTRIALISING MALAYSIA

Table 3.1 Trend of DFI flows in industrial projects granted approval, 1971–88

Year	No. of projects approved	Foreign equity (M$m)[a]	Total equity (M$m)[a]	%	Growth rate % p.a.[b] FE	DE	TE
1971	304	96.4	563.4	17.1			
1972	355	149.0	359.3	41.5	54.6	−55.0	−36.2
1973	473	254.1	544.9	46.6	70.5	38.3	51.7
1974	525	264.1	759.1	34.8	3.9	70.2	39.3
1975	461	155.3	564.5	27.5	−41.2	−17.3	−25.6
1976	425	114.1	458.5	24.9	−26.5	−15.8	−18.8
1977	400	107.9	357.9	30.1	−5.4	−27.4	−21.9
1978	428	177.8	480.2	37.0	64.8	21.0	34.2
1979	484	495.6	1254.7	39.5	178.7	151.0	161.3
1980	460	248.2	752.9	33.0	−49.9	−33.5	−40.0
1981	613	495.3	1709.1	29.0	99.6	140.5	127.0
1982	481	527.6	1921.5	27.5	6.5	14.8	12.4
1983	498	296.3	1022.4	29.0	−43.8	−47.9	−46.8
1984	749	275.4	1213.4	22.7	−7.1	29.2	18.7
1985	625	324.9	1823.7	17.8	18.0	59.8	50.3
1986	447	524.5	1878.8	27.9	61.4	−9.6	3.0
1987	332	750.7	1529.3	49.1	43.1	−42.5	−18.6
1988 (Jan–May)	193	614.3	1056.2	58.2	–	–	–

Notes: [a] All amounts measured in current values.
[b] FE = foreign investment; DE = domestic investment; TE = total investment
Source: MIDA.

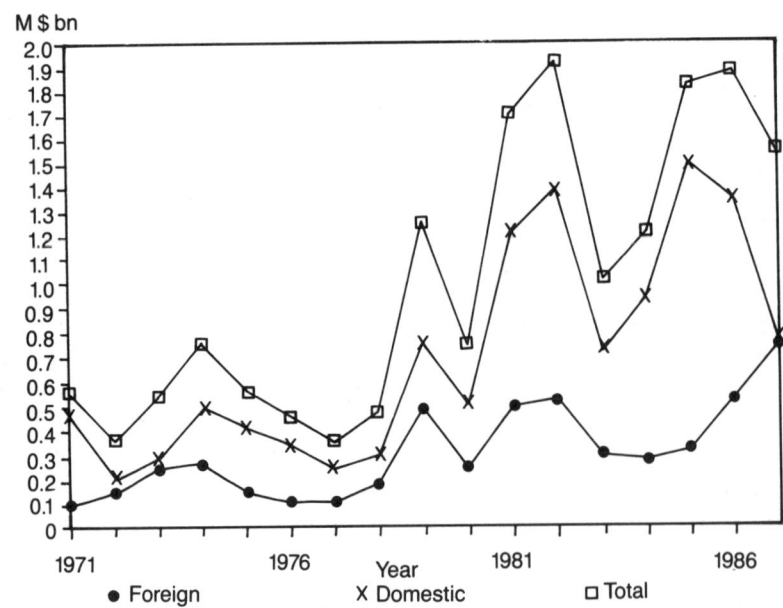

Figure 3.1 Approved equity investment trend in the Malaysian manufacturing sector, 1971–87
Source: MIDA.

Table 3.2 Distribution of approved projects by degree of foreign participation, 1984–7

	No. of approved projects				Proposed called-up capital (M$m)				Loan (M$m)			
	1984	1985	1986	1987	1984	1985	1986	1987	1984	1985	1986	1987
Wholly Malaysian-owned	380	321	177	105	486.9	869.1	751.5	420.1	1224.5	1606.6	628.4	491.8
Wholly foreign-owned	24	30	30	81	27.4	24.4	56.4	436.7	50.0	67.6	65.0	963.2
Joint Ventures:												
Malaysian majority	276	214	158	87	570.6	804.9	504.2	419.9	1080.7	2012.0	873.0	624.5
Foreign majority	61	48	69	49	112.2	98.4	196.2	212.0	152.4	146.8	261.1	269.6
Equal ownership	8	12	13	10	16.3	26.9	370.5	40.6	80.1	30.2	1456.9	55.0
TOTAL	749	625	447	332	1213.4	1823.7	1878.8	1529.3	2587.7	3863.2	3284.4	2404.1
In percentages:												
Wholly Malaysian-owned	50.7	51.4	39.6	31.6	40.1	47.7	40.0	27.5	47.3	41.6	19.1	20.5
Wholly foreign-owned	3.2	4.8	6.7	24.4	2.3	1.3	3.0	28.6	1.9	1.7	2.0	40.1
Joint Ventures:												
Malaysian majority	36.8	34.2	35.3	26.2	47.0	44.1	26.8	27.5	41.8	52.1	26.6	26.0
Foreign majority	8.1	7.7	15.4	14.8	9.2	5.4	10.4	13.9	5.9	3.8	7.9	11.2
Equal ownership	1.1	1.9	2.9	3.0	1.3	1.5	19.7	2.7	3.1	0.8	44.4	2.3

Source: MIDA.

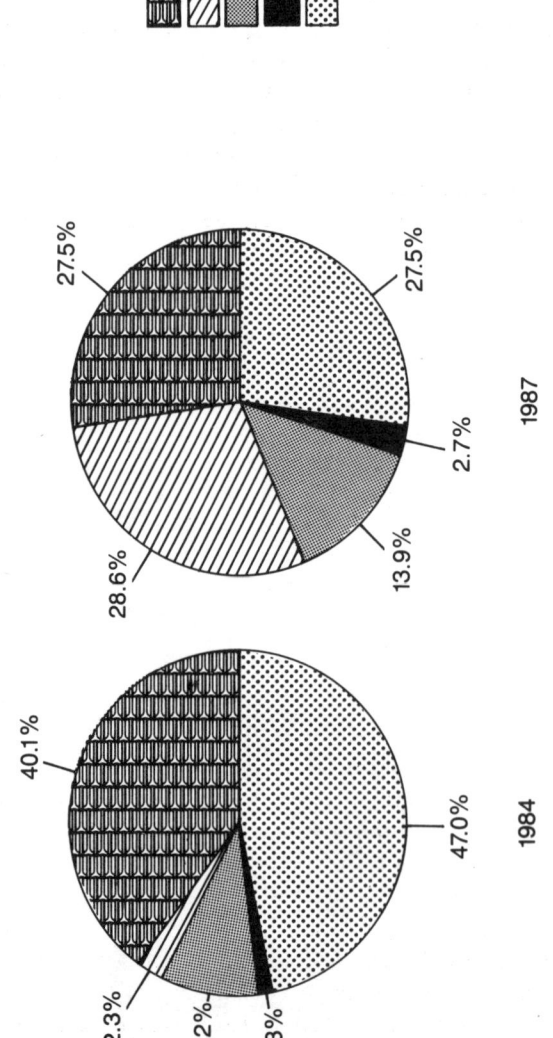

Figure 3.2 Proposed called-up capital, 1984 and 1987
Source: MIDA.

foreign- and majority foreign-owned ventures accounted for only 3.2 per cent and 8.1 per cent respectively of proposed capital investment in 1984, the proportion of such firms approved in 1987 rose to 24.4 per cent and 14.8 per cent respectively.

It must be recognised that the above statistics refer only to the *proposed* called-up capital in *approved* projects; the *actual* investment may be less because the final paid-up capital may be considerably less than the proposed called-up capital, and moreover, some of the approved projects may actually not be implemented. According to MIDA, 20–25 per cent of projects approved during the last ten years failed to get off the ground (see *Star*, 4 May 1988). The main reasons cited were lack of finance, difficulty in finding marketing outlets, and difficulty in getting approval owing to red tape.

The cumulative stock of DFI in 3,302 manufacturing firms in *actual* production as at the end of 1986 is as indicated in Table 3.3. As can be seen, by the end of 1986, close to 32 per cent of the total paid-up capital value of the companies in production was foreign owned. This represents a slight decline from 37.8 per cent in 1981, consistent with the above observed trend that new DFI approved declined considerably over 1982–5. Foreign sourcing of loans, however, escalated over 1981–6, from less than one-quarter of total outstanding loans to 60 per cent.

Table 3.3 DFI stock in manufacturing firms in actual production, 1981–6

Year	No. of firms	Paid-up (M$m)			Loan (M$m)		
		Total	Foreign	%	Total	Foreign	%
1981	2,749	7,227	2,734	37.8	2,662	629	23.6
1983	2,963	9,643	3,218	33.4	3,483	896	25.7
1986	3,302	14,550	4,590	31.5	10,117	6,036	59.7
% p.a. 1981–6		15.0	10.9		30.6	57.2	

Source: MIDA

The above estimates of *actual* DFI *stock* derived from MIDA's survey of approved companies in production correspond quite closely with the estimates derived from another independent source on DFI, the Department of Statistics' *Financial Survey of Limited Companies*. Out of 893 manufacturing firms with annual sales exceeding M$5 million covered in 1985, 30.3 per cent of their equity share capital was held by non-residents (see Table 3.4). This represents a decline from 37.9 per cent in 1978. It is interesting to note that, while foreign ownership of equity in foreign-majority controlled firms declined during 1978–85, it actually increased slightly in the locally controlled firms.

As expected, foreign equity participation tends to be concentrated in the larger-sized firms (see Table 3.5). In 1983, while foreign equity accounted for less than 20 per cent of the total paid-up capital of manufacturing firms with

Table 3.4 Equity capital stock ownership structure in the manufacturing sector, 1978 and 1985 (%)

Items	All limited company		Locally controlled		Foreign controlled	
	1978	1985	1978	1985	1978	1985
Total equity share capital: Percentage	100.0	100.0	100.0	100.0	100.0	100.0
Value (M$bn)	4.47	11.49	2.91	8.99	3.05	2.50
Held through nominee companies in Malaysia	3.4	8.9	4.5	10.9	1.1	1.8
Held directly by other companies in Malaysia	30.2	44.9	42.9	54.3	5.2	11.5
Held directly by other Malaysian residents	28.6	15.8	38.8	18.3	9.9	7.1
Held directly by non-residents (individuals & companies)	37.9	30.3	13.8	16.6	83.8	79.6

Source: Calculated from Department of Statistics, *Report of the Financial Survey of Limited Companies*, Government of Malaysia, Kuala Lumpur, 1978 and 1985.

Table 3.5 Ownership of paid-up capital of companies in production by race, industries and size of company, 1983

Industry paid-up capital	No.	Bumiputra M$	%	Non-Bumiputra M$	%	Malaysian M$	%	Non-Malaysian M$	%	Total M$	%
Below M$250,000	712	8,243,706	10.83	58,878,188	77.36	67,121,894	88.19	8,989,013	11.81	76,110,907	100.0
M$250,000–499,999	516	19,215,694	10.46	145,498,544	79.21	164,714,238	89.67	18,969,483	10.33	183,683,721	100.0
M$500,000–999,999	482	50,308,724	15.44	221,143,791	67.89	271,452,515	83.33	54,286,363	16.67	325,738,878	100.0
M$1,000,000–1,999,999	442	103,343,173	17.82	366,416,465	63.17	469,759,638	80.99	110,266,542	19.01	580,026,180	100.0
M$2,000,000–9,999,999	614	497,899,244	19.60	1,221,664,217	48.10	1,719,563,461	67.70	820,429,984	32.30	2,539,993,445	100.0
M$10,000,000 and above	197	1,730,612,989	29.15	2,002,607,970	33.73	3,733,220,959	62.87	2,204,574,631	37.13	5,937,795,590	100.0
Sub-Total	2,963	2,409,623,530	24.99	4,016,209,175	41.65	6,425,832,705	66.63	3,217,516,016	33.37	9,643,348,721	100.0

Source: MIDA

less than M$2 million paid-up capital, they constituted over 37 per cent of the total paid-up capital for firms with over M$10 million paid-up capital.

Among the domestic investors, the proportion of Bumiputra ownership also increased directly with the size of the companies, consistent with the fact that there is a tendency for foreign joint ventures in Malaysia to seek Bumiputra investors as partners to comply with the NEP requirements (see Table 3.5). This is further confirmed by the fact that, among the 173 member firms in the Malaysian International Chamber of Commerce and Industry (MICCI), which largely represents the international business community in Malaysia, Bumiputra share of equity in 1986 amounted to 21 per cent, whereas the non-Bumiputra share was only 7.7 per cent.

MANUFACTURING OUTPUT AND EMPLOYMENT CREATION

Table 3.6 summarises our estimate of the share of foreign-majority-controlled firms in overall output and employment generation in the manufacturing sector of Malaysia in the period 1974–85, based on data compiled from the Department of Statistics' annual *Industrial Surveys*. In 1974, foreign-majority-controlled firms accounted for only 11.3 per cent of the manufacturing establishments, but they contributed nearly half of the total gross output value, over one-third of total employment and 47 per cent of fixed assets value. There has been a steady decline in the contribution of foreign-majority-controlled firms since then. By 1985, foreign-controlled firms accounted for less than 8 per cent of the number of firms, 35 per cent of output, 19 per cent of fixed assets, and 29 per cent of employment. (The apparently low share of fixed assets may be misleading since only book values are reported. A larger

Table 3.6 Share of manufacturing industries by foreign majority-controlled firms, 1974–85

	Year	No. of establishments	Revenue/ Output (M$'000)	Fixed Assets (M$'000)	Total Employment
Total	1974[a]	4,696	10,113,040	3,025,909	281,241
	1979[a]	4,987	24,670,666	5,974,208	418,010
	1985	5,820	45,585,892	21,385,875	476,260
Foreign	1974[a]	532	5,040,766	1,408,852	94,098
	1979[a]	457	10,379,298	2,027,948	136,820
	1985	444	15,798,293	3,989,999	137,347
Foreign as %	1974[a]	11.3	49.8	46.6	33.5
	1979[a]	9.2	42.1	33.9	32.7
	1985	7.6	34.7	18.7	28.8

Note: [a] refers to Peninsular Malaysia only.
Source: Department of Statistics, *Industrial Survey*, Government of Malaysia, Kuala Lumpur, various years.

amount of capital depreciation may have been reported by foreign firms owing to the accelerated depreciation allowance given, and the larger establishments of foreign firms.)

It is likely that the contribution of foreign-controlled firms has increased since 1985 in view of the observed DFI trends since 1985 but, unfortunately, more up-to-date information is not yet available.

It must be recognised that the above statistics pertain only to the direct contribution of foreign-controlled firms to the manufacturing sector in Malaysia. The indirect contribution would be significantly larger, but unfortunately there are no aggregate statistics that provide a reasonable estimate of its magnitude at the macroeconomic level.

SECTORAL PATTERN OF DFI

Table 3.7 shows the distribution of DFI stock in manufacturing firms in actual production by industrial sectors as of the end of 1986. As can be seen, the degree of foreign participation, as measured in terms of paid-up capital ownership, is highest in the scientific and measuring equipment industry (87 per cent), beverage and tobacco industry (67.5 per cent) and electrical and electronics industry (50.7 per cent). It is lowest in the wood-based industry (7.88 per cent), plastic industries (13 per cent) and paper product industry (16 per cent). The predominance of foreign ownership, when measured in terms of fixed assets, is even more pronounced in the top three sectors mentioned above.

DFI BY COUNTRY OF ORIGIN

While Singapore and the United Kingdom have for historical reasons been the most important source of DFI for Malaysia's manufacturing sector, the role of Japan has been rapidly increasing in recent years.

Table 3.8 summarises the composition of DFI stock in manufacturing firms in production by country of origin as of the end of 1986 and compares it to the composition of foreign equity in projects approved in 1986–7. Several salient features can be highlighted. Firstly, up until 1986, Singapore remained the biggest source of foreign equity stock in Malaysia's manufacturing sector, accounting for close to 30 per cent of total foreign paid-up capital. Japan ranked second with about 20 per cent, followed by UK (16 per cent), US (6 per cent) and Hong Kong (6 per cent). If we include foreign loans as part of the DFI measure, however, then Japan emerged as the largest source of DFI stock with 43 per cent, followed by UK (21 per cent) and Singapore (14 per cent).

The rapid rise in the yen value since late 1985 has resulted in a massive increase of Japanese DFI. While Japanese DFI in the late 1970s and early 1980s was mainly targeted at the USA and the EEC region, with negligible relocation to the Southeast Asian region, the picture has changed considerably recently.

Table 3.7 Distribution of employment and capital structure by industry of companies in production as at 31 December 1986

Industry	% Paid-up capital						% loan	Fixed asset %
	Malaysia							
	Bumiputra	Chinese	Indian	Others	Foreign	Total	Foreign	Foreign
Food Manufacturing	35.34	25.28	1.05	12.20	26.12	100.00	13.63	25.69
Beverages & tobacco	16.23	9.93	0.39	5.94	67.51	100.00	58.53	70.28
Textile & textile products	26.23	16.74	1.15	17.88	38.01	100.00	24.09	52.51
Leather & leather products	25.76	20.91	0.73	12.35	40.25	100.00	0.00	46.35
Wood & wood products	32.25	45.40	0.52	13.95	7.88	100.00	40.42	8.45
Furniture & fixtures	37.13	14.87	0.39	36.01	11.60	100.00	9.84	16.10
Paper & paper products	34.35	32.94	0.68	16.02	16.01	100.00	27.64	19.08
Chemical & chemical products	50.37	9.23	0.47	7.81	32.12	100.00	54.26	21.21
Petroleum & coal	54.45	1.57	0.11	0.75	43.11	100.00	98.43	37.03
Rubber products	25.60	22.34	1.22	14.77	36.07	100.00	26.44	41.38
Plastic products	18.90	51.95	0.35	15.92	12.87	100.00	6.92	14.59
Non-metallic products	29.57	19.83	0.38	20.69	29.54	100.00	53.50	30.65
Basic metal products	42.35	16.71	0.40	4.98	35.56	100.00	74.25	32.58
Fabricated metal products	21.91	28.54	0.36	24.39	24.80	100.00	6.52	22.85
Machinery manufacturing	22.60	16.66	0.54	32.76	27.44	100.00	11.25	38.76
Electrical & electronic products	24.76	14.61	0.25	9.71	50.68	100.00	25.85	76.61
Transport equipment	51.82	13.25	0.79	12.20	21.94	100.00	77.35	21.41
Scientific & measuring equipment	4.90	6.58	0.09	1.55	86.88	100.00	92.66	90.27
Miscellaneous	39.23	19.90	2.84	6.94	31.08	100.00	40.73	45.82
Total	34.76	19.98	0.64	13.08	31.54	100.00	59.66	34.03

Source: Calculated from MIDA data.

Table 3.8 Sources of foreign equity in industrial companies in production, 1986 and in approved projects, 1980-7

	Foreign investment in companies in production at end of 1986									Approved foreign called-up capital				
	Value (M$'000)				Share					Value (M$'000)		Share		
Country of origin	Paid-up capital	loan	Loan + paid-up capital	Fixed assets	Paid-up capital	Loan	Loan + paid-up capital	Fixed assets		1980-6	1987	1980-6	1987	
Singapore	1,338,560	160,629	1,499,189	1,168,725	29.4	2.7	14.2	17.2		309,210	134,615	11.6	17.9	
Japan	913,623	3,735,997	4,649,620	1,741,860	20.1	61.9	43.9	25.7		486,548	230,848	18.3	30.8	
United Kingdom	708,627	1,474,246	2,182,873	889,202	15.6	24.4	20.6	13.1		236,509	26,122	8.9	3.5	
United States of America	279,229	240,464	519,693	673,459	6.1	4.0	4.9	9.9		188,887	61,272	7.1	8.2	
Hong Kong	270,679	240,024	510,703	415,214	5.9	4.0	4.8	6.1		148,872	27,828	5.6	3.7	
Australia	136,791	11,597	148,388	163,165	3.0	0.2	1.4	2.4		159,092	29,650	6.0	3.9	
Holland	120,093	170	120,263	466,712	2.6	0.0	1.1	6.9		195,165	n.a.	7.3	n.a.	
West Germany	119,815	47,086	166,901	151,883	2.6	0.8	1.6	2.2		79,804	10,056	3.0	1.3	
Switzerland	101,287	3,683	104,970	251,919	2.2	0.1	1.0	3.7		34,140	n.a.	1.3	n.a.	
Denmark	84,558	6,435	90,993	49,471	1.9	0.1	0.9	0.7		5,199	3,625	0.2	0.5	
Canada	56,802		56,802	86,367	1.2	0.0	0.5	1.3		28,528	11,205	1.1	1.5	
Sweden	36,889	2,427	39,316	31,227	0.8	0.0	0.4	0.5		15,891	624	0.6	0.1	
Thailand	31,646	370	32,016	76,939	0.7	0.0	0.3	1.1		39,378	655	1.5	0.1	
Indonesia	30,391	150	30,541	75,813	0.7	0.0	0.3	1.1		34,456	800	1.3	0.1	
Philippines	28,877		28,877	73,657	0.6	0.0	0.3	1.1		33,065	100	1.2	0.0	
India	27,573	19,457	47,030	41,526	0.6	0.3	0.4	0.6		39,260	26,500	1.5	3.5	
Taiwan	24,734	29,959	54,693	29,438	0.5	0.5	0.5	0.4		58,483	118,460	2.2	15.8	
France	13,092	4,639	17,731	28,798	0.3	0.1	0.2	0.4		23,406	15,050	0.9	2.0	
Norway	8,410	1,231	9,641	9,313	0.2	0.0	0.1	0.1		10,265	n.a.	0.4	0.0	

New Zealand	6,914		6,914	5,932	0.2	0.0	0.1	0.1	6,165	n.a.	0.2	0.0
Arab Countries	4,812	4,886	9,698	7,956	0.1	0.1	0.1	0.1	29,322	n.a.	1.1	0.0
Italy	3,946	9,919	13,865	4,989	0.1	0.2	0.1	0.1	21,848	5,680	0.8	0.7
Korea	3,153		3,153	4,376	0.1	0.0	0.1	0.1	24,408	1,995	0.9	0.3
Belgium	2,605	3,695	6,300	13,819	0.1	0.1	0.1	0.2	13,290	4,090	0.5	0.5
Brunei	848	5,750	6,598	950	0.0	0.1	0.1	0.0	144	n.a.	0.0	n.a.
Bahamas	200	1,500	1,700	771	0.0	0.1	0.0	0.0	4,867	3,570	0.2	0.5
Sri Lanka	38	n.a.	38	72	0.0	0.0	0.0	0.0	n.a.	100	n.a.	0.0
Austria	1	n.a.	1	1	0.0	0.8	0.8	0.8	17,689	n.a.	0.7	n.a.
Pakistan												
Yugoslavia	n.a.	n.a.	n.a.	n.a.	n.a.	n.a.	n.a.	n.a.	600	n.a.	0.0	n.a.
Bermuda	n.a.	n.a.	n.a.	n.a.	n.a.	n.a.	n.a.	n.a.	n.a.	720	n.a.	0.1
People's Republic of China	n.a.	n.a.	n.a.	n.a.	n.a.	n.a.	n.a.	n.a.	n.a.	n.a.	n.a.	n.a.
Panama	n.a.	n.a.	n.a.	n.a.	n.a.	n.a.	n.a.	n.a.	n.a.	n.a.	n.a.	n.a.
Mauritius	n.a.	n.a.	n.a.	n.a.	n.a.	n.a.	n.a.	n.a.	n.a.	n.a.	n.a.	n.a.
Others	197,014	31,514	228,528	317,132	4.3	0.5	2.2	4.7	417,836	29,722	15.7	4.0
	4,551,207	6,035,828	1,0587,035	6,780,686	100.0	100.0	100.0	100.0	2,663,746	750,715	100.0	100.0

Source: Calculated from MIDA data.

Table 3.9 The top five countries in terms of paid-up capital by industrial sector as at 31 December 1986

	Food manufacturing			Beverages & tobacco			Textile & textile products			Leather & leather products		
Country		Paid-up M$	%		Paid-up M$	%		Paid-up M$	%		Paid-up M$	%
No.1	Singapore	245,882	37.6	UK	157,915	38.6	Japan	231,512	48.7	Singapore	2,214	11.0
No.2	UK	118,859	18.2	Singapore	146,125	35.8	Singapore	123,355	25.9	Others	17,847	89.0
No.3	Switzerland	79,827	12.2	Hong Kong	73,143	17.9	Hong Kong	56,399	11.9			0.0
No.4	Denmark	74,915	11.5	USA	21,589	5.3	W. Germany	24,840	5.2			0.0
No.5	Japan	23,578	3.6	Denmark	6,755	1.7	Australia	13,343	2.8			0.0
Total		654,171			408,631			475,486			20,061	

	Wood & wood products			Furniture & fixtures			Paper, printing & publishing			Chemical & chemical products		
Country		Paid-up M$	%		Paid-up M$	%		Paid-up M$	%		Paid-up M$	%
No.1	Japan	34,606	44.9	Singapore	9,605	68.9	USA	35,774	55.0	USA	135,118	26.6
No.2	Singapore	21,819	28.3	W. Germany	1,200	8.6	Singapore	17,527	26.9	UK	103,711	20.4
No.3	Taiwan	4,768	6.2	Korea	1,145	8.2	Hong Kong	7,869	12.1	Singapore	77,837	15.3
No.4	UK	3,924	5.1	Australia	601	4.3	UK	3,020	4.6	Hong Kong	56,331	11.1
No.5	Hong Kong	3,289	4.3	Norway	585	4.2	Taiwan	275	0.4	Indonesia	29,777	5.9
Total		77,079			13,934			65,055			508,017	

	Petroleum & coal			Rubber products			Plastic products			Non-metallic mineral products		
Country		Paid-up M$	%		Paid-up M$	%		Paid-up M$	%		Paid-up M$	%
No.1	UK	164,127	42.6	Singapore	76,857	46.1	Japan	14,841	44.2	Singapore	206,761	50.9
No.2	Japan	105,240	27.3	UK	24,445	14.6	Singapore	10,732	32.0	UK	58,250	14.3
No.3	Holland	105,184	27.3	Australia	22,762	13.6	Hong Kong	2,288	6.8	Japan	46,356	11.4
No.4	Hong Kong	254	0.1	USA	7,770	4.7	Belgium	1,569	4.7	Australia	42,438	10.4
No.5	Indonesia	68	0.0	W. Germany	7,658	4.6	USA	1,378	4.1	Sweden	26,289	6.5
Total		385,381			166,875			33,579			406,603	

	Basic metal products	Paid-up M$	%		Fabricated metal products	Paid-up M$	%		Machinery manufacturing	Paid-up M$	%		Electrical & electronic products	Paid-up M$	%
Country				Country				Country				Country			
No.1	Japan	136,438	43.3	No.1	Singapore	104,488	50.0	No.1	Singapore	34,836	41.0	No.1	Japan	137,238	27.8
No.2	Singapore	101,345	32.1	No.2	Japan	33,836	16.2	No.2	Japan	27,030	31.8	No.2	Singapore	102,675	20.8
No.3	Canada	52,156	16.5	No.3	Australia	24,226	11.6	No.3	USA	10,509	12.4	No.3	Hong Kong	33,855	6.9
No.4	UK	7,849	2.5	No.4	Hong Kong	11,272	5.4	No.4	UK	4,982	5.9	No.4	USA	33,337	6.8
No.5	Australia	7,509	2.4	No.5	Switzerland	9,400	4.5	No.5	W. Germany	2,758	3.2	No.5	UK	28,562	5.8
Total		315,317		Total		208,728		Total		84,962		Total		493,785	

	Transport equipment	Paid-up M$	%		Scientific & measuring equipment	Paid-up M$	%		Miscellaneous	Paid-up M$	%		Total	Paid-up M$	%
Country															
No.1	Japan	97,879	51.1	No.1	W. Germany	20,602	49.2	No.1	USA	13,400	34.6	No.1	Singapore	1,338,560	29.4
No.2	Singapore	43,508	22.7	No.2	USA	8,509	20.3	No.2	Japan	7,417	19.2	No.2	Japan	913,623	20.1
No.3	UK	17,411	9.1	No.3	Switzerland	7,129	17.0	No.3	W. Germany	5,263	13.6	No.3	UK	708,627	15.6
No.4	W. Germany	12,105	6.3	No.4	Singapore	2,695	6.4	No.4	UK	3,876	10.0	No.4	USA	279,229	6.1
No.5	USA	7,790	4.1	No.5	Japan	1,600	3.8	No.5	Switzerland	2,971	7.7	No.5	Hong Kong	270,679	5.9
Total		191,673		Total		41,870		Total		38,728		Total		4,551,207	

Source: Calculated from MIDA data.

Japanese DFI flow has escalated, particularly in Thailand in 1987, and, although not as massive, a dramatic increase in Japan DFI has also been observed in Malaysia (see Table 3.8). Japan DFI accounts for over 30 per cent of total foreign equity in approved projects in 1987, more than twice that contributed by the two next-largest investing countries (Singapore and Taiwan).

Table 3.9 further breaks down the pattern of DFI stock composition by sectors as at the end of 1986. While Singapore was the leading DFI country in seven industrial sectors, Japan topped other DFI countries in textiles, wood-based products, plastic, basic metal products, electrical/electronics and transport equipment, and came in second in petroleum-based industries, fabricated metal products, machinery and 'miscellaneous' industries. The USA and UK came in first in two sectors each (paper and chemicals for the former and beverage/tobacco and petroleum products for the latter); while West Germany dominated the scientific equipment industry.

PERFORMANCE AND PROFITABILITY TRENDS OF DFI

As has been repeatedly emphasised in the theoretical literature on DFI and TNCs, any rigorous analysis of the economic impact of DFI requires detailed project-level information and specific assumptions about what the alternative situation might have been were the particular DFI contribution to the project withdrawn. Macro-level statistics concerning the performance of TNCs or DFI-dominated firms as a whole may be misleading in as much as they do not allow the separating out of various interacting factors, for example, high profitability of TNCs may reflect not so much the superior technology or more efficient management of these foreign firms, but rather their monopolistic domination of certain sectors, access to tariff protection, etc. The determinants of such macro-level performance measures need to be investigated independently. There is also the danger that the aggregate statistics may mask significant inter-sectoral as well as intra-sectoral differences among the TNCs.

The above caveats notwithstanding, it is nevertheless still useful to derive some aggregate performance measures that may throw some light on the differences between locally controlled and foreign-majority-controlled firms, based mainly on data from the annual *Financial Survey of Limited Companies in Peninsular Malaysia* conducted by the Department of Statistics. A total of 893 manufacturing firms with annual turnover exceeding M$5 million were covered in the latest available survey (1985). Although this represents only 15.3 per cent of the total number of manufacturing firms covered by the Department of Statistics' annual *Industrial Survey*, it accounts for 91.4 per cent, 87.1 per cent and 60 per cent of the latter's output, fixed assets and employment respectively. As such, the findings from the survey are likely to be reasonably representative of the industry as a whole, with bias in the direction of excluding many of the smaller locally controlled firms. Out of the 893 firms included in the survey in 1985, 188 or 21 per cent were foreign subsidiaries, while only 7 (0.8 per cent) were branches of foreign companies registered abroad.

Profitability trend

The rate of return on capital is calculated for foreign and locally controlled firms for selected years over 1971–85. Four measures are used: return on fixed assets, return on shareholders' funds, return on equity, and return on sales. Both before-tax and after-tax profit estimates are used (since actual tax payments are not available, tax *provision* figures are used as proxies instead). The results are as given in Tables 3.10 and 3.11. As can be seen, foreign-controlled firms clearly outperformed locally controlled firms on all four measures in every year, typically by a factor of more than two. The rate of return differentials are typically bigger when post-tax profit is used as the profitability measure rather than pre-tax profit. While no clear long-term trend is observed, the rate of return appears to have declined sharply in 1985 with the onset of the sharp economic recession in the country in 1985–6.

The generally higher profitability performance of foreign-owned ventures compared with locally controlled firms is also confirmed in the 1986 and 1987 *Malaysian Manufacturing Future Survey* (see Sieh, 1986, 1987).

Export propensity

While foreign investment in the Malaysian manufacturing sector has traditionally been domestic market oriented, government efforts since the early 1970s have been to encourage greater export of manufactured goods. Export-oriented foreign investment is in particular encouraged through various incentives.

Table 3.12 compares the export to revenue ratio of foreign and locally controlled firms, respectively, over 1971–85. As can be seen, both foreign and locally controlled firms have increased their export orientation over time. Foreign-controlled subsidiaries on the whole appear to have had a slightly higher export propensity than local firms since the mid-1970s, while foreign branch companies have consistently been export oriented, with export propensities as high as 80–90 per cent.

Import propensity

A major concern often voiced about TNCs is their propensity to import raw materials, parts and components from overseas (typically from their parent companies or affiliates), rather than to source them locally. Hence, the concern with setting local content as a performance criterion in the investment promotion and regulation framework of many LDCs.

Table 3.10 Before-tax profitability estimates of manufacturing firms, by ownership, 1970-85

Measure	1970	1971	1972	1973	1974	1975	1976	1977	1978	1979	1980	1981	1982	1983	1984	1985
Return on total assets:																
Locally controlled companies	13.0	8.0	11.9	34.8	18.7	7.4	13.7	12.3	16.9	23.6	20.2	13.7	10.6	8.0	14.3	8.0
Foreign subsidiary	26.1	23.0	25.0	36.0	34.2	18.2	22.8	25.8	31.7	41.2	43.3	36.0	30.5	29.5	26.8	19.3
Foreign branch	37.3	26.7	31.4	38.1	58.6	22.1	34.8	44.3	50.3	62.7	75.5	24.9	8.2	5.4	7.2	3.0
All companies	20.9	15.7	18.6	35.5	27.0	12.6	18.0	18.0	23.0	31.5	30.0	22.1	17.5	13.9	17.5	10.3
Return on shareholders' funds:																
Locally controlled companies	10.8	7.4	11.6	30.0	17.0	7.4	13.2	13.9	17.8	24.4	19.7	13.4	9.9	10.2	15.5	10.0
Foreign subsidiary	21.0	17.3	19.7	27.8	27.4	18.6	22.1	23.7	28.0	32.4	32.7	26.3	22.3	21.9	19.7	13.8
All companies	18.4	13.9	17.2	30.5	23.9	13.3	18.0	19.3	23.2	29.8	27.1	19.9	15.6	15.1	17.1	11.3
Return on equity capital:																
Locally controlled companies	12.1	7.9	12.3	37.8	21.0	8.4	14.7	15.1	19.9	29.5	26.5	18.1	13.2	12.8	21.5	12.8
Foreign subsidiary	28.4	22.9	26.2	41.8	42.9	24.5	29.5	32.9	38.9	50.7	56.4	52.9	45.7	49.3	44.8	30.6
All companies	22.6	16.5	20.4	41.8	33.0	16.0	21.5	22.9	28.1	40.3	40.3	31.5	24.3	23.3	27.4	16.7
Return on sales:																
Locally controlled companies	4.3	3.2	4.8	10.2	6.1	2.6	4.1	3.8	5.0	6.4	5.4	3.8	3.3	3.8	6.1	4.4
Foreign subsidiary	9.3	6.8	7.2	9.8	8.1	6.2	6.7	6.9	7.8	8.2	8.1	7.1	6.4	6.7	6.3	5.1
Foreign branch	2.7	2.7	3.6	3.6	4.1	3.1	3.5	4.1	4.4	5.0	5.7	3.8	4.3	4.1	3.0	1.7
All companies	5.6	4.8	5.7	9.2	6.8	4.1	5.0	4.9	6.0	7.1	6.6	5.2	4.7	5.1	6.2	4.6

Source: Department of Statistics, *Report on the Financial Survey of Limited Companies*, Government of Malaysia, Kuala Lumpur, various years.

Table 3.11 After-tax profitability estimates of manufacturing firms, by ownership, 1970–85

Measure	1970	1971	1972	1973	1974	1975	1976	1977	1978	1979	1980	1981	1982	1983	1984	1985
Return on total assets:																
Locally controlled companies	7.0	2.6	5.7	22.2	10.3	1.7	6.5	5.6	9.7	14.8	13.3	8.8	6.2	4.7	10.8	2.9
Foreign subsidiary	17.4	13.8	15.5	23.9	21.9	10.5	13.8	16.5	19.9	28.2	30.5	26.0	21.1	20.1	17.9	10.5
Foreign branch	24.3	15.8	17.1	22.2	31.5	10.3	16.2	22.1	29.7	34.0	41.8	13.4	5.1	3.7	4.4	1.2
All companies	13.1	8.3	10.6	23.0	16.1	5.8	9.8	9.9	13.8	20.5	20.2	15.1	11.4	8.9	12.6	4.5
Return on shareholders' funds:																
Locally controlled companies	5.8	2.4	5.6	19.1	9.3	1.7	6.3	6.3	10.2	15.2	13.0	8.5	5.8	5.9	11.7	3.7
Foreign subsidiary	14.0	10.4	12.2	18.5	17.5	10.7	13.4	15.1	17.6	22.1	23.0	19.0	15.4	14.9	13.1	7.5
All companies	11.6	7.4	9.8	19.7	14.3	6.1	9.7	10.6	14.0	19.4	18.3	13.6	10.1	9.7	12.3	4.9
Return on equity capital:																
Locally controlled companies	6.5	2.6	5.9	24.1	11.5	1.9	7.0	6.8	11.4	18.5	17.4	11.5	7.7	7.5	16.2	4.7
Foreign subsidiary	18.9	13.8	16.3	27.8	27.4	14.0	17.8	21.0	24.4	34.7	39.7	38.2	31.6	33.5	29.4	16.6
All companies	14.2	8.8	11.6	27.1	19.7	7.4	11.7	12.6	16.9	26.2	27.2	21.5	15.8	14.9	19.7	7.3
Return on sales:																
Locally controlled companies	2.3	1.0	2.3	6.5	3.3	0.6	2.0	1.7	2.9	4.0	3.5	2.4	1.9	2.2	4.6	1.6
Foreign subsidiary	6.2	4.1	4.5	6.5	5.2	3.6	4.0	4.4	4.9	5.6	5.7	5.1	4.4	4.5	4.2	2.7
Foreign branch	1.7	1.6	1.9	2.1	2.2	1.4	1.6	2.1	2.6	2.7	3.2	2.1	2.7	2.8	1.8	0.7
All companies	3.5	2.5	3.3	5.9	4.1	1.9	2.7	2.7	3.6	4.6	4.4	3.6	3.1	3.3	4.4	2.0

Source: Department of Statistics, Report on *The Financial Survey of Limited Companies*, Government of Malaysia, Kuala Lumpur, various years.

Table 3.12 Export and import propensity of manufacturing firms, by ownership, 1970–85

	1970	1971	1972	1973	1974	1975	1976	1977	1978	1979	1980	1981	1982	1983	1984	1985
Export/Revenue (%):																
Locally controlled companies	20.2	20.4	21.3	25.3	22.3	23.1	25.5	27.7	24.9	31.9	62.2	35.2	31.9	34.5	35.0	35.3
Foreign subsidiary	13.1	31.0	16.3	22.3	27.5	22.9	29.8	32.6	36.1	35.7	35.8	32.9	37.7	37.7	46.7	41.8
Foreign branch	73.3	86.1	85.5	81.7	84.9	89.0	89.7	88.7	89.0	91.7	89.9	92.5	76.8	74.1	76.7	75.6
All companies	32.2	36.2	28.1	31.4	32.7	29.1	33.0	34.6	34.1	38.4	53.0	37.4	35.7	36.6	40.3	38.1
Import/Expenditure (%):																
Locally controlled companies	−19.5	−36.6	−19.4	−22.1	−24.9	−19.9	−14.3	−17.0	−20.9	−23.0	−24.1	−22.2	−23.2	−22.0	−18.4	−18.7
Foreign subsidiary	−35.6	−31.5	−29.7	−39.2	−44.8	−48.9	−48.8	−46.4	−48.2	−50.0	−52.6	−48.2	−42.6	−39.6	−40.1	−48.7
Foreign branch	−6.3	−4.2	−4.0	−3.7	−3.3	−2.7	−3.7	−2.7	−2.6	−2.4	−2.0	−6.2	−3.2	−0.2	−0.1	−0.2
All companies	−21.2	−28.8	−21.9	−27.0	−31.2	−29.9	−26.2	−26.2	−29.4	−32.8	−34.4	−32.3	−31.3	−29.3	−26.7	−29.3

Source: Department of Statistics, *Report on the Financial Survey of Limited Companies*, Government of Malaysia, Kuala Lumpur, various years.

Table 3.13 Investment propensity of manufacturing firms, by ownership, 1970–85

	1970	1971	1972	1973	1974	1975	1976	1977	1978	1979	1980	1981	1982	1983	1984	1985
Investment in fixed assets/profit (%)																
Locally controlled companies	216.1	396.8	252.8	73.8	130.0	271.7	139.2	133.8	97.9	80.6	116.7	140.7	148.3	168.2	106.6	159.4
Foreign subsidiary	62.7	72.0	77.1	62.1	70.9	92.9	52.1	51.2	52.8	50.6	53.3	64.7	76.1	62.3	75.7	85.9
Foreign branch	45.3	48.3	68.0	35.3	25.8	32.2	18.8	14.7	11.0	20.7	16.5	26.2	34.2	47.1	32.8	56.6
All companies	104.0	151.8	133.7	66.3	88.8	144.3	87.4	83.8	71.1	62.1	77.0	91.6	101.5	104.4	93.5	129.7
Investment in fixed assets/FA in Malaysia (%)																
Locally controlled companies	28.0	31.6	30.0	25.7	24.4	20.1	19.0	16.5	16.5	19.0	23.6	19.3	15.8	13.5	15.2	12.7
Foreign subsidiary	16.4	16.5	19.3	22.3	24.3	16.9	11.9	13.2	16.7	20.8	23.1	23.3	23.2	18.4	20.3	16.6
Foreign branch	16.9	12.9	21.3	13.4	15.1	7.1	6.5	6.5	5.5	13.0	12.4	6.5	2.8	2.6	2.4	1.7
All companies	21.7	23.9	24.9	23.5	24.0	18.2	15.8	15.1	16.3	19.5	23.1	20.3	17.7	14.5	16.3	13.4
Net investment income outflow/profit (%)																
Locally controlled companies	−6.1	−4.6	−6.1	−1.9	−3.5	−10.4	−7.0	−5.8	−3.6	−3.9	−3.4	−4.3	−10.6	−31.6	−25.6	−43.8
Foreign subsidiary	−52.4	−53.7	−49.0	−52.0	−55.2	−59.0	−63.1	−58.9	−56.6	−59.9	−58.7	−60.0	−57.1	−55.5	−58.2	−42.1
Foreign branch	n.a.	n.a.	n.a.	−63.2	−56.2	−53.5	−50.7	−50.4	−61.2	−56.9	−5.3	−59.5	−69.3	−80.1	−83.2	−75.7
All companies	−41.1	−42.3	−35.9	−28.6	−36.5	−43.5	−38.2	−35.7	−32.6	−35.1	−35.9	−39.1	−40.4	−46.3	−39.3	−43.2
Net investment income outflow/revenue (%)																
Locally controlled companies	−0.3	−0.1	−0.3	−0.2	−0.2	−0.3	−0.3	−0.2	−0.2	−0.2	−0.2	−0.2	−0.4	−1.2	−1.6	−1.9
Foreign subsidiary	−5.1	−3.9	−3.7	−5.3	−4.6	−3.8	−4.3	−4.1	−4.5	−5.0	−4.9	−4.4	−3.8	−3.8	−4.0	−2.5
Foreign branch	n.a.	n.a.	n.a.	−2.3	−2.3	−1.7	−1.8	−2.1	−2.7	−2.8	−3.3	−2.3	−3.0	−3.3	−2.5	−1.3
All companies	−2.3	−2.0	−2.1	−2.6	−2.5	−1.8	−1.9	−1.8	−2.0	−2.5	−2.4	−2.0	−1.9	−2.3	−2.4	−2.0

Note: Profit refers to profit before tax.
Source: Department of Statistics, *Report on the Financial Survey of Limited Companies*, Government of Malaysia, Kuala Lumpur, various years.

Table 3.12 also shows the import to total expenditure ratios for foreign and locally controlled firms respectively over 1971–85. The data show that foreign subsidiaries clearly have a higher tendency to import raw materials and components than firms which are under local majority control. While local firms on average appear to import around 20 per cent of their input purchases, the ratio appears to hover around 40–50 per cent for foreign subsidiaries.

Outflow of investment income

Another major concern of government planners as regards TNCs is the fear that they would repatriate their profits to their home countries rather than reinvest in the host country. To provide a basis for further analysis, several indicators related to this issue can be calculated:

new investment/profit ratio
new investment/fixed asset ratio
net investment income outflow/profit ratio
net investment income outflow/revenue ratio.

Table 3.13 shows the behaviour trends of these indicators over 1971–85 for the foreign and locally controlled firms respectively. As can be seen, foreign firms repatriated a much higher proportion of their profits as investment income out of the country, compared with the net investment income outflow for locally controlled firms. At the same time, the rate of new investment or reinvestment in Malaysia as a proportion of profit is lower for foreign-controlled firms than for local firms. This suggests that reinvestment by foreign subsidiaries is lower than what it could be due to the repatriation of profits to their parent countries.

Tax revenue contribution

In addition to creating employment, TNCs are expected to contribute tax revenues to the government. As Table 3.14 shows, however, foreign subsidiaries appear to pay a lower rate of taxation (as a proportion of total profit before tax) than locally controlled firms. This is probably due to the various investment incentives being provided, especially to foreign investors, or because foreign investors have a higher propensity to receive such incentives than local firms.

In interpreting the above findings it should be recognised that the underlying data sources pertain only to firms with turnovers exceeding M$5 million per year (M$1 million before 1979). To the extent that the smaller firms, which are excluded from this survey coverage, tend predominantly to be local firms, it is almost certain that the data presented underestimate the real differences between locally controlled firms and foreign subsidiaries.

Table 3.14 Tax as a percentage of total profit of manufacturing firms, by ownership, 1970–85

	1970	1971	1972	1973	1974	1975	1976	1977	1978	1979	1980	1981	1982	1983	1984	1985
All limited companies	37.1	46.9	43.2	35.2	40.2	54.0	45.8	45.0	39.9	35.0	32.5	31.6	33.0	35.8	28.2	56.3
Locally controlled	45.8	67.5	51.9	36.2	45.3	76.9	52.1	54.9	42.7	37.5	34.4	36.2	41.8	41.6	24.5	63.3
Foreign controlled	33.4	39.8	37.9	33.5	36.1	42.6	39.6	36.0	37.1	31.6	29.5	27.7	30.8	32.0	33.3	45.7
Foreign branches	34.8	41.0	45.7	41.8	46.2	53.2	53.3	50.0	41.0	45.7	44.6	46.3	37.9	31.3	39.1	59.5

Source: Computed from Department of Statistics, *Report on the Financial Survey of Limited Companies*, Government of Malaysia, Kuala Lumpur, various years.

It should also be noted that the post-tax profitability of foreign subsidiaries, as measured in terms of return on *equity capital*, is generally high by international standards. This is especially so in the 'boom' years of 1974, 1978–80 and 1983–84, when the average profitability of foreign-majority firms exceeded 20 per cent and, in some cases, even 30 per cent. This relatively high profitability pattern confirms various impressionistic views that Malaysia is a relatively attractive place for DFI. Indeed, available data pertaining to the profitability of US DFI over 1979–84 do show that the return to investment in Malaysia has been rather high compared with most other less developed countries (*Business International*, 29 November 1985). Case studies of individual TNCs also confirm this general impression of Malaysia as a country with a good track record as far as profitability is concerned.

CASE STUDIES OF TRANSNATIONAL CORPORATIONS

Main Issues

Although the economic performance of the country has been relatively robust during the last two decades, as evidenced by an average real GDP growth rate of over 7 per cent during 1970–85, the external changes that have taken place since the early and mid-1980s have had a profound impact on the Malaysian economy. Like most developing countries that are increasingly dependent on the economic well-being of the industrial countries, Malaysia has been negatively affected by the various policy adjustments that are being implemented in these countries as a result of their economic slowdown and increasing unemployment. Indeed, Malaysia experienced a severe recession over 1985–6, recovering in 1987 and 1988.

Besides decreasing public sector spending, the slow growth in Malaysia during 1985–6 has also been attributed to sluggish private sector investment. In the past, private investment has played a significant role in the growth of the economy, but this has weakened relatively since the early 1980s. The ratio of private gross fixed capital formation to GNP declined steadily from 20.2 per cent in 1980 to 18.0 per cent in 1984, 15.1 per cent in 1985, 11.6 per cent in 1986, and 11.3 per cent in 1987.

The Malaysian government responded to these influences through various policy adjustments and initiatives, although the results have been mixed so far. Given the relatively low growth scenario during the 1985–7 period, and the likelihood of only moderate improvement during the rest of this decade, Malaysia faces numerous development adjustment problems and issues ahead. These problems and issues need to be addressed with new policy initiatives or development strategies. In the context of industrial development, the more significant issues are the need to be more outward-looking and internationally competitive; the need to create a conducive investment climate; the need to expand the country's industrial base and technological capability; and the need to increase employment opportunities and skills.

While these are general issues that can be fully addressed only within the larger context of the IMP and other new macroeconomic policy initiatives, they nevertheless provide important background, or the context for this study, insofar as DFI constitutes an important component within the overall development framework. Through in-depth case studies of twenty-six TNCs operating in Malaysia, we hope to throw light on the extent to which TNCs have effectively contributed towards industrial development in the country. In particular, the case studies will highlight the following main issues:

- employment creation by the TNCs;
- equity structure and restructuring within the NEP guidelines;
- inter-industry linkages;
- decision-making processes within the TNCs; and
- negotiation processes between government agencies and the TNCs.

Profile of TNCs selected

A summary profile of the twenty-six parent TNCs selected for case studies by the study team is given in Table 3.15. As can be seen, the selected TNCs represent a broad geographical spread (four from the UK, six from the USA, five from Japan, seven from Europe, two from Australia, one from Canada and one from South Korea), covering a wide spectrum of industrial sectors, including both mature and technology-driven sectors, and final consumer goods as well as intermediate goods industries. Many of these TNCs are conglomerates or integrated industrial groups with involvement in several related product groups, although some have more specialised product lines. Most are among the top players in their respective industries in the world, and all have tens or hundreds of operational units in many different countries.

A summary profile of the Malaysian operations of these TNCs is given in Table 3.16. As can be seen, many of these TNCs have more than one plant/subsidiary operation in Malaysia producing more than one line of product (e.g. Monsanto has both a chemical plant as well as a semiconductor component plant in Malaysia, while Matsushita has seven subsidiaries producing different electrical product lines). About 40 per cent of the TNCs selected are export oriented, while the other 60 per cent are domestic market oriented. Most of the firms have been in operation in Malaysia since the early 1970s, but some of these have expanded significantly only in the 1980s. Several on the list are relative newcomers. In terms of equity structure, all export-oriented operations have majority foreign control (mostly 100 per cent wholly foreign-owned), while domestic-market-oriented firms tend to have a lower degree of foreign control, with several having less than 50 per cent foreign equity share. The domestic-market-oriented firms all have dominant share in the Malaysian market.

Table 3.15 Profile of parent TNCs

Parent TNC	Country	Total turnover 1986 (billion)	Total employment 1986 ('000)	Ranking	Operation in Malaysia
BAT PLC	UK	£19.1	305.36	20% share of world tobacco market outside socialist world	Malayan Tobacco Co. Bhd.
ICI PLC	UK	£10.1	121.8	4th largest chemical co. in Europe (6th in the world); 3rd largest industrial in UK (17th in Europe, 46th in the world)	Chemical Co. Malaysia Bhd.
Metal Box PLC	UK	£1.11	26.9	11th largest engineering co. in Europe	FIMA-Metal Box Bhd.
Unilever	UK-Holland	G 55.4	298	World's largest agricultural & food group; 4th largest industrial in Europe (18th in the world)	Lever Brothers (M) Sdn. Bhd.
Colgate-Palmolive Co.	US	US$ 4.98	37.9	6th largest US parachemical, 70th largest US industrial	Colgate-Palmolive (M) Sdn. Bhd.
Goodyear Tire & Rubber Co.	US	US$ 9.10	121.6	World's largest tyre & rubber products manuf.; 33rd largest US industrial	Goodyear Malaysia Bhd.
Monsanto Co.	US	US$ 6.88	51.7	5th largest chemical in USA (13th in the world); 51st largest US industrial	Monsanto (M) Sdn. Bhd.

Hewlett-Packard Co.	US	US$ 7.10	82	4th largest computer co. in USA; 56th largest industrial in USA	Hewlett-Packard Group
Motorola Inc.	US	US$ 5.89	94.4	7th largest electronics co. in USA; 62nd largest industrial in USA	Motorola Malaysia Group
Intel Corp.	US	US$ 1.36	21	23rd largest electronics co. in USA; 200th largest industrial in USA	Intel Malaysia Group
Hitachi Ltd	Japan	¥ 4848	161.3	2nd largest industrial co. in Japan (13th in the world; 3rd largest elec. eng. co. worldwide)	Hitachi Group
NEC	Japan	Y 2450	90.1	42nd largest non-US industrial co. in the world	Pernas-NEC Telecommunications
Matsushita Elec. Ind. Co. Ltd	Japan	¥ 1483 (US$ 16.8)	134.8	2nd largest electrical equip. co. in Japan (4th in the world); 15th largest industrial co. worldwide	Matsushita Group
Nippon Sheet Glass Co. Ltd	Japan	¥ 209	6.0	2nd largest glass manuf. co. in Japan	Malaysian Sheet Glass Bhd.
Toray Industries Inc.	Japan	¥ 542	11.4	Largest Japanese manuf. of synthetic fibres; 20th largest chemical co. in the world; 39th largest industrial co. in Japan	Pen-Group
Henkel KGaA	W. Germany	DM 8.72	32	5th largest chemical co. in W. Germany (14th in Europe)	Henkel Oleo- Chemical (M) Sdn. Bhd.

Table 3.15 continued

Parent TNC	Country	Total turnover 1986 (billion)	Total employment 1986 ('000)	Ranking	Operation in Malaysia
Robert Bosch GbH	W. Germany	DM 21.7	147.4	Largest automotive equipment manuf. in W. Germany; 9th largest industrial co. in W. Germany	Robert Bosch (M) Sdn. Bhd.
Siemens AG	W. Germany	DM 47.0	363	largest electrical co in Europe (4th largest in the world); 28th largest industrial co. in the world	Siemens Group
T.L.M. Ericsson	Sweden	SKr 31.6	68.2	One of the world's leading suppliers of telecom. systems & services; 131st largest non-US industral co. in the world	Ericsson Group
N.V. Philips G.	Holland	G 55.0	346.9	2nd largest manuf. of electrical equipment in Europe (5th in the world); 9th largest European industrial (29th in the world)	Philips Group
Nestlé	Switzerland	US$ 17.2	154.8	12th largest non-US industrial co. in the world	Nestlé Group

C.C. Friesland Cooperative	Holland	n.a.	n.a.	One of the largest dairy products manuf. group in the world	Dutch Baby Malaysia Industry Sdn. Bhd.
BATA	Canada	n.a.	75	Largest rubber footwear manuf. group in the world	BATA (Malaysia) Sdn. Bhd.
Pacific Dunlop	Australia	A$ 2.4	25.4	One of the largest industrial co in Australia	Ansell Group
BHP Co. Ltd	Australia	A$ 8.76	61	One of the world's largest mining & metal groups; largest co. in Australia	John Lysaght (M) Sdn. Bhd.
Hyundai	S. Korea	US$ 14	156	2nd largest industrial co. in S Korea, 25th largest non-US industrial co. in the world	Sime-Hyundai Wood Industries Sdn. Bhd.

Source: Fortune Magazine, Kompass Directories, Moody Directories

Table 3.16 Profile of TNC operations in Malaysia

Parent TNC	Operation in Malaysia	Equity (%)	Plant/Subsidiaries No.	Employ.	Sales (M$m)	Year Established	Production Characteristics
BAT PLC	Malayan Tobacco Co. Bhd.	64.5	1	n.a.	687	1956	tobacco manuf.; domestic market oriented
ICI PLC	Chemical Co. Malaysia Bhd.	50.1	4	516	521	1963	agro-chemicals, fertilisers, industrial chemical & paints; mainly domestic market oriented
Metal Box PLC	FIMA-Metal Box Bhd.	48	4	886	109	1958	food packaging manuf.; mainly domestic market oriented
Unilever	Lever Brothers (M) Sdn. Bhd.	70	2	1,200+	n.a.	1952	food & household/personal products manuf.; domestic market oriented
Colgate-Palmolive Co.	Colgate-Palmolive (M) Sdn. Bhd.	85	1	310	148	1961	household & personal care products; domestic market oriented
Goodyear Tire & Rubber Co.	Goodyear Malaysia Bhd.	51	1	780	129	1972	rubber tyre manuf.; domestic market oriented
Monsanto Co.	Monsanto (M) Sdn. Bhd.	51	1	n.a.	26	1971	chemical (weed-killer); domestic market oriented, 30% export through Singapore
Hewlett-Packard Co.	Hewlett-Packard Group	100	2	2,200	300	1972	opto-electronic components; 100% export
Motorola Inc.	Motorola Malaysia Group	100	3	8,900	>1,000	1972	electronic components; 100% export
Intel Corp.	Intel Malaysia Group	100	2	2,500	150	1972	electronic components; 100% export
Hitachi Ltd	Hitachi Group	90–100	3	1,900	n.a.	1972	semiconductor manuf.; 100% export
NEC	Pernas-NEC Telecommunications	35	1	230	94	1974	telecommunication switching equipment; domestic market oriented
Matsushita Elec. Ind. Co. Ltd	Matsushita Group	73	7	5,950	924	1965	consumer electrical products; domestic market oriented
Nippon Steel Glass Co. Ltd	Malaysian Sheet Glass Bhd.	44	2	850	n.a.	1971	sheet & float glass manuf.; domestic market oriented

Company	Subsidiary	%				Year	Description
Toray Industries Inc.	Pen-Group	100	5	4,770	300	1971	synthetic fibres & textile manuf.; export oriented
Henkel KGaA	Henkel Oleo-Chemical (M) Sdn. Bhd.	50	1	98	33	1982	oleo-chemical manuf.; mainly export-oriented
Robert Bosch GmbH	Robert Bosch (M) Sdn. Bhd.	100	1	1,800	n.a.	1972	automotive parts manuf.; mainly export-oriented
Siemens AG	Siemens Group	100	2	1,538	79	1973	electronics components & semiconductors manuf.; 100% export
T.L.M. Ericsson	Ericsson Group	30–70	3	980	>100	1970	telecommunication switching equipment, mobile phone, PABX manuf.; domestic market oriented
N.V. Philips G.	Philips Group	50–100	3	2,000+	>70	1968	audio-electronics products (export-oriented); PABX equipment & electronic lighting domestic market oriented
Nestlé	Nestlé Group	60	5	1,800	n.a.	1962	consumer food manuf.; domestic market oriented
C.C. Friesland Cooperative	Dutch Baby Malaysia Industry Sdn. Bhd.	50.1	1	460	109	1963	dairy products & health food manuf.; domestic market oriented
BATA	BATA (Malaysia) Sdn. Bhd.	64	2	2,000+	92	1957	rubber footwear manuf.; domestic market oriented; 10% exported
Pacific Dunlop	Ansell Group	75	6	1,200	200	1974	rubber gloves manuf.; 100% export
BHP Co. Ltd.	John Lysaght (M) Sdn. Bhd.	100	1	40	n.a.	1968	steel roofing products; domestic market oriented
Hyundai	Sime-Hyundai Wood Industries Sdn. Bhd.	30	1	141	10	1987	wood-based furniture manuf.; mainly export oriented

Source: MITI.

Table 3.17 Forms of transnational corporate involvement in selected industries in developing countries

Industry and sector	Major forms of TNC involvement	Market orientation	Main TNC advantage
Food and beverage processing			
Branded food	Foreign direct investment, joint ventures	Domestic	Product differentiation, marketing
Textiles and clothing			
Man-made fibres	Foreign direct investment, licensing, turnkey projects	Domestic	Advanced process and product technologies
Clothing	Subcontracting	Exports	Marketing skills
Clothing (specialist)	Licensing, foreign direct investment	Exports	Product differentiation, marketing skills
Pharmaceuticals	Foreign direct investment, licensing (in conjunction with foreign direct investment)	Domestic	Product differentiation, rapid technological innovation
Fertilisers	Joint ventures	Domestic	Technology, management and marketing
Industrial chemicals	DFI, joint ventures	Domestic some export	Process technology, integrated market
Basic metals/non-metallic minerals	Joint ventures	Domestic	Process technology
Automobiles			
Foreign assembly	Licensing	Domestic	Technology, management and marketing
Foreign production	Foreign direct investment		
Electrical power equipment	Joint ventures	Domestic	Technology, management and marketing
Semiconductors	Foreign, direct investment, subcontracting	Exports	Rapid technological innovation, integrated market
Consumer electronics	DFI, joint venture, OEM arrangement	Exports	Product differentiation, technology and marketing
Telecommunication equipment	Joint ventures	Domestic	Rapid technological innovation

Source: MITI.

In examining the impact and contribution of the TNCs, the study found significant and systematic differences in the behaviour of TNCs that are domestic market oriented and those that are export oriented. Table 3.17 summarises the broad pattern of differences in the form of TNC involvement by sectors, and their key advantage factors as can be derived from a review of the literature (see e.g. UNCTC 1987 and other sectoral studies by the UN Centre on Transnational Corporations). The TNCs selected for our case studies do indeed exhibit characteristics that largely conform to the broad pattern identified in Table 3.17.

For example, both the telecommunications equipment manufacturers (Ericsson and NEC) in Malaysia involve joint ventures, their main contribution being seen as technology and innovative leadership. The resource-based industries such as glass-making (Nippon Sheet Glass), palm-oil processing (Henkel), rubber footwear (BATA) and fertilisers/industrial chemicals (ICI) similarly involve joint ventures, with their main contribution being seen as process technology and, in the case of Henkel, integrated market access. Export-oriented industries, such as semiconductor components and textiles, on the other hand, tend to be 100 per cent owned by the foreign parent TNCs, their main advantages being advanced process/product technologies and integrated market access. Finally, for the domestic market-oriented food and beverage processing TNCs in Malaysia, their main comparative advantage appears to lie in established product differentiation (branded goods) rather than technological sophistication per se.

Employment creation

Overall, in absolute numbers, most of the companies covered by our case studies have contributed sizeably to the creation of employment opportunities in Malaysia. The TNCs in the electronics industry, in particular, have contributed significantly towards employment growth in the manufacturing sector, especially in the 1970s and early 1980s.

However, the employment creation record of the TNCs is less impressive when examined in terms of labour utilised per unit of capital. On the whole, it is observed that the investment projects initiated by the TNCs are relatively more capital intensive than their respective industry averages. Moreover, it is noticed that the capital intensity of investment projects appears to be increasing over time (even after adjustment for inflation), suggesting that a fairly significant shift towards higher capital- and technology-intensive production is occurring. This is particularly so for the TNCs in the electronics industry: among all the TNCs in the electronics industry covered in our case studies, a rather significant increase in the level of automation has been observed over the last six to eight years. Thus, productivity has increased significantly with very little or no increase in labour. Consequently, although outputs have more than doubled over the last few years for these TNCs, the level of employment has increased by less than 10–20 per cent. Indeed, one company indicated that it was carrying excess labour that it had not retrenched, partly in anticipation of future expansion and partly because of its alleged corporate philosophy to retain and redeploy workers wherever possible.

Equity structure and NEP restructuring

The issue of equity restructuring seems to be a crucial concern for the domestic-market-oriented companies. This is not so for export-oriented companies since the government does not impose local equity requirements on them. For the domestic-oriented TNCs, the NEP imposed a requirement of divesting up to 51 per cent of their equity to local Malaysians by 1990. However, considerable uncertainties exist concerning the minimum restructuring requirement. A 30 per cent figure was interpreted as the minimum requirement by the foreign investors interviewed, even though the conditions of approval of manufacturing licences sometimes carry higher requirements. Among the domestic-market-oriented TNCs interviewed, especially those established prior to the NEP, the strong feeling expressed was that they should be given the opportunity to maintain majority ownership and control. Thus, while they would be willing to divest part of their equity control, they would resist losing majority control if at all possible.

At present, most domestic-market-oriented companies have complied with the minimum equity restructuring requirement of 30 per cent; examples would include Lever Brothers (M) Sdn. Berhad, Colgate-Palmolive (M) Sdn. Berhad and ICI Malaysia. In several of these cases, it appears that the government has accepted the 30 per cent restructuring as 'adequate', and has not pressed for a higher level of divestment. However, some of the TNCs interviewed have been prepared to divest close to, or even more than, 50 per cent of their equity.

It has often been argued that the imposition of this local equity participation condition has dampened the inflow of DFI and reduced the propensity of existing TNCs to expand their investments in Malaysia. This is an issue that needs detailed comprehensive surveys at the firm level covering all relevant sectors and investors by country of origin, but indications from our limited case studies are that existing companies, despite their reluctance to comply, have nevertheless decided to compromise in order to be allowed to expand their activities. Factors such as fiscal incentives, favourable rates of return to their investments, political stability and non-radical unionism appear to have outweighed the equity conditions imposed by the Malaysian government.

Some companies, in fact, have taken a 'far-sighted' approach and have offered to restructure before being 'asked' to do so. However, a certain amount of delay appears to have occurred in the case of some other companies trying to come to terms with the restructuring requirements. In at least one case, the parent company took a 'hard' line and did not undertake to divest its 100 per cent equity holding. However, after repeated applications for expansion and diversification into new products were turned down by the government, the company finally decided to compromise. The original 'hard' line was attributed to bad experiences encountered by another subsidiary operation of the parent company in India where the locals were given a majority share.

One issue of concern raised by more than one TNC interviewed is the allowable price at which the equity of TNCs can be divested. The present Capital Issue Committee (CIC) guidelines appear to be too restrictive, and in effect force the TNCs to sell their shares at prices significantly below market prices. It is this factor, rather than the fear of losing control, that is preventing the TNCs concerned from divesting their shares earlier.

Another issue relates to the difficulty of finding suitable local Bumiputra partners willing to take the shares up for divestment. Some TNCs interviewed indicate that this has been a problem, especially in recent years, owing to recession and the increasing budget tightness of government-owned Bumiputra institutions.

Management control

It must be borne in mind that equity ownership by Malaysian interests in companies where TNCs are participating does not necessarily mean management control. With some exceptions, nearly all the TNC operations interviewed appear to be effectively controlled by expatriates who are personnel from the parent companies. This is particularly apparent in companies:

(a) that are dependent on the foreign partner to provide the technical know-how (generally accompanied by a licence or technical assistance agreement); and

(b) that are dependent on the foreign partner to provide market access.

Nevertheless, some outstanding exceptions should be noted. Intel, for example, has had a Malaysian managing director for many years. Similarly, Henkel has had a Malaysian managing director right from the start.

More generally, a trend towards indigenisation of management, particularly at the second rung, has been observed among the TNCs studied. Although most of the key posts are still held by expatriates in most of the TNCs interviewed, efforts have been made to Malaysianise most of the next-in-line senior positions. This is generally practised by US and Europe-based TNCs to minimise the costs of employing expatriates. However, there appears to be a tendency among Japanese companies to retain a higher proportion of expatriates at the senior level. In at least two companies studied, the Malaysian counterpart managers have complained that the Japanese practised exclusive management control, where local Malaysian managers are not adequately consulted.

Inter-industry linkages

Except for the resource-based operations (rubber, wood and palm oil), there is little evidence that the companies interviewed have managed to acquire a significant proportion of their raw material or intermediate input requirements from local sources (although some efforts have been made by some of them to increase such purchases). Subcontracting systems, involving a stable ancillary supplier-purchaser relationship, are as yet not well developed. This state of affairs may not be totally their fault because there are a number of inhibiting factors making inter-industry linkages minimal. These factors include:

(a) The nature of some of the industries represented by the selected companies still requires a large proportion of raw materials and other inputs from overseas as these inputs, not available locally, represent 'work in progress', to be further processed (e.g. semiconductor components, chemical resins, dairy produce).
(b) There are certain tie-ups between the local subsidiaries and their parent companies or other affiliate companies overseas for the bulk procurement of raw materials and other inputs for reasons of economies of scale. This applies to companies like Nestlé and DBIM.
(c) For most of the companies interviewed, the question of the quality and reliability of local raw materials supply and ancillary services always crops up. In many cases, local TNC operations may have little choice but to obtain their raw material and other inputs from or through their parent companies to maintain quality.

Interviews with the TNCs also indicate that a number of their operations in Malaysia have expanded over the years through *upstream* and *downstream integration*, rather than horizontal diversification. Notable cases are the introduction of testing operations and the proposed introduction of wafer fabrication by several semiconductor component manufacturers. Such front-end and back-end integration results in internalised inter-industry linkages rather than linkages with third-party firms.

Local decision-making autonomy vs. global strategic requirements

The issue of the extent of local decision-making autonomy versus the global strategic framework of the corporations is of key concern in understanding how the local TNCs' investment and operating behaviour can be influenced. Obviously, a TNC with relatively centralised systems of decision making will be less susceptible to leverage by local factors than one which practises a more decentralised style of management.

Decision making at the firm level covers various aspects, the major relevant ones being:

(a) future investment decisions including capacity expansion and product diversification;
(b) identification of technology and sourcing of capital equipment and machinery;
(c) sourcing of raw materials, components and intermediate products; and
(d) marketing channels and policies.

Investment decisions

In terms of future investments, the case studies indicate that, while the final decisions are generally made by the parent companies, the local management often appear to have played a major initiating and lobbying role in such decisions. This finding suggests that future Malaysian government strategies in promoting foreign investments should consider the potential role of locally based managers (in most cases, expatriates sent from the parent companies) as valuable 'insider' allies. These managers can be extremely important in influencing the decisions made at the headquarters in view of the fact that:

1. As 'insiders', they have intimate knowledge of how corporate decisions are made, who the key decision makers are, and how they can best be influenced, what competition there is, etc. They can help package the investment and bid much better than Malaysian government officials who lack such knowledge. In addition, being 'insiders' to the TNCs concerned, they often have prior knowledge of proposed projects and investment opportunities coming up, and thus can help the government to target its promotion activities rather than 'shoot in the dark' through a general promotion mission.
2. Their local knowledge and experience of the local investment climate constitutes a comparative advantage when compared with decision makers at the headquarters, and hence they have greater credibility in putting up a convincing case that Malaysia is a conducive place for investments than Malaysian government officials, who may be regarded with mistrust (since governments always emphasise only the good things).
3. Local expatriate managers have to compete for projects with their affiliate companies around the world, and this means that their track records (either in Malaysia or elsewhere) will have considerable influence on the headquarters corporate planners. Thus, getting those with good track records to argue on behalf of Malaysia may help sway decisions at headquarters.

The above observation implies that while it is important to send investment missions to other industrial countries, it is equally important that local expatriate management be 'cultivated' so that they can play an active role in promoting additional investments in Malaysia.

Technology sourcing

In terms of technology identification and the sourcing of capital equipment and machinery, our case studies indicate that it is generally the parent companies which make the decisions or give technical advice to local subsidiaries on these matters. It is often in the interest of the parent companies to maintain this type of relationship, as in some cases the parent companies are also the technology suppliers. This situation may also apply to local subsidiaries at the initial stage when they still lack the expertise to determine their need for technology, capital equipment and machinery. Finally, a number of TNC operations in Malaysia were found to be taking over 'used' equipment from other affiliate operations of their parent companies.

A number of exceptional cases do exist, however, where the power of decision making to source equipment and machineries has been decentralised to the local operations. One Japanese TNC interviewed, for example, has opted for American machinery even though one of its affiliate companies in Japan was lobbying to sell its machinery to them. In the Sime-Hyundai joint venture, the process technology is sourced completely independently from Hyundai through an evaluation committee set up by Sime Darby itself.

Sourcing of raw materials, components and intermediate inputs

The case studies indicate that most of the TNCs are totally independent of their parent companies in terms of sourcing decisions, with the exception of TNCs that practise bulk purchasing for their subsidiaries. Most local TNCs indicate that they try to buy from the cheapest source, if possible from Malaysian suppliers. The relatively poor performance in terms of local sourcing by many of the TNCs interviewed is blamed on the lack of price competitiveness or quality/reliability of local suppliers. Indeed, a common complaint by the TNCs interviewed is that there is a shortage of domestic ancillary services and industries.

Marketing channels and policies

A big contrast exists between export-oriented and domestic-oriented TNCs with respect to marketing decisions. The domestic-oriented companies have no reason to be dependent on their parent companies, and thus tend to have great autonomy in the marketing channels and methods that they choose to adopt in line with local conditions. Over the years, companies like Lever Brothers (M), Colgate-Palmolive (M), Nestle and BATA have established their own relatively efficient marketing/sales networks.

However, for export-oriented companies in global industries (including those in the electronics industry and rubber products industry), dependence on their parent companies is more pronounced because:

(a) the latter have established regional marketing networks all over the world; and
(b) they have also centralised expertise and knowledge of the needs of each market consumer segment.

This means that the local subsidiaries do not need to be concerned with marketing; the outputs are channelled to designated regional marketing centres, or according to specific custom orders directed to them from the parent/regional headquarters. Through such functional divisions, the local manufacturing operations are assured of access to international markets without incurring extra costs. For this service, there are several cases – from our case studies – in which the local subsidiaries have to pay a marketing fee.

It is of interest to note that, in several cases, the advantage of tying up with a foreign TNC – as perceived by the local partner or local management – lies more in the market access provided by the TNC than in the technology that it may bring. The case of Sime-Hyundai and Ansell are good examples of this comparative advantage in marketing access.

Profitability and performance

The case studies of the selected TNCs show that, in most cases, the companies have achieved respectable returns in recent years. Indeed, most of the investment project applications submitted by the TNCs indicate short pay back periods and achievement of hurdle rates typically exceeding 20 per cent in the first five years. Generally, the export-oriented industries performed better than the domestic-oriented TNCs on a pre-tax basis, i.e. even before tax incentives (which favour export-oriented TNCs more) are taken into account.

Domestic-oriented TNCs engaged in more traditional and slower-growing product lines (e.g. construction materials, agricultural chemicals) tended to perform less well. There was also evidence of one project which performed poorly owing to political compromise – the assembly plant was located in one of the less-developed states in the country and the company had to expand production capacity rapidly to fulfil large annual production targets in the short time set by the government agency (which was the main customer). The orders could not be sustained by the government agency, and as a result the company had to cut back drastically and eventually close down the plant operation. It could be argued that the poor performance of the project was caused by poor locational choice and bad procurement planning on the part of the government agency.

The above observations notwithstanding, it is fair to conclude from the case studies that TNCs are generally rather profitable in Malaysia. Indeed, a major issue emerging from our analysis of the financial performance of the TNCs is the healthy cash surplus that some of them have been able to build up, which they were not able to reinvest in Malaysia owing to a perceived lack of viable projects and, in a couple of cases, uncertainty over the future direction of the NEP. The policy implication arising from this is the need for the government to re-examine more closely its efforts to promote reinvestment and expansion of existing TNCs, as opposed to attracting new DFI to come in.

Overall perception and assessment of Malaysia's investment climate

The companies interviewed in the case studies were asked to rank their overall assessment of the strengths and weaknesses of Malaysia's investment environment. Political stability turns out to be the most important factor valued by the TNCs interviewed, followed by attractive investment incentives, good infrastructure and a ready supply of a trainable labour force. On the negative side, the most significant disadvantage appears to be the limited size of the domestic market and, hence, the lack of reinvestment opportunities. Indeed, several of the domestic-oriented TNCs covered by our case studies were found to have accumulated sizeable cash reserves that could not be reinvested for want of viable projects. In addition, the relatively high corporate tax rate has been cited by some as a disincentive, not necessarily for the moment (when many still enjoy tax holidays) but in the longer term.

The findings from our case studies are generally consistent with those from another independent source of information relating to TNC perception of government policies and administrations – the MICCI *Business Assessment Surveys* for 1983 to 1986. The annual surveys basically poll the chief executives of the foreign companies on their general perceptions of the efficiency of government agencies, NEP guidelines and government regulations, the provision of services and infrastructure, the investment climate and business prospects. The main observations from the surveys are as follows:

1 There has been a general improvement in the speed of government approvals by the various government agencies, as indicated by the increased percentages of firms giving government agencies 'adequate' and 'good' ratings. For the Ministry of Trade and Industry (MTI) and MIDA in particular, the 'good' rating increased considerably in 1986,
2 The firms' perceptions of government's 'reasonableness' (in dealing with them) during the 1983–6 period seems to be fair – indicating that a good percentage of these firms give a 'good and adequate' rating on matters such as NEP equity guidelines, racial composition of staff and licensing arrangements.
3 The firms are fairly satisfied with the services and infrastructure facilities provided by the government. The 'good' ratings were given to items like availability of finance, availability of qualified labour, industrial relations, most forms of transport and public utilities like water supply.
4 Although a large percentage of the firms (36.4 per cent) viewed the

investment climate in 1986 as unchanged, an increasing number were of the view that the climate had improved. The percentage increased to 33.5 per cent for the 1986 situation from 12.4 per cent for the 1985 situation. More than half the firms, (53.2 per cent) believed that business prospects for 1987 would improve when surveyed.

NOTE ON DATA SOURCES

No single government agency is responsible for collecting statistics and monitoring development trends concerning DFI in general and DFI in the manufacturing sector in particular. A variety of sources exist, but each has its limitations. A brief review of the more relevant data sources actually utilised in this study is given below.

Department of Statistics

At the most macro-level, the Department of Statistics develops estimates of the various components of the long-term capital flows in the national accounts. The Department of Statistics also conducts an annual Financial Survey of Limited Companies which covers all companies with annual sales exceeding M$5 million (M$1 million before 1979), including manufacturing establishments. While quite informative, the survey unfortunately does not provide a breakdown by specific industries. There is also a rather long time-lag (the 1985 survey was published only in March 1988).

Malaysian Industrial Development Authority

By far the most up-to-date and readily accessible source of data series on DFI in the manufacturing sector is MIDA. Two major statistical data series on DFI are compiled by MIDA: the first provides an estimate of the expected flow of DFI, while the second provides an estimate of the actual stock of DFI.

1 Statistics on investment project applications received and granted approval. The key statistics covered include proposed capital called-up, proposed loans and potential employment creation, and are now published quarterly after a very short time-lag. Although providing an excellent source on the latest trends, these statistics are not wholly reliable as a measure of actual DFI performance since they refer to planned/approved undertakings rather than actual implementation. The full approved investment amount is credited to the year of approval, even though actual disbursement may be over a number of years. Moreover, considerable delays between approval and implementation often occur, and some projects are subsequently shelved or abandoned. Thus, the approval statistics are likely to overstate the actual investment. On the other hand, actual investment flows may also be understated owing to the fact that various minor

reinvestments or expansion/improvement projects by existing companies may not require approval under the ICA, and hence escape recording in the official statistics. Indeed, until recently, no breakdown was given between approved new ventures and approved major projects by an existing establishment.

2   Statistics on approved manufacturing firms in actual production based on annual surveys. The key statistics covered include the stock of paid-up capital, outstanding loan and book value of fixed assets by ownership, and employment by race cross-tabulated against industrial groups. Other statistics are covered in the survey, but most are not fully computerised, including basic economic variables like output, value added and investment. There is usually about a one-year lag in the publication of the information.

For analysis of the cumulative performance of DFI at the aggregate and sectoral level, the latter source is clearly more useful, although the former tends to be more frequently cited.

Ministry of International Trade and Industry (MITI)

The Industries Division of MITI maintains the most comprehensive source of information on DFI in industry in the form of manual administrative files containing all correspondence between the MITI, the companies and other government agencies. While rich in details on individual companies, almost no interfirm statistics are compiled from them. The amount of information available on particular companies varies tremendously.

A standard-format questionnaire has been designed by the Evaluation Development and Planning Section of the Industries Division to capture various key data of the individual companies. This was administered in 1986/7, but so far the computerisation work is incomplete, so no statistical analysis of this potentially rich database can be carried out as yet.

Other sources

In addition to the above data sources from the government, various ad hoc surveys and studies have been carried out by academic researchers from time to time. A notable effort to introduce a regular survey is the Malaysia Manufacturing Future Survey initiated by Arthur Anderson, similar in content to other annual surveys conducted in North America, Europe and Japan since 1982. However, the sample size appears to be too small and the response rate too low for the data to be used with confidence. Another regular annual survey by the Malaysian International Chamber of Commerce and Industry (MICCI) provides useful insights into the business assessments of the top executives of the internationlly orientated firms (mostly TNCs).

REFERENCES

Malaysian International Chamber of Commerce and Industry (MICCI), Annual Business Assessment Survey.

Sieh-Lee Mei Ling and Susan Tho Lai Mooi (1986) *Malaysia Manufacturing Futures Survey 1986 Report*, Faculty of Economics and Administration, University of Malaya, Kuala Lumpur.

Sieh-Lee Mei Ling and Susan Tho Lai Mooi (1987) *Malaysia Manufacturing Futures Survey 1987 Report*, Faculty of Economics and Administration, University of Malaya, Kuala Lumpur.

UNCTC (1987) *Transnational Corporations in the Man-made Fibre, Textile and Clothing Industries*, United Nations Center for Transnational Corporations, New York.

4

FREE TRADE ZONES AND INDUSTRIAL DEVELOPMENT IN MALAYSIA

Rajah Rasiah

The development of Free Trade Zones (FTZs)[1] in Malaysia since 1972 has generally been geared towards generating employment as well as investment and accelerating industrial growth (Ministry of Finance, 1988). This followed the introduction of the New Economic Policy (NEP) in 1970, which earmarked the industrial sector as the main engine of growth to spearhead poverty eradication and economic restructuring.[2] At that time, the World Bank, the United Nations (through the United Nations Industrial Development Organisation (UNIDO) from 1976), the Asian Productivity Organisation (APO), the Asian Development Bank (ADB) and the Organization for Economic Co-operation and Development (OECD) were actively promoting FTZs in East and Southeast Asia.[3]

While FTZs have played a vital role in the spread of transnational capital in the Southeast Asian region (with the possible exception of Singapore), their role in other Asian countries has not been as significant. Although foreign capital has been operating in Hong Kong and in FTZs in South Korea and Taiwan, industrialisation efforts in these economies have been driven primarily by domestic capital. Thus, foreign capital in FTZs has been of only limited significance in the high industrial growth rates in these countries. In the case of Malaysia, despite foreign dominance of several key high-technology industries (such as electronics), FTZs played a relatively modest role in the expansion of domestic industrial capital. Nevertheless, since the mid-1980s, backward linkage opportunities have grown strongly as international developments have encouraged the growth of domestic subcontracting firms.

The significance of FTZs for the industrial development of Malaysia will be evaluated in light of these issues. After providing a brief account of the growth of FTZs in Malaysia, the early phase of production in FTZs is described, followed by an assessment of the shift towards more capital-intensive production, closing with an examination of the implications of FTZs for industrial development in Malaysia.

GROWTH OF FTZs IN MALAYSIA

The slackening pace of industrialisation in the mid-1960s and the worsening unemployment problem caused the Malaysian government to review the import-substituting industrialisation (ISI) policy prevailing then. By 1970, the national unemployment figure was 8.0 per cent, and as high as 15.2 per cent in the state of Penang (Rajah and Mukunden, 1989: 6). The contribution of manufacturing to GDP in the 1960s remained small, hovering around 9 per cent in both 1960 and 1964 (World Bank, 1983: 153). In 1968, the government enacted the Investment Incentives Act to overcome the problem of internal market saturation – then seen as the main barrier to manufacturing expansion (see Hoffman and Tan, 1975) – through export promotion. Thus, ISI was gradually displaced by export-oriented industrialisation (EOI) from the late 1960s. The Investment Incentives Act offered generous benefits to encourage firms to export goods manufactured in Malaysia (Malaysia, 1976: 366). Under this Act, exemptions from company tax, relief from payroll tax, investment tax credit, depreciation allowances, export incentives, tariff protection and exemption from import duty and surtax were granted to approved companies (Malaysia, 1971: 149). The Malaysian Industrial Development Authority (MIDA), established in 1965, and the various state economic development corporations began to woo such investors. With this switch, manufacturing sector growth began to pick up; the contribution of the manufacturing sector to GDP increased to 12.2 per cent in 1970, 14.4 per cent in 1975 (Malaysia, 1976: 362), 18.0 per cent in 1981 (World Bank, 1983: 153), and 23.9 per cent in 1988 (Bank Negara, 1988: 167).

The Investment Incentives Act was augmented by the Free Trade Zones Act of 1971. The most attractive platform for export-oriented firms to emerge was the FTZs and licensed manufacturing warehouses (LMWs).[4] Following the FTZ Act, FTZs were specially designed and developed by state economic development corporations for firms manufacturing products for export.

FTZs are essentially special industrial estates where the normal trade regulations do not apply.[5] In this regard, Penang and Selangor states took the lead by earmarking FTZs as important centres to spearhead their own industrialisation efforts (see Kamal and Lo, 1975; Rajah, 1987; Goh, 1988). Malaysia's first FTZ was opened at Bayan Lepas (Penang) in 1972. By 1987, Malaysia had ten FTZs, four of which were located in Penang, three in Selangor, two in Malacca, and one in Johore (see Table 4.1[6] and Figure 4.1) The total developed area within FTZs reached 538.32 hectares in 1989. In 1987, the 100 FTZ firms in Malaysia had M$1,429.2 million in fixed assets and employed 68,877 workers.

Regionally, the state of Penang had 58 per cent, i.e. the lion's share, of developed FTZ space in 1989. Penang also had 55 per cent of FTZ firms;

INDUSTRIALISING MALAYSIA

Figure 4.1 Free Trade Zones in Peninsular Malaysia, 1989
Source: based on unpublished MIDA data, 1989.

Table 4.1: Free Trade Zones in Malaysia, 1987

	Developed area (ha)[a]	No. of firms	Fixed Assets (M$m)	Employment
Penang	310.54	55	691.6	37,068
Bayan Lepas	150.94	41	524.2	28,911
Prai	146.94	12	134.0	5,861
Prai Wharf	4.73	1	26.4	1,824
Pulau Jerejak[b]	7.93	1	7.0	472
Selangor	100.52	29	631.3	24,456
Sungai Way/Subang	42.77	21	399.5	16,355
Ampang/Ulu Kelang	36.47	7	195.1	7,077
Telok Panglima Garang	21.28	1	36.7	1,024
Malacca	26.49	16	106.3	7,353
Batu Berendam	18.48	12	93.2	5,924
Tanjong Kling	8.01	4	13.1	1,429
Johore	100.77	–	–	–
Pasir Gudang-JPA[b]	100.77	–	–	–
Total	538.32	100	1,429.2	68,877

Notes:
[a] 1 January 1989 figures.
[b] Pulau Jerejak and Pasir Gudang-JPA are not listed as FTZs in certain MIDA pamphlets. Some MIDA pamphlets also list Senai in Johore as an FTZ. The author's listing is based on interviews and unpublished information from MIDA and PDC.
Source: MIDA (1989); Penang Development Corporation, unpublished data, 1989.

Penang's FTZ firms held 48 per cent of FTZ fixed assets and generated 54 per cent of FTZ employment in 1987. The Bayan Lepas FTZ, the biggest FTZ in Malaysia in 1987, had 41 firms, with fixed assets worth M$524 million and 28,911 employees (see Table 4.1).

TECHNOLOGY AND THE LABOUR PROCESS IN THE 1970s

The early phase of EOI was generally characterised by low value-added labour-intensive production. Falling profit rates, in the face of rising wages and competition, encouraged such internationalisation of industrial production. The United States Government relaxed its customs regulations 806.3 and 807.0 to help US firms reduce production costs by relocating labour-intensive, low value-added production processes abroad (Moxon, 1974: 29; cited in Lim, 1978: 17; UNCTC, 1987: 54–5). This was followed by similar customs legislation in the Federal Republic of Germany, Japan and the United Kingdom, though their restrictions were still comparatively tighter than those of the United States (United Nations, 1987: 54–5). In the case of the textile and apparel industry, the relocation process was strongly tied to quota restrictions imposed under textile and garment agreements signed by importers such as the US and the European Economic Community (EEC), particularly the Multi-Fibre Arrangement (MFA), which came into existence in 1974 (United Nations, 1987: 21). In the 1970s, FTZ textile (but not apparel) firms were more capital intensive than electronics firms. However, foreign firms locating in Malaysian FTZs in the 1970s were generally more labour intensive.

Electronics, electrical, textile and apparel manufacturing formed the core of firms relocating into Malaysia's FTZs. When foreign firms began relocating production in Malaysia, most of their machinery was brought in by the parent firms. However, some new machines were also designed to take better advantage of the new labour force available (see Lim, 1978). Foreign, especially US, capital relocated labour-intensive processes abroad, where low wage and other production costs as well as other attractive conditions prevailed.[7]

Until the early and mid-1980s, new machinery in the electronics industry generally replaced only human energy. With the assembly of electronics/electrical components and products growing into large-scale operations, problems of assembly-line manufacturing had to be addressed. Working conditions were often terrible: in semiconductor firms, for instance, die bonding was done by workers who had to align, aim and bond wires one unit at a time with the aid of maskless high-powered microscopes (Rajah, 1989: 347), and workers performing test operations and assembly were exposed to concentrated acids and other hazardous chemicals.

With textile firms operating in the FTZs, the processes of spinning and weaving have always been capital intensive. For instance, two large subsidiaries in Penang, jointly owned by Hong Kong and Japanese capital, reported in 1985 that the best workers could handle 20–30 conventional weaving machines (installed since 1972). However, in the same firms, about 1,600 conventional weaving machines were operated by 180 line workers on average in each shift. As workers handled several machines, they were not confined to particular locations. None the less, the machines require great discipline and constant attention and the accident rate was relatively high. Skilled quality control inspectors were also needed to spot and amend weaving defects quickly. Additionally, the working environment left much to be desired. In the sizing department, for instance, where chemicals and starch are applied to the yarn, workers had to endure searing heat. In other departments, noise was a particular problem and was exacerbated by the absence of adequate protective clothing.[8]

With such technology, productivity can normally be increased only by intensifying work tasks in shortened shifts and/or by introducing several shifts. But in Malaysia productivity was raised without shortening shifts. Workers were confined to their task locations and were disciplined for talking or moving around. The absence of unions in the electronics industry and the circumscribed unions in the electrical, textile and apparel industries helped ensure that this was a convenient and profitable strategy for foreign capital.

Workers in Malaysia's FTZs have been advertised as dexterous to help encourage foreign investment. Many workers, however, their health permanently damaged, have been forced to leave; workers often complained of headaches, failing eyesight, sore eyes and backstrain (Tan, 1986: 20). Several workers in the textile industry have actually gone deaf. Management often encouraged senior workers to retire by granting them special bonuses. They were then replaced with new workers starting at lower wages. Similarly, workers who frequently complained of exhaustion and illness have been induced to retire early (Rajah, 1987). In electronics firms, long hours of scope work adversely affected the eyesight of workers. Intensification of work tasks and frequent substitution of workers were made easy by the existence of a large pool of industrial labour.

Female workers have generally been preferred for their dexterity and willingness to work for lower wages (see Lim, 1978). As female incomes are viewed socially as only supplementary to male incomes, this has been used to legitimise lower wages for women. Since employers did not mind transient labour, high labour turnover (Tan, 1986: 27, Rajah, 1987) has helped firms to keep wage levels generally low. For example, the average monthly wage of women workers in the electronics industry was M$137 in May 1974, M$163 in May 1977, and M$222 in May 1980 (MIDA, 1983: 26) during years of very high inflation by Malaysian standards. Young, inexperienced and docile school leavers have provided the bulk of the labour sought (see Lim, 1978; Kamal *et al*, 1985; Rajah, 1987).

Companies usually operated on a system of three 8 hour shifts and a typical work week of six days. As wages were low, workers often worked overtime on the seventh day when the firms required them. Electronics workers and textile workers who worked in the FTZs from 1973 to 1979 claim that they came home so tired that they hardly had enough energy to do anything else but sleep (Rajah, 1989: 348). In addition, several studies have shown that the productivity of these workers declined considerably over time (see Lim, 1978; Kamal *et al.*, 1985).

TECHNOLOGY AND THE LABOUR PROCESS IN THE 1980s

Competition provided the main impetus for changes in production in FTZ factories. With declining product prices, product cycles have become shorter, and firms have increased their investments to enhance competitiveness and profitability. Whilst changes in product and production technology in textile and apparel firms seem to have taken place slowly (see Clairmonte and Cavanagh, 1981), semiconductor and telecommunication firms have exhibited more rapid change in both respects (see Rajah, 1989). In addition, in textile, knitting, semiconductor and telecommunication firms, which collectively contribute more than half of the employment generated in Malaysia's FTZs, production has become highly capital intensive. However, in consumer electronics, electrical and apparel firms, production technology remains very labour intensive.

While textile firms were much more capital intensive than electronics firms in the 1970s, the picture has changed. Unlike in the electronics industry, where firms in Malaysia's FTZs use some of the most sophisticated assembly and test machines, in the textile and apparel industry, there is some lag between the technology used in parent firms compared with their Malaysian subsidiaries. Person–machine ratios in the electronics industry have increased more rapidly than in the textile industry. Besides, in the six textile firms surveyed, automated machines were used only in the processes of pirn winding and weaving as indicated earlier, several machines used in 1972 are still being used. However, a change in technology since 1986 in weaving, where air-jet looms were expected to replace conventional weaving machines completely by 1990, person–machine ratios are rising. Even so, the person–machine ratio is expected to be 1:11 by 1990, only slightly higher than the 1:9 mean for conventional machines.[9] In any case, the air-jet looms which have been installed so far have raised productivity by three to four-fold. However, the ratio is not expected to change considerably in spinning, where technological change has not been as significant. Also, the six-day work week is expected to remain unchanged. Two Japanese firms reported that the excess space that has emerged from the fewer machines now used in weaving had been used by the spinning department to increase production levels. In addition, once the transition to air-jet looms is complete, four firms claim that skilled quality control inspectors will be phased out completely as the new machines guarantee defect-free weaving, thus displacing skills in the manufacturing labour process further. Moreover, the reduced noise and dust fibre levels are still above permissible levels.[10] For example, Tan (1988: 3–4) found that, of the 274 workers she studied, 37 females were suffering from byssinosis.

Productivity in knitting is far superior to that for weaving. For instance, double jersey weft knitting exceeds the weaving rate by a factor of 5 to 3, while production in warp knitting is 30–60 times faster than in weaving (UNCTC, 1987: 77). In one Hong Kong knitting firm in the Bayan Lepas FTZ, weft knitting, dyeing and finishing have been completely computerised, while other processes, such as collar knitting, are still semi-automated. In the whole of Asia, their computerised machines – from West Germany and Japan – were second only to those used in Japan.

In apparel firms, several skilled tasks – such as sewing – have remained labour intensive. Microelectronic technology, particularly in computer-aided design (CAD) – introduced in the clothing industry for grading and laying up garments as early as 1972 – made its way to Malaysia only in the mid-1980s. It was first introduced in 1984 by a foreign firm with LMW status in Penang. By 1989, four foreign firms, including one located in the Bayan Lepas FTZ, had installed such technology. Unlike semiconductor and telecommunication firms, where production processes have rapidly shifted to automated technology, the diffusion of microelectronic technology in apparel firms has taken place only in certain processes, such as grading and plotting. This is similar to consumer electronics, in that the change has taken place mainly to increase precision and when it was found to be more efficient. In fact, the most automated apparel firm in Malaysia claims that wastage of fabric – which forms about 65 per cent of production costs – is the main reason for installing auto-controlled machines. But highly skilled tasks, such as sewing, have remained labour-intensive, in fact, dexterity tests are carefully conducted in apparel firms before workers are assigned to skilled tasks.

In consumer electronics firms, the worker–machine ratio is still 1:1, with assembly lines still highly decomposed. For example, conveyor belts move along parallel lines, where seated workers attach specific components onto printed circuit boards and assemble stereo sets. One Dutch consumer electronics firm had twenty-five such assembly lines in 1988. Low skills are clearly evident as workers perform highly fragmented tasks, where almost the only attribute required is fast, nimble fingers. Meanwhile, the automation of printed circuit board insertions in three consumer electronic and electrical firms has not involved any vertical recomposition of work tasks. Instead, the horizontal integration of work tasks with such automation has only reduced drudgery and increased precision.

In semiconductor and telecommunication firms, products have become more sophisticated. The kind of precision needed in the manufacture of some of these products is beyond the capability of manual operations. For example, the sub-micron chip can be made only with the aid of computers, (*International Business Week*, 10 June 1985: 89–90). The miniaturisation process is now so developed that more than a million circuits can now be inserted within a minimum line width of sub-microns (see Lalor, 1986: 24). Products are increasingly equipped with more functions, and are generally cheaper and smaller too. This is why automation in Malaysia has gained momentum in industries that assemble components, especially semiconductors and telecommunication components.

Production processes have undergone tremendous transformation. Crises often provide opportunities for more rapid replacement of old forms of production with new ones (see McFarlane, 1988). The crisis of the semiconductor industry in the mid-1980s saw firms incorporating more efficient production techniques, of which Just-In-Time (JIT), Materials Requirement Planning (MRP), Materials Resource Planning (MRP1), Integrated Materials Resource Planning (MRP2), automation and the related reorganisation of labour have been the most significant.[11]

JIT and MRP control techniques have become a common feature of the electronics components sector, where demand fluctuations are highly volatile (see Rajah, 1989). Fifteen semiconductor and two telecommunications firms interviewed stated that their manufacturing processes were organised along JIT principles. The introduction of JIT has markedly reduced machine set-up time and increased the flexibility of production systems. It has also reduced inventory buffers, errors and defects, idle time, surplus workers, excess machine capacity and problems of insufficient preventive maintenance. All the semiconductor and telecommunication firms in Penang, and US firms in other Malaysian FTZs have introduced the four-shift system, which has sharply reduced shift change time (see Rajah, 1989).[12]

Among other things, the spread of JIT has turned FTZs in Malaysia into important sites for integrated tail-end production for electronics components firms. For example, one US firm reported that the incorporation of JIT and automation technology from 1984 has halved the required factory space. About half its labour force was made redundant, with international restructuring required as well. To centralise production at proximate sites to reap the benefits from JIT, the firm moved assembly and test operations from the Caribbean to use the excess capacity at the Bayan Lepas FTZ factory (Rajah, 1988: 34).

However, even in highly automated plants, the production of certain products – such as cerpacks and flatpacks – is still done manually. Two firms reported the existence of separate lines for such products, which are not economic to automate because of the small volumes involved. One semiconductor firm reported that workers using manually operated machines requiring microscope work are given a scope allowance of M$7.20 monthly (Rajah, 1987: 226). In contrast to the 1970s, when workers wore no masks, such work is currently performed with the aid of protective shields for the eyes. In the case of automated operations, operators do aligning for only one set of units through the scope. Once this is done, subsequent units within each batch are aligned automatically.

Although automation began in Malaysia from the late 1970s, its impact was accelerated by the mid-1984 crash in the electronics industry worldwide. A Japanese firm, with an average worker–machine ratio of 1:12, was the most automated in 1988. The most automated American firm had a worker–machine ratio of 1:8. The most automated process within this firm was tape-bonding, where one worker handled 10 machines. Four other American firms had a worker–machine ratio of 1:6, while another four had a ratio of 1:4.

Workers operating automated machines need different types of skills. Such new skills include statistical process control (SPC) methods, basic programming and knowledge of the specific additions they are integrating the products with. Promising workers are now given specialised training within the firms. Upon successful completion of such training, they are promoted to positions as technicians or quality control inspectors. For example, one worker, who started as an operator in 1976 now holds the post of general foreman. His monthly salary has increased to M$2,100. Semiconductor and telecommunication firms now prefer a portion of their line workers to be skilled. Such skilled and better-paid workers are more inclined to stay with their employers.

In the 1970s, labour in FTZs merely followed instructions from the parent plants. Since then, there has been some increase in local management control of the production process in electronic components factories, which has enhanced their role in the decision-making process. Malaysian professionals are now called over more frequently to parent plants to help reorganise and rationalise production there. Local experts from Malaysia, with knowledge and experience of the tail-end stages (assembly and final testing) of production in Malaysia, help link them up better with the earlier stages (R&D and wafer fabrication) in the parent plants. In fact, such rationalisation and reorganising of the labour process have led two American semiconductor firms to relocate end-of-line wafer fabrication processes in Malaysia.

More importantly, some Malaysian managers frequently visit the parent plant abroad to help improve organisation of the production lines. One such manager developed a production system that incorporated JIT and product planning for the parent firm in the USA. Eight US firms reported that Malaysian professionals have been absorbed by their parent firms to work on such strategic planning. Eight firms also reported that models of machines modified and perfected to JIT work-flow requirements are now used in their parent plants as well.

OWNERSHIP AND CONTROL

In general, foreign capital has almost completely dominated FTZ firms. At the end of 1988, as in the 1970s US firms in FTZs were fully owned, while firms from Western Europe were either fully owned or jointly owned with other foreign investors. Only in a few limited cases did European firms share equity with Malaysian capital. Precima (which produces watch components in the Sungai Way FTZ) is a rarity: its equity breakdown in 1986 was 30 per cent Malaysian and 70 per cent foreign (Swiss and British). In the case of Japanese firms, some shared equity with local capital. For example, Malaysian capital held 20 per cent equity in Kanebo, a major textile firm in the Prai FTZ, 10 per cent equity in Hitachi, a major semiconductor firm in the Bayan Lepas FTZ, and 10 per cent equity in Koa Denko, an electronics components firm in the Batu Berendam FTZ. However, the Pen group of five large textile firms in Penang is now completely owned by Toray (Japanese capital), as is the case with electronic firms, such as NEC Malaysia, situated in the Telok Panglima Garang FTZ. The Pen group in Penang was initially controlled by Hong Kong's Textile Alliance, with a small proportion of equity held by Malaysians.

Foreign capital controlled all firms where they held 50 per cent equity or more. The situation was somewhat similar in the case of joint ventures between local and foreign capital where Malaysian capital held more than 50 per cent of equity. Most such firms were still controlled by foreign capital, though local capital was dominant in terms of equity. For example, Clarion – which assembles car radios and stereos, and had an equity breakdown of 55 per cent Malaysian and 45 per cent Japanese – had a Japanese managing director and was essentially controlled from Japan. Although Malaysians held 51 per cent equity in KESP – a semiconductor subcontracting firm which does assembly test functions such as burn-in – it was still foreign controlled, although the foreign equity was split (29 per cent Singaporean and 20 per cent Taiwanese).

According to data on paid-up capital, foreign capital held 80.8 per cent of overall equity in Malaysian FTZs in 1987 (Table 4.2). Foreign capital was clearly dominant in textiles (97.8 per cent), electric and electronics (89.9 per cent), scientific and measurement instruments (96.5 per cent), and others (80.9 per cent). Also, the major FTZ industries of electric and electronics and textiles (including knitting and apparel) – which together accounted for 59 per cent of FTZ firms and 57 per cent of the paid-up capital in FTZs – are almost completely owned by foreign capital.

In 1982, Japanese capital controlled twenty-eight firms – the largest number in Malaysian FTZs (see Table 4.3). The Americans were a close second, with twenty-six firms. Only in six small firms was there a majority of

Table 4.2 Paid-up capital in Free Trade Zone firms, 1987

Industry	No. of firms[a]	Paid-up capital Local %	Paid-up capital Foreign %	Paid-up capital Total M$m
Food	2	70.1	29.9	1.1
Beverage/tobacco	1	21.5	78.5	108.0
Textiles	11	2.2	97.8	213.0
Wood	2	65.6	34.4	53.1
Chemicals	2	54.3	45.7	12.3
Petroleum/coal	1	100.0	0.0	0.6
Rubber	3	65.4	34.6	23.0
Plastic	3	49.3	50.7	4.2
Non-metal	3	86.7	13.3	1.5
Fabricated metal	6	65.4	34.6	8.9
Machinery	6	21.7	78.3	23.7
Electric/electronic	48	10.1	89.9	174.0
Transport	1	100.0	0.0	8.1
Scientific/measurement	7	3.5	96.5	31.3
Others	6	19.1	80.9	15.7
Total	102	19.2	80.8	678.5

Note: [a] Figures include two firms approved but not yet in production in 1987.
Source: MIDA unpublished data (1989).

Table 4.3 Ownership of Free Trade Zone firms, 1982

Country	Penang	Selangor	Malacca	Total	%
Japan	13	14	1	28	31.5
USA	15	9	2	26	29.2
West Germany	10	–	2	12	13.5
Malaysia	4	–	2	6	6.7
Switzerland	2	1	1	4	4.5
Hong Kong	3	–	1	4	4.5
Others[1]	6	1	2	9	10.1
Total	53	25	11	89	100.0

Note: [1] Others refer to other nations and joint-ventures with equal ownership.
Source: Anazawa (1985–6: 105).

locally controlled equity. Most Japanese firms were found in textiles and garments and in electronics. American firms in Malaysian FTZs were mainly found in the electronics sector. German firms were mainly concentrated in medical instruments and electronics. Hong Kong capital, which was dominant in the textile sector in the 1970s, had sold much of its equity to Japanese interests by the mid-1980s. The few remaining Hong Kong firms in Malaysian FTZs are mainly in knitting, apparel and consumer electronics. Meanwhile, the withdrawal of privileges under the Generalised System of Preferences (GSP) from the Asian NICs in 1988 further encouraged industrial relocation in Malaysia. Consequently, some Taiwanese and new Hong Kong capital ventured into the FTZs, as well as into non-FTZ industrial estates, in Malaysia.[13]

Owing to the lack of new information, analysis of the ownership of FTZ firms is based on 1982 data (see Table 4.3). Japanese capital controlled the highest number of firms (31.5 per cent), with US capital a close second (29.2 per cent); the other major interest was German (13.5 per cent). There were only six (6.7 per cent) Malaysian firms. While the forty FTZ firms surveyed point to the strong possibility of Japanese and American firms retaining their positions, it is highly likely that Hong Kong and Taiwanese firms, which began relocating production in Malaysian FTZs in the late 1980s, may have swelled their numbers.

While most US firms are still 100 per cent owned, since about 1980 there has been a greater tendency for foreign capital to encourage equity participation by local managerial personnel in their firms. For instance, fifteen semiconductor firms and one telecommunications firm reported that, since the early 1980s, local managers have been allowed to hold a small percentage of shares to encourage the notion of a corporate family. Despite such efforts, however, there is as yet no indication of moves to encourage more broad-based local ownership. The corollary of foreign equity is control over production. There is frequent liaising – by telephone and telex – between parent firms and subsidiaries in Malaysia. As a result, although day-to-day operations in American firms are under the control of local management, strategic decision making is still done abroad. However, local management has an important role in decisions about capacity, targets and the inputs to be used. Four US semiconductor firms and one Canadian telecommunications firm surveyed were run completely by Malaysians. But, unlike in American electronic components firms, most top positions in textile, apparel and scientific/measurement instrument firms are still held by foreigners. Likewise, in Japanese, Taiwanese and Hong Kong firms – mainly involved in the textile and apparel industries – foreign personnel even made important decisions on day-to-day operations.

UNIONS AND WAGES

With the exception of the electronics industry, unions are allowed in FTZ firms. However, Malaysian unions have little room for manoeuvre. The Industrial Relations Act of 1967 – following the Trade Union Ordinance of 1959 – empowers the Minister to grant recognition to individual unions (Shoesmith, 1986: 116). Following the Act, in their early years of existence pioneer industries and those in FTZs were exempted from the otherwise mandatory collective bargaining obligations. Thus, in the early phase, there were no unions in FTZ firms, a major plus factor that helped attract large American electronics firms to Malaysia.

However, unions were gradually allowed in several FTZ industries. The Textile Workers' Union (TWU) of Penang successfully unionised Woodard Textile Mills, which employed 2,300 workers, in March 1978 (*Ibid*: 178), followed by Pentex in December 1978. Subsequently, other textile workers were unionised. Similarly, the National Union of Rubber Products Workers successfully unionised in the FTZs, beginning with the registration of 400 workers from PLAAT, now owned by domestic capital but at that time controlled by German interests. The Electrical Industry Workers' Union (EIWU), formed in 1972, also began unionising firms, such as Granek, which is classified within the electrical sub-sector.

But the electronics industry, which employed more than 80,000 workers in 1988, by and large remained free of unionisation (*Star*, 23 September 1988: 1). Earlier efforts in 1974 by the EIWU to register electronics workers were rejected by the Registrar of Trade Unions (Shoesmith, 1986: 179). In June 1988, the American Federation of Labor and Congress of Industrial Organizations (AFL–CIO) filed a petition calling for the withdrawal of duty-free privileges under the GSP from Malaysia, claiming that the Malaysian government had denied freedom of association and the right to organise and to bargain collectively (*Star*, 24 September 1988: 1). In late 1988, the Labour Ministry finally allowed in-house unions in electronics firms. The formation of an in-house union in the RCA factory in Kuala Lumpur has since met with considerable resistance from management.

Some Japanese firms had allowed in-house unions even before the decision. Yet, apart from these Japanese firms and RCA, the other electronics firms are still without even in-house unions. American firms still oppose unions vehemently. The Malaysian–American Electronic Industry (MAEI) has strongly voiced its unhappiness over the decision to allow unions in the electronics firms (*New Sunday Times*, 25 September 1988). An American semiconductor firm in Penang threatened to relocate to Bangkok, where it had unused factory premises.

The in-house unions in Japanese electronics firms have been management creations comprised of 'friendly and manageable' worker members willing to cooperate with management representatives; inevitably, these unions serve the interests of management. Meanwhile, many American firms have introduced worker–management committees similar to the in-house unions found in Japanese firms. These 'quality of company life' committees (QCLC), were composed of employee representatives (professionals and workers alike), and were run by the companies' personnel managers and managing directors.

The absence of independent unions has meant that management has dictated the terms with labour. Nine managing directors of American component firms in the Bayan Lepas, Sungai Way and Ulu Kelang FTZs, for instance, stressed that their presence in Malaysia would be seriously undermined if unions were allowed in their firms. With the absence of independent unions that can actively defend workers' rights, workers in electronics firms have been quite helpless in dealing with management.

While strong independent unions can play an important part in influencing working conditions, their efficacy is also conditioned by broader economic and political forces, such as government policy, unemployment levels and international economic conditions. For example, while some textile workers' unions are noted for their militancy and success in collective bargaining (see Shoesmith, 1986), wages in the textile industry are still generally lower than in the electronics components sector, where there was no independent union until 1989. Also, management representatives are often well-connected ex-government officials, which does not help labour.

Unlike in South Korea, where wages in local firms are higher than in foreign firms operating in FTZs (see Irvan, 1986), foreign firms in Malaysian FTZs pay considerably higher wages than most local firms. In 1988, average monthly wages for skilled and unskilled workers in eighteen of the twenty-four local firms outside FTZs interviewed – two textile, twelve garment and ten supporting – were lower than M$300. In contrast, average salaries for unskilled and semi-skilled workers in FTZ textile and garment firms were in the range M$320–340 monthly. Since labour turnover in the spinning and weaving industry is very high, most workers earned between M$300–400 monthly. Highly skilled workers, particularly sewing and knitting machine operators in the apparel and knitting industry, earned above M$700 monthly.

Most skilled workers, however, earned M$400–550 monthly. These wages are all for an 8 hour day, six days a week.

Labour control methods have also become more refined, but developments in the semiconductor and telecommunication components industries in FTZs indicate that the major stimulus to change in the production process has been competition. Furthermore, the incorporation of JIT techniques and automation is rapidly increasing the proportion of the technical workforce. Management, therefore, now have to contend with a labour force which is increasingly becoming more skilled and better paid, though eight firms have employed temporary contract workers, at low wages, during periods of high demand.

Average monthly compensation for the relatively more automated electronics firms in 1988 ranged from M$550 in a small American semiconductor firm to M$600 in a large American semiconductor firm (Rajah, 1987). Meanwhile, particularly productive operators in one firm earned as much as M$800 monthly. These figures include allowances for food, scope work, shift work and bonuses. Since these salaries were for a 6 hour, 5.7 day work week, they were significantly higher than in the textile industry. Average wage levels in electronics component firms in 1988 were, in fact, the highest in Malaysian FTZs. However, highly skilled workers performing sewing operations in the apparel industry were reported to earn as much as M$900 monthly. None the less, although the apparel industry had the highest paid individual workers, relatively unskilled workers earned less than M$400 monthly, and were generally paid according to piece-rate arrangements, while workers operating automated plotting and grading tasks earned M$400–500 monthly.

In both textile and knitting firms, there appear to be deliberate efforts to automate workers in order to check spiralling wages. All six textile firms and one knitting firm interviewed reported that competition and relatively longer product cycles made it 'uneconomic' to pay higher wages. Low wages and deplorable working conditions in the textile industry are considered to be the main reason for the high labour turnover experienced.[14] However, in the case of the apparel industry, the two firms interviewed reported that competition for skilled sewers is the main reason for their 'exceptionally high' wages.[15]

Working conditions in the electronics components industry have improved considerably in the more automated firms. The eye strain associated with long hours of scope work seem to be declining, while work shifts have been shortened to 6 hours. Labour control is more lax as workers are now allowed to talk, while the living conditions of workers are better. Workers can now afford a room for two, with each paying about M$50 monthly.[16] All seventeen components firms cited the considerable increase in skills, knowledge and functions of local managers and professionals working in the firms as an important factor in the overall rise in wage levels. These firms are also aware that their wage levels are significantly higher than in firms with unions. The fear of workers forming unions may be an important reason for the relatively high wages in the electronics components industry. The other reason given was the huge profit margins of these firms; thus profitability has positively influenced workers' wages.

However, during the crisis from mid-1984 to 1986, even in the automated semiconductor firms wages were slashed for all levels of staff. Although the management of one firm, where salaries were slashed by 10 per cent in 1985, claimed that the workers had consented to this reduction, the absence of unions allowed such decisions to go uncontested. While the workers were certainly aware of the reductions, they had been led to believe that the alternative was for the firm to go bankrupt, thereby leaving everyone jobless. Since 1987, three components firms are reported to have re-employed workers retrenched during 1984–6 as temporary contract workers on lower wages, to meet increased demand for semiconductors since 1987.

In small consumer electronics firms, where automation is still limited, things have not changed much. One firm paid a meagre M$300 monthly average compensation in 1988, such wages were comparable to those paid by textile firms in the FTZs. Workers from these firms also complained of being drowsy and tired and of failing eyesight and being unsure of their future. Working conditions within these firms were generally deplorable. One firm making cheap radio cassette players claimed that similar products are made in Hong Kong and Taiwan by means of a 'putting-out' system where housewives work cheaply in their own homes. Even managers in this firm were paid significantly lower salaries than those in the semiconductor firms. The executive director, for instance, earned only as much as some ordinary managers in semiconductor firms. The managements of these smaller, very labour-intensive consumer electronics firms claim that higher wages would drive them out of Malaysia. Yet the situation of these workers was still generally better than that in local electronics support and textile firms.

As noted earlier, unions were excluded from the electronics industry until 1988, as the state feared an exodus of these firms if unions were allowed. Recently, American semiconductor and telecommunications firms have offered better wages than are available in unionised firms to justify their claim that unions are unnecessary in the electronics industry. The absence of unions is also a major reason why the electronics labour force in Malaysia is extremely flexible. Despite the existence of unions, wages in textiles are significantly lower than in electronic components firms, notwithstanding the impact of competition among apparel firms, which seems to have pushed up wages of skilled workers.

IMPACT ON MALAYSIA'S INDUSTRIAL DEVELOPMENT

While FTZs seem to generate employment and foreign exchange, the operations of FTZ firms and other macroeconomic developments, particularly since the mid-1980s, appear to have favoured greater transfer of technology and growth of linkages. This section assesses the impact of FTZs on the industrial development of Malaysia.

Employment

Employment is perhaps the most important benefit Malaysia has derived from FTZs (see Table 4.4). From 21,243 in 1973, employment in FTZs reached its peak of 81,688 in 1984, with the greatest expansion taking place during the years 1973–80. Even the first oil shock of 1973–5 did not adversely affect this growth. However, the global recession following the second oil crisis of 1979–80 and the 1984–5 downturn in the electronic components industry, led to firms reducing their workforces in 1981–2 and 1985–6. Overall FTZ employment levels were not too badly affected in 1981, mainly because of the relocation in Malaysia of labour-intensive firms after Singapore restructured its incentives to promote more capital-intensive and higher value-added industries (Kamal and Young, 1985; Rajah, 1987). The decline in FTZ employment in 1985 was much sharper, falling by 16.8 per cent, mainly in the electronics components industry.

Table 4.4 Free Trade Zone firms and employment, 1972–87

Year	No. of firms (a)	FTZ employment ('000) (b)	Change %	Mean firm employment	Malaysian manufacturing employment ('000) (c)	(b)/(c) %
1972	14	–			231.5	
1973	28	21.2	–	759	294.0	7.2
1974	41	25.6	20.5	624	419.0	6.1
1975	51	31.7	24.0	622	398.2	8.0
1976	56	42.1	32.5	752	448.0	9.4
1977	61	46.9	11.5	769	502.5	9.3
1978	66	53.3	13.7	808	538.3	9.9
1979	73	59.5	11.7	815	652.1	9.1
1980	78	67.1	12.6	860	750.5	8.9
1981	84	72.5	8.1	863	779.8	9.3
1982	89	69.8	–3.9	784	796.2	8.8
1983[a]	98	74.8	7.2	763	800.3	9.3
1984	104	81.7	9.2	786	844.0	9.7
1985	104	68.3	–16.4	657	828.0	8.2
1986	111	70.6	3.4	636	810.0	8.7
1987	100	68.9	–2.4	689	920.6	7.5

Note: [a] FTZ figures from 1983 are for firms approved and in production.
Sources: 1972–82 FTZ figures for no. of firms and employment are from Warr (1986); 1983–87 FTZ figures are from unpublished MIDA data; Ministry of Finance (1989).
Figures for Malaysian manufacturing employment are from annual Treasury *Economic Report*, various issues.

Despite fears that the supposedly footloose electronics industries would leave, with automation encouraging relocation back to the developed countries (Kaplinsky, 1985; Kamal and Young, 1985), there was little emigration of FTZ firms from Malaysia. Equity restructuring – such as the transfer of Mostek to Thomson, and subsequently to International Device Technology (IDT), and the absorption of Monolithic Memories (MMI) by Advanced Micro Devices (AMD) – often involved rationalisation and reorganisation, leading to retrenchment by some of these firms. For example, AMD retrenched 800 workers from the two MMI plants it absorbed in the Bayan Lepas FTZ in 1987.

Meanwhile, mean permanent employment by firms has fallen sharply as a consequence of the shift to more capital-intensive production and greater labour flexibility. From 759 in 1973, mean firm-employment, which peaked at 863 in 1981, had fallen to 636 in 1986, rising only marginally to 689 in 1987 (see Table 4.4). In electronic components firms, the introduction of JIT techniques also contributed to falling levels of employment. Thus, leaving contract workers aside, the recent upsurge in demand for workers in FTZs is mainly caused by a new wave of firms, particularly in consumer electronics, relocating to Malaysia since 1987.

While workers generally enjoy better wages when the industry is booming, the converse has often been the case during recessions. For example, labour shedding, reduced wages and other inducements – such as bonus payments – for voluntary retirement were common in electronic components firms between mid-1984 and early 1987. In fact, two firms shortened their work week to three days and four days respectively in 1985, slashing wages by 20 per cent and 10 per cent in the process. In the case of the firm which reduced salaries by 20 per cent, many employees, including managers and engineers, were also given the impression that the firm was on the verge of retrenching employees without the payment of any compensation. As a result, instead of 'eventually getting retrenched' without any retrenchment benefits, many chose to leave 'voluntarily' with some bonus inducement. The firm's management claimed that it was in danger of going bankrupt as a result of poor orders. They then restructured the assembly line, shifting sharply to more capital-intensive production, while retaining most of their technical staff. Not surprisingly then, all the semiconductor firms and two telecommunication firms reported that the proportion of technical staff has increased tremendously since 1984 (Rajah, 1987). Others, including managers, have been trimmed, while retraining has frequently been done. The forty-eight electric and electronics firms accounted for 67.8 per cent of FTZ employment in 1987 (see Table 4.5). Textiles (12.1 per cent) and scientific/measurement instruments (6.2 per cent) firms were the other major employment generators. Since these industries are dominated by foreign capital (see Table 4.2 above), FTZ employment depends strongly on transnational firms.

Table 4.5 FTZ employment characteristics by industry, 1987

Industry	No. of firms[a]	Bumiputra	Chinese	Indian	Other	Foreign	Total	%[b]
Food	2	428	195	16	0	1	640	0.9
Beverages/tobacco	1	261	236	79	0	2	578	0.8
Textiles	11	4,376	2,624	1,321	40	44	8,404	12.1
Wood	2	341	63	35	0	1	440	0.6
Chemicals	2	81	100	14	7	1	203	0.3
Petroleum & coal	1	24	1	0	0	0	25	0.0
Rubber	3	742	210	316	9	3	1,280	1.8
Plastic	3	193	123	53	0	4	373	0.5
Non-metal	3	83	11	11	50	0	155	0.2
Fabricated Metal	6	113	62	43	2	3	223	0.3
Machinery	6	822	711	177	2	0	1,712	2.5
Electric/electronics	48	27,637	11,158	8,061	255	93	47,204	67.8
Transport equipment	1	231	194	41	5	1	472	0.7
Scientific/measurement	7	2,340	950	973	9	25	4,297	6.2
Others	6	2,097	602	879	8	10	3,596	5.2
Total	102	39,768	17,240	12,019	387	188	69,602	100.0
%[b]		(57.1)	(24.8)	(17.3)	(0.6)	(0.3)	(100.0)	

Notes:
[a] Figures are for firms in production. Thus, information used here includes two firms already in production that were not yet approved in 1987.
[b] Percentages rounded.
Source: MIDA, 1989.

The ethnic breakdown of FTZ employment in 1987 shows the Bumiputras (57.1 per cent) almost proportionately represented, with the Chinese (24.8 per cent) considerably lower, and the Indians (17.3 per cent) significantly higher than their respective national demographic proportions (see Table 4.5). Much of the Bumiputra and Indian labour force is on the lower occupational rungs as operators. In fact, in the forty firms surveyed, 75 per cent of the professionals were Chinese, far outnumbering both Bumiputras (7.5 per cent) and Indians (10 per cent). Expatriate employment, which is concentrated in top managerial and technical positions, accounted for 0.3 per cent of overall FTZ employment. Most expatriates were found in the electric and electronics (93), textiles (44) and scientific/measurement instrument (25) industries.

Despite the rapid introduction of more capital-intensive technology in FTZ firms recently, the survey showed that the overall gender breakdown was still strongly skewed towards female labour (73.2 per cent). Electronics firms had the biggest proportion of female workers (76.4 per cent), followed by textile and garment firms (69.5 per cent). Only one firm (Hong Kong owned), in the Bayan Lepas FTZ, reported a higher proportion of male workers (60 per cent) overall.

Export performance

In 1982, value added in FTZ firms totalled M$944 million. This constituted 10.2 per cent of the national manufacturing value added of M$9,246 million (Ministry of Finance, 1985: 95). The electronics industry contributed 76.4 per cent of the FTZ value added (Warr, 1986: 192).[17] Regionally, value added in Selangor (54 per cent) far exceeded that in the main FTZ state, Penang (28 per cent).

FTZ firms dominate manufacturing sector exports. From a share of 1 per cent in 1972, FTZ exports rose to 52.3 per cent in 1982, after peaking with a 74.5 per cent share in 1979 (see Table 4.6). Although official figures are not available for 1983–8, the dominance of electronics exports – which contributed more than 30 per cent of all manufactured exports during 1986–8 (almost entirely from FTZs) – points to the continued dominance of FTZ firms.[18] Three major American semiconductor firms reported that more than 65 per cent of their worldwide profits in 1988 were generated in Malaysia.[19]

Table 4.6 FTZ and non-FTZ manufactured exports, 1972–82

Year	FTZ exports M$	%	Non-FTZ exports M$	%	Total exports M$
1972	6.9	1.0	715.7	99.0	722.9
1973	223.7	20.0	895.0	80.0	1,118.7
1974	448.8	26.5	1,241.8	73.5	1,690.6
1975	723.3	36.2	1,297.1	63.8	2,020.4
1976	1,157.3	46.6	1,327.7	53.4	2,485.2
1977	1,153.5	43.1	1,522.1	56.9	2,675.6
1978	2,179.3	59.5	1,485.1	40.5	3,664.4
1979	3,622.5	74.5	1,237.4	25.5	4,859.9
1980	3,872.4	61.3	2,446.8	38.7	6,319.2
1981	3,818.9	59.8	2,564.7	40.2	6,383.6
1982	3,930.3	52.3	3,581.2	47.7	7,511.5

Sources: adapted from Warr (1986: 190); Bank Negara Malaysia (1989).

Technology transfer

In the 1970s, apart from the transfer of dexterous and some technical and middle-line managerial skills, most studies show that there has been little technology transfer in the FTZ (see Lim, 1978; Rajah, 1987; Rajah and Mukunden,, 1989; Chan *et al.*, 1983). With weak linkages and close control from abroad, local firms benefited little from the operations of FTZ firms. Additionally, most key technical and managerial posts were held by expatriates.

The situation in the 1980s improved slightly in textile and apparel firms. The number of foreigners per firm declined from 10–18 in the 1970s to 4–8 in 1989. However, all key technical and managerial posts in textile firms were still held by foreigners, mainly professionals from Japan and Hong Kong. In apparel firms, although the overall figures were similar, some local professionals were found in key managerial posts. The mean expatriate employment figure for the eleven textile and garment firms was four in 1987. While local firms situated outside FTZs far outnumber foreign firms, the former are very much smaller in size than the latter. As discussed earlier, production technology in textile and apparel firms has not changed much. Most machines of the 1970s still remain.

While there has been little technology transfer in textile firms, apparel firms have seen a higher degree of technology transfer. One deputy factory manager claimed that, if it were not for market constraints, Malaysians could produce apparel products similar to those of Hong Kong and Japanese firms.[20]

Perhaps the greatest transfer of technology has been recorded in telecommunications and semiconductor firms. A survey (MIDA/JICA/JETRO, 1989) has shown that local ancillary firms, particularly mould and die manufacturers, have benefited tremendously from technology transfer from FTZ firms. One firm stated that local engineers have on several occasions developed automated machines that are now mass produced by local ancillary firms which export all over the world. One such product is a semi-automated die-attach machine, which was recently subcontracted to a local firm. Additionally, engineers in a telecommunication firm have perfected modules, relays and other designs used in telecommunication products.

In the case of semiconductor firms in Malaysia, however, technology development has been limited to machinery. In the 1970s, the semiconductor industry in Malaysia was nothing more than an off-shore enclave where management merely executed instructions from parent firms (Rajah, 1987). In the 1980s, particularly since 1985, changes in the dynamics of production have enabled local management to gain some control of the production process, although foreign capital remains the dominant interest (see Rajah, 1988: 32–5). For example, as noted above, professionals from Penang often advise the parent firm on how better to integrate the firm's global production processes. In fact, such rationalisation and reorganisation have led two major American firms to relocate end-of-line (EOL) wafer fabrication processes in the Bayan Lepas and Sungai Way FTZs. Six American firms have also reported that managers from their Malaysian subsidiaries frequently visit the parent plants to improve the organisation of the production lines. One manager, for example, was key in the development of a production system incorporating JIT and product planning into the corporation worldwide.

Eight American electronics components firms reported that twelve of their professionals have been absorbed by their parent firms to work on strategic planning. While this involves a brain drain from Malaysia, it shows that some FTZ personnel have been able to advance their know-how and careers in the firms' interest. In addition, one firm reported that Malaysian machine models modified for JIT specification are now also used in the parent plants (Rajah, 1987). In another case, when one firm began replacing old machinery with automated machinery during 1984–6, 200 engineers were sent to the USA for training. But all training is limited to production technology. There is no training for product development, which is still retained within the parent firms. Expenditure on technical training has also been on the increase (see Rajah, 1990). While training programmes in Japanese firms differ and are generally on a smaller scale, the transfer of production technology is significant all round.

The rapid change in production techniques constantly requires retraining. Unlike in the USA, where opposition to retraining is strong, the absence of unions and weak labour laws in Malaysia have ensured a more docile and malleable workforce. Thus, in an industry where technology changes swiftly, the presence of a highly skilled technical labour force that adapts quickly to new technologies with little resistance is certainly a major positive factor for retaining production in Malaysia (see Rajah, 1987; *South*, 1987). Foreign firms are now increasingly subcontracting machinery prototypes to local firms. In one firm, a mobile unit – composed of engineers and technicians – frequently redesigns and modifies existing machinery to improve efficiency.

The rapid shift towards more capital-intensive production has undoubtedly displaced many workers but has also raised the skills of the remaining workers. The fact that workers now have more technical knowledge and work more line processes suggests that some form of multiskilling is occurring.[21] Inevitably, this has been one of the major reasons for the decline in the overall workforce. For instance, one firm with 100 workers per shift tending manual die-bonding lines in 1978, had only 30 workers in 1989, though production volumes had increased. Such restructuring of production processes has increased the proportion of technical personnel.

The second channel for technology transfer – which has become more significant lately – is subcontracting. The significance of this development is discussed below.

Linkages

Linkages between FTZ firms and the domestic economy in the 1970s and early 1980s were quite marginal. During 1972–82, the use of local raw materials and local suppliers hovered around 2.3–4.9 per cent and 0.2–2.8 per cent respectively (see Table 4.7). While the FTZ firms' high export figures satisfied the government's export-oriented policy preference, they had few forward linkages. These percentages had changed little between 1983 and 1988 for the electronics firms interviewed. Nevertheless, textile materials from foreign firms in FTZs are increasingly purchased by domestic subcontractors that produce garments for export (see Rajah and Mukunden, 1989).

However, backward linkages were found to have been more important, as in the purchase of capital equipment. As Table 4.7 shows, from an exceptionally high figure of 78.2 per cent in 1972, when very few firms were in operation in the FTZs, the domestic component dwindled to 8.3 per cent in 1982.[22] Although this percentage fell further during 1983–8 (mainly owing to the import of automated machinery for electronic components firms and, to a lesser extent, textile firms),[23] domestic supplies of machines and services to FTZ firms have been on the increase.[24]

While the use of local raw materials and equipment has remained marginal in FTZs, recent developments in the international economy have given some impetus to the growth of local subcontracting firms. The rising cost of imports caused by the yen appreciation, the withdrawal of GSP privileges from the Asian NICs as well as changing production techniques that favour proximate suppliers have created greater opportunities for subcontracting firms in Malaysia. Consequently, ancillary firms that have business contacts with the electronics firms in Malaysia now undertake auto-precision turning work, precision engineering and plastic mould-parts fabrication. They manufacture automation systems, precision plastic moulding products, plastic extrusion products and moulds, and do stamping, tooling, die making and packaging. For example, in 1987, there were an estimated sixty local mould and die subcontractors, with a total annual sales turnover of M$40–50 million (MIDA/JICA/JETRO, 1989: 1).[25] MIDA *et al.* (1989) have also found that mould and die manufacturers who service the electric and electronics industry have emerged as a response to requests from foreign semiconductor firms located in FTZs. In fact, interviews show that the largest local subcontractor in Malaysia, who recorded a sales turnover of M$4.3 million in 1987, had enjoyed tremendous financial and engineering support from American semiconductor firms in the Bayan Lepas FTZ before being able to service them. In 1987, local subcontractors provided 20 per cent of the M$150 million worth of moulds and dies supplied to the electronics industry in Malaysia.

In 1987, with the exception of Ipoh and its environs (where there were four firms), the other mould and die subcontractors were located close to the FTZs of Penang (nineteen firms) and Selangor (thirty-seven firms) (MIDA/JICA/JETRO, 1989: 2). The bigger subcontractors supplied around 70 per cent of their sales turnover to FTZ firms, and the remaining 30 per cent were mainly exported (Teh, forthcoming). On average, supporting firms sold 40–50 per cent of their products to FTZ firms (MIDA/JICA/JETRO 1989: 8).

Table 4.7 Raw materials, capital equipment and sales of Free Trade Zone firms, 1972–82 (M$m)

Year	Raw materials[a]			Capital equipment			Sales		
	Local	Imported	Local % of total	Local	Imported	Local % of total	Local	Foreign	Local % of total
1972	0.2	4.1	4.6	1.6	0.4	78.2	–	6.9	–
1973	3.7	155.7	2.3	19.8	47.7	29.4	0.3	223.7	0.2
1974	12.1	362.2	3.2	67.0	157.1	29.9	5.6	448.8	1.2
1975	20.4	517.9	3.8	74.6	93.6	44.3	4.2	723.3	0.6
1976	26.3	751.3	3.4	8.4	50.6	14.2	17.9	1,157.3	1.5
1977	38.0	736.3	4.9	13.0	64.9	16.7	12.6	1,153.5	1.1
1978	47.2	1,508.2	3.0	16.8	67.1	20.0	23.2	2,179.3	1.1
1979	51.6	1,820.0	2.8	53.7	185.2	22.5	58.1	3,622.5	1.6
1980	61.8	2,654.7	2.3	14.7	165.3	8.2	2.9	3,872.4	0.1
1981	72.8	2,501.8	2.8	19.7	178.4	10.0	36.4	3,818.9	0.9
1982	109.5	2,914.4	3.6	16.8	184.8	8.3	113.9	3,930.3	2.8

Note: [a] Purchases from within FTZs are classified as imports.
Source: adapted from Warr (1986:190).

CONCLUDING COMMENTS

It is clear that FTZs have contributed considerably to the growth of Malaysia's economy, have attracted a sizeable portion of Malaysia's manufacturing investment and have been responsible for significant employment creation and export performance. Additionally, particularly since the 1980s, the FTZs have provided an environment for technology transfer and the growth of local linkage firms.

While the signs augur well for the development of Malaysia as a niche for foreign capital to relocate tail-end stages of productive capital, much depends on how Malaysia fits into their plans. At this juncture, although the share of Malaysian manufacturing equity in FTZ firms is small, the contribution of these firms to exports, wages and employment is large. However, unless domestic capital begins to control more, national industrial strategies will continue to be constrained by conditions set by foreign capital. The consequences of such foreign domination may become more serious if major trading powers – such as the USA, the EEC and Japan – withdraw trade benefits provided by the General Agreement on Tariffs and Trade (GATT) before domestic industrial capital matures. This is particularly important because trade benefits were among the major reasons for foreign manufacturing firms to operate in Malaysian FTZs.

Also, as FTZ activity is tied to the vicissitudes of the world economic environment, global economic downturns can have serious implications, as shown by the widespread retrenchments in electronics firms during the 1985–6 downturn, which caused overall manufacturing employment to fall.

As the current macroeconomic scene favours the agglomeration of tail-end stages of production in major regional markets, including the Asia–Pacific, the government should emphasise technology transfer and the development of local linkage firms, particularly in the machine, plastic and chemical engineering industries, by providing special incentives and easy access to credit and market information, and by setting up a centralised engineering R&D agency to assist these firms. Large-scale industrialisation needs the back-up of supporting firms, as was rightly pointed out in the Industrial Master Plan (IMP), and has been demonstrated by South Korea and Taiwan (see Westphal et al., 1984; Fransman, 1986). Also, instead of expanding university undergraduate enrolment,[26] the government should expand skilled labour training programmes. Most firms report that skilled personnel comparable to those in Singapore can be found in Malaysia, but not in sufficient quantities (see *South East Asia Digest*, 9 June 1989: 12).

NOTES

Information in the paper is mainly based on research carried out by the author during 1986–9 covering twenty electronics firms, nine textile and garments firms, one electrical firm, two scientific and measurement instrument firms and eight other foreign supporting firms in FTZs. In addition, the survey also covered six local supporting firms situated outside FTZs that had backward linkages with FTZ firms, two textile firms, twelve garment firms and four other supporting firms. Several unpublished documents from MIDA and Penang Development Corporation (PDC) have also been used.

Since the forty FTZ firms studied were among the 100 in production in 1987, $N = 100$; $n = 40$ (i.e. 40 per cent).

1. FTZs in other countries are often referred to as export processing zones (EPZ).
2. The NEP had the twin objectives of eradicating poverty and restructuring society to eliminate the identification of race with economic function (by 1990) (Malaysia, 1981: 31).
3. For a brief exposition of the underlying rationale behind the promotion of FTZs in East and Southeast Asia, see Rajah (1989: 344–5).
4. LMWs were introduced to encourage the dispersal of industries and to enable the location of factories producing at least 80% for export and whose raw materials/components are mainly imported where the establishment of FTZs is neither practical nor desirable. These establishments are accorded similar facilities and incentives as those in FTZs (Ministry of Finance 1988: 56).
5. FTZs (for companies producing entirely for export; in exceptional cases, firms exporting not less than 80 per cent of production can be considered for location) lie outside the Principal Customs Area (PCA); thus, goods imported to and exported from PCA are not liable to customs duty. However, goods imported from and exported to the PCA are liable to customs duty unless exemptions have been approved by the Treasury (Ministry of Finance, 1988: 55). In addition, FTZ firms enjoy some of the most generous tax incentives, such as pioneer status (which provides complete exemption from corporate and development tax for 5–10 years) and investment tax allowance.
6. Unpublished information from MIDA (1989) showed no firms in the Pasir Gudang Johore Port Authority (JPA) FTZ in 1987.
7. This economic situation, coupled with political developments in the Pacific rim, saw the US government promoting the Pacific Basin as a region for US corporate domination (see Muto, 1977).
8. For instance, the noise level in conventional weaving machines was as high as 106 dBA, which surpassed the permissible level of 90 dBA (Tan, 1988: 4).
9. In fact, one large Japanese firm claimed 30 workers would be operating 350 air-jet looms in the weaving department during each shift by 1990.
10. For example, the mean dust concentration in the blowing area in one mill was 2.01 mg/m^3, which exceeded the Threshold Limit Value (TLV) by ten times! The same paper also reported that the processes of carding, combing and roving in four mills exceeded the TLV. Noise levels where air-jet looms were installed reached 99 dBA (Tan, 1988: 3, 4).
11. See Rajah (1989) for a brief explanation of these concepts.
12. When demand rises, the work week is extended with overtime. The shortening of the work week during periods of low orders enables firms to save overhead costs. The flexible use of workers allows effective rotation between tasks, which is essential for JIT, where work is done when needed, in the necessary quantity, at the necessary time (Rajah, 1988: 33). Eight firms stated that, since 1987, they had been employing low-wage contract workers to meet the exceptionally high orders.
13. Each foreign subsidiary plant is counted as a separate FTZ firm.
14. One textile firm which experienced a labour turnover of 50 per cent in 1988 reported that it is contemplating reducing its labour force by shifting to more capital-intensive production.
15. One Hong Kong garment firm reported that it was going to raise the wages of skilled sewers, by raising their wage ceiling from M$900 to M$1,000 monthly.

Despite rising wages for skilled jobs in the apparel sub-sector, the two firms interviewed reported that it was still less economic to automate several skilled processes in Malaysia.
16 Some could even afford to purchase – mainly through hire-purchase arrangements – household items, such as television sets and cassette players, after meeting family commitments.
17 For example, 90 per cent of FTZ exports in 1974 came from the electronics industry (Datta-Chaudhuri, 1984: 86).
18 Sales, however, slowed slightly in 1988, thereby giving rise to fears of a possible slump in the electronic components industry in 1988.
19 These figures should, however, take into consideration the likelihood of transfer pricing, which may deflate the declared values of imports and inflate export values of firms operating in tax havens like Malaysian FTZs. The implications of this for Malaysia could be serious as inflated exports may actually exaggerate the export performance of the manufacturing sector.
20 The deputy factory manager also reported that the demand for apparel products is strongly tied to brand names.
21 As was argued by Sayer (1986), the very fact that workers are now in control of more processes (due to job enlargement) is itself enough to suggest that reskilling is taking place.
22 Electronics firms alone purchased M$181.5 million (90 per cent) of the M$201.6 million worth of capital equipment bought by FTZ firms in 1982 (Warr, 1986: 190). Imports comprised 92.4 per cent of the total purchased by electronics firms in FTZs.
23 Electronic components firms began shipping rapidly automated machines to Malaysia from 1983 after automated machinery was first introduced in 1979. In the case of textile firms, auto-controlled pirn winding machines and air-jet looms were mainly introduced from 1986, while knitting, apparel and machining firms began introducing CNC machines mainly from 1983.
24 FTZ firms, particularly semiconductor firms, have been instrumental in developing local machinery firms since the 1980s.
25 This figure does not include several in-house manufacturers.
26 The lack of a large mass of skilled labour in Malaysia to provide the base for industrialisation is glaring (see MIDA/JICA/JETRO, 1989; *New Straits Times*, 29 July 1989, p. 3). Efforts by the government to place greater emphasis on skilled training would not only help but also ease the serious graduate unemployment problem since the mid-1980s.

REFERENCES

Anazawa, M. (1985–6) 'Free Trade Zones in Malaysia', *Hokudai Economic Papers*, Vol. XV

Bank Negara Malaysia (1988) *Annual Report, 1987*, Kuala Lumpur.

Bank Negara Malaysia (1989) *Annual Report, 1988*, Kuala Lumpur.

Chan L.H. *et al.* (1983) 'Women Workers in Malaysia: TNCs and social contradictions' paper presented at the seminar on 'Industrialisation and the Labour Process in Asia', Copenhagen.

Clairmonte, F. and Cavanagh, J. (1981) *The World in Their Web*, Zed Press: London.

Datta-Chaudhuri M.(1984) 'The Role of Free Trade Zones in Employment Creation and Industrial Growth in Malaysia', in E. Lee (ed.) (1984) *Export Processing Zones and Industrial Employment in Asia*, ARTEP, Bangkok, pp. 69–94.

Fransman, M. (1986) 'International Competitiveness, Technical Change and the State: The Machine Tool Industry in Taiwan and Japan', *World Development*, 14/2/; 1375–96.

Goh B.L. (1988) 'Foreign Investment and Market Fluctuations – Experience in the Penang Labour Market', paper presented at the seminar on 'Foreign Investment and Employment Generation in Asia and Pacific', Tokyo, 15–17 November.

Hoffman, L. and Tan, T.N. (1975) 'Pattern of Growth and Structural Change in West Malaysia's Manufacturing Industry 1959–68', in David Lim (ed), *Readings on Malaysian Economic Development*, Oxford University Press, Kuala Lumpur.

Irvan, A. (1986) 'Real Wages and Class Struggle in South Korea', *Journal of Contemporary Asia*, 17,4; 385–408.

Kamal S. and Lo F.C. (1975) 'Industrialization Strategy, Regional Development and the Growth Centre Approach: a case study of West Malaysia', report submitted at United Nations Center for Regional Development (UNCRD) seminar, 'Industrialisation Strategies and the Growth Pole Approach to Regional Planning and Development: The Asian Experiences', Nagoya.

Kamal S. and Young, M.L. (1985) 'Penang's Industrialisation: Where do we go from here?', paper presented at Malaysian Economic Association (Northern Branch) Convention on 'The Future of Penang', 6–8 May.

Kamal S. *et al.* (1985) 'Young Workers and Urban Services in Penang: A Summary Report', paper prepared for the policy seminar, 'Services for Young Urban Workers', Penang, 26 July.

Kaplinsky, R. (1985) 'Electronics-based Automation Technologies and the Onset of Systemofacture: Implications for Third World Industrialisation', *World Development*, Special Issue, 13: 423–40.

Lalor, S.E. (1986) 'Overview of the Micro-electronic Industry in Selected Developing Countries', *Industry and Development*, 16: 23–58.

Lim, Linda (1978) 'Multinational Firms and Manufacturing for Export in Less-developed Countries: the case of the electronics industry in Malaysia and Singapore', PhD dissertation, University of Michigan, Ann Arbor

McFarlane, B. (1988) 'Growth and Cycles in Southeast Asian Development', *Journal of Contemporary Asia*, 18(2): 119–38.

Malaysia (1970) *Second Malaysia Plan, 1971–1975*, Kuala Lumpur.

Malaysia (1976) *Third Malaysia Plan, 1976–1980*, Kuala Lumpur.

Malaysia (1981) *Fourth Malaysia Plan, 1981–1985*, Kuala Lumpur.

MIDA (1983) 'Review of the Electronics Industry in Malaysia and Policy Recommendations for its Development', Electrical and Electronics Division, Kuala Lumpur, August.

MIDA (1989) 'Statistics on the Manufacturing Sector, 1989' (unpublished).

MIDA/JICA/JETRO (1989) 'Moulds and Dies', a study on selected industrial product development in Malaysia compiled by Malaysian Industrial Development Authority, Japan International Cooperation Agency (JICA) and Japan External Trade Organisation (JETRO).

Ministry of Finance (1972–88) *Economic Report*, Kuala Lumpur, various issues.

Muto, I. (1977) 'The Free Trade Zones and the Mystique of Export-Oriented Industrialisation', *Free Trade Zones and Industrialisation in Asia*, Special Issue of *AMPO: Japan–Asia Quarterly Review*, pp. 9–32.

Rajah R. (1987) 'Pengantarabangsaan Pengeluaran and Pembahagian Buruh Antarabangsa: Kajian Kes Industri Separa Konduktor di Pulau Pinang', M.Soc.Sc. dissertation, Universiti Sains Malaysia.

Rajah R. (1988) 'The Semiconductor Industry in Penang: Implications for the New International Division of Labour (NIDL) Theories', *Journal of Contemporary Asia*, 18,1: 24–46.

Rajah R (1989) 'Labour Process in the Electronics Industry in Penang', in P. Limqueco (ed.), *Partisan Scholarship: Essays in Honour of Renato Constantino,* Journal of Contemporary Asia Publishers, Manila.

Rajah R (1990) 'The Electronics Industry in Malaysia: Implications for Neo-Classical and Neo-Marxist Theories', paper presented at Post-Graduate Research Seminar Series, Faculty of Economics, University of Cambridge, Cambridge, 21 March.

Rajah R and Mukunden, M. (1989) 'The Significance of the Textile and Garment Industry in Penang's Economy', paper prepared for the Malaysian Economic Association (Northern Branch) seminar, 'The Textile Industry in Malaysia: Challenges and Choices', Penang, 11–12 August.

Sayer, A. (1986) 'New Developments in Manufacturing: the just-in-time system', *Capital and Class,* 30: 43–72.

Shoesmith, D. (1986) *Export Processing Zones in Five Countries: The Economic and Human Consequences,* Asia Partnership for Human Development, Hong Kong.

South (1987) 'Scoring of the Chip War', July.

South East Asia Digest (1989) 'Still a foreign enclave', 9 June, 3: 1, 7, 12.

Tan, B.K. (1986) 'Women Workers in the Electronics Industry', in Hing A.Y. and T. Rokiah, (eds), *Women and Employment in Malaysia,* Special Issue of *Manusia dan Masyarakat.*

Tan, G.L. (1988) 'Occupational Health Studies of Workers in the Textile and Electronics Industries in Malaysia', paper presented at the CIDA/TWAS Conference on 'The Role of Women in the Development of Science and Technology in the Third World', Trieste, Italy, 3–7 October.

Teh, Alfred (forthcoming) 'The Penang Supporting Industry', in *Changing Dimensions of the Electronics Industry in Malaysia,* Malaysian Economic Association (Northern Branch), Penang.

UNCTC (1987) *Transnational Corporations in the Man-made Fibre, Textile and Clothing Industries,* United Nations Center for Transnational Corporations, New York.

United Nations *Yearbook on Industrial Statistics: National Tables,* New York, various issues.

Warr, P.G. (1986) 'Malaysia's Industrial Enclaves: Benefits and Costs', in T.G. McGee, *et al.* (eds), *Industrialisation and Labour Force Processes: A Case Study of Peninsular Malaysia,* Research School of Pacific Studies, The Australian National University, Canberra.

Westphal, L.E., Linsu Kim and Amsden, A.H. (1984) 'Republic of South Korea', *World Development,* 12, 5/6: 505–33.

World Bank, (1983–7), *World Development Report,* Oxford University Press, Oxford, various issues.

5

MALAYSIAN MANUFACTURING SECTOR LINKAGES

Leslie O'Brien

The industrialisation strategies of the 'second-tier NICs' of East Asia have been heavily reliant upon inputs of foreign capital into manufacturing. It has been hoped that direct foreign investment, through the medium of transnational corporations, would bring in capital and managerial experience, aid in the transfer of technology as well as give access to markets which might otherwise be closed to the countries concerned.

Critics of the policies which have sought to attract such foreign capital have argued that foreign companies entering into manufacturing production in the newly industrialising countries are little more than 'run-away shops', i.e. short-term phenomena which extract far more than they contribute to the economies of the countries that play host to them. Although some of the foreign-owned firms operating in East Asia have proved to be footloose, many of the fears about the short-term nature of such investments seem to have been unfounded. This raises the question of the long-term implications of direct foreign investment, both for development theory and for development strategy. (For some of the empirical details and theoretical debates, see Norlund *et al.*, 1984; Yoshihara, 1985; Hamilton, 1986; Jomo, 1986; Hewison, 1989; Limqueco *et al.*, 1989.)

There are long-running debates – in economics, industrial geography and other social science disciplines – which focus on industry, technology and size differentials in the capacity of firms to form linkages within, and thus aid the development of, the national economies in which they operate (see, for instance, Chenery and Watanabe, 1958; Hirschman, 1958; Yotopoulos and Nugent, 1973, 1976; Taylor and Thrift, 1982a, 1982b). While industrial sector, technology and firm size are of critical importance in this debate on linkages, the question of the ownership of firms should not be ignored. This latter issue is particularly important in the Malaysian context, where foreign ownership of the manufacturing sector has been – and still is – widespread. We would also argue that the issue of ownership is of significance because of the association between ownership and control or decision making, and all that this implies for complementarity with government developmental policies and strategies.

In examining differentials by industrial sector and ownership, this study seeks to make a contribution both to the debate concerning the long-term impact of direct foreign investment in the newly industrialising countries, as well as to the discourse concerning such differentials in the capacity of manufacturing companies to stimulate linkages within the national economy.

MANUFACTURING IN MALAYSIA

For the purposes of this study, the manufacturing sector in Malaysia is seen as comprising three elements: first, the longest-established import-substituting section, which produces goods such as food and drinks, some simple metal products, some electrical products and the like; secondly, companies manufacturing resource-based, mainly export-oriented products such as latex rubber and timber products; and thirdly, companies involved in the production of non-resource-based products, such as electrical goods and electronic components, for sale on the world market.

Most industries and types of product and process technology are to be found in Malaysia's manufacturing sector: from those using low levels of technology to produce such low-technology goods as certain types of foodstuffs and articles like garments, through medium-technology production of certain chemical products, to some high-technology elements in the electronics and rubber industries (e.g. companies producing silicon logs; companies involved in the production of latex rubber goods such as surgical gloves and condoms). (For further methodological and empirical details, see O'Brien, 1989a, 1989b.) Manufacturing in Malaysia also comprises 'light' industries, such as those producing textiles and garments, as well as government-sponsored 'heavy' industry, including the manufacture of the Malaysian car, cement plants, steel mills and the like.

According to indicators such as share of GDP and contribution to exports earnings and to job creation, manufacturing is now the single most important sector of the Malaysian economy. In the past thirty years, the rapid expansion of this sector has transformed Malaysia from an agriculture-based economy into a second-tier NIC (Limqueco *et al.*, 1989).[1] The manufacturing sector today is of great absolute and relative significance. Of critical interest, however, is whether this key sector of the Malaysian economy is capable of self-sustained reproduction, or whether it is dependent upon the outside world for inputs and for markets.

Investment goods and consumption goods

To what extent is Malaysia's manufacturing sector nationally integrated, and to what extent is it dependent upon external sources for such critical components as production equipment and product inputs? One way to gauge the potential for Malaysian manufacturers to be independent is to ascertain the relative weight or strength of the investment goods producing industries within the manufacturing sector.² The end use of a product must be known before a valid classification can be made. Before we can make a judgement about whether a product is a capital or a consumer good, we should know who is likely to buy (private individual/family, business enterprise) and why.³

Following Hoffman (1958), manufacturing industries were classified as being essentially investment or consumer goods producers when it was considered that at least 75 per cent of their productive output was directed to one or the other of these sectors. As detailed in Table 5.1, this produced an

Table 5.1 Type of goods produced, by industry, 1985

	Value added (M$'000)	%
I. *Consumer goods*:		
Food	1,745,099	12
Beverages & tobacco	812,459	6
Textiles & garments	578,511	4
Leather	6,222	–
Furniture	99,848	1
Paper	137,274	1
Electrical/electronics	1,832,470	13
Transport	524,486	4
Sub-total	5,736,369	41
II. *Intermediate and investment goods*:		
Wood[a]	653,568	5
Paper[a]	137,274	1
Chemicals[a]	1,907,632	14
Petroleum and coal	391,138	3
Rubber[a]	621,095	4
Plastic[a]	228,386	2
Non-met.minerals*	825,952	6
Basic metal[a]	465,451	3
Fabricated metal[a]	365,201	3
Machinery	247,049	2
Electrical/electronics*	1,832,470	13
Transport	524,486	4
Scientific/measurement	75,43	1
Sub-total	8,275,139	59
TOTAL	14,011,508	100

Note: The output of industry does not lend itself to any neat classification scheme. The above classification scheme is based on an understanding of the end use of the greater majority (>75 per cent) of the output. In three instances, productive output is almost equally divided between consumption and investment goods. In these cases, the industry has been placed in both categories.
[a] indicates those industries that are more likely to produce intermediate than final-finished products.
Source: Calculated from Department of Statistics *Industrial Survey 1985* data in Malaysian Industrial Development Authority (MIDA), *Statistics on the Manufacturing Sector, 1988*: 29, Table XXXIII(i).

estimate that 59 per cent of the output of the manufacturing sector comprises investment goods, and 41 per cent comprises consumption goods.

Dependence of the manufacturing sector

With such a high percentage of output consisting of investment goods, we might expect that Malaysian manufacturing would display at least a degree of self-sufficiency. However, we must also ask whether the investment goods made in Malaysia are used in Malaysian manufacturing. Also, do the unfinished products and components made by Malaysian manufacturers constitute inputs for other domestically manufactured goods? Macro-level data suggest that this is not the case.

In 1988, a scant 2 per cent of value added in Malaysian manufacturing came from machinery production. This included the manufacture of agricultural machinery and equipment, woodworking machinery, office equipment and the like. It also included the assembly and reconditioning of diesel engines and turbines, boilers and generators, some of which are used in manufacturing (calculated from MIDA, n.d.). This domestic output of machinery and equipment, although quite diverse, was insufficient to meet local demands. As the following data on imports reveal, Malaysian manufacturers are very dependent on both finished and unfinished inputs from abroad. In 1986, for instance, 23 per cent of all imports were consumption goods, 29 per cent were investment goods and 48 per cent intermediate goods. In that year alone, the importation of investment goods cost the country M$7,973 million. Nearly one-third (31 per cent) of these imports was machinery of some type, most of which found final use in the manufacturing sector (the remainder consisted of transport equipment and metal products). Furthermore, although half the value added in the large investment goods producing sector of Malaysian manufacturing comprises intermediate goods, imports of intermediate goods are also considerable; in 1986, the importation of intermediate products cost M$13,379 million and 73 per cent of this amount was for components and other manufacturing inputs (Bank Negara Malaysia, 1987: 194, Table 6.15). This inflow of capital equipment and components is indicative of the growth and expansion of the manufacturing sector in particular, as well as of the overall economic development of the country.

If the foreign sales of Malaysian manufactures were sufficient to offset the costs of imported machinery, the end result would be positive in balance-of-payments terms. However, what is this imported machinery used to manufacture? Are these machines and other imported investment goods being used to manufacture Malaysian-made capital equipment which will reduce the country's dependency on imports at some time in the future? Are the commodities produced destined for the local or the world market, and what does this imply for the creation of linkages between manufacturers in Malaysia? We will attempt to answer these questions, in the first instance by way of an industry-level analysis of production and consumption.

In terms of size and pattern of ownership, the manufacturing sector in Malaysia is quite diverse. In terms of output and value, however, the sector is very narrowly based. In 1988, nearly half (48 per cent) of value added in the sector came from just three industries – food and beverages (17 per cent), chemicals (16 per cent) and electrical and electronic products (15 per cent). A further 10 per cent of value added was accounted for by the combined output of non-metallic mineral products, iron and steel and non-ferrous metal basic industries (calculated from MIDA, 1989: 29–30).

Furthermore, as will be demonstrated below, some of these industries have a limited capacity to generate forward and backward linkages and thus aid in the creation of an interdependent manufacturing sector that has both depth and breadth. All the manufacturing industries are obviously connected to the national economy through their use of such infrastructural facilities as sewerage, roads, railways, harbours, airports, water, electricity, postal services and the like, and through their employment of labour. Most also source their printing and packaging material from local producers. As we shall see, however, marked differences exist beyond this point. These variations are, in part, due to the uneven global distribution of natural resources, but are also a consequence of the policies and practices of the companies which comprise the manufacturing sector.

The majority of the inputs for one of the main industry groupings, food and beverages, are local in origin. Tropical fruits and nuts, vegetables, fish, edible palm oil and so on are available locally in abundant supply. Linkages thus exist in the economy between agricultural producers, middlemen[4] and manufacturers. Grains such as wheat, barley and rye, of course, do not grow in the tropics, and thus they – or flour made from them – must be imported. In addition, some specialist substances, such as the bacteria used in yeast production or the wort used in some of the 'locally produced' beers, come from abroad. In these instances, linkages would be formed between traders and manufacturers. The output of the food and beverage industries consists entirely of consumer non-durables, much of which is directed to the domestic market. Some high-quality foodstuffs, as well as processed palm oil (a major food industry product), are sold on the world market (the latter is used in the manufacture of soap or margarine, some of which is re-imported into Malaysia). Links are thus created between manufacturers, local wholesale and retail businesses, as well as those involved in import–export trade. That goods such as food and beverages are produced in Malaysia – rather than abroad – is an asset, rather than a liability, both for the economy as a whole and, more specifically, for the industrialisation of the country. The production of consumption goods, however, does not have the same developmental potential as the production of investment goods. This is because the final product is consumed and is not a component of something else that could be made in Malaysia.

Another major manufacturing sub-sector is the chemicals industry. In the Malaysian context, although many of the products manufactured involve high-technology knowledge, the process technologies used tend to be relatively simple. There are a few technologically sophisticated companies, producing industrial chemicals or products such as carbon black that require complex and/or automated machines. On the whole, however, manufacturing chemicals mainly consist of a great deal of mixing of compounds imported from abroad, using machinery imported from abroad. Thus at the input end of the chemical industry, as in the case of food and beverages, multitudinous links exist between traders and manufacturers.

Approximately 20 per cent of the output of this industry comprises consumer non-durables, e.g. pharmaceuticals, for the local market. The remainder is for industrial use, and comprises goods such as adhesives, fertilisers, gases, paints and polyvinyls. These are sold both domestically and elsewhere in Asia. Thus, at the output end, manufacturer–market–manufacturer networks prevail. As with foodstuffs, sale on the domestic market of most consumer non-durables has little developmental potential because it involves little more than mixing compounds of formulas developed in the larger drug houses in the West. The production of intermediate goods such as industrial chemicals, however, represents one of the few areas where Malaysia is able to supply its own – albeit somewhat reconstituted – inputs. As such, the chemical industry is one industry that is likely to generate both forward and backward linkages and, in so doing, lead to greater diversity in the manufacturing sector.

In terms of value added, the electrical and electronics industry is not the most important manufacturing activity in Malaysia. The practice of intra-firm transfer pricing (to maximise profits) distorts the measurement of the real significance of this sub-sector. A different picture emerges when we look at the contribution of the industry to exports. In 1988, manufactured products contributed 48.6 per cent of the country's total exports. Well over half (56.3 per cent) of manufacturing exports was contributed by the electrical/electronics industry.[5]

As the designation suggests, this industry has two major components. On the one hand is the electrical industry, concerned with the assembly of medium-technology consumer durables such as air-conditioning units, radios, TV sets and low-to-medium-technology intermediate goods such as switch gear. On the other hand is the electronics industry, involved with the production – mainly the assembly – of semiconductor devices that are the components of both consumer durables and investment goods. There is quite a lot of local input into the industry in so far as low-technology components are concerned. For instance, for the electrical side of the industry, casings for refrigerators, washing machines and television sets are usually furnished by local suppliers who use aluminium, steel or copper sheeting – imported from abroad – to form the shapes required, or utilise foreign-manufactured polymers to extrude or form plastic parts. Many of the more sophisticated components are either not available locally or are sourced abroad by preference. This is as much due to the continued location of such production abroad as to the lack of technological capacity in Malaysia. For instance, Malaysia has a well-established glass industry, yet cathode picture tubes for use in television sets are not made there. Even though Malaysia has the capacity and technology to produce motors, most are imported fully finished or in the form of parts for assembly in Malaysia. Some switch gear is assembled in Malaysia and some imported, whilst most paints and varnishes are locally produced. At the input end, therefore, electrical product manufacturers might be expected to have links both with other local producers as well as with importers. As regards output, some consumer durables produced by the electrical industry are sold on the local market, but a great deal – especially air-conditioning units – is sold abroad. At the output end, therefore, there are some links with other manufacturers within the country, but most of the associations are between manufacturers and sales companies or international traders.

The situation is somewhat different for electronics, due to its recent development, competition between manufacturers and the consequent high degree of secrecy which surrounds many of the production processes. Until recently, all the silicon logs – which comprise the base material of most semiconductor devices – were developed in the USA and Japan. (One or two foreign firms in Malaysia are now beginning to produce these on-site.) They were then air-freighted to Malaysia for slicing and polishing, and then re-exported to the USA or Japan for chemical etching with circuit designs. Once this was done, the wafers were then re-imported into Malaysia for dicing and attachment to fairly simple metal lead-frames, of which many are now made in Malaysia.

Much of the output of this industry is sold on the world market. At the input end, therefore, links exist between the electronics companies and the local market, at least in so far as the supply of low-technology components is concerned. Most other transactions take place at the subsidiary-to-subsidiary level, that is, within companies. At the output end, our own primary data (elaborated on below) suggest that foreign-owned electronics companies forge very few links with the local economy.

Inputs into the three main mineral and metal industries consist of local natural resources such as clay, tin and sand. There is also some processing of imported raw materials (e.g. there is some smelting of aluminium and iron/steel in Malaysia). Scrap metal steel and aluminium are also smelted. A great many factories, however, use foreign-made machinery to roll, press, form or cut aluminium, steel or copper coils, and aluminium, steel or copper sheets, imported from abroad.

Much of the output of these three industries consists of intermediate goods. These range from the production of cement through to simple nuts and bolts to a great variety of forged, moulded, extruded, rolled and pressed metal products to supply the local building and construction industry.[6] Thus, at both the input and output ends, there are a great many forward and backward linkages in these industries. These industries include a considerable number of small and medium-sized enterprises. Although their combined output contributes only 10 per cent of value added in the manufacturing sector, they seem to have considerable developmental potential (Federation of Malaysian Manufacturers, 1986; Bank Negara Malaysia, 1987: 188, Table 6.13; 194, Table 6.15; Malaysia, 1989: 16, Chart 2.3; 194–5, Table 8.10; and MIDA, 1989).

The above analysis hints at the pattern of dependency and independence of the manufacturing sector. Since it is based on macro-level data, it is unable to reveal much about the decision-making process, and thus has limitations. We need to know whether – given the present structure of opportunities – the manufacturing sector is likely to become more independent in the not too distant future. We will attempt to address this by referring to primary data gathered on the policies and practices of a wide variety of companies in the manufacturing sector in Malaysia.

SURVEY RESULTS

Data have been gathered on eighty-six companies in the Malaysian manufacturing sector.[7] The companies in the study were selected from a listing of companies provided by the Malaysian Industrial Development Authority (MIDA).[8] Information was provided concerning the name and location of the firm, industry, employment size and majority ownership by nationality. This MIDA list was then divided into those companies that were majority Malaysian owned and those that were majority foreign owned. These companies were then further classified by employment size into small establishments (defined as having fewer than 250 employees), medium sized (251–1,000 employees) and large and very large (more than 1,000 employees) ventures. Fifteen small, fifteen medium and fifteen large Malaysian-owned and fifteen small, fifteen medium and fifteen large foreign-owned companies (plus appropriate substitutes) were then selected at random from each of the six categories and became the subject of research. There were insufficient large and very large Malaysian-owned companies to fill the cell tables, so medium-sized companies were substituted; four cells are empty.

Although industry was not the basis of sample selection, the companies in the study are spread across a range of industries in the manufacturing sector. They include such low-technology industries as food, beverage and tobacco production, medium-technology industries such as basic metal products and fabricated metal products, and high-technology areas such as chemicals, petroleum and electrical/electronics production. Some are fully locally owned and controlled, some are Malaysian/foreign joint ventures, some are 100 per cent foreign owned and controlled. Most of the foreign capital invested in these companies is headquartered in Singapore, Japan, the USA or Australia. Location was not held constant; thus, the geographical distribution of the companies follows the contours of industrial development in Malaysia, i.e. some were located in the Penang/Butterworth region, many were in the Klang Valley, a few around Malacca and the rest in the industrial zones of Johore.

Of the companies in the study, 57 per cent were involved in the production of investment goods and 43 per cent in the production of consumption goods. In this respect, the sample population very closely approximates the structure of production of the manufacturing sector as a whole (Table 5.1), and similarly raises the question of the extent to which this type of investment goods/consumption goods division is an indication of some degree of self-sufficiency in the sector. A further parallel between the total and the sample populations can be found in the output of components. As detailed in Table 5.1 above, at the macro-level at least half of the output of the investment goods producing sector came from industries making intermediate rather than finished products. In the sample population, this tendency is even more marked: 90 per cent of those companies classified as producing investment goods manufactured intermediate products. The sample data thus represent an excellent opportunity for further exploring the question of the extent to which intermediate products made in Malaysia contribute to local sourcing for production.

Variations by industry

Each of the companies studied was asked to supply comprehensive data about what they produced, and to specify where they obtained the equipment they used to manufacture their products. They were also asked a variety of questions regarding their inputs and outputs, i.e. details of what raw materials or components were used in the production process, where they were obtained from, and whether they were procured from suppliers inside or outside the country. The companies were also asked to provide information about their marketing and distribution systems.

On the issue of production equipment, the companies in the study reflected the dependency on imports found at the macro-level. Two-thirds of the companies used nothing but foreign-made machinery, equipment and instruments to manufacture their made-in-Malaysia products, while one-third of the companies had some local input (see Table 5.2). Not one company in the study used only made-in-Malaysia equipment to manufacture 'made-in-Malaysia' products.

There was a tendency for foreign-owned companies – or those originally established as foreign owned but since restructured to have majority local ownership – to source their production equipment from the country in which they were headquartered. For instance, British companies would import new or used production equipment from the UK, US-owned companies would import from the USA and so on. Importation of both heavy machinery and instrumentation from East Asia, especially Japan, was very common. This held true irrespective of who owned and controlled the company in question. Thus, there were instances of some US-owned and controlled companies in Malaysia sourcing the majority of their production equipment from Japan, Taiwan or Korea; however, there was no instance of a Japanese-owned and controlled company being reliant upon other than Japanese machinery. This pattern is a reflection of the limited development of manufacturing in the first instance in countries like Australia, the decline of such industries as exist there, as well as in the USA and the UK, and the ascendancy and growing domination of Japan, Korea and Taiwan in this regard.

Table 5.2 Source of production equipment and instrumentation

Region	Number
Northeast Asia (especially Japan)	19
Northeast Asia and USA	7
USA	9
Australia and Northeast Asia	18
UK and Northeast Asia	4
Sub-total	57 (66%)
Some Malaysian input	29 (33%)
Total	86

There were twenty-nine companies in the study that had some Malaysian content in their production equipment. Twelve of the twenty-nine merely modified equipment that was essentially manufactured elsewhere, but some of the equipment of seventeen of the companies was fully locally manufactured. Nearly all of these had machine shops of their own, as was the case for a considerable number of factories that utilised only imported machinery. The difference in the case of the former is that their machine shops were used not only for repair or minor modification purposes, but also for in-house import-substitution production.

Machinery manufactured locally tended to be lower-technology production equipment, used by companies operating in low-to-medium-technology industries. For example, four of the twenty-nine companies were food manufacturers, one was a furniture manufacturing company, another produced prefabricated housing, while nine produced fabricated metal products. One rubber company manufactured 80 per cent of its own production equipment.

Other companies that used some locally manufactured production equipment were located in industries which might be expected to exhibit some degree of self-sufficiency – for instance, three of the twenty-nine were machine engineering operations. Only two were located in a high-technology industry; both were electronics companies that had formulated a policy which included the aims of rationalising some expenditure and attempting to transfer technology to Malaysia by using their machine shop to manufacture their own production equipment. Irrespective of the level of technology of the industry, or of the product or process technology, instrumentation associated with machinery was always sourced abroad.

One clear pattern which emerged in this section of the study was that those companies that modified or manufactured their own production equipment were much more likely to be locally rather than foreign owned and controlled; fifteen had upwards of 51 per cent Malaysian equity, another six were majority Malaysian owned and controlled. This suggests that local ownership and control may aid the development of a more self-sufficient and interconnected manufacturing sector. (The issue of ownership and control will be explored in greater depth in a later section of this chapter.)

As far as the generation of linkages through raw material or component inputs is concerned, an examination of the company data by industry strongly confirmed the analysis we offered concerning inputs and outputs at the macrolevel (see Table 5.3). The essentially resource-based food and beverage companies in the study were highly reliant on local raw materials, as were the rubber and non-metallic mineral companies. These types of companies were least likely to source their inputs from abroad. The electrical/electronics and chemicals companies were least likely to have linkages within the local economy. Electronics companies in particular, reliant as they are on high-technology components produced in the OECD countries, were the least likely to source in Malaysia and the most likely to source from abroad.

As far as the creation of linkages within the national economy through outputs is concerned, a slightly different pattern emerged. Companies that

Table 5.3 Source of inputs by industry

Industry	<50% sourced in Malaysia (n=44)	>50% sourced in Malaysia (n=28)
Food and beverages/rubber	30	70
Non-metallic minerals	17	83
Chemicals	73	27
Fabricated metal/machinery engineering	68	32
Electrical/electronics	73	27
Electrical	(44)	(56)
Electronics	(88)	(12)
Total	61	39

sourced the majority of their inputs domestically also tended to sell their goods on the local market. Although the chemical and fabricated metal industry companies in the study sourced a high proportion of their inputs abroad, they sold a high proportion of their output on the domestic market. Electrical and electronics industry companies in general, especially the electronics companies, displayed a tendency both to source their inputs from and to direct their outputs to the world market.

Table 5.4 Destination of outputs (market), by industry

Industry	<50% sold in Malaysia (n=23)	>50% sold in Malaysia (n=49)
Food and beverages/rubber	20	80
Non-metallic minerals	17	83
Chemicals	9	91
Fabricated metal/machinery engineering	5	95
Electrical/electronics	69	31
Electrical	(33)	(67)
Electronics	(88)	(12)
Total	32	68

The number and value of linkages forged at the input and the output aspects of production vary by industry, and from one company to another within the different industries. What other factors influence the creation, or otherwise, of linkage effects?

Variations by ownership

Overall, the manufacturing sector conforms with the New Economic Policy (NEP) requirement of a corporate sector that is 70 per cent local, 30 per cent foreign owned. However, key areas of the manufacturing sector, especially the electrical/electronics, beverage and tobacco and scientific and measurement industries, are majority foreign owned (O'Brien, 1989a). Our macro-level data are insufficient to tell us exactly how great a proportion of the capital goods sector is foreign owned. The survey was structured so as to cover both foreign and local ownership and control[9] patterns, thus we would not expect it to reveal much about foreign capital domination or under-representation. An examination of our data reveals only a slight tendency towards greater foreign capital investment in the capital goods sector. Of the companies that were majority locally owned and controlled, 41 per cent were engaged in the production of consumer goods, 59 per cent produced capital goods. In the case of the majority-foreign-owned companies, the ratio was 35 per cent consumer goods production to 65 per cent capital goods production.

This difference is of little significance, other than reflecting that foreign capital is prepared to invest in any manufacturing activity in Malaysia likely to return a profit. Clearly the production of consumer goods in a society such as Malaysia – with its expanding population, rising incomes and escalating 'wants' – is not to be ignored.

What our data do reveal is a marked tendency for locally owned and controlled manufacturing companies to forge more links with the national economy than their foreign-owned and controlled counterparts. Companies that were majority Malaysian owned and controlled were highly likely to obtain their supplies locally: 32 per cent obtained at least 75 per cent of their inputs from Malaysia, while 68 per cent obtained at least half their inputs locally. Among the foreign-owned and controlled companies, the reverse was the case: 65 per cent obtained at least 75 per cent of their inputs from suppliers outside Malaysia, 76 per cent obtained at least half their inputs abroad.

This pattern can be explained by reference to a number of factors. Firstly, the locally owned companies were more likely to be involved in the production of lower-technology products than their foreign-owned counterparts; thus, inputs were more likely to be available in Malaysia than would be the case for the higher-technology components of higher-technology products. Secondly, the locally owned companies were more likely to be involved in the production of resource-based products than their foreign-owned counterparts. Lastly, the establishment of networks and the cultural factor of familiarity in the supply of inputs need to be taken into account. Managers of the locally owned and controlled companies were much more familiar with supply networks within Malaysia than the expatriate managers of the foreign-owned and controlled companies. Conversely, managers of the locally owned and controlled companies were much less familiar with overseas supply networks than their expatriate manager counterparts. Local managers of the foreign companies seemed to have an awareness of local supply networks but tended to be doubtful of the quality of such Malaysian-made equivalent products as were available, and were usually employed by firms that had established supply networks abroad. Whatever the reason or combination of reasons that explains the greater likelihood of local companies to source their inputs from within Malaysia, the fact that they do so is an indicator of their creation and maintenance of more local linkage effects than is the case with the foreign-owned and controlled companies.

A second indication of differences as regards the establishment of, or lack of, links between the manufacturing companies in the study and the wider Malaysian economy can be found in data obtained on marketing policies and practices. In the case of the locally owned companies, 76 per cent sold at least three-quarters and 81 per cent sold at least half their productive output on the Malaysian market, compared with 37 per cent of the foreign companies selling at least three-quarters and 55 per cent selling at least half their products in Malaysia. Only 5 per cent of the local companies sold 0–24 per cent of their output overseas, compared with 41 per cent of the foreign companies selling up to a quarter of their productive output abroad. This suggests that foreign capital is invested across the board in the manufacturing sector (i.e. in import-substituting as well as in export-oriented industries).

CONCLUSIONS

Where might we expect more linkage effects to be formed? A high proportion of the paid-up and fixed capital assets of the food and beverage industry is foreign owned, owing to the presence of a few large transnational firms. The multitude of small, locally owned and controlled companies, however, increases the likelihood of linkages in this sub-sector of manufacturing. Like the food industry, the chemical and electrical industries do not involve such high technology as to preclude local ownership, and – as we have found – local ownership increases the likelihood of local links.

Where might we expect few local linkages to be formed? The electronics industry has been characterised by high technology and therefore considerable foreign ownership and control. Local linkages are not precluded by this combination of factors, though they are more likely to be limited to lower-technology inputs, and subject to both cost considerations as well as company policy encouraging linkages with the local economy.

The above data show that industry and size are critical to the formation of linkages with the local economy. They also show the significance of ownership in this regard. We might expect that small-scale, low-technology, foreign-owned firms might contribute more to the local economy than large, high-technology TNCs. The latter may not be footloose, but they seem to have a limited capacity to stimulate the economy.

NOTES

1. Whether 'full-blown' or 'second-tier', newly industrialised countries are locked into a global system of economic interdependence. By comparison, post-colonial dependencies are essentially extractive economies, typified by a large proportion of the ownership and much of the control of the economy held by the former colonial 'masters' from which the country recently obtained formal political 'independence'.
2. Investment goods are the 'equipment' of a factory. They are a part of the fixed capital assets of an enterprise. They are purchased as investments so as to be able to produce something else. Consumer goods, by contrast, are ends in themselves. Once manufactured and sold, they are 'consumed', i.e. used up sooner (e.g. consumer non-durables like food) or later (e.g. consumer durables like radios, TVs, refrigerators). Not all the productive output of some factories is goods that have reached the final form in which they will be used. They may be 'finished' in so far as the particular step in the division of labour in production is concerned, but they cannot stand alone. They are thus 'intermediate' goods. Such intermediate products may be components of consumer goods or of investment goods.
3. An example I have used elsewhere (O'Brien, 1990) is the question whether a bed,

for instance, is a capital/investment good or a consumer good. I have argued that, if it is purchased by a household for domestic use, then we can clearly see that it is a consumer durable. If, however, it is purchased by a hotel or motel owner, this would not be the case. Such a bed might not 'produce' something else, but it is clearly purchased as an investment made with the aim of producing wealth.
4 It seems reasonable to assume that factory-to-factory linkages (i.e. direct supply) would exist only between subsidiaries of one parent company, and that independent producers would source their inputs through intermediaries. Research by Goh (1987) on the creation of linkages in the manufacturing sector in Penang suggests that this is the case.
5 The only other export-oriented manufacturing industries of note are textiles, clothing and footwear, which contributed 8.9 per cent, and petroleum and chemical products, which together contributed 8.1 per cent (Malaysia, 1989: 16 and 194, Table 8.10).
6 This industry category also produces pewter, a consumer durable sold on the world market.
7 Information on the operating principles and practices of the companies was obtained by a variety of methods. Between 1987 and 1989, several research visits were made to Malaysia. Each of the companies was contacted. All available published material was collected from the firms. Structured and unstructured interviews were conducted with the chief executive officer (or a delegate), production manager and personnel manager of each of the companies. In nearly every instance, a site tour was arranged so that the production process could be viewed and an assessment made of the conditions of work in the factories involved.
8 There are approximately 17,000 companies in the manufacturing sector in Malaysia. Approximately 88 per cent of these are very small, family owned and operated establishments. Under the Industrial Coordination Act (ICA) of 1975, every existing or proposed manufacturing company with 25 or more full-time employees and shareholder funds in excess of M$250,000 is required to obtain a manufacturing licence. The ICA has been amended several times, e.g. on 12 December 1985 so that only companies employing 50 or more people and with shareholder funds of M$1 million or more were required to obtain a licence. The ICA was further amended on 24 October 1986. Now, only companies with more than 75 full-time employees, or shareholder funds in excess of M$2.5 million, are required to license and thus come under MIDA scrutiny. Thus, the MIDA database represents the 'modern' face of manufacturing in Malaysia.
9 Control of the firms was estimated by a variety of methods, including questions concerning the structure of the board of directors of the companies, and information obtained about short-, medium- and long-term decision making.

REFERENCES

Bank Negara Malaysia (1987) *Annual Report 1986*, Kuala Lumpur.
Chenery, H.B. and Watanabe, T. (1958) 'International comparisons of the structure of production', *Econometrica*, 4: 487–521.
Federation of Malaysian Manufacturers (1986) *1986 Directory*, 17th edition, Kuala Lumpur.
Goh, B.L. (1987) 'Linkages between the Multinational Corporations and Local Supporting Industries – A case study of Penang', Urban Research Unit, Research School of Pacific Studies, The Australian National University (unpublished).
Hamilton, F.E. (ed.) (1986) *Industrialization in Developing and Peripheral Regions*, Croom Helm, London.

Hewison, K. (1989) *Power and Politics in Thailand*, Journal of Contemporary Asia Publishers, Manila and Wollongong.
Hirschman, A.O. (1958) *The Strategy of Economic Development*, Yale University Press, New Haven, Conn.
Hoffmann, W.G. (1958) *The Growth of Industrial Economies*, translated from the German by W.O. Henderson and W.H. Chaloner, Manchester University Press, Manchester.
Jomo, K.S. (1986) *A Question of Class: Capital, the State and Uneven Development in Malaya*, Oxford University Press, Singapore.
Limqueco, P., McFarlane, B and Odhnoff, J. (1989) *Labour and Industry in ASEAN*, Journal of Contemporary Asia Publishers, Manila and Wollongong.
Malaysia (1989) *Mid-Term Review of the Fifth Malaysia Plan, 1986–1990*, Government Printers, Kuala Lumpur.
MIDA [Malaysian Industrial Development Authority] (1989) *Statistics on the Manufacturing Sector 1988*, Kuala Lumpur.
MIDA [Malaysian Industrial Development Authority] (n.d) *Directory of Approved Companies in Production as at 31 December, 1982, Supplementary Listings*, Kuala Lumpur.
Norlund, I., Wad, P. and Brun, V. (1984) *Industrialization and the Labour Process in Southeast Asia*, Institute of Cultural Sociology, University of Copenhagen, Denmark.
O'Brien, L.N. (1989a) 'The Relative Significance of Foreign Investment in the Manufacturing Sector in Malaysia', paper presented to the Institute of Australian Geographers 23rd Annual Conference, Adelaide, 13–16 February.
O'Brien, L.N. (1989b) 'Technology Transfer and the Skilling of Labour in the Manufacturing Sector in Malaysia', paper presented to Malaysia Society of the Asian Studies Association of Australia Sixth Colloquium, Sydney, 10–11 June.
O'Brien, L.N. (1990) 'Indices of Industrialisation: Capital Goods Production in Malaysia', *Journal of Contemporary Asia*, 20, 4: 509–20.
Taylor, M.J. and Thrift, N.J. (1982a) 'Industrial Linkage and the Segmented Economy: 1. Some Theoretical Proposals', *Environment and Planning A*, 14: 1601–13.
Taylor, M.J. and Thrift, N.J. (1982b) 'Industrial Linkage and the Segmented Economy: 2. An Empirical Reinterpretation', *Environment and Planning A*, 14: 1615–32.
Yoshihara, K. (1985) *Philippine Industrialization: Foreign and Domestic Capital*, Oxford University Press, Singapore.
Yotopoulos, P.A. and Nugent, J.B. (1973) 'A Balance Growth Version of the Linkage Hypothesis: a Test', *Quarterly Journal of Economics*, 87, 2: 157–71.
Yotopoulos, P.A. and Nugent, J.B. (1976) 'In Defence of a Test of the Linkage Hypothesis', *Quarterly Journal of Economics*, 90, 2: 334–43.

6

MALAYSIAN RURAL INDUSTRIALISATION STRATEGIES IN NATIONAL PERSPECTIVE

Ashwani Saith

This paper addresses the potential role of rural industrialisation in contemporary Malaysian economic development. In considering rural industrialisation as a policy instrument, a distinction can be drawn between an approach that regards it as a strategy for initiating or relocating industrial enterprises in the countryside, and an alternative, though not a mutually exclusive approach that treats it as a strategy that adopts as its objective the generation of rural non-farm incomes primarily through encouraging the migration of the rural workforce to industrial enterprises located in contiguous local urban centres. Focusing on the Malaysian context, selected aspects of the rural non-farm sector are profiled using diverse sources. Finally, selected strategic issues are discussed in the context of the revised development strategy enunciated in the Fifth Malaysia Plan; themes relating to industrial location, linkages and leakages, and migration receive special attention.

RURAL INDUSTRIALISATION: LOCATION OR LINKAGE?

How is the term 'rural industrialisation' to be interpreted in the Malaysian context? No unique and universally appropriate definition can be elicited from the diverse experiences of 'rural industrialisation' in the process of economic development. It would be useful, before proceeding to the Malaysian case, to seek some definitional clarity.

Two alternative approaches

Two alternative – though partially overlapping – approaches to the theme need to be distinguished. In the first, which we might for convenience label the *locational approach*, the primary criterion adopted for the definition of rural industry is its location in a designated rural area. This views the policy instrument primarily as a device for furthering objectives related to physical and spatial planning. Most frequently, in this approach, rural industrialisation is a safety valve for controlling problems of urban industrial concentration, with all its negative externalities. Regional or rural dispersal are motivated, in essence, by objectives of urban development planning. Such an approach includes the relocation of urban industries to lower-order urban (and ultimately to rural) centres, as well as the initiation of new industrial enterprises at a faster rate in the industrial hinterland than at its core.

In sharp contrast to this is the *linkage approach*. Here, the rural industrial sector is viewed from the rural end, and the key criterion for defining an industrial enterprise or other economic activity as 'rural' is whether it generates significant developmental linkages with the rural sector. One simple index of the intensity of linkage effects could be the percentage of the gross output value of the enterprise that is accounted for by the rural sector, either through receipts for rural raw materials purchased by the enterprise, or through income flows received in the form of wages or profits for labour or capital provided by the residents of the rural sector. Restricting the index to the disposition of the value added by the enterprise would be inappropriate since it would exclude the linkage through the raw material purchases made in the rural sector. This linkage index also restricts itself to the direct effects generated by the production of the output.

Two modifications could make the quantitative measurement of linkages still more meaningful. Firstly, the notion could be widened so as to include the capital equipment expenditures of the enterprise as well; secondly, the index could be based on both the direct as well as the indirect rural linkages generated by the production of one unit value of gross output. However, as a quick proxy, the simple direct linkage index would suffice. If a separation is made between the raw material, labour and capital linkages, the index could also throw up a useful classification of the industrial enterprises by type and intensity of linkage. For multi-product enterprises, indices could indicate the type and intensity of rural linkages with respect to each product line, or with respect to each factor of production. These indices could range between zero and unity with respect to direct linkage effects, though the inclusion of indirect effects generated through the multiplier could raise the direct-cum-indirect linkage index to levels greater than one. The problem remains of having to mark an arbitrary threshold level such that an enterprise with a linkage index above it could be thought of as being a 'rural' enterprise. The choice of the cut-off level would have to depend upon local circumstances and objectives, with an eye to the sensitivity of the results to minor variations in the cut-off level.

The locational and linkage approaches could yield quite different profiles of 'rural industry'. On the one hand, not all industries located in designated rural areas would necessarily display high levels for the linkage index. This might be especially true where modern medium- or large-scale industrial enterprises are being coaxed through incentives to relocate their plants in designated rural areas. While taking the pressure off the urban centre, it might still leave the high urban linkage effects more or less intact. On the other hand, from the point of view of the linkage approach, location per se is of no consequence. What matters is the linkage effect, and this could be high or low irrespective of the location, at least in principle. Realistically as well, there could be several types of industries which, though located in the smaller urban centres, nevertheless display exceedingly high rural linkages, through a high dependence on either rural labour and/or rural raw materials within production processes that are labour and raw material intensive.

Which approach is more meaningful depends upon the objectives of policy and the concrete circumstances of the economy. It is necessary to emphasise though that the generation of rural linkages is not contingent upon a deep rural location. Whether a locational criterion is superimposed on the linkage criterion would depend upon the ease with which resources, including the rural labour force, could move from their rural residential locations to the urban work-places. Where settlement patterns are thin and scattered and where infrastructural development levels are high – especially those relating to mobility, i.e. transport and information flow systems – labour force migration would provide a viable alternative to rural plant location without a loss in the level of rural linkage.

In what follows, the theme of rural industrialisation is viewed in the context of strategies for rural income and employment generation within the poorer rural sector communities; as such, preference will be given to the linkage approach, and rural industrialisation will be understood as the sub-sector of the mainstream industrial sector that displays sufficiently strong rural linkages, irrespective of whether such enterprises are located in designated rural areas or not. The following four categories will be utilised: (i) rural located, rural linked (RLoc–RLink); (ii) rural located, urban linked (RLoc–ULink); (iii) urban located, urban linked (ULoc–ULink); (iv) urban located, rural linked (ULoc–RLink). ULoc will then refer to all urban-located industries and RLoc to all rural-located ones; ULink will refer to all urban-linked industries and RLink to all rural-linked ones. The three categories connected through location or linkage with the rural sector generally cover a remarkably wide variety of activities and enterprises, ranging from petty household-based cottage and handicraft production activities to large-scale, relatively complex industrial plants. These specific characteristics will become relevant in the context of discussion relating to concrete situations.

Development objectives

What are the objectives assigned to rural industrialisation strategies in developing countries? A summary enunciation of these will also provide a checklist of possible criteria for the evaluation of specific country policies and performance. The first, overarching objective is usually employment generation. However, this is not enough since such employment could be generated at unacceptably low levels of productivity, as in the case of poor rural households which accept implicit wage rates that are well below the poverty-line equivalents as part of a strategy of economic survival under harsh conditions. It is therefore necessary to introduce the second objective of income generation; but here again, while high productivity could generate high incomes (i.e. value added), the share of the workers (i.e. the rural poor) might be as low as before if the labour market conditions are either saturated or monopsonistic, as might well happen when individual rural workers are confronted by large-scale, profit-seeking private or institutional employers. Hence, the necessity to introduce the third-level objective, that is, ensuring acceptable levels of income generation for the target group, i.e. the labour force drawn mainly from the rural poor. But even then, the conditions under which the labour is performed might have other serious objectionable features about it: labour organisation might be banned; worker safety might be low; working conditions might be of the sweat-shop type; and there might be obnoxious features relating to the exploitation of subordinated categories of labour, i.e. women and children. Thus, worker welfare levels constitute the fourth objective.

From a wider developmental point of view, it is necessary to introduce a few more criteria for judging success. The fifth objective, thus, might address itself to the question of growth. Do the enterprises (or activities) display a dynamic investment behaviour, or are the surpluses from the enterprises disposed of mainly as consumption by those who are in receipt of the components of the value added? In this context of dynamic effects, a vital objective is raising the level of industrial skill formation in the countryside. Sixthly, again stressing the need for generating rural linkages, the question of positive linkages with the agricultural sector and its population – which does not participate directly in these higher-productivity rural industries – could legitimately be raised. This bifurcates into two aspects: one concerns the relationship of rural industrialisation to local agricultural development; the other concerns the transfer and sharing of the benefits of the additional incomes generated by rural industries to the agricultural population. (The first would form one, but not the only, way of contributing to the fulfilment of the second.) Thus, a full listing of the objectives would include the generation of: employment, higher productivity, wages, worker welfare and participation, internal accumulation, skill formation, agricultural development and positive spin-offs for the agricultural population not directly engaged in rural industry.

RURAL INDUSTRIALISATION STRATEGIES

RURAL NON-FARM ACTIVITIES IN MALAYSIA

The rural non-farm sector is notorious for its heterogeneity everywhere, and Malaysia is no exception. At one end are the rural industrial estates and the rural agri-processing industries, which in the Malaysian case can be quite large scale. At the other end of the range are the part-time, seasonal, household-based non-farm activities (NFA) of marginalised agriculturists. Within these extremes are a variety of full-time specialised operations (e.g. traditional handicrafts, new non-farm occupations generated by the process of economic growth), and these could have a variety of organisational and ownership characteristics. As such, it is not surprising that in Malaysia, as elsewhere, systematic statistical information on the NFA sector is hard to come by (see Saith, 1989).

NFA, rural poverty and inequality

What is the relationship between NFA and the incidence of rural poverty and inequality? Do NFAs perform the function of reducing inequality, or of exacerbating it at the micro-level, say within a village? Since NFAs are important for poor rural households for supplementing meagre agricultural or farm incomes, they are likely, other things being the same, to reduce the poverty of the household concerned. But such activities are known to be important for all strata of rural households; this raises the question of whether NFA incomes tend to reduce or to worsen inequality, and the effect that any such worsening might have on processes of agrarian differentiation. These questions are again important, but unanswerable with the present database. Some partial evidence is available, and will be used in an illustrative manner.

With respect to the issue of poverty, some direct macro evidence is provided by data from various – though not always strictly compatible – socioeconomic surveys conducted on a nationwide basis. The findings (reported in Malaysia, *Fifth Malaysia Plan, 1986–1990 (5MP)*, 1986: 86) reveal some interesting patterns in this regard. While the incidence of rural poverty declined from 58.7 per cent for the entire rural sector in 1970, to 47.8 per cent in 1976, and to 24.7 per cent in 1984, the composition of the rural poor remained remarkably stable over the period. Comparing all rural poor in 1970 and 1984, smallholders formed 52.6 per cent in 1970 and 57.9 per cent in 1984. For padi farmers, the figures are 17.5 per cent and 16.7 per cent; for estate workers, 8.4 per cent and 4.0 per cent; and for fishermen, 4.0 per cent and 2.4 per cent respectively. The last group is rural sector industries, and here the percentage was 17.5 per cent in 1970 and 19.0 per cent in 1984. The reduction in the overall incidence of poverty has therefore taken place in part through a decline in the internal incidence of poverty within each group, and partly through a redistribution of the rural population from groups which had a high incidence of poverty in favour of groups which had low rates.

In this regard, the poverty-alleviating role of the rural industries group was very powerful. In 1970 the incidence of poverty in this group was the lowest at 35.2 per cent; in 1984, it was down to 10.0 per cent. But alongside this, its share of the rural population had increased dramatically from 29.1 per cent to 46.9 per cent (which is in keeping with the previous findings on the changes in the occupational and industrial profile of the rural labour force). Thus, the processes of rural industrialisation, which have been operative in the rural sector in Malaysia, have contributed in both ways towards the overall reduction in poverty.

With respect to the impact of NFA on rural income inequality, one frequently encountered hypothesis is that such incomes tend to be redistributive in nature since the poorer sections of the population have higher participation levels forced upon them by their poverty. Such a hypothesis could be defended using the experience of the East Asian countries. However, where initial rural inequalities are very high, such relationships might become inoperative, as the rural rich might manage to gain disproportionately from such lucrative NFA opportunities as exist. This could be especially so when access to these activities is interfaced with the local rural bureaucracy.

Some evidence for rejecting this hypothesis in the Malaysian rural context is provided by a field study (Shand, 1985) carried out on a stratified random sample of 600 farmers within the Kemubu irrigation project in Kelantan, and a second control sample of 300 farmers from adjacent areas outside the irrigation project. The relevant findings may be summarised briefly. Firstly, non-farm incomes were not evenly distributed between households. For 1980, a normal year, 40 per cent of the households in the project sample had no non-farm income; another 33 per cent had non-farm incomes of up to M$1,000 per household; and the remaining 27 per cent had non-farm incomes in excess of M$1,000. The corresponding percentages for the control (non-project) sample were: 33 per cent, 36 per cent and 31 per cent. This indicates that there was a high degree of inequality in the distribution of non-farm incomes. Secondly, concentration coefficients estimated for different sources of income showed that net padi income had relatively low inequality, since inequalities in land ownership had been moderated by an inverse relationship between farm size and productivity. The ratios were 0.17 and 0.18 for the project and the control samples, respectively. Other farm income tended to be more unequally distributed, with coefficients of 0.37 and 0.26, respectively. This yielded, on the whole, low inequalities in the distribution of total net farm income, with coefficients of 0.21 and 0.23. However, in sharp contrast, the concentration coefficients for the distribution of non-farm income were extremely high, at 0.56 and 0.55 respectively, which had the effect then of raising the degree of inequality in the distribution of total household income to high levels, with coefficients of 0.35 and 0.39.

One explanation for this could be that the poorer households would lack the ability to initiate a non-farm enterprise on their own, while the richer and better-connected ones would not. Thus, the former group would have to generate their non-farm incomes through operations in the local labour markets, which in a depressed region like Kelantan might not be buoyant enough to provide any significant income-earning opportunities. Indeed, the study cites the local shortage of demand for unskilled and skilled labour as one contributing factor in explaining this negative impact of non-farm incomes.

Rural NFA enterprises and entrepreneurs

Within the heterogeneity of the rural NFA sector, enterprises and entrepreneurs stand at the other end of the spectrum from the one occupied by the rural NFA labour force and the petty agriculturists who combine cultivation with part-time NFA activities, often organised within the household. But even among these enterprises and entrepreneurs, there is considerable internal variation. The field is dominated by the giant institutional entrepreneurs, e.g. the Regional Development Authorities (RDAs) and the Federal Land Development Authority (FELDA), and by the firms, frequently quite large-scale, in the industrial estates in the rural and the semi-urban areas. Such firms usually have strong links with their institutional or private sector parents and/or partners. The discussion of the rural industrial estates will be held in abeyance and it will be dealt with in a relatively detailed manner in an analysis of the linkages of such enterprises. Here, attention is therefore focused on the other component: that constituted by small-time, relatively independent private sector rural entrepreneurs who usually operate on a tiny scale. The subject of the discussion will be rural NFA Bumiputra entrepreneurs. This topic is especially important. As was seen, rural industry makes a positive contribution to poverty alleviation and, if rural Bumiputra entrepreneurs, functioning on a small scale, were found to be the agents of this rural industrialisation, the process would make a second contribution to the objective of 'restructuring' society. Therefore, from the government or planning vantage point, the experience of such entrepreneurs and enterprises is of special interest.

However, virtually no systematic data are available on this theme, and exclusive reliance will be placed upon a 1983 field survey of 387 rural Bumiputra entrepreneurs operating in the NFA sector (Chee, P.L., 1985). This was not a scientifically selected sample and, as such, the findings based upon it cannot be used for making any wider generalisations. Even so, it does yield very useful insights; in any event, the sample size is quite large. The findings are used here to elicit important characteristics of the entrepreneurs and their experience. How successful were they? And if they were not, why not?

In terms of the economic characteristics of the enterprises, the large majority were tiny, employing fewer than five workers; very few employed more than twenty workers. For all manufacturing enterprises, the Census of

Manufacturing for 1981 shows an average of 28.3 workers per enterprise. The value of fixed assets employed per enterprise in rural enterprises was under M$50,000 for nearly 90 per cent of them, whereas the average figure for the entire manufacturing sector was ten times as large. The value of fixed assets per worker in 70 per cent of the rural enterprises was under M$5,000, but the figure in the entire manufacturing sector was 3.6 times that. Finally, the value of sales for 56 per cent of the rural units was under M$5,000. Thus, the rural enterprises were tiny on all counts, though there was some variation internally. More than half of them were in the food manufacturing sector. But in a significant number of cases (30.3 per cent), the enterprise had subsequently diversified into new product lines.

Data on the year of establishment of these 387 enterprises provide some very useful indirect information. Seen per quinquennium since 1950, it turns out that until 1969, the average number of starts per year was about two only. Since then, there has been a clear trend of acceleration: for 1970–4, the number of starts was about five per year; for 1975–9, it jumped to twenty-five, and in the years 1980–3, it rose further to thirty-seven. To the extent that this index and its trend can be read as proxies for the overall buoyancy of the rural NFA sector, it indicates a remarkably favourable period of rapid expansion. This trend is also consistent with the very sharp changes discussed earlier in the structure of the rural labour force in terms of both the occupational as well as the industrial profiles. They also correspond, of course, with a period of rapid economic growth in both the agricultural as well as the industrial sectors, and as such appear to be plausible.

What are the origins of the rural entrepreneurs? Are they 'rural' simply by virtue of their enterprises being categorised as 'rural', or do they have genuine rural social origins? This is an important question with significant social and economic implications. The survey shows that as many as 200, or 53.6 per cent, had fathers who were either farmers or fishermen by occupation; another 7.5 per cent had fathers who were labourers or craftsmen. Indeed, as many as 42.9 per cent of the entrepreneurs themselves had these occupations prior to starting the enterprise. Thus, there is evidence that the majority are genuinely rural; this is also indicative of considerable occupational mobility.

How did they perform? Data on the monthly income per entrepreneur reveal that 53.9 per cent earned less than M$500. Assuming a family size of five, and a dependency ratio of 2.5, this implies a per capita income of just M$200, which does not compare favourably with the median household income of M$581 per month for Bumiputra households in Malaysia in 1984 (*5MP*, 1986: 99). Even if the income per entrepreneur is conjecturally treated as family per capita income, it does not appear to be an indicator of success as an entrepreneur. On the other hand, such 'quick' surveys almost invariably underestimate this variable, which it is in the interests of the entrepreneur to understate. However, at the top end, 71 entrepreneurs, or 19.0 per cent, had incomes between M$1,000 and M$3,000; and another 28 (or 7.5 per cent), above M$3,000. This is one clear criterion for measuring success, but the study added three others to separate the 'very successful' and the 'unsuccessful' cases from the full sample: the age of the enterprise; the development of new product lines, etc.; and the entrepreneur's own perceptions. A composite index based on these considerations then classified 38 as being very successful, and 107 as being failures.

What accounts for the failures and successes, and is there a recognisable pattern? Some very useful conclusions emerge. Firstly, it turns out that being rural in social origin does not necessarily help in being successful. Ninety-three, or 86.9 per cent, of the 107 failures had grown up in villages, compared with 50.0 per cent of the very successful ones. As many as 80, or 74.8 per cent, of the failures had fathers who were farmers or fishermen, as against 31.6 per cent of the very successful group. It also turns out that the failures were concentrated in the smaller size groups: 94, or 87.9 per cent, owned enterprises with fixed assets under M$10,000 in value, whereas 33, or 86.8 per cent, of the very successful enterprises were above this level; 102, or 95.3 per cent, of the failures employed fewer than 5 workers, as against 17, or 44.7 per cent, for the very successful cases. The enterprises which failed were also much more specialised in food production alone. Considering the cited causes of success, 80 (or 21.4 per cent, the largest single figure) replied 'good market'; while this cause and/or 'hard work' accounted for 40.5 per cent of the cases; 'luck, timing, opportunity, and God's help' brought up the rear, and were together worth just 1.3 per cent of cases! Other variables positively associated with success were education to a mild extent, though the role performed by the knowledge of a second language, especially English, was particularly important. Interestingly, but perhaps not surprisingly, 'specialised training received by the entrepreneur' was quite unrelated to failure or to success.

The role of government assistance does not appear to have been powerful in helping these enterprises in the initial years. As many as 60.3 per cent of the total sample of 387 had had to rely exclusively on their own resources for the seed capital. At the same time, 316, or 82.1 per cent, cited lack of capital as the 'main problem in getting started'; and 266 or 71.3 per cent had no government assistance in the first three years of operation. Furthermore, at the time of the survey, 284, or 76.1 per cent, made no sales at all to government agencies. This must not be read to imply that linkages to government agencies could have had no role to play in the highly successful cases. It is possible that it was the same small group of entrepreneurs who did rely on loans from government agencies and who made substantial sales to them. Indeed, *a priori* reasoning, coupled with some casual observation of this type of industrial enterprise, supports the idea that this argument could have a great deal of validity.

The general conclusion which emerges is then one which discounts the deduction of high dynamism from the age profile of these rural enterprises. The acceleration does testify to buoyant and rapid expansion. In part, this could be explained by the direct support programmes of the various large-scale institutional entrepreneurs under whose umbrella such small-scale rural entrepreneurs might have been nourished. But the evidence suggests that, while this might account for a small minority of them having been very successful, it had few linkages with the rest, or the majority of them. The majority, it is argued, saw the economic opportunities – generated by the high economic growth of the economy coupled with the extremely favourable terms of access to government bureaucracy and development agencies created for the Bumiputra community by the restructuring policies – but because of limitations associated with their social origins were unable to make the most of them. The implications of these findings are not entirely optimistic with respect to using the small-scale rural Bumiputra entrepreneur as the prime mover in any rural industrialisation policy. It might be argued that, when underwritten by government agencies, they appeared to have had noticeable success; but that can hardly form the main plank of a replicable prototype.

PERSPECTIVES ON MALAYSIAN RURAL INDUSTRIALISATION

It will be apparent from the eclectic nature of the previous section that any attempt at formulating strategies for rural industrialisation in Malaysia has to contend with an extreme paucity of data. This being unavoidable, the discussion in this section will use the diverse information assembled from mixed sources as the basis for developing skeletal arguments about some rural industrialisation policies implicit in the Fifth Malaysia Plan for 1986–90. It will be prefaced by observations culled from the Fifth Plan document's scattered references to rural industrialisation or allied themes, and highlights some pivotal features of the Plan strategy. This is followed by a closer look at these identified features, dealing sequentially with themes related to linkages (especially rural) of urban industrial enterprises, and, subsequently, with selected policy aspects of the programme of rural urbanisation which constitutes a special 'development thrust' for accelerating rural development in the Fifth Plan period.

Rural industrialisation in the revised spatial strategy

The reoriented spatial strategy takes cognisance of the weaknesses inherent in the previous one. There was excessive industrial and infrastructural dispersal within the federal planning framework where state governments were perhaps more enthusiastic than prudent in the proliferation of townships and industrial estates within their boundaries. Such regional dispersal strategies therefore had but a 'marginal impact' (*5MP*, 1986: 354), and in effect wasted national resources. The revised strategy can be summarised in terms of its *two guiding principles* and *three operative elements*.

Looking at the underlying principles, or premises, the first could appropriately be labelled *regions over states*.

Planning and programming on the state basis ... have limitations since this approach fails to capture the benefits of any large-scale project in a particular state that spread to adjoining states, and neither does it recognize the fact that metropolitan areas provide specialized services to spatial units far beyond their state boundaries. ... Planning programmes on a multi-state basis can lead to a reduction in overlapping investments and duplication of infrastructural projects. Besides, it can also widen the scope for the sharing of state resources as well as interstate cooperation in joint projects.... In this respect, [the Fifth Plan will] emphasize regions as a framework for analysis, both inter and intraregionally, rather than states, as was adopted in previous Plans.
(5MP, 1986:166)

Sabah and Sarawak are to be treated as single-state regions.

The second guiding principle can be summarised in the phrase *people-prosperity over place-prosperity*.

One of the strategies for reducing regional disparities is to move people to where the jobs are or the people-prosperity strategy. This is carried out by accelerating growth in the leading areas, either within or outside the region, which enjoy some measure of comparative advantage and economies of scale, while, at the same time, facilitating the smooth operation of the labour market to encourage workers to move so that they are able to reap higher returns from their labour inputs. The other strategy is to move jobs to where the people are or the place-prosperity strategy. Programmes implemented under this strategy are designed to provide employment to the population living at particular locations, and population movements into these areas, if any, constitute a minor element. Both these approaches have advantages as well as trade-offs. In the past, programmes to reduce interstate disparities placed heavy emphasis on the place-prosperity strategy to the extent that too many locations with limited resources were developed. Consequently, growth was dispersed over too many centres in the country to reap the benefits emanating from economies of scale.
(5MP, 1986: 200)

In the future, the balance between the two principles is to be redressed in clear favour of people-prosperity.

This new strategy is enunciated best through specifying its three constituent operative elements. The first is the policy of controlled concentration of industrial location

on existing growth centres enjoying agglomeration economies so that existing infrastructure, communications, ancillary services and skilled manpower can be more fully utilized. Such a strategy, based on market forces and efficiency criteria, is necessary in the light of the recession, structural adjustment, and financial prudence.
(5MP, 1986: 358)

While dispersed townships and industrial estates are to be de-emphasised, reliance is placed on the development of a Western Industrial Corridor. Weak spots along the length of the Corridor are to be further developed, with further lateral sub-arteries of spontaneous and planned development to follow in due course. Six regional centres are to receive concentrated attention; of the four in Peninsular Malaysia, three are in this Corridor.

The second policy element is that of facilitating migration on an intra-regional basis though not on an inter-regional one.

> One or several centres in a region will be developed to attract the rural–urban migrants as well as those who move from smaller to larger towns, thereby reducing the inter-regional flow of migrants from the less to the more developed regions of the country.
>
> (*5MP*, 1986: 201).

The rationale underlying this is that migrants have been found to display stronger economic attributes than the average members of the sending areas, so that discouraging inter-regional movement would prevent a deterioration in inter-regional disparities.

The first two elements – industrial locational concentration and migration – are complementary in nature and form the cutting edge of the new people-prosperity strategy. The development needs of the residual population, mostly in rural areas, are then addressed by the third constitutive element – the policy of rural urbanisation. As such, this element would appear to form a substrategy within place-prosperity incorporating *in situ development*. But this would be misleading, as unpackaging the rural urbanisation policy reveals a strong dose of controlled population movements at local level.

Rural urbanisation itself has three sub-policies:

(a) 'estatisation', involving agricultural development based on a new emphasis on estate-type management for smallholders. The basic objective is to rationalise this sector and make it more competitive. For this, various support and institutional policies come into play, including the development of cooperatives, group farming, consolidation of uneconomic holdings, etc.;
(b) 'industrialisation', implying the promotion of village or other small-scale industries or non-agricultural economic activities; and
(c) 'villagisation', or the regrouping of traditional villages to foster the development of rural growth centres (*5MP*, 1986: 318). Here, the intention is to move rural populations in low-density areas into clusters with a critical minimum size of 2,500 persons. The fresh site would be a newly constructed township, complete with new housing and infrastructural and welfare facilities.

However, with regard to rural industry, which is of immediate concern, it is difficult to identify any new initiatives or reorientations; the implicit policy would appear to be one of continuity, with the added expectation that the formation of the rural urban centres with concentrated infrastructural facilities would provide the necessary boost to generate some extra buoyancy to this traditionally marginalised sector.

With the background provided by the empirical observations above, it is appropriate, at this stage, to relate the analytical regional framework of the Fifth Plan to the two definitional approaches discussed earlier with respect to rural industrialisation, i.e. their locational and linkage aspects. It was argued that, from the policy point of view, location per se was not crucial. What mattered was whether or not the industrial enterprise generated significant economic and development linkages with the rural sector, regardless of whether it was actually situated within designated rural areas or not. What has to be established in the Malaysian context is whether or not the industrial location policy proposed – including the position of village industry within it – is likely to create such linkages in adequate measure. To investigate this vital issue, the impact of past industrial development in both sectors would have to be analysed with reference to its linkages, and, against that experience, the likely impact of the new people-prosperity-type industrial location policies on future trends will have to be assessed. Unfortunately, the database is far from adequate for forming any hard conclusions, but piecemeal information from scattered sources can be juxtaposed to sketch the outline of a picture which arguably captures some important features faithfully.

Two specific areas will be discussed. The first is concerned with the economic linkages generated by specific categories of industry – e.g. those in Free Trade Zones, industrial estates, etc. – which are not directly located in villages or prime rural areas. The other concerns some aspects of the proposed rural urbanisation programme.

Available evidence (see Saith, 1989) suggests that, even under the previous policy regime of industrial *dispersal*, the dynamic role of migration was at best rather weak, and at worst quite negligible. There is a need, within the context of the new strategy of relative industrial concentration, to demonstrate that a weaker policy (in this regard) than before will turn out to yield stronger results than before. In short, too much must not be expected of migration as a developer of rural areas; the implication for appropriate *in situ* rural development policies is obvious.

Economic linkages of industrial enterprise

The question concerning the economic linkages generated by the manufacturing sector is directed at the spread effects of the main operative element of the revised spatial strategy. Migration acts as the instrument which links labour, including rural labour, to the concentrated centres of industrial activity. We have argued that the backward development linkages of migration with the sending region and sector are likely to be weak.

But the wage bill of the workforce forms the minor fraction of the total value added by the sector, so it remains possible for the sector to generate powerful spread effects through the direct and indirect impact of the production of the rest of the value added. Indeed, the rationale as well as the justification of the reorientation of regional and industrial dispersal policies was predicated upon the existence of precisely such effects. Much depends upon the extent to which this stipulation is realistic. One indication of this might be provided by a review of the experience of the past in this respect.

The usual disclaimer about statistical limitations has to be invoked and, once again, the treatment will be eclectic and draw its materials from three prime sources: Malaysia (1983), which is focused on the economic impact of the industrial estates; UNIDO (1985), which includes a study on the analysis of the linkage effects of the Malaysian manufacturing sector; and *MIPS* (1984), for information about the operation of Free Trade Zones (FTZs) and licensed manufacturing warehouses (LMWs). The discussion in this section will centre on the strength and pattern of these spread effects. These cover the direct and indirect multiplier effects on income and on employment of the growth in the manufacturing sector, as specified by its recent technological and industrial profile. The pattern of sourcing raw material purchases will be noted. Three basic constituencies with which these spread effects – or conversely, leakages – will be identified are:

(a) the domestic economy in relation to the rest of the world;
(b) the different states, and indirectly, through this, the regional groupings of states according to per capita income strata;
(c) the sectors of origin of regional GDP, again at the state level.

In itself, such information is relevant for anticipating the likely impact of industrialisation along the lines of the recent past. While these are constituencies of obvious interest with respect to the objectives of generating spread effects in favour of both the rural sector and the Bumiputra community, deductions will have to be made in an indirect manner, though some direct information will become available.

First, consider the national level. Data on the estimated final demand multipliers and on the backward and forward linkages of the different sectors of the economy point to a leakage of about one-third to the rest of the world. The analysis of direct and indirect inter-industry linkages for eleven industrial groups suggests that, for most cases, the total multipliers were lower for the Malaysian economy (using the 1975 input–output matrix) than for Korea (and Japan and the USA), but were also below those of most other economies in the Association of South East Asian Nations (ASEAN). This also held true when the multipliers were netted for import leakages. The conclusion is that inter-industrial linkages were more weakly developed in the Malaysian economy, and import leakages were correspondingly higher than elsewhere. The comparison with the Korean economy, at a similar level of per capita GNP, is sharp in every case, except in some natural resource based sectors.

The point about the import-leakage propensity is especially important in relation to the leading growth sectors of recent Malaysian industrial growth, viz. in the electronics and textiles industries located in the Free Trade Zones and the licensed manufacturing warehouses. Data for 1982 – which are consistent with trends in the previous decade – reveal the following characteristics.

Firstly, both FTZs and LMWs are dominated by the 'electronics and electricals' and the 'textiles and garments' industries, and exports account for 97.2 per cent and 96.5 per cent of their total sales, respectively. Extreme specialisation is combined with extreme export orientation.

Secondly, domestic linkages through material purchases are remarkably weak. Local raw materials as a share of all raw material purchases account for 3.6 per cent and 10.6 per cent, respectively, while local shares of capital equipment purchases were 8.3 per cent and 24.0 per cent in these manufacturing sectors. The combined weighted percentages were 3.9 per cent for FTZs and a relatively higher 12.2 per cent for LMWs. Before endorsing the 'superior' linkages of the latter, they should be compared with the figures for the domestic sector, which would undoubtedly show an extreme contrast.

Thirdly, FTZ firms have an average employment of 830 workers, while LMWs average 381, making them quite large sized. They are skill extensive, and can therefore rely on a relatively under-skilled workforce. As such, production skill formation could not be said to be an external effect created by FTZ or LMW employment.

Fourthly, in terms of linkages generated through employment, the contribution of the sector is substantial. The labour force is overwhelmingly female, young and unskilled or semi-skilled, and is drawn primarily from direct or indirect rural migrants. It is also underpaid. While the share of wages in value added (at 37.1 per cent and 34.3 per cent, respectively) is boosted by the low capital intensity of operations (in FTZ firms, the cumulative wage bill during 1972–82 was 18 per cent greater than the cumulative expenditures on local and imported capital equipment for the same period, reckoned without adjusting for changes in relative prices), average wages are relatively low. In 1982, they averaged M$4,983 and M$3,515 in FTZ and LMW firms, respectively, The corresponding figures for 1971 were 85 per cent and 67 per cent of the average wages in the manufacturing sector of the country. The true difference would be somewhat higher, since the FTZs and the LMWs account for about 25 per cent of the employment of the aggregate manufacturing sector. The conclusion is inescapable that the FTZ enclaves have been grafted onto the economy with negligible domestic linkages, except through the employment side. LMWs show marginally stronger material linkages than the FTZs, but this advantage is negated through lower wages. The dispersed location of the LMWs does not seem to have had any impact on the magnitude of domestic linkages.

The pattern of linkages of industrial development in states, stratified according to their income status (including that in rural industrial estates), is based on materials provided by Malaysia, (1983). As such, the analysis is restricted to the industrial estate sector, though, given its internal diversification and regional and sectoral dispersal, the picture which emerges should have considerable general validity. Four sets of observations will be made covering: the sectoral profile; the inter-state pattern of linkages generated; the inter-sectoral pattern of linkages profiled by state; and the share of Bumiputras.

Sectoral profile

Over the 1968–81 period, the total number of industrial estates rose from 11 to 88. In 1968, there were *no* rural estates, but between 1979 and 1981 they improved their share from 36.9 per cent to 46.6 per cent (Malaysia, 1983: 2–15). However, in 1981, their share of the total planned area declined to 24.2 per cent; while their share of the developed area was lower still at 21.3 per cent, and the actually occupied area was just 14.2 per cent. Only 32 per cent of the developed area of the rural industrial estates (RIEs) was occupied, while in the semi-urban industrial estates (SIEs) and the urban industrial estates (UIEs) the percentages were higher at 44 per cent and 65 per cent, respectively.

While the RIEs had 14.2 per cent of the occupied area, their share in employment generated was even lower, at 5.2 per cent, with UIEs and SIEs taking up 66.4 per cent and 28.4 per cent, respectively.

With respect to employee income generated, the RIEs' performance was again further down the relative scale. They generated just 3.7 per cent of the total employee income, as against 68.8 per cent and 27.5 per cent for the UIEs and the SIEs, respectively. Thus, RIEs, while making up 46.6 per cent of the *number* of estates, generated a mere 3.7 per cent of the total employee income – a telling statistic.

The internal industrial profile is summarised by industrial diversification coefficients. These estimate the divergence of the weighted share of the different industries within any estate with respect to the overall pattern in all the estates put together. The index varies between zero and unity. A higher value implies a higher divergence from the overall industry mix, and hence is indicative of a higher degree of specialisation. The UIEs are highly diversified, with an index of 0.28, while the indices for the SIEs and the RIEs, 0.58 and 0.82 respectively, suggest increasing specialisation as estates move away from the urban areas. These indices exclude the FTZs, which, of course, are highly specialised and would transform the comparison. The low diversification of the RIEs is due to their heavy concentration on resource-based industries.

There is also a clear pattern with respect to the economic profitability of the different categories of industrial estate. Using commercial prices for the land, rather than the official (artificially low) prices at which land allocations were made, Malaysia (1983) survey data indicate that, of a total of 59 cases, 9 of the 12 UIEs showed internal rates of return (IRR) in excess of 100 per cent, while only one had a negative IRR. Of the 23 RIEs, on the other hand, only 2 had an IRR greater than 100 per cent, while as many as 6 had negative IRRs. (The SIEs occupied an intermediate position.)

Linkage impact at state level

Three types of linkages will be mentioned: those pertaining to the gross output value of the state; household income (defined as wages and salaries) generated by the industries; and employment created by the estates. Both direct and indirect effects induced through the appropriate multiplier will be noted at the state level. (In order to derive these, Malaysia (1983), converts the national input–output matrix into separate state-level matrices through the use of industrial location quotients, derived from the Census of Manufacturing data.)

The 'high-income group' (HIG) of states comprises only Selangor, and involves 14 (16.1 per cent) of the 87 industrial estates used in the analysis, but accounts for 48.4 per cent of the direct gross value added (DGVA) by all 87 estates (Perlis, with one estate, and belonging to the 'low-income' group, is excluded). The 'middle-income group' (MIG) of states, consisting of Penang, Perak, Negeri Sembilan, Malacca, Johore and Pahang, accounts for 46, or 52.9 per cent, of the estates and 46.7 per cent of the DGVA effect. The 'low-income group' (LIG) – Kedah, Kelantan and Trengganu – has 18, or 20.7 per cent, of the estates and 3.1 per cent of DGVA. The shares of the Eastern states (ESG), Sabah and Sarawak, are 10.3 per cent and 1.8 per cent, respectively. It is clear then that the poorer states, which are also the ones with dominating rural sectors, are losers with respect to the generation of DGVA. The position is somewhat worse if both the DGVA and the indirect or induced gross value added (IGVA) are also included. The HIG share in IGVA is 53.9 per cent, while the LIG share is reduced to only 1.8 per cent. The reason for this disparity is that the more articulated state economy of HIG can internalise much more of the IGVA than can the weakly developed economies of LIG states. The IGVA:DGVA ratio is 1.01 for HIG, but just 0.54 for LIG.

With respect to the impact on household incomes (HY) within the state, the HIG share of total household income (THY) is 48.5 per cent, and the ratio IHY:DHY is 0.57. The corresponding figures for the LIG are 3.5 per cent and 0.36 respectively. In terms of the overall impact of such HY generation on the total value added in the state, the industrial estates' share accounted for 5.9 per cent for HIG, 4.1 per cent for MIG, and 1.2 per cent for LIG.

Turning to the employment effects, HIG is responsible for 34.1 per cent of the direct employment effect (DE) of industrial estates, MIG for 58.3 per cent, LIG for only 4.9 per cent and ESG for a mere 2.7 per cent. Comparisons with respect to employee income (IE) generated, which is related to the HY effect, are somewhat more favourable for the HIG states. The ratio of IE:DE was 1.60 for HIG and 1.39 for LIG, implying that, for every worker directly employed in the industrial estates, additional employment of 1.60 and 1.39 workers was induced through indirect effects elsewhere in the state. Once again, when considering the total employment effect as a percentage of the total employment in the state, the share was highest for HIG at 22.6 per cent, compared with just 2.8 per cent in LIG, and a negligible 1.8 per cent in the ESG. Clearly, the poorer agricultural states could hardly have felt the direct and indirect employment-generation impact of industrial estates.

It should be noted that a significant number of the establishments in industrial estates are not new establishments but ones which have relocated from elsewhere in the economy. Thus, of the 82 establishments in the estates in LIG, 30 (or 36.6 per cent) had been relocated, while 41 of the total of 230 in HIG (or 17.8 per cent) were in this category. Thus, relocations, at least in terms of *numbers*, appear to have moved in favour of the poorer states, suggesting that relocations could be designed to take advantage of the significantly lower wages there.

Intra-state sectoral linkages

The methodology also allows the gross value added (GVA) and the employment (E) effects to be subdivided within each state according to the sector to which they accrue. Thus, the extent to which an expansion of final demand, i.e. production, in the industrial estates generates GVA and E linkages in agriculture, mining and quarrying, manufacturing, trade, transport and storage, and the services sectors can be estimated separately. Special interest would attach, in the present context, to the impact of industrial estates on the agricultural sector, and, in particular, to the impact of *rural* industrial estates in poor states on their general economy. Unfortunately, the effects cannot be separated by source, i.e. with respect to UIEs as against RIEs. As an approximate proxy, however, it might be noted that the RIEs are located mostly in the poorer agriculturally biased states, whereas the UIEs tend to the other end of the economic spectrum; in other words, the relative incidence of RIEs within all estates in any state is likely to be positively correlated with its income status. This proxy variable is neither entirely satisfactory nor entirely unrealistic. (Unfortunately, Malaysia (1983) did not also estimate the linkage effects for different states with respect to the different types of industrial estates.)

How was the indirectly generated gross value added shared between the different sectors of the economy? The statewise pattern is interesting and can be summarised in a few points. Firstly, taking the country as a whole, of the M$3.8 billion of IGVA generated, only 7.0 per cent accrued to agriculture. Mining and quarrying accounted for just 0.9 per cent, and manufacturing for 22.1 per cent. Thus, the three commodity sectors together are beneficiaries of only 30 per cent of the IGVA. The remaining 70 per cent goes to trade, transport and storage and services. This overall pattern suggests that the linkages of the industrial estates with the commodity sectors is weak, especially with respect to agriculture. Secondly, if HIG and LIG states are compared, some striking variations emerge. Thus, in Kedah, the share of agriculture was 0.8 per cent; of manufacturing, 8.2 per cent and of the commodity sectors together, 9.2 per cent. Having received only 1.4 per cent of the total IGVA in the first place, Kedah state found that a staggering 90.8 per cent of this amount accrued to the non-commodity, 'soft' sectors. For Kelantan, the share of the commodity sectors was a negligible 2.1 per cent of its 0.2 per cent share of the total IGVA. By comparison, the commodity sector accounted for 38.8 per cent of IGVA in Selangor state, a percentage which was related to its fat 53.9 per cent of total IGVA at the country level. Thirdly, looking at the distribution of the IGVA generated for the entire manufacturing sector (which formed 22.1 per cent of the total IGVA, as seen), Selangor alone accounted for as much as 63.7 per cent of it, while the share of LIG was 0.6 per cent!

The pattern of distribution of the indirect employment effect – estimated at 318,590 for the country – follows a parallel pattern. Of this number, agriculture accounts for 12.3 per cent; mining and quarrying for 0.8 per cent, and manufacturing for 11.5 per cent. The commodity sectors together take up 24.6 per cent, of which the remainder goes to the trade, transport and services sectors. Once again, the poorer and non-industrial states display high percentages – sometimes over 90 per cent – for the share of the non-commodity sectors. As before, of the total IE-effect jobs estimated for the manufacturing sector, viz. 36,619, 49.4 per cent are in HIG and only 1.1 per cent in LIG. The corresponding figures for the agricultural sector are 39,126, 74.7 per cent and 1.5 per cent respectively.

Pertinent to the question of linkages is the issue of the sourcing of raw materials purchases by industrial estates. What is the share of intra-state sources in sourcing? Survey data reveal a few important features and also permit a contrast with the FTZ estates. UIEs (excluding FTZs) purchase 21.7 per cent of their material inputs from within the state, 22.7 per cent from other states, and 55.6 per cent from overseas. The corresponding figures for SIEs and RIEs are 17.4 per cent, 35.8 per cent and 46.8 per cent; and 9.1 per cent, 32.0 per cent and 58.8 per cent, respectively, and reveal the very high import leakages of the industrial estates. But the rates are even higher for the FTZs, at 11.3 per cent, 3.0 per cent and 85.7 per cent respectively for the three sources.

Impact on restructuring

Some brief comments might be in order about the contribution of this form of industrialisation to the restructuring of Malaysian society. The index is the degree of participation of the Malay population in employment with respect to the ownership of establishments, as well as their suppliers.

With respect to *direct* employment generated, Malays constitute 56.6 per cent of the workforce, suggesting that the objective was met. However, with respect to the *indirect* employment effects, the share of Malays is lower at 33.7 per cent, and yields a share of 43.2 per cent in the total (direct and indirect) employment effect.

Malays are also under-represented in the ownership structure of paid-up capital for a sample survey of firms. Their share in UIEs is 14.9 per cent, as opposed to 30.7 per cent for non-Bumiputras and 54.4 per cent for foreign owners. For SIEs and RIEs, the corresponding percentages are: 29.1 per cent, 34.8 per cent and 36.1 per cent; and 12.5 per cent, 36.0 per cent and 51.5 per cent respectively. Within the UIEs, FTZ firms obviously display a pattern skewed even further in favour of foreigners. What is startling is the remarkably low share of Bumiputra owners at the rural level where their population shares are the highest.

Considering the ownership of various supplier firms linked to the firms in the industrial estates, the data again reveal under-representation of Malays. For suppliers of parts and components and of repair and maintenance services, their shares are about 10 per cent or less. For suppliers of raw materials and providers of transport and other miscellaneous services, the Malays' shares are somewhat higher, though they come near their shares in the state population in only a few states – notably in Trengganu and Kelantan.

The overall thrust of the analysis of linkages seems to be that the present structure of the Malaysian economy has powerful leakages. These exist at the national level, but also very clearly with respect to the weaker regions of the domestic economy. Here, there are direct leakages to the overseas sector but, more significantly, the internal economic centre of gravity is such that it appears to suck in most of the additional value added from industrialisation towards this industrialised heartland. Another aspect worth noting in this context is the relative lack of integration between the industrial and agricultural sectors, at least at the level of the state economies. This is evidenced by the lack of any correlation between states when ranked by their state per capita GDPs generated by the agricultural sector as against the manufacturing sector. The rank correlation coefficient is -0.39. Mining and quarrying and manufacturing per capita income profiles were similarly unrelated – the rank correlation coefficient here being -0.12. Agricultural and mining profiles were themselves unrelated ($r = 0.22$), while the block of manufacturing, construction, trade and transport, utilities and services were all strongly related to one another. This implies a segmented economic structure where there exist very weak linkages between the agricultural, mining and manufacturing (and allied) sectors. In such a framework, a growth impulse imparted to the manufacturing industry is unlikely to spill over in any significant manner to the agricultural sector. The various findings based on the data drawn from diverse sources in this section corroborate this argument. When there is such structural separation at the sectoral level, industrial policies of spatial dispersal can have, at best, only very limited value as generators of linkages for the local, agricultural sub-economies in which they are embedded by policy choice. The weak, if not dismal, performance of the industrial estates programme in this regard is explicable in these terms. On the whole, it is arguable that it failed to meet any of its stated objectives to any significant extent.

Rural urbanisation: some policy-oriented remarks

The topic is approached from a strategic vantage point. Does the preceding analysis of the context of planned rural urbanisation underwrite the role that the revised spatial (and implicit inter-sectoral) development strategy, i.e. the new people-oriented approach, assigns to it? And even if the answer is affirmative, are the policy instruments assigned to the programme of rural urbanisation sufficient, and sufficiently strong, to deliver the goods? Do these instruments clash in a serious manner with others directed at other development objectives of the Plan? Are adequate resources identified for implementing these policies; and, where this involves private sector investment, do appropriate institutional and market instruments exist for coaxing such investments to flow in the desired magnitude and direction?

These are all essential questions. This final section will restrict itself, however, to a small set of related observations on these themes. The analysis of the domestic linkage effects of industrialisation supported the view that, under the policy of industrial dispersal to industrially underdeveloped and rural regions, very few dynamic linkages were generated which benefited the local, especially rural, populations of such regions. This could be seen as justifying the revision in favour of regrouping over-dispersed industrialisation in higher-order urban centres, in order to make the industrialisation process more efficient.

But it would be fallacious to argue on the basis of the relative failure of the lapsed 'place-prosperity' policy – of which industrial dispersal was a prime component – that the new 'people-prosperity' policy would achieve superior results *with respect to the generation of positive linkages with the poorer regions and with the rural poor*. Indeed, given also the conclusions of the analysis of the linkage effects of migration on the rural sector, the net impact of the revision could well imply a net loss in the performance relative to these objectives. The crucial conclusion to be drawn must be that, so long as the agricultural and the industrial sectors remain as structurally delinked as at present, an exclusively spatial or locational policy of dispersal will not work; but then neither will one of spatial concentration.

This has the immediate implication that strong emphasis must continue to be placed in the short and medium terms upon other policies which orient themselves directly to the target variables, viz. rural poverty incidence, inter-regional disparities, etc., as well as on medium- and long-term policies which create the preconditions for the achievement of these objectives through the linkages which are, at present, too weak. Indeed, these two should be treated as different dimensions of a single, coherent long-term policy.

This introduces some imponderable factors. The nature of this long-term policy, or rather strategy, could vary quite radically, depending upon the assumptions made about the external economic environment. Consider two alternative scenarios. In the rosy world where, as is assumed implicitly with regard to the Fifth Plan targets, economic growth picks up as, hypothetically, world economic demand and prices for Malaysia's primary sector exports return to their previous upward trajectory, the present people-prosperity strategy could transform the agricultural sector in the space of perhaps fifteen to twenty years. Migration would draw off the agricultural population working in structural conditions with low productivity. Labour market scarcities, which were beginning to emerge in several regions of the economy in the recent past, would encourage mechanisation and restructuring, thus raising agricultural productivity further. In such a scenario, at the end of another successful run of national economic growth, there would still remain pockets in agriculture where low absolute or relative productivity would call for explicit subsidisation policies for the residual rural producers. But the per capita incomes of the rural poor would, in the main, have been lifted through absorption into a high-productivity industrial workforce. If the basic premises underlying such a strategy were found plausible, it could legitimately be argued that rural industrialisation of the kind which required rural location would be largely irrelevant, since the necessary linkages would be generated through the structural transformation engineered through inter-sectoral migration. It could be argued, at least with some justification, that this is perhaps the main scenario which underpins the new strategy.

However, there are three major difficulties with this approach. Firstly, the international economy might not recover sufficiently, or soon enough, and then perhaps for not long enough. As such, the policy might not be sufficiently risk averse. Secondly, the required transformation of the economy might take much longer under Malaysian conditions, where the growth linkages are restricted, as well as also concentrated, and this would raise the issue of whether or not, in this long transition, something more should not be done about those at the far end of the queue. Thirdly, even if successful, it might only exacerbate the inter-regional and inter-state disparities in the economy, and this might not be acceptable beyond a point in the federal system.

There is much to be said, therefore, for strengthening the 'place-prosperity' and *in situ* elements in the strategic framework to a very substantial extent. In this frame of reference, the potential role of rural industrialisation would need to be looked at afresh. Such a programme, if successful, could provide insurance for the possibility that the revised 'people-oriented' policy might encounter some of the difficulties listed above, by generating an alternative source for raising the productivity and the labour absorptive capacity of the rural sector. More important, if it were linked to a programme of agricultural development within an appropriate macro-level, but also micro-level institutional framework, it could create the preconditions under which *subsequent* policies of industrial dispersal could succeed in developing local intra-regional as well as local inter-sectoral linkages.

This raises issues concerning the conditions necessary for rural industrialisation to succeed in terms of these objectives, especially in the poorer regions. At this juncture, the role assigned to rural industrialisation within the Fifth Malaysia Plan, as well as in the new underlying strategy, needs to be examined. In the present *ex ante* context, such a consideration is constrained to general and qualified observations, which will also draw in, where appropriate, pointers from the East Asian experiences. These remarks will be directed at the three elements of the programme of rural urbanisation: smallholder agricultural commercialisation, villagisation and village industry.

Certain important choices exist with regard to the development of the smallholder agricultural sector. Thus far, a significant part of the agricultural sector's growth has been generated by the estates, which have highly concentrated spatial patterns. The spread effects of such growth have been relatively weak. Both major governmental interventions in agricultural development – large irrigation schemes for rice, and the FELDA land development schemes – have been extremely expensive options in terms of rural income generation and labour absorption. There is bound to exist a sharp trade-off with smaller-scale, more dispersed schemes of the *in situ* type, which rely on local participation and resources for construction, maintenance and management. It is worth noting that the development cost for settling one family in FELDA schemes has risen to approximately three times the value of fixed assets per worker on average in the manufacturing sector of the country, while the annual returns to the settler are no higher on a per capita basis than those accruing to the industrial worker in the form of wages, even excluding the non-wage component of value added. Similarly, the remarkably high rice subsidies could not only have a high opportunity cost but also raise the supply price of labour artificially, with negative effects for local rural industrial possibilities. Employment could be created more cheaply and through more dynamic processes.

The other aspect worth mentioning is the institutional one. The experience of the successful major East Asian economies strongly suggests that land reform could have a very powerful growth-inducing impact on the rural sector. It would greatly raise the absorptive capacity of agriculture with respect to inputs; at the same time, through incorporating marginalised sections of the rural population into the land-owning structure, it would ease the problems of labour absorption. At present, there is a strong tendency, which will be accelerated by the estatisation policies since the mid-1980s, for increased mechanisation and labour displacement. The objective of encouraging competitiveness through this method of raising productivity could conflict with the objective of widening the base of the rural growth process. Cooperative and group farming solutions could provide a compromise, though their effects could be inegalitarian if not preceded by some type of land reform. Such a reform could also obviate the need for agricultural subsidies in certain sectors, to the extent that these subsidies were designed to support the incomes of poor farmers. Taiwan, with its effective land reform and agricultural development policies oriented towards what was essentially a smallholding peasantry, did without subsidies and, indeed, drew a substantial surplus out of agriculture for industrial development. The Malaysian situation at present is more like the contrasting Korean one as far as the present *policy mix* is concerned. But, structurally, other policies might prove both desirable and feasible.

On the element of villagisation and local infrastructure provision in small rural growth centres, there is a risk of making a mistake born out of optimism about the role of infrastructural development in inducing economic growth in unfavourable economic circumstances. One could accept the argument that current population densities do not allow for the easy provision of services, or provide a concentrated enough source of demand for rural industrial products, and that rural industries, which would usually depend upon the availability of labour, would not find high enough concentrations of population to draw upon. However, it is preferable to proceed with caution, if past experience in Malaysia – as, for instance, with the Village Rehabilitation Scheme – and elsewhere is any guide. The programme is likely to be inordinately expensive and subject to the standard lengthy list of possible reasons for the scheme to go wrong. The experience of settlements illustrates this almost universally. There could also be real trade-offs. An alternative could be to place resources into developing micro-level infrastructure without interfering with the settlement patterns, except in obviously necessary cases. This might be prudent in the initial phase because of uncertainty with regard to the strata of rural or semi-urban settlement, which is likely to become the focal point of local economic growth. The assumption that such focal points can automatically be induced through the prior placement of 'infrastructure' has been falsified almost universally. Furthermore, given the expense involved, it is doubtful if this scheme could be considered a cost-effective replicable prototype. Finally, it is the type of scheme that inherently precludes popular local participation, which any viable strategy of rural development needs.

One important aspect of infrastructure is that it could facilitate the outmigration of local resources – both skilled and unskilled labour, as well as raw materials – as easily as the process of local development. When it is viewed as it should be, as an enabling, but passive factor in promoting local development, the focus of attention shifts to other necessary, but missing factors. Thus, in Taiwan, a spatially dispersed infrastructure generated a wide spatial spread in rural growth partly because of the absence of a strong gravitational pull exerted by an overdeveloped central economic core. The opposite was illustrated in the Korean case, where none of the policies of regional dispersal made any serious impact in the face of pulls exerted by Seoul and Pusan. In Malaysia, infrastructural provision in the absence of successful local development could well lead to a process closer to the Korean case.

What is clear is the need to integrate the three elements of the rural urbanisation policy within a consistent economic rather than bureaucratic framework. This integrated policy then has to be articulated through state or regional policies. Without this, the third element, village industry, is unlikely to be successful. There is a danger of repeating the thinking which was implicit in the policy of dispersing rural industrial estates earlier at a higher level. That, coupled with the township development programme, could be repeated in some respects at the lower level of aggregation of the planned rural growth centres.

Some of the elements of a hypothetical policy framework might be tentatively mentioned. In a poor agricultural region, the process starts with *agricultural* development. The initial steps in rural industry would then be to take advantage of the backward and forward linkages generated by this growth. The same would also apply to other natural resource based growth. One crucial area in this is the agricultural processing industry, which could provide substantial linkages to the local economy. This industry should be organised, wherever possible, on a small-scale basis, since this has the advantage of starting a growth process at a dispersed level based on the internally generated surpluses of agricultural development. In this regard, while the small-scale rice-milling sector has shown dynamism, government policies towards it have been negative on the whole. Fiscal incentives have generally favoured large-scale firms. In rice milling, part of the motivation seems to have been to protect the capacity utilisation of the already functioning large-scale plants under public ownership, even though the small-scale sector was at least as efficient in economic terms (Vokes *et al.*, 1982).

In this process of internalising the linkages of local growth through the small-scale sector, the institutional framework is of great import. Interesting models are provided, for instance, by the Kedah Development Authority (KEDA), and the parallel Muda Agricultural Development Authority (MADA). Both allow for considerable internal diversification, but also vertical integration so as to minimise the leakage of local value added to sources outside the constituency. This is particularly true of KEDA. The danger here is of overcentralisation and lack of participation of the rural poor, whose status could be reduced to that of the working poor. Here, there are possibilities of generating lower-level participative groupings of workers who could provide a collective entrepreneurship for rural enterprises.

MADA's industrial company is mostly owned by its farmers through the agricultural cooperatives, though the degree of farmers' control over decision making might still be rather limited. Yet equity ownership, unlike the KEDA case, gives the farmers some dividends from the profits of the company. Within such a company, there could be further possibilities of effecting an agriculture–industry link, so difficult to establish under the institutional framework of private ownership. Another possibility could be to use farmers' cooperatives and group farms, envisaged as part of the rural urbanisation scheme, as the basic institutional units for the initiation of non-farm activities and rural industrial enterprises. This arrangement would also generate dynamic linkages between agriculture and industry which they could not achieve by themselves.

The next stage is the diversification of the region's industrial sector specifically into those groups of industries which are connected through backward linkages with the extant production pattern of the region. Clearly, there would be limits beyond which such efforts could become inefficient.

To a certain extent, this sequential pattern of development assists in solving the fundamental problem of demand. The development of the agricultural sector is of crucial importance, since in a poor agricultural region the additional demands generated could create further possibilities of industrial self-provisioning with the region. This could be rationalised through local government purchase policies for a wide range of products which could be internally produced. In the Malaysian context, where the share of the government sector is substantial, significant multipliers could be generated in this manner.

The role of rural sector exports, other than those through the FTZ type of connection, is likely to come up against the two gaps, viz. the positive wage and negative skill, which would restrict competitiveness in the traditional labour intensive types of products. In the present situation, the generation of rural exports on any significant scale is likely to remain a difficult proposition.

For the poor agricultural regions in Malaysia, there is no short-cut to industrialisation. Indeed, the danger frequently comes from impatient attempts at short-circuiting the process and grafting on to the under-developed economy of the state a range of relatively advanced industries which generate multiplier effects that the local economy does not have within its economic strength to internalise. There is only slender evidence in the Fifth Malaysia Plan document of any systematic and articulated policy towards rural industry. On the basis of the analysis of this paper, this is an important lacuna, since, in the Malaysian situation, the rural industrial sector could perform a crucial linking function in an inter-sectorally and inter-regionally articulated, balanced process of development.

REFERENCES

Chee, P.L., (1985) 'A Survey of Bumiputra Entrepeneurs in Peninsular Malaysia', in S. Mukhopadhyay and Lim C.P. (eds), *The Rural Non-Farm Sector in Asia*, APDC, Kuala Lumpur.

Malaysia (1983) *The Development of Industrial Estates: An Evaluation and Import Studies*, 2 vols.

Malaysia (1986) *Fifth Malaysia Plan, 1986–1990*, Kuala Lumpur.

Mehmet, O. (1986) *Development in Malaysia*, Croom Helm, London.

MIPS (1984) *Final Reoprt of the Malaysian Industrial Policies Studies Project*, IMG Consultants Pty Ltd, Sydney (restricted circulation).

Saith, A. (1989) *Location, Linkage and Leakage: Malaysian Rural Industrialisation Strategies in National Perspective*, Institute of Social Studies, The Hague.

Shand, R.T. (1985) 'Agricultural Development, Non-Farm Employment and Rural Income Distribution: A Case Study in Kelantan, Malaysia', Paper presented to the 'International Seminar on the Role of Rural Industries for National Development in the Asian Region', KREI/APDC, Seoul.

UNIDO (1985) *Medium and Long Term Industrial Master Plan: Malaysia, 1986–95*, Vol. III, Part 7, (a) *Executive Highlights*, (b) *Analysis of Linkage Effects*, MIDA, Kuala Lumpur.

Vokes, R.W.A., Wells, R.J.G. and Fredericks, L.J. (1982), *Rice Processing in Kedah, Malaysia: An Economic and Technical Survey*, Human Settlements Division, A.I.T., Bangkok.

7

TECHNOLOGY TRANSFER IN THE MALAYSIAN MANUFACTURING SECTOR
Basic issues and future directions

Anuwar Ali

The process of technology transfer has been defined as 'a process in which a country is free to choose autonomously, from among different alternatives of scientific and technological knowledge, those which are best suited to its natural conditions and to its development objectives, its capacity for assimilation and its pattern of living' (Capriles, 1977). The process itself is thus complex, requiring the fulfilment of a number of prerequisites, including the willingness of the licensor to transfer the desired technology, an acceptable price for the technology, and the capacity of the host country to acquire such technology. However, in most developing countries, including Malaysia, experience suggests that technology has not been effectively transferred or acquired in the sense defined above.

This paper has several objectives:

1. To highlight some of the basic issues relating to technology transfer in manufacturing;
2. To review the progress of technology transfer in Malaysia in recent years;
3. To examine the existing administrative framework with respect to technology transfer; and
4. To outline other aspects of technology development in the future.

BASIC ISSUES IN TECHNOLOGY TRANSFER

A number of important issues have been identified in the literature concerning technology transfer to developing countries in recent years (see e.g. Cho, 1988; Contractor, 1981; and UNCTC, 1987), including:

- the limited choice of technologies available in practice owing to the oligopolistic nature of technology supply;
- the imperfect markets for technology transactions;
- the significance of technology pricing as a transfer pricing mechanism by MNCs;

- the weak bargaining position of less developed country (LDC) firms vis-à-vis technology suppliers due to intensifying competition among LDCs;
- the restrictive terms and conditions of technology transfer;
- the lack of adaptive capacity of technology recipients;
- the low absorptive capacity and poor research and development (R&D) of the recipients; and
- the continuing dependence on technology suppliers owing to the rapid pace of technological change.

Limited choice of technologies available

In spite of the increasing pace of technological developments and their commercialisation worldwide, the actual choices open to developing countries as far as usable technologies are concerned may be rather limited in practice. One of the principal reasons for this is that much of the world's useful technology is in the hands of a small number of large and powerful enterprises, mainly in the industrial countries, whose domestic laws confer *proprietary rights* over most forms of technology while imposing obligations and/or restrictions upon those permitted by the owner to make use of such technology. Contractor (1981) reported that 'there were, on average, only five alternative global suppliers of a similar technology that a prospective licensee could have turned to'. This concentration of technology-generating capacity can be related to the fact that major R&D activities are actively promoted mainly by large multinational companies (MNCs); for example, thirty firms accounted for two-thirds of private basic research in the United States.

Given the rapid pace of technological change within the industrial countries, many developing countries are in no position to reduce the technological gap that exists between them and the former, let alone be on par with the industrial countries. To stay competitive, therefore, many firms in developing countries have become increasingly dependent upon technology suppliers in the industrial countries for the supply of technology as embodied in capital equipment and know-how. To a large extent, therefore, the choice of technology is basically determined either by large industrial MNCs or by technology suppliers in the industrial countries.

Imperfect market for technology transactions

Technology transfer into developing countries must also be seen in the context of technology transactions taking place under very imperfect market conditions, which generally favour technology suppliers. Aside from the oligopolistic nature of technology supply, the ability to choose and assimilate imported technology in developing countries like Malaysia has also been hampered by the lack of indigenous technical know-how. Technology buyers from developing countries often lack sufficient knowledge and information about the technology they hope to acquire from their potential suppliers. Unlike mass commodity sellers, technology suppliers generally do not disclose detailed information about their product to potential buyers until all transactions are completed to protect the proprietary value of the product. Technology buyers lacking technical sophistication often have little choice but to agree to purchase the technology they need without sufficient knowledge of its eventual functional value.

Furthermore, technology transfer is often 'packaged' with foreign technical expertise and capital equipment bundled together, which may lead to hidden additional costs, thus making it difficult to evaluate the actual price of the technology. The 'price', as expressed in direct costs, may be only a small proportion of the full cost, as the technology sale is generally accompanied by restrictive conditions that add to the true cost of the transfer.

In view of the above factors, supplier–buyer relations in international technology transactions have been described as a 'bilateral monopoly', where the price tends to be determined through a series of negotiations between the two parties (Cho, 1988). If both parties are equal in their relative bargaining positions (regarding information and availability) in the negotiating process, then the final negotiated price will be closer to the price determined in a competitive market. But if one party is in a stronger bargaining position, the final negotiated price is more likely to deviate from a competitive market price. Thus, where buyers have less than sufficient information and knowledge about the technology, suppliers are in a position to capture a greater share of potential economic rents from the sale of such technology.

Technology pricing as a transfer pricing mechanism

A large part of international technology transfer actually takes place between parent MNCs and their overseas subsidiaries or joint venture partners in developing countries. In such cases, the pricing of the technology transferred may be dictated by transfer pricing considerations to minimise taxation on their corporate income. Thus, in a country like Malaysia, where the withholding tax rate on repatriation of royalty payments due under technical agreements is lower than the corporate profit tax rate, technology may be overpriced to minimise other, especially income, taxation.

Weakening bargaining position of LDC firms

The bargaining position of LDC firms in relation to MNCs and foreign technology suppliers over technology transfer has tended to weaken in recent years owing to intensifying competition among LDCs for foreign investments in general, and 'high-tech' investments in particular. In addition, in 'high-tech' industries, characterised by rapid changes in technology, developing countries often lack the ability to catch up and, as such, are much more vulnerable and dependent upon foreign technology suppliers willing to provide the latest technological innovations.

Restrictive terms and conditions of technology transfer

Technology suppliers are often in an advantageous position to dictate the terms and conditions of technology transfer, basically in order to secure big returns and to protect the competitive position of the suppliers. Such high returns may take the form of profits earned, not only through equity participation but also from sales of intermediate goods, capital equipment, spare parts and technical services, not to mention the possibility of transfer pricing.

In this respect, the price paid to acquire a particular technology may also reflect the lack of technical, financial, legal and commercial expertise essential to obtain information about the technology and the various options which may exist. This disadvantage is particularly prevalent among the smaller firms, which are generally domestically owned and controlled. Their larger counterparts, on the other hand, tend to have greater access, either because of their superior organisational ability or because they are established through joint ventures with foreign MNCs.

Lack of adaptive capabilities

The modification by MNCs of processes and products to suit host country circumstances is dependent on many factors, including the type of technology, the local social and economic environment, and the parent companies' perception of their subsidiaries' or joint venture partners' capacity to operate efficiently and profitably in the long run. Generally, not many foreign-controlled firms appear willing to adapt their products to suit local conditions (Frank, 1980).

Product adaptation is likely to occur among manufacturers of import-substitution goods, especially consumer goods. But for products which face international rather than country-specific demands, firms may prefer to train service personnel, rather than simplify the products, to maintain certain minimum standards and quality. Firms are also reluctant to develop a new product or modify an existing one if the market, especially in a developing country, is not large enough to recover the costs involved.

Low absorptive capacity and R&D

Even if MNCs are willing to accommodate domestic firms' desires for technology transfer, the ability of the latter to acquire and adapt new technology also depends on the host country's capacity to absorb new information, as defined by the skills of its people and its policies towards technology transfer as well as information generation and dissemination in general. It is in these areas that developing countries are yet to develop their full potential.

One major constraint in the process of technology adaptation and development in developing countries is related to the insistence of technology licensors on the use of their usual machinery suppliers, usually from their own countries. Hence, they generally contract foreign engineering designers. This also reflects the generally weak industrial base of developing countries, principally due to their low technological absorptive capacity and poor R&D activities. Even domestic manufacturers are often reluctant to try domestic technologies even if they are available. To them, this would be a much more risky proposition compared with the use of tested foreign technologies.

The low absorptive capacity mentioned above is further complicated by evidence that most MNC subsidiaries do not undertake R&D because such activities are generally handled by the parent companies. Those companies which do undertake R&D tend to confine such activities to simple experimental development and application research (Sim, 1978; Rahim Bidin, 1983).

TRENDS IN INTERNATIONAL TECHNOLOGY TRANSFER

In principle, the transfer of technology can manifest itself in many ways, the more important ones being:

- exchange of information and personnel through technical cooperation programmes;
- direct employment of foreign experts;
- imports of machinery and equipment and related literature;
- contractual purchase of a given technology or know-how through licences and agreements for the right of access to or use of particular technologies protected by trademarks, patents, licences, etc.
- internalised technology transfer from parent companies to subsidiaries overseas through direct foreign investment; and
- books, journals and other forms of published information, either in the public domain (e.g. libraries) or through private information services.

In their quest for technology, either to establish new industries or to improve existing production techniques, developing countries have resorted to most of the above methods, either singly or in combination. However, there are virtually no systematic data on most of these modes or forms of technology transfer, not only in Malaysia, but also in most other developing countries. The most commonly available data usually relate only to technology transfer through formal contractual agreements between private enterprises on the one hand, and technical aid programmes between governments.

Despite the absence of comprehensive data, it is generally believed that the flow of direct foreign investments worldwide has significant implications for the extent and nature of technology transfer. In particular, large MNCs are increasingly becoming the most significant source of technology. From the developing countries' point of view, foreign investments from industrial countries are expected to be accompanied by technology transfers through the flow of information, the use of patents and trademarks, and the use of production processes and engineering designs, apart from the employment of foreign personnel and the import of machinery and plant equipment. However, much of such technology transfer takes place through internalised modes, and does not get recorded in any official statistics, although there is increasing use of formal contractual agreements, even between MNCs and their subsidiaries.

INTERNATIONAL TECHNOLOGY TRANSFER TO MALAYSIA

Technology transfers to Malaysia, as measured by the number of formal contractual agreements concluded, have increased rapidly in recent years. As shown in Table 7.1, the Ministry of Trade and Industry approved a total of 1,432 agreements during the 1970–87 period, with the number increasing since 1980. While the number of agreements averaged fewer than sixty a year before 1980, the average number nearly doubled after 1980. This reflects the increasing pace and diversity of industrialisation, particularly marked since the mid-1970s.

The fact that 52.6 per cent of all agreements approved during the period were in the form of technical assistance and know-how agreements, while another 22.2 per cent were in the form of management services and joint-venture agreements, reflects the pattern of technology transfer to the Malaysian manufacturing sector. It also indicates the shift from the 'packaged' to the 'unpackaged' type of foreign capital investments in relation to the technology transfer process.

Table 7.2 shows that Japan accounted for a substantial proportion (32.2 per cent) of all agreements signed between 1975 and 1987. The other countries that have been important in this context are the United Kingdom and the United States, accounting for 13.7 per cent and 10.6 per cent, respectively. The increase in the number of agreements signed with Japanese technology suppliers has been particularly marked since 1980, perhaps partly due to the government's Look East policy as well as the increasing international role of Japan as an industrial technology exporter.

The importance of Japan as a technology supplier to domestic industries becomes even more evident if one examines figures on imports of capital equipment or machinery, which constitute one element of technology transfer. Since the mid-1970s, for example, 34–40 per cent of Malaysia's machinery needs originated from Japan. Only the United States, among the other industrial countries, came close to Japan in this respect. Even then, its share was well below that of Japan's, i.e. an average of 26 per cent during the same

Table 7.1 Types of technology transfer agreements, 1970–87

Type of agreements	1970	1971	1972	1973	1974	1975	1976	1977	1978	1979	1980	1981	1982	1983	1984	1985	1986	1987	Total	%
Technical assistance and know how	9	15	33	34	28	27	30	21	48	54	57	64	48	61	71	51	50	53	754	52.6
Management	–	1	13	5	3	12	7	7	11	13	13	6	10	13	10	6	10	5	145	10.1
Joint venture	–	2	7	6	7	6	6	4	7	8	14	22	14	14	17	9	19	11	173	12.1
Service	4	2	9	5	5	12	5	1	12	3	6	7	2	7	2	1	1	1	85	5.9
Trade-marks/patents	3	2	4	3	6	1	5	–	4	4	4	8	8	7	1	19	33	30	142	9.9
Turnkey and engineering	–	–	–	–	–	–	–	–	–	–	5	5	4	4	6	–	1	–	25	1.7
Others[a]	–	–	–	–	–	–	–	–	–	–	15	19	8	25	12	10	9	10	108	7.5
Total	16	22	66	53	49	58	53	33	82	82	114	131	94	131	119	96	123	110	1,432	100.0

Note:
[a] Others include supply and purchase, sales, marketing and distribution.
Source: Unpublished data, Ministry of Trade and Industry.

Table 7.2 Technology transfer agreements by country of origin, 1975–87

Countries	1975	1976	1977	1978	1979	1980	1981	1982	1983	1984	1985	1986	1987	Total	%
Japan	22	21	7	32	21	32	35	33	46	39	33	38	37	396	32.2
United Kingdom	10	6	4	13	11	20	17	6	19	11	14	21	17	169	13.7
USA	6	4	1	9	8	11	14	10	18	12	13	12	12	130	10.6
India	3	5	8	7	5	5	4	4	4	2	6	1	–	54	4.4
West Germany	–	1	4	6	11	9	11	10	2	2	3	2	5	66	5.4
Australia	3	2	1	–	4	10	5	6	2	5	3	9	3	53	4.3
Hong Kong	1	–	3	3	2	9	2	3	2	7	4	7	7	50	4.1
Singapore	3	2	2	1	2	4	7	5	3	8	2	3	4	46	3.7
France	2	4	–	–	2	–	7	–	4	1	–	4	3	27	2.2
Italy	1	1	–	1	1	2	–	–	–	–	2	1	1	10	0.8
Panama	–	–	3	–	1	1	–	1	2	2	–	5	1	12	1.0
Switzerland	–	–	–	2	1	–	3	1	1	2	1	1	1	14	1.1
Norway	–	–	–	–	1	1	–	2	2	2	5	–	2	14	1.1
South Korea	–	1	–	1	–	–	–	2	4	6	1	3	1	19	1.5
Others	7	6	–	7	17	9	26	12	24	22	9	16	16	171	13.9
Total	58	53	33	82	87	113	131	95	131	119	96	123	110	1,231	100.0

Source: Unpublished data, Ministry of Trade and Industry.

Table 7.3 Technology transfer agreements, by industry groups, 1975–87

Industrial group	1975	1976	1977	1978	1979	1980	1981	1982	1983	1984	1985	1986	1987	Total	%
Electronic and electrical	17	9	5	21	15	19	16	19	15	21	20	12	29	218	17.7
Fabricated metal	8	3	5	7	16	6	14	7	12	3	9	22	21	133	10.8
Chemical	3	–	4	19	8	11	21	5	15	17	16	15	18	152	12.3
Transport equipment	5	4	–	5	7	10	11	11	22	17	20	15	4	131	10.6
Food	4	7	2	2	8	14	15	4	21	6	10	8	8	109	8.9
Textiles	6	7	2	4	–	8	5	2	5	6	1	7	2	55	4.5
Basic metal	–	5	3	3	5	7	10	13	5	5	1	1	2	60	4.9
Wood and wood products	4	1	6	5	4	–	–	4	1	6	–	4	1	36	2.9
Pulp, paper, printing and publishing	–	–	–	–	–	–	–	–	–	–	3	4	1	8	8.6
Rubber and rubber products	6	–	1	2	5	8	14	2	7	5	4	13	8	75	6.1
Non-metallic mineral products	1	6	1	1	7	5	4	16	9	17	7	7	12	93	7.6
Hotel and tourist complex	–	5	1	–	2	4	2	4	8	7	4	4	1	42	3.4
Plastic	1	–	2	–	3	5	6	1	2	7	–	4	–	31	2.5
Others	3	6	1	13	7	17	13	6	9	2	1	7	3	88	7.1
Total	58	53	33	82	87	114	131	94	131	119	96	123	118	1,231	100.0

Source: Unpublished data, Ministry of Trade and Industry.

period. Other important suppliers have been West Germany and the United Kingdom.

Table 7.3 shows that most of the agreements approved during the 1975–87 period were in the electronics and electrical industries (17.7 per cent), fabricated metal industries (10.8 per cent), chemical industries (12.3 per cent) and transport equipment (10.6 per cent). These three industries accounted for more than 50 per cent of all agreements signed, reflecting the strong need for technology transfers to these relatively technology-intensive industries.

The increasing number of technology transfer contracts and agreements recorded in recent years has also been reflected in significantly greater outflows of royalty payments from the country. Unfortunately, there is no single reliable source of data on royalty payments for technology transfers. An attempt has been made to derive estimates of such outflows from three different sources, each of which suggested different conflicting trends (see Anuwar Ali and Wong Poh Kam, 1988).

Data derived from the Bank Negara Exchange Control Department lumped together rent payments with royalty payments, covering only transactions above M$10,000. The Inland Revenue Department, on the other hand, lumped interest and royalty payments together. Finally, the Ministry of Trade and Industry started estimating royalty payments, based on technical agreements approved, only in the last few years.

Tables 7.4, 7.5 and 7.6 summarise the relevant data derived from the three sources. Bank Negara estimates suggest a total outflow of about M$241 million in 1987 (including rents), against about M$73.1 million from the IRD (excluding rent, but including interest payments). The MTI estimate of M$275 million royalty payments for 1985 is the highest, but this figure pertains to total expected royalties for the next five years, not actual royalty outflows for the year.

Such conflicting data and the crude aggregative nature of the estimates reflect the current state of relative ignorance about the cost of technology

Table 7.4 Receipts and payments of rent and royalties, 1980–8

Year	Receipts M$'000	Payments M$'000	Net balance M$'000
1980	47,013	146,521	−99,508
1981	13,884	171,207	−157,323
1982	33,975	212,944	−178,969
1983	10,561	192,676	−182,115
1984	20,771	203,857	−183,086
1985	24,764	201,067	−176,303
1986	20,010	204,366	−184,356
1987	21,427	240,552	−219,125
1988 (1 Qtr)	4,053	60,088	−56,035

Source: Bank Negara Malaysia estimates.

Table 7.5 Interest and royalty payment outflows from Malaysia, 1982–7

	M$m
1982	43.54
1983	47.19
1984	74.75
1985	48.31
1986	61.60
1987	73.11

Source: Unpublished data, Inland Revenue Department.

Table 7.6 Estimated total royalties for approved technology transfer agreements by year, 1985–7

Year	Total net sales M$m	Total royalty payments M$m	% of net sales
1985	9,273.2	275.4	2.75
1986	23,608.3	203.0	0.85
1987	8,118.4	177.4	2.20

Source: Unpublished data, Ministry of Trade and Industry, Technology Transfer Unit.

transfer. A better system for measuring and monitoring technology transfer payments is definitely needed to provide a sound basis for policy analysis.

Policy implications for manpower training and R&D

From the above observations concerning the mechanisms of technology transfer, especially through MNCs, two policy implications emerge that should be given immediate attention by policy makers.

Manpower training

At the present stage of Malaysia's industrial development, manpower training must be reviewed as an integral part of the technology transfer process. Most Malaysian-based subsidiaries of MNCs (as well as Malaysian companies purchasing technologies through licensing agreements) are still largely at the stage of learning to absorb transferred process technology, rather than at a stage of improvement and innovation. Consequently, an integral programme of manpower training is critically needed to enable Malaysian engineers and skilled labour to assimilate the skills in order to be able fully to exploit the transferred technology.

In this regard, it would be most appropriate to incorporate manpower training provision as a criterion for evaluating and approving direct foreign investments in the future. For domestic market-oriented investments, and more particularly for projects involving significant public investment, firms should commit themselves to a particular level of ongoing manpower training commensurate with the requirements to operate and manage the transferred technology fully. This training can be in the form of formal training programmes at overseas plants or subsidiaries, in-house training, or setting up a training institute that can offer training for both employees of the firms as well as other workers. This concept of manpower training as an 'offset investment', if implemented with carefully designed guidelines, will help further to improve the rate of manpower skill development in the country.

R&D

Despite the significant amount of new technology that is continuously being introduced by various MNCs operating in the country, there has been very little indigenous effort by local R&D institutions (universities and the various public sector R&D centres) to work with these MNCs further to accelerate the pace of technology assimilation and its diffusion beyond the MNCs. In view of the global corporate policies of many of these MNCs to limit their R&D spending in countries like Malaysia, it is up to the local institutions to take greater initiatives to offer their services to the MNCs, receiving in return, the benefits of access to new technologies, exposure to practical problems and needs of the marketplace, and opportunities to learn from the skills and knowledge of those in the field. In this regard, new strategies should be adopted to encourage and promote greater university and R&D institution linkages with the MNCs in the immediate future. Some obvious possibilities include:

(a) greater linkages between Universiti Sains Malaysia and the electronics-based MNCs in the Northwest region of Peninsular Malaysia. The Malaysian Institute of Microelectronic Systems (MIMOS) should also seriously consider expanding its R & D activities in this region, rather than concentrating on the Kelang Valley area alone;
(b) greater linkages between the palm-oil-processing and petrochemical-based MNCs and Universiti Teknologi Malaysia in the southern region.

POLICY FRAMEWORK AND APPROVAL MECHANISM FOR ROYALTY PAYMENTS

Overview of existing framework

The present institutional and policy framework for regulating technology transfer from other countries has evolved over the years. Prior to 1968, manufacturing companies had only to submit any technology transfer agreements to Bank Negara under the Foreign Exchange Control Act in support of any royalty or technical fee remittances overseas. Since Bank Negara was then mainly concerned with the amount of remittances, agreements were not subjected to screening.

The Investment Incentives Act of 1968 was basically designed to attract foreign investment by providing total or partial tax relief to companies involved in new manufacturing projects or expanding into new products. Companies granted these incentives were subjected to certain conditions, one of which required them to submit all agreements signed with foreign companies for government approval. Following the implementation of the Industrial Coordination Act of 1975, the Technology Transfer Unit (TTU) was established within the Ministry of Trade and Industry for the specific purpose of screening all types of agreements. Under the ICA, all manufacturing firms requiring licence registration are also required to have any agreement signed with any foreign companies screened by the Technology Transfer Unit.

Technology Transfer Unit (TTU)

Functioning principally as a screening unit for agreements signed between Malaysian and foreign companies, the TTU has four main objectives:

1. to ensure that the agreement will not be prejudicial to the national interest;
2. to ensure that the agreement will not impose unfair and unjustifiable restrictions or handicaps on the Malaysian party;
3. to ensure that the payment of fees, wherever applicable, will be commensurate with the level of technology to be transferred and will not have any adverse effect on Malaysia's balance of payments;
4. to ensure meaningful transfer of technology.

Policy guidelines on technology transfer

The TTU was established to function under a broad set of policy guidelines concerning the provisions of any agreement on technology transfer deemed acceptable by the Malaysian government. The guidelines have been revised on various occasions to reflect the changing needs of the industrial sector.

Prior to the establishment of the TTU, domestic companies under licence generally had to bear higher direct costs for technology as demanded by their technology suppliers. The mode of calculating technical assistance and royalty fees also tended to favour the technology suppliers. Since then, the TTU has insisted that all technical fees or royalty payments should be based on net sales rather than gross sales; this has been defined as gross sales less sales discounts or returns, transport costs, insurance, duties, taxes and any other charges. A rate of 1–5 per cent of net sales is normally considered acceptable. The practice of itemisation of services under separate agreements and capitalisation of know-how fees and royalties is, however, not encouraged.

If no technical assistance fees are involved, domestic industries may have to pay substantial emoluments to acquire production engineers or management personnel from overseas. However, the TTU has issued a set of guidelines relating to such payments to minimise the production costs of domestic industries. For agreements of indefinite periods, the Unit insists that the duration of agreements should be adequate for full absorption of the technology. The life of any patent relating to technology is also taken into consideration. The period should be limited to no more than five years. Any extension of the five-year period should be made with the approval of the Ministry, which will insist on conditions and grounds, such as upgrading the technology transferred.

Even if we can assume that the direct costs of technology transfer are not excessive, domestic manufacturers might still be disadvantaged substantially if restrictive conditions are imposed in agreements signed with foreign technology suppliers. These might include restrictions on export outlets, the level of technology transferred and domestic R&D activities.

The MTI has, however, tried to eliminate such restrictions to allow domestic manufacturers more room to expand their operations. For instance, if the technology suppliers insist on export restrictions, the Ministry will demand that consent for sales outside the restricted territories should not be unreasonably withheld. At the very least, the Ministry requires the technology suppliers to allow their domestic licensees to export to other ASEAN countries.

A few technology suppliers insist on fixing the price of the licensed product, while others insist that Malaysian licensees purchase all material inputs and components at prices fixed by the supplier. The first restriction appears to be more common; such tie-in purchases strengthen the position of the technology supplier (in many cases, a multinational company), and thus enable it to maximise its gains by selling over-priced components, intermediate inputs, capital equipment and spare parts. Furthermore, the obligation to purchase key inputs from the technology supplier enables the supplier to monitor the activities of the Malaysian licensee, including constant checks on the production figures of the domestic licensee for the purpose of determining technical or royalty fees.

To avoid such situations, the TTU has laid down a number of guidelines for the purchase of components or intermediate inputs, including:

- the domestic licensee should determine alternative sources of supply as far as possible;
- a clause binding the domestic licensee to purchase all imported components and supplies through the technology supplier should be avoided, unless no suitable alternative source is available;

- if a provision is included such that components and imported supplies will be obtained through the technology supplier, the domestic licensee should seek to include the following stipulations: (i) prices to be based on internationally competitive prices, with the manner of determining such prices described; and (ii) the most favoured licensee clause will apply to pricing.

Even though the technology to be imported or developed can be identified and chosen, the deficiencies of skilled labour, including R&D personnel, may still prevent its efficient implementation. The scarcity of skilled industrial labour has often been a major constraint on the transfer of technology to Malaysia. It is therefore a policy of the government that adequate training be provided at the technology supplier's plant facilities as well as at the local plant.

Existing policy on remuneration for technology transfer

The cost of technology transfer to domestic industries is to a large extent influenced by the bargaining strength of the foreign technology supplier, the Malaysian company or subsidiary or joint venture partner, as well as by the Ministry of Trade and Industry. Each of these parties has its own view of the value of technology and its own preferences as to how it should be transferred.

It is in this context that the MTI – while sharing the Malaysian company's desire to acquire technology at low cost – has to make its calculations based on long-term national interests rather than returns to the firm alone. Such considerations include the social costs and benefits of each type of technology, the linkages with other industries, the use of domestic resources, the direct costs of technology (e.g. royalties) as well as hidden costs, such as possible overpricing by the technology supplier of inputs to the local party. There are two basic methods for remunerating the transfer of technology agreed to by the Ministry: lump-sum payments and running royalty payments.

Lump-sum payment

This type of payment is generally permitted in selected cases in which the technology can be fully and completely transferred and absorbed by the licensee. This normally involves payments for less sophisticated technology or production techniques which do not need any continuous flow of technical assistance from the licensor.

Lump-sum payments are generally disliked by technology-importing countries as they appear to be unattractive to the local licensees because of the extra sum involved, apart from the substantial investments needed for plant, machinery and working capital, especially in the initial stages. Furthermore, payments have to be made before the licensees are really sure of their projects being successful.

When permitted by the Ministry, these payments are made in instalments. Initial lump-sum payments in addition to royalties are discouraged. If such payments are requested, they should be only for the recovery of actual expenses incurred by the licensor for preliminary services provided to the licensee.

Running royalty payments

The Ministry prefers that royalty payments are linked to production performance or sales receipts, whereby the computation is generally calculated as a percentage of 'net sale' or ex-factory price. The rate is usually fixed at 1–5 per cent of 'net sales'. The rate usually approved by the Ministry is 2% of net sales if the technology transferred is not highly sophisticated.

The Ministry has adopted a number of criteria in evaluating the amount of fees to be paid by the Malaysian licensee. For less sophisticated technology and assembly operations, a royalty fee *not exceeding 2 per cent of net sales* is usually permitted. (For motor vehicle assembly, where assembly operations are basically involved, royalty payments are discouraged.)

However, a certain amount of flexibility has been introduced in the Ministry's evaluation of royalties exceeding the general guideline of 2 per cent of net sales. Such flexibility would occur in the following cases:

- highly sophisticated technology, e.g. wafer fabrication;
- projects involving high 'local content', e.g. if more than 50 per cent;
- export-oriented industries;
- heavy industries; and
- priority industries, e.g. automotive component parts.

The above guidelines are rather broad in that, for example, what constitutes a 'heavy industry' is not spelt out. It is therefore not possible to get automatic approval for applications requesting royalty rates above 2 per cent of net sales, and case by case assessment is carried out in practice.

In addition to the above, the TTU also appears to take into consideration two other factors as internal working guidelines in its evaluation of royalty rates.

Equity consideration. When the foreign licensor holds a majority share in the licensee company, the rate allowed may be lower than when the licensor does not hold any equity at all or is a minority equity holder, on the grounds that in the latter case it does not have any other way to get a return from its investment in technology development.

Profit consideration. The TTU also uses a general indicator stipulating that the total amount incurred by the licensee for such payments should not exceed 25 per cent of gross profits or 50 per cent of net profits of the company. This criterion is used as an additional check to ensure that payments for technology transfer by a domestic firm are within reasonable bounds.

An examination of records of TTU approvals in recent years indicates that the TTU has, in fact, been fairly flexible in approving applications with royalty rates exceeding 2 per cent of net sales. Of the 251 agreements with royalty payments approved during the 1985–7 period, only 89 (or 35.5 per cent) had royalty rates less than 2 per cent. Another 86 (or 34.2 per cent) were approved with 2–3 per cent, of royalty rates, while the rest (30 per cent) were approved at a royalty rate of 3 per cent and more. Overall, about 10 per cent of the approved agreements had royalty rates of 5 per cent or higher. It is also of interest to note that:

- the industries with the highest proportion of approved agreements above the 2 per cent level included food, beverages and tobacco, chemicals, rubber products, machinery, electrical machinery and appliances, and transport equipment.
- in the rubber products sub-sector, more than 80 per cent of the agreements submitted during the 1985–7 period were approved with more than 2 per cent royalty payments, while in the electrical goods sector, 5 out of 44 cases were given royalty rates exceeding 5 per cent.

To a large degree, these observations indicate the extent to which the Ministry of Trade and Industry has been flexible, not only in attracting investments into priority industries, but also in accommodating the increasingly technological needs of these industries in the form of new machinery, equipment and processes, as well as management expertise and marketing know-how. One example of such industries is the resource-based rubber products sub-sector, which attracted substantial interest among foreign investors in 1987–8.

NEED FOR A NEW DIRECTION FOR TECHNOLOGY DEVELOPMENT

In the medium and long term, a more systematic and comprehensive approach to the issue of technology transfer is clearly needed. Despite the many issues and constraints discussed above, it is clear that if Malaysia is to achieve the ambitious targets of its Industrial Master Plan (IMP), both domestic manufacturers and their foreign counterparts have to be encouraged to adopt a more aggressive approach towards raising the technological level of their production. Indeed, many of the issues identified have already been noted in the IMP, albeit in rather general terms. Several broad policy recommendations have been put forward, but there appears to be very little that deals specifically with the issue of increasing the effectiveness of technology transfer by multinational companies.

In this respect, the role of the Ministry of Science, Technology and Environment in promoting technology transfer needs to be taken into consideration in addition to that of the Ministry of Trade and Industry. The October 1987 decision by the Coordinating Council for Industrial Technology Transfer to set up a Committee to Formulate a Plan of Action for Industrial Technology Development in support of IMP implementation is a step in the right direction. As a result of this initiative, a number of studies are currently being undertaken with the following objectives:

- to assess the state of the art of industrial technologies in the country;
- to assess the effectiveness of current programmes designed to promote innovation in industrial technology;
- to identify the constraints and problems hindering domestic industrial technology development;
- to identify the existing level of technology within particular industrial sectors as well as the key technologies crucial to the development of relevant sectors, and to assess their respective strategic importance;
- to formulate selective sectoral technology plans in line with the priority product groups identified for each sector by the IMP;
- to formulate technology enhancement programmes for the various product groups;
- to establish concrete technology development strategies to promote systematic technological development; and
- to formulate pragmatic policy instruments necessary to ensure achievement of the technology development strategy.

CONCLUDING REMARKS

A resilient industrial structure with a strengthened technological base can contribute to sustained long-term industrial growth. Equally importantly, this structure must be flexible enough to respond to changing opportunities generated by either domestic or international demand. The bases for the comparative advantage that Malaysia has had in the past are now changing. Two main factors have influenced this change: changes in international exchange rates, particularly yen appreciation, and the emergence of new technologies in the industrial countries.

The yen appreciation has affected the industrial competitiveness of Japan's traditional exports, culminating in policy adjustments favouring high-technology or knowledge-intensive industries. This, in turn, has affected the position of Asian NICs in terms of heavy industrial goods exports, and that of ASEAN and other countries in terms of consumer goods exports.

The emergence of new technologies in the industrial countries and the consequences of the oil price increases in the 1970s are still making a significant impact on the global industrial environment. These are to be found in areas such as micro-electronics, communications, robotics, bio-technology, laser technology and new materials technology. The wide application and dissemination of these new technologies in the advanced industrial countries have had a profound impact on the basic structure of industrial production in terms of production costs, productivity and industrial relocation, thereby changing the international pattern of comparative advantage. Furthermore, technology transfer is often 'packaged', with foreign technical expertise and capital equipment bundled together, which may lead to hidden costs, thus making it more difficult to evaluate the price of each component of the technology.

This suggests that Malaysia ought to prepare itself better for the necessary structural adjustments envisaged by the IMP. Policies towards this end must include comprehensive rationalisation programmes for declining industries as well as modernisation programmes for existing industries, including small-scale industries. All this requires expansion of the country's technological capability.

A major bottleneck in industrial expansion is the relatively weak scientific and technological infrastructure in the manufacturing industries. This arises partly because of Malaysia's relatively recent efforts to promote export-oriented industrialisation due to its historical reliance on traditional export commodities. This situation has hindered not only the rapid expansion of the country's industrial base, but also the country's technological capability.

As indicated earlier, Malaysia should therefore develop a coherent and comprehensive plan designed to upgrade domestic industrial technology by increasing the country's ability to acquire and adapt imported technology as well as its capacity to innovate. This means that an array of policy instruments and a clearly identified institutional framework must be established. Furthermore, it is also possible to enhance the functions of existing research institutions, including the Standards and Industrial Research Institute of Malaysia (SIRIM), the Malaysian Institute of Microelectronic Systems (MIMOS) and other related agencies.

In pursuit of developing a technological base as well as upgrading levels of science and technology in the future, two priorities should be followed:

1 expanding R&D activities, especially applied and developmental research, in areas in which the country has a comparative advantage; and
2 expanding and strengthening human resource development to increase the availability of the high-level manpower required for work in all branches of science and technology.

For a developing country like Malaysia, the government must play an increasingly important role in industrial R&D, in terms of both policy direction and direct research involvement. This is because the results of R&D activities have some attributes of a pure public good. Without government encouragement and financial support, the amount of R&D activity in society would become less than optimal, since social benefits would be greater than private benefits over time.

Secondly, doing research is an extremely risky enterprise, and at this stage Malaysian society has not developed an adequate mechanism to bear part of the inventor's costs and risks. This also means that the government's role becomes crucial.

Lastly, technological development requires substantial infrastructural support of various kinds, including education and training, technical extension services, development of public-private sector linkages, and a legal framework (i.e. patent laws) to enforce property rights to sustain and enhance such technological innovation.

REFERENCES

Anuwar Ali and Wong Poh Kam (1988) *Assessment Study on Transnational Corporations in Malaysia*, UNCTC/UNDP – Malaysia Project, Kuala Lumpur.

Capriles, R.S. (1977) 'Technology Transfer and the Industrialists in Latin America', *Impact of Science on Society*, 27, 3.

Cho, K.R. (1988) 'Issues of Compensation in International Technology Licensing', *Mir*, 28.

Contractor, F. (1981) *International Technology Licensing*, Heath and Co., Lexington, Mass.

Frank, I. (1980) *Foreign Enterprise in Developing Countries*, Johns Hopkins University Press, Baltimore, Md.

Rahim Bidin (1983) 'The Situation and Experiences Relating to Technology Transfer Issues in Malaysia', paper presented at the National Seminar on Technology Transfer Policy and Planning, 12–14 December, Kuala Lumpur.

Sim Ah Ba (1978) *Decentralization and Performance: A Comparative Study of Malaysian Subsidiaries of Different National Origins*, Monograph Series of Faculty of Economics and Administration, University of Malaya, Kuala Lumpur.

UNCTC (1987) *Transnational Corporations and Technology Transfer: Effects and Policy Issues*, United Nations Center for Transnational Corporations, New York.

8

ELECTRONICS AND INDUSTRIALISATION
Approaching the 21st century
David O'Connor

The Malaysian economy is being rapidly transformed from one overwhelmingly dependent on primary commodity exports to one with a large and increasingly diversified industrial base. The process of industrial development has accelerated in recent years, with external factors like the 1985 Plaza Accord having had a major impact. Yet, other countries have faced similar external conditions but few have benefited to the same extent as Malaysia. Thus, one must look in part to Malaysia's favourable domestic environment to explain its strong economic performance. Among the more important elements have been political and macro-economic stability, a relatively open trade and investment regime, and competitive labour and land costs. High growth places strains of its own on the economy, which some countries cope with better than others. For example, labour and land costs have risen with rapidly growing demand. While there is reason to expect, given the resilience the economy has exhibited to date, that high growth can be sustained for some time, there are still formidable challenges to be faced.

By most indicators, the performance of the Malaysian economy, in particular the manufacturing sector, has been impressive over the last two decades. From 1970 to 1987, the share of manufactures in total merchandise exports rose from roughly 20 per cent to 45 per cent (Bank Negara Malaysia, 1988), where it remained in 1990 (World Bank, 1992). As a share of gross domestic product (GDP), manufacturing value added (MVA) increased from only 12.2 per cent in 1970 to 24.4 per cent in 1988 and the share has continued to grow since. As of 1988 the manufacturing sector employed over 1 million people, or roughly 17 per cent of the labour force; by 1990 that share had risen to almost 20 per cent.

As impressive as the performance has been thus far, it may not be easy to sustain through the 1990s, for several reasons. First, the rapid growth of the last two decades has depended heavily on foreign direct investment in light (labour-intensive) manufacturing. Labour costs have risen steeply over the last decade, making Malaysia less competitive than some of its neighbours in labour-intensive industries. Moreover, given the central role of foreign investment in the manufacturing sector, there are lingering doubts about whether or not domestic capital is capable of substituting for foreign capital over the long run as the driving force of industrial capital accumulation. Furthermore, efforts by the government to diversify the country's industrial base away from light industry have been fraught with difficulties. For instance, the drive into heavy industries has not only proved very costly, but also failed to reduce significantly the country's reliance on foreign corporations to supply critical technological, managerial and other inputs.

When the government first embarked upon a strategy of export-oriented industrialisation in the early 1970s, a primary objective was to reduce the economy's vulnerability to swings in world commodity prices. Ironically, the direction industrialisation took in the first decade and a half left the country hardly less vulnerable to volatile world markets. For, a single industry – electronics – dominated industrial sector growth – and especially growth in manufactured exports – throughout this period. Moreover, within that industry the Malaysian economy came to be specialised in a very narrow subset of activities, namely the assembly (and later testing) of semiconductor devices. These critical components of virtually all electronic equipment, from calculators to communications systems, have been one of the most dynamic growth areas in the global electronics industry over the last few decades. They have also been one of the most highly cyclical markets, alternating every few years between feast and famine. When world semiconductor markets were down, predictably the Malaysian electronics industry would slump, and this in turn would have ripple effects throughout the economy.

Also, by the late 1970s, the semiconductor industry was beginning to apply its products to its own production lines. In short, microprocessors (the powerful logic chips which make up the 'brains' of any microcomputer) were helping firms to automate the assembly of their products. What had historically been a very labour-intensive activity was no longer so. Some observers extrapolated automation trends and predicted that before long the labour content of an assembled chip would be so small that there would be no cost advantage to performing the assembly in a low-wage country like Malaysia. Then, by this logic, the multinational corporations would close up shop and move back to their home bases in the industrialised countries. Fearful of that prospect, policy makers asked what would be left behind if the companies withdrew. In the decade that the multinationals had been enjoying generous tax holidays and other government incentives, had they been transferring technology which would enable an indigenous electronics industry to survive in their absence? Many suspected the answer was 'no'.

Thus began a critical reappraisal of the direction export-oriented industrialisation had taken to date. By this time, however, there was already too much history behind the development of the electronics industry simply to write it off, however far short of expectations it may have fallen. Between 1973 and 1985, gross output in the electronics industry rose at an annual rate of 38 per cent and employment at 16 per cent. By 1985, gross electronics and electrical industry exports amounted to M$6 billion, or 50 per cent of all manufactured exports. (In 1990, 53 per cent of all OECD manufactured imports from Malaysia consisted of electronics and electrical machinery; World Bank, 1992.) The value added in this industry constituted 15 per cent of manufacturing value added in 1985. Electronics employment stood at 81,600, or roughly 17 per cent of manufacturing employment, just prior to the industry slump of 1985. Semiconductor operation accounted for 72 per cent of the electronics industry's output and employment and an even higher share of electronics exports.

The skewed structure of Malaysia's electronics industry can be seen from the figures in Table 8.1, which show the 1982 shares of industrial electronics, consumer electronics and electronic components in total electronics industry output for Malaysia as well as a number of other Asian countries.

Table 8.1 Output shares of major sectors of the electronics industry, 1982 (%)

Sector	Malaysia	Singapore	Korea	Japan
Industrial	5.7	14.8	16.0	35.9
Consumer	8.7	33.8	38.6	32.2
Components	85.6	51.6	45.4	31.9
Total output (US$bn)	1.78	2.48	4.0	43.7

Source: MIDA/UNIDO (1985).

Policy makers found themselves caught on the horns of a dilemma. They wanted to reduce the country's dependence on the semiconductor industry, while at the same time coaxing the participants in that industry to 'do more' in Malaysia – i.e. to introduce more technology-intensive operations and build up various supplier and supporting industries. Many were concerned that, should they exert too much pressure on the foreign semiconductor firms, they might end up killing the goose that lays the golden egg. Still, something needed to be done.

THE INDUSTRIAL MASTER PLAN: THE ELECTRONICS SECTOR STRATEGY AND RECENT PERFORMANCE

This dilemma had not been substantially resolved by the mid-1980s. By that time, the government was also beginning to reassess the wisdom of its thrust into heavy industries. Rather than address the various problems piecemeal, it decided that a comprehensive review of industrial development strategy was in order. Thus, it enlisted the technical support of the United Nations Industrial Development Organization (UNIDO) and the financial support of the UN Development Programme (UNDP) to prepare a draft Industrial Master Plan (IMP). Almost two years in preparation, the plan was completed in mid-1985 and, in a somewhat modified form, ratified by parliament. It took effect at the beginning of 1986, covering a planning horizon of ten years. While at the time certain targets (e.g. for exports) appeared overly ambitious, before the end of the 1980s it had become apparent that they were in fact overly conservative. Few if any anticipated the tremendous boost that would be given to Malaysia's manufactured exports by the revaluation of the yen and the appreciation of the Korean won and Taiwanese dollar. More important, however, than the numerical projections was the fact that the IMP signalled the government's resolve to address certain structural weaknesses which had in the past hampered broad-based industrialisation.

The electronics industry was one of several industrial sectors for which detailed development strategies were mapped out. Given the aforementioned importance of the sector in terms of its contribution to manufacturing value added, exports and employment, the future development of this industry would no doubt have a strong impact on overall economic performance. Left to itself, would the industry become more balanced in structure or would the semiconductor segment continue to dominate? What sort of strategy would enable other segments to grow more rapidly without jeopardising the growth in value of semiconductor exports? Within the semiconductor segment per se, would there be any significant increase in local value added and, if so, how would that occur? These were certain of the key sector-specific issues to be addressed. Beyond that, there was the broader question of what relationship the development of the electronics industry would bear to that of other industrial sectors. Would it continue to be a 'high-tech' export enclave, or could it evolve stronger linkages with other industries?

In 1985, on the eve of the implementation of the Industrial Master Plan, the output structure of the electronics industry had not changed substantially from that represented in Table 8.1 above. Components – in particular semiconductors – dominated, with consumer electronics a distant second. Some 59,500 workers were employed by semiconductor firms and another 12,100 by consumer electronics firms (Department of Statistics, 1985). Industrial and professional electronics production was minuscule, with most of what did exist consisting of communications equipment. At the same time, within the semiconductor sector, virtually all the operations consisted of assembly (and in some cases testing), with almost all direct production materials imported and relatively little local value added. Ownership patterns differed across sectors. In semiconductors, with one exception, all firms were wholly foreign owned. In consumer electronics, joint ventures were more common, but only in the case of those producing primarily for the domestic market. Export-oriented firms in this sector were also largely foreign owned. Overall, the industry was heavily export oriented, with all semiconductor output exported and a high proportion of consumer electronics output as well.

The semiconductor sector

High employment and low domestic value added were the two prominent features of the semiconductor sector in the mid-1980s. The government was reluctant to exert too much pressure on semiconductor manufacturers to raise domestic value added for fear that they would choose instead to invest elsewhere and thereby jeopardise a major source of employment. The accustomed image at the time was of a 'footloose' industry, willing and able to relocate on short notice to another country which offered more attractive conditions. It was because of the perceived threat of withdrawal that the government exerted much tighter control over workers' organisations in the electronics industry – effectively banning them until recently – than in other industries. The price workers would have to pay for keeping their jobs, it was argued, was low wages. Finally, the government felt compelled to offer generous tax incentives to foreign investors in the semiconductor industry (although in this respect the semiconductor industry was not unique) to compete with the incentives offered by other countries in the region.

In the early 1980s, the image of the industry began to change in a number of respects. First, automation of assembly and testing made the industry far less labour intensive than it had been in the past. Thus, prospects for the industry providing substantial new employment opportunities in the future began to dim. At the same time, the utilisation of sophisticated microprocessor-controlled and computerised machines required a growing cadre of engineers and technicians to program, install, maintain, troubleshoot and repair them. The amount of know-how required by the personnel working in the assembly and test facilities was increasing, and the importance of accumulated experience in raising operator efficiency and plant productivity was growing. Thus, given the 'sunk investments' of firms in training local personnel and the amount of time that would be required to train personnel to the same level elsewhere, the transfer costs of moving a facility out of Malaysia were substantial. In addition, multinationals were shipping a growing volume of their tested chips directly to customers in the region, which meant that their Malaysian subsidiaries had to acquire considerable expertise in customer support and service. To close down the Malaysian operation would disrupt supplier–customer links which had taken some time and effort to develop. In short, the industry was less footloose than it might have been during the days when local operations consisted largely of 'line girls' performing manual assembly under microscopes.

These developments had a number of implications. First, the growing capital intensity of the industry meant that, in the future, capital costs would weigh more heavily and semi-skilled labour costs less heavily in corporate calculations of the optimal location for a semiconductor plant. Secondly, while semi-skilled labour was becoming less important an input, skilled engineering and technician labour was becoming more important. Thus, relative costs of skilled labour would figure more prominently in determining the comparative advantages of different locations. Thirdly, as automation increased, demand rose correspondingly for a variety of specialised tooling like jigs and fixtures for automated assembly and test equipment. Though not related to assembly automation per se, there was also a demand for stamping dies (to make lead frames, the multi-legged connectors that allow integrated circuits to be placed on printed circuit boards), cutting tools for trimming the lead frames, and moulds for injecting epoxy resin to make plastic integrated circuit packages.

Initially, some of the large foreign semiconductor firms set up in-house machine shops to handle their tool and die maintenance. As the variety and precision of tooling requirements increased with automation, special automation support centres were established. These became a valuable training ground for Malaysian process engineers. Over time, Malaysia has developed one of the richest pools of expertise in semiconductor assembly and test automation in the world. Some of those engineers and technicians trained while working for the foreign semiconductor firms have gone on to establish or join local engineering companies, which now serve as subcontractors to the foreign firms. A number of local engineering companies in the area of the Bayan Lepas Free Trade Zone in Penang have grown from small shops to large suppliers of specialised tooling to semiconductor firms. In order to qualify as vendors, they have had to upgrade their engineering capabilities substantially. To meet the very tight tolerances required, they must use precision machinery (e.g. electrostatic discharge machines) and be well versed in statistical process control. One firm went from making a semi-automatic die bonder on contract for a leading US semiconductor firm to exporting units, e.g. to a semiconductor contract assembler in Korea. Also, at least one local firm has become a supplier of burn-in test boards, connectors and racks used by semiconductor firms in their final testing operations.

Thus far, no local company has been able to enter the area of supplying direct materials – beyond tin solder – for semiconductor assembly houses. The quality and precision requirements for those materials are generally beyond existing capabilities of most local firms. For example, lead frames are a part which requires very precise stamping operations to achieve the required tolerances. In addition, the quality of the metal alloys is critical to ensuring reliable performance of the chips attached to the frames. Moreover, these components are subject to large economies of scale. A handful of Japanese metalworking companies have come to dominate this business, and even many of the large US semiconductor companies that do not make their own lead frames source from those companies. One US company that has long made its own lead frames in Penang is National Semiconductor, which also does contract lead frame manufacture for other semiconductor firms in Malaysia. Some of the leading Japanese lead frame manufacturers have also invested in Malaysia in recent years, including Mitsui Hi-Tec and Kitako Electronics. As semiconductor firms in Malaysia continue to introduce new package configurations – especially as they move to small outline packages, surface mount devices, and devices with high lead counts – they require closer support from their lead frame vendors. The introduction of just-in-time inventory methods into their assembly operations has also enhanced the desirability of having short supply lines to their materials suppliers. Finally, the revaluation of the yen has substantially raised the costs of continuing to source supplies from Japan. Thus, it seems likely that a growing volume of local lead frame requirements will be sourced from Malaysia-based producers in the future. Indeed, with the new investments, Malaysia is well positioned to become a regional lead frame supplier.

The semiconductor assembly business does not use that many direct materials other than lead frames, gold and aluminium wires, epoxy resins, ceramic substrates, and the wafers themselves, which account for the overwhelming share of material costs in most devices. Even if all the other materials besides wafers were to be sourced locally, local value added would rise by probably less than 10 per cent. To add significant local value in manufacturing, it would be necessary to fabricate the wafers locally. Currently, Malaysia does have at least one major investment in the preparation of wafers for fabrication, by the leading Japanese silicon wafer supplier. This operation involves the slicing of wafers from silicon ingots and their subsequent polishing and, for some products, deposition of an epitaxial layer. The actual processing of wafers – commonly known as diffusion or fabrication (fab) – is the most capital- and technology-intensive part of the semiconductor manufacturing process. Until fairly recently, most semiconductor firms in the industrialised countries kept that part of their operation within their home bases or in other industrialised countries. The situation has begun to change, in part because a growing number of developing countries – most especially the Asian newly industrialising countries (NICs) – have acquired access to know-how and technology to perform their own wafer fabrication. In some cases the route to such acquisition was through joint ventures established with leading developed country semiconductor producers. In other cases, the source of technology was purchase of a turnkey facility. In the case of the semiconductor industry, however, the notion of 'turnkey' is misleading, since each new wafer fab facility requires extensive 'fine tuning' before it can achieve acceptable yields of good wafers. In short, there are very sizeable learning economies, many of which are plant specific but others of which are more generic. Semiconductor engineers with experience in 'ramping up' a new fabrication facility are a very important asset to a country which is hoping to build up its wafer fabrication capacity. To the extent that local engineers lack such experience, the industry would initially need to rely on costly expatriate staff or consultants.

Wafer fabs tend to place much greater demands on infrastructure and to require a larger number of specialised supporting industries than assembly. A reliable electrical power supply is an especially important requirement, so that countries with underdeveloped electricity generating capacity are not likely candidates for the location of wafer fabs. Large quantities of pure water are also needed. As for supporting industries, speciality gas and electronics-grade chemical suppliers are critical. Of course, such supporting industries do not develop in a vacuum without a sizeable user industry, yet the feasibility of setting up such industries may depend on the base of skills and know-how in related areas, the general level of engineering capability (for example, in chemical engineering), as well as the availability of low-cost supplies of raw materials. Since certain of the gases required in wafer fabrication are volatile and therefore difficult to transport, while the chemicals must meet very high standards of purity (and transport adds to the risk of adulteration), not having a local supply may substantially increase the costs of wafer fab.

Malaysia is still at a slight disadvantage relative to the Asian NICs in terms of its skill base and supporting industries to develop wafer fab on a large scale. (In terms of physical infrastructure there are few constraints.) These disadvantages may diminish in coming years, however, as Malaysia has already attracted a few investments in wafer fab which should serve to develop a local skill base. Still, until a larger number of fabs are set up, it is doubtful whether a sizeable supporting industry will emerge. The first few investments in wafer fabs have not been very sophisticated technologically. In one case, the company introduced only a 'bump metallisation' process, the back end of wafer fab rather than the whole process. In the second case, the wafer fab is for a simple product, namely discrete transistors, rather than integrated circuits (ICs). Taiwan's Hualon Microelectronics Corp. had plans to build a large wafer fab in Kedah state, at least before the recent semiconductor slump put many firms' investment plans on the back burner.

What explains the increased interest in Malaysia as a possible site for wafer fab investments? There are a couple of factors. First, competitive conditions have been changing rapidly in the international semiconductor business. In particular, US producers are coming under more intense pressure from Japanese firms. They have lost almost completely in the market for dynamic random access memories (DRAMs) and their market shares are eroding in a number of other products as well. Faced with such pressures, they are seeking to cut costs however possible. Now that it has been demonstrated that wafer fab can be done quite competitively in certain NICs, they may be more willing to risk investing in a country like Malaysia. Moreover, while product cycles are very short in certain types of devices, other devices have much longer lives. Their process technology has matured to the point where it is relatively simple to transfer the process to a country without advanced semiconductor processing know-how. For example, there is still a sizeable demand for transistors, linear ICs, standard logic devices, even earlier-generation microprocessors and microcontrollers. They could continue to be manufactured in the developed countries but, given the scarcity of high-level engineering resources in those countries, firms would often prefer to devote these resources to producing state-of-the-art products while transferring the more mature products elsewhere. Moreover, the process equipment transferred has in all likelihood been fully depreciated, so capital costs are minimal.

For many if not most types of semiconductor devices, Asia now constitutes the fastest-growing (not yet the largest) market. For example, given the overwhelming concentration of consumer electronics production in the region, discrete transistors and linear ICs, which are used heavily in consumer applications, find their major market outlet in Asia. There may be sizeable inventory cost savings of locating wafer fab close to assembly, since inventories are not tied up in transit between the two facility sites. With new just-in-time inventory methods, this is particularly important. In addition, there may be certain technical reasons for establishing closer links between wafer fab and assembly and testing. Quick feedback from assembly to wafer fab is desirable to be able to identify in a timely fashion possible sources of low yields and to fine tune the process. Also, the backward integration by many Malaysian semiconductor plants into wafer probe test operations, which are the bridge between wafer fab and assembly, brings them one step closer to the front end. Malaysian engineers working in wafer probe must be able to interpret the test results in order to help diagnose problems occurring in fabrication. To do so effectively, they must not only maintain close communication with fab operations but be thoroughly versed in fab process technology as well. While this is not quite tantamount to knowing how to operate a wafer fab, it is the next closest thing. Thus, it would not be surprising if Malaysia were to witness further investments in wafer fabrication in coming years.

Given the paucity of domestic electronics firms engaged in the production of equipment of their own design, there is still little demand for local IC design services. Thus, even if wafer fab should come to Malaysia, it would probably be geared initially to the requirements of large foreign-owned electronics equipment manufacturers for standard (or 'commodity') chips. Yet, in recent years, the highest growth rates in world chip markets have been registered by non-standard (i.e. application specific) ICs (ASICs). These include both custom and semi-custom chips designed to the requirements of a specific customer or use. The tremendous advantage of ASICs from the point of view of the user firm is that they enable it, at relatively low cost, to differentiate its product in the market from those of its competitors. ASIC design capability is a critical element of a niche market strategy, since it permits frequent design modification and thereby enables the innovative firm to stay one step ahead of the competition. A profitable niche does not usually remain a niche for long, so the firm that has found it must be ready to move on to exploit new opportunities once others enter and compete down prices. In Taiwan, where there are many small firms designing new consumer electronics novelty items and add-on boards and peripherals for personal computers, the demand for IC design services is quite substantial and a number of ASIC design houses have sprung up in recent years. In Singapore, by way of contrast, until recently the dearth of local firms making innovative products has stifled the development of an ASIC design industry. Over time, if Malaysia should be able to spawn a sizeable number of small, innovative hardware suppliers, the demand for ASIC design can be expected to grow. Even with relatively low-volume demand, a local ASIC design industry might emerge, with fabrication contracted to silicon foundries in Singapore or elsewhere. A much larger volume of local ASIC demand than currently exists would be required to justify the establishment of a domestic ASIC silicon foundry.

In the short term, it may be more valuable to develop local printed circuit board (PCB) design capability. The likelihood seems greater at present that local firms would require PCB design and fabrication services than that they would require ASIC design and fabrication.

The diversification thrust of Malaysia's electronics industry: consumer electronics

A key recommendation of the electronics sector strategy of the IMP was that the electronics industry should become more diversified, with an initial emphasis on building up the consumer electronics sector. At the time of the IMP, there were already a few relatively large export-oriented consumer electronics operations, including Sharp-Roxy, Thomson, General Electric (now a part of Thomson) and Philips. Still, consumer electronics exports were minuscule as compared with semiconductor exports. The logic behind the emphasis on consumer electronics had several elements. First, consumer electronics generates a large demand for components – not only semiconductors but passive components, printed circuit boards, picture tubes, tuners, speakers, etc. Thus, a larger installed capacity of consumer electronics equipment production would create a sizeable market and make possible cost-effective local production of a growing number of components. Secondly, since components for consumer electronics are generally less sophisticated than those for industrial/professional electronics – yet similar in terms of production know-how – starting with consumer electronics could provide valuable experience which would enable component producers over time to meet the tougher precision and reliability requirements for industrial applications. Thirdly, it was anticipated that, owing to rising costs and labour scarcities in Singapore, more and more consumer electronics firms would migrate across the Causeway to southern Malaysia. A further advantage of consumer electronics is that it remains more labour intensive than semiconductor assembly/testing. Thus, as demand for semi-skilled (mostly female) labour tapers off in the latter sector, consumer electronics expansion could take up some of the slack.

The growth of the consumer electronics sector in the last several years has been impressive. From 1987 to 1988, consumer electronics exports jumped by two-thirds to M$2.5 billion. One important impetus to that growth has been the revaluation of the currencies of Japan, Taiwan and Korea against the US dollar. Japanese firms in particular have significantly expanded their consumer electronics investments in Malaysia. An additional motivation for such investments has been to circumvent trade restrictions on Japanese exports to the US and European markets. (Other countries in the region – notably Thailand and Indonesia – have received sizeable consumer electronics investments in recent years as well.) Examples of some of the major investments in Malaysia include:

- JVC – a partially owned Matsushita affiliate – has invested in a plant in Shah Alam Industrial Estate to produce portable cassette players, compact disk players and car audio systems for export;
- Sharp and Matsushita have both made Malaysia one of their worldwide production centres for colour TVs, and Sony made a major investment in a plant which should have been shipping 800,000 sets by end-1991;
- Hitachi, JVC, Sony, Mitsubishi and Sharp-Roxy are all investing in the production of video cassette recorders (VCRs) in Malaysia. Hitachi also intends to make key VCR components like recording heads and tape drive mechanisms in Malaysia. This set of investments, when complete, will make Malaysia the third-largest VCR exporter in the world after Japan and Korea.
- Malaysia has also become a leading exporter of microwave ovens, again largely as a result of Japanese investment, e.g. by Sanyo.

The consumer electronics industry in Malaysia has begun to move beyond low-cost assembly. Sharp, for example, has begun exporting in small volume the first locally designed colour TV set to other countries in the region (*Financial Times*, 28 September 1989). In the case of audio equipment, a European electronics company is planning to market a Malaysian-designed variation of the 'Walkman' radio. For a number of years Motorola's Malaysian subsidiary has been involved in product design for two-way radios and electronic pagers. It seems reasonable to expect more such activities to be performed in Malaysia in the future. For, given the scarcity of design engineers in many industrialised countries, it is likely that multinational firms will seek to utilise their more costly home-based engineers to design higher-value-added state-of-the-art products. They could be expected to tap engineering resources in lower-cost locations to design lower-value-added, less technologically sophisticated products.

A few locally owned firms have taken an interest in performing their own research and development (R&D). One, PK Electronics Sdn. Bhd., makes uninterruptible power supplies (UPS), air conditioner controls, and other products. Out of a workforce of 200, it has five engineers and between ten and twenty people developing its own products. Normally it first sells its products in the domestic market until the bugs are worked out and then begins to export (*Electronics Engineering*, December 1989). Another, Eastrade, was started by a mechanical engineer who had worked with Motorola's R&D operation in Malaysia. Eastrade started out making electronic toys and now makes radios under an OEM (original equipment manufacturer) agreement with Sony, which provides the company with detailed specifications of product designs. For this reason, up until now it has had little need for its own product development capabilities. Since the company would like greater autonomy, it is exploring a joint venture with a foreign firm which possesses its own R&D capability and recognised brand name. Thus far, the company has had difficulty locating qualified R&D engineers in the area around Penang, its manufacturing base; currently it has an R&D staff of only three (*Electronics Engineering*, November 1989).

Besides limited availability of personnel, other constraints are faced by local firms interested in doing more of their own product development. For example, Penshin Components Sdn. Bhd. of Penang (a capacitor maker which has diversified into OEM supply of car stereos) claims that its own engineers have designed some models it sells but that the tooling costs per model are very high, due in part to the limited local toolmaking capability. A strict OEM relationship (i.e. where the local firm does none of its own design) can obviate this problem if the customer supplies the tooling. When custom tooling must be ordered and fabricated abroad, there can be considerable delays which add to costs.

The growth of the component industry

The component industry has already begun to respond to the growing number of assembly investments. Between 1987 and 1988, the number of component firms in production rose steeply. While some of those were export-oriented semiconductor operations, the bulk were for other sorts of components, including resistors, diodes, capacitors, transformers, power supplies, coils and filters, and loudspeakers. Thomson-CSF of France has built a new plant in Penang which is reputed to be the world's fourth-largest passive component (capacitor) factory (*Far Eastern Economic Review*, 26 October 1989). In addition, Hitachi, which has for some time made colour picture tubes (CPT) in Singapore, has transferred electron gun assembly to Malaysia, with CPT production possibly to follow. Meanwhile, a large Taiwanese CPT manufacturer (belonging to Tatung) has built a factory in Malaysia for small (14≡) tubes, which will ultimately have a capacity of 600,000 a year. A number of component suppliers have also started up to supply the large demand from VCR manufacturers.

These developments in the component sector should strengthen the foundations of Malaysia's electronics industry. Yet the fact remains that the major investments in this field have been made by wholly foreign-owned companies, usually suppliers from Japan or elsewhere who have followed their major customers to Malaysia. Even if small Malaysian companies would like to expand capacities to supply the large volumes demanded by export-oriented foreign firms, they may have difficulty raising the capital to do so.

Moreover, it takes time to build up the capabilities to set up and operate large-scale production facilities; a firm cannot grow from a shopfront operation to a high-volume manufacturer overnight. Thus, customers in a hurry to develop local component sources may find bringing their own suppliers from abroad to be the least-cost route.

The entry of high-volume component manufacturers into Malaysia may strengthen the competitiveness of the large, mostly foreign-owned equipment suppliers, but the advantages to smaller Malaysian-owned equipment suppliers are apt to be more modest. For, the large component vendors often have little interest in filling the small batch orders of a large number of small users, preferring to concentrate on servicing their large customers. One development which may work to the advantage of small equipment manufacturers is the entry into Malaysia of a sizeable number of small and medium-size Taiwanese component and materials suppliers (*Electronic World News*, 15 January 1990: 18). Those companies are more accustomed to servicing a large and diverse customer base, given Taiwan's own industrial structure. Thus, to limit such investments, as some have proposed (see, e.g., UNIDO, 1990: 62), on the grounds that they compete with local suppliers and supporting industries, seems counterproductive.

The rapid growth in the component sector as well as in consumer electronics is reflected in Table 8.2. The value of consumer electronics production increased almost three-fold from 1986 to 1988 while employment doubled. In the case of components, output value almost doubled and employment increased by 44 per cent.

Table 8.2 Growth trends in consumer electronics and components, 1986–8

	No. of establishments at end-year[a]	Ex-factory value of own mfd. products (M$'000)	Paid employees at end-year
Radios, televisions and sound recording equipment[b]:			
1986	15	792,257	11,144
1987	19	1,393,273	17,387
1988	25	2,248,674	23,109
Semiconductors and other electronic components:			
1986	55	5,694,325	57,459
1987	43	7,506,916	71,344
1988	69	9,947,937	82,436

Notes: [a] This refers to establishments with 100+ employees.
[b] Certain consumer electronics goods may not be included here.
Source: Department of Statistics, *Monthly Manufacturing Statistics*, Kuala Lumpur, May 1989.

ELECTRONICS

New developments in industrial/professional electronics

Just as labour-intensive consumer electronics operations have been shifting out of Singapore to Malaysia (mostly to Johore state), so too the labour-intensive computer peripheral assembly operations – mostly disk drive subassembly and assembly – are shifting out of Singapore to lower-cost locations. Some major firms have moved into Thailand – notably Seagate Technology, which began transferring assembly of hard disk drives (HDDs) to Bangkok in the early 1980s, and more recently Micropolis. Malaysia has played host to a number of leading HDD suppliers in recent years, including Conner Peripherals and Maxtor. In addition, suppliers of HDD components like read-write heads have begun to invest in order to cut costs as well as provide better support to their customers. Sony has invested in a major facility to manufacture floppy disk drives and may later make HDDs and optical disk drives in Malaysia as well (*Electronic World News*, 6 November 1989; *Financial Times* Survey, 28 September 1989). Japanese disk drive component suppliers which have decided to invest in Malaysia include Kobe Precision and Hitachi Metals. A few local firms have found some opportunities in supplying HDD makers with metal parts like the aluminium die castings that form the drive's base plate and cover. One local firm making die cast parts for disk drives had acquired experience as a supplier to a Japanese motorcycle manufacturer and later to the manufacturer of the national car, Proton.

In addition to disk drives, a few other types of office automation equipment are either produced or soon to be produced in Malaysia. Hewlett-Packard, for example, is making electro-photographic assemblies for facsimile machines and copiers. A study performed by the Malaysian Industrial Development Authority (MIDA), Japan International Co-operation Agency (JICA), and Japan External Trade Organisation (JETRO) notes that, while the 'assembly of photocopying machines, facsimile machines and word processors requires technical elements which are not involved in the assembly of radio cassette tape recorders, air-conditioners and other electronic equipment ... with the provision of necessary equipment and appropriate work guidance, the assembling work of office electronic equipment in Malaysia would become possible' (MIDA/JICA/JETRO, n.d.). The Japanese firm, Toshiba, was reported to be studying the feasibility of opening an office automation equipment facility in Malaysia to assemble copying machines, facsimile machines and key phones (*Business Times*, 12 August 1989). Another major planned investment in this field is a plant to be built by Brother Industries of Japan. Initially, it would make plastic key pressings and spring parts for electronic typewriters. Eventually it could produce micromotors, print head units, and other parts and components for facsimiles, printers and copiers (*Business Times*, 9 June 1989).

The telecommunications equipment sector

In the case of telecommunications equipment, most local production has traditionally been focused on the requirements of the hard-wired network operated by Syarikat Telekom Malaysia (STM), the recently corporatised successor of Jabatan Telekom Malaysia (JTM). The two major suppliers of switching equipment to that network – NEC of Japan and Ericsson of Sweden – have local manufacturing joint ventures. In addition, Ericsson introduced mobile cellular telephones into Malaysia in the mid-1980s and has been a major supplier of equipment to the cellular market ever since. It is not known whether cellular telephones are currently made in the country, though Ericsson has a licence to make them and it seems probable that it is exercising it. Besides Ericsson, another leading supplier of cellular equipment, Motorola Communications, has a large presence in the country, though traditionally its main products have been two-way radios (or 'walkie-talkies') and pagers.

In the case of NEC and Ericsson, both have begun to export subassemblies of their switching and multiplexing equipment as a way of filling up capacity idled by a slowdown in STM's network expansion plans. The main supplier of subscriber equipment to the domestic market, a locally owned firm named Uniphone, has also received enquiries from foreign firms interested in marketing its telephone sets abroad. Another leading international telecommunications equipment supplier, Northern Telecom of Canada, has long performed production for export in Penang's Bayan Lepas Free Trade Zone. Its major products are components and subassemblies for its equipment, including transformers, capacitors, fuses, dynamic receivers and printed circuit boards. It also assembles telephone sets. In the case of transformers, prototypes are built and tested in Penang. Also, a new private branch exchange (PBX) system is to be transferred directly from design in North America to prototype production in Malaysia. To handle such requirements, the Malaysian operation is acquiring new equipment for reliability testing.

Software development

Some mention should be made of the software industry in Malaysia, given the rapid growth of the world software business. A number of leading information technology (IT) equipment suppliers have come to recognise the strategic importance of building up their software and service businesses. There are two principal reasons for this shifting emphasis. First, hardware is becoming an ever more competitive business with shrinking profit margins. This is a result of the large number of new entrants combined with the increasing standardisation of hardware. Second, and relatedly, software represents a growing share of total system cost for many IT systems. Software increasingly sells machines. Without strong software support, equipment vendors find themselves at a worsening competitive disadvantage. At the national level, Singapore has targeted software as an area for development in accordance with its emphasis on promoting human capital-intensive industries. Compared with hardware manufacturing, software development has an extremely high value added per square metre of space, an important consideration in countries where real estate values have become exorbitantly high.

Malaysia's software industry is as yet relatively small. As in other countries where large computer systems are imported, there are local distributors who help customers develop applications software for their mainframes or mini-computers. These are of diminishing importance as the local market becomes increasingly dominated by small systems – mostly desktop and notebook personal computers (PC) and workstations. While many PC users rely primarily on off-the-shelf packages, there is some demand for local-language versions of such packages as well as for customised versions better adapted to specific users' requirements. Successful local PC and workstation distributors need to be able to provide their customers with more than off-the-shelf hardware and software. As the Malaysian economy becomes more dependent on computers, the local market should provide entry opportunities for shrewd software entrepreneurs. If niche marketing is appropriate anywhere, it is likely to be in software. To compete in standard packages with the likes of Microsoft, Lotus and WordPerfect may be courageous but it is also foolhardy. Collaboration with such firms in the 'localisation' of popular packages may be a more feasible route.

Software for export has not yet evolved into a significant activity in Malaysia. Recently the government has begun to offer incentives for foreign investors in this field. The first investor was the German computer firm Nixdorf (subsequently merged with Siemens). The plan was to establish a software development centre, employing 50–100 professional personnel to develop banking and insurance applications which run on a version of the UNIX operating system supported by the Open Software Foundation (OSF). (It is not known whether the Malaysian software centre has survived the reorganisation of Nixdorf that followed its merger with Siemens.) Among the factors cited by the company in its selection of Malaysia were: (i) the availability at low cost of well-educated computer graduates; (ii) the new government incentives on offer to software exporters; (iii) the well-developed telecommunications infrastructure in the country (Computertimes Section, *New Straits Times*, 4 August 1988). Malaysia appears intent on strengthening its UNIX programming capabilities; in September 1989, for example, it hosted an international seminar on 'Current Developments and Future Trends of UNIX-based Systems', with speakers from both of the leading rival UNIX camps – the OSF (to which IBM belongs) and the ATT-supported 'Archer group'.

A potential future advantage for Malaysia's software industry is the critical shortage of software engineers in certain industrialised countries, most especially Japan. Japanese firms have been able to address the software bottleneck in part by boosting programmer productivity and rationalising the software production process, but it is likely that they will come to rely more on low-cost labour for offshore programming in the future. There may be limits, however, to how far the early stages of software development – conceptualisation and detailed design – can be de-localised, since they require close coordination and communication between customer and software designer. Still, as with hardware so in the software industry there is a range of development jobs of differing degrees of complexity. Presumably, international software companies will assign their high-paid engineers in the industrialised countries to the more complex and demanding jobs for which they can command a price premium while looking to economise on more routine jobs through use of lower-paid engineers in developing countries. India has perhaps been the most successful so far in capitalising on the software skill shortage in industrialised countries; in the process, it has raised its software exports from a mere US$17 million in 1985–6 to approximately US$100 million by 1989 (*Electronic World News*, 5 November 1990: 16).

ISSUES FOR THE FUTURE OF MALAYSIA'S ELECTRONICS INDUSTRY

Strengthening domestic electronics and related firms

The first and most critical question confronting Malaysia's electronics industry is the sustainability of its historic growth rate in coming years. With the industry having registered healthy growth – despite cyclical downturns – for two decades now, why should sustainability be an issue? There are three reasons. First, the recent wave of expansion of consumer electronics and, to a lesser degree, industrial electronics investment was the result in large measure of adjustments to correct imbalances in the international economic environment, in particular through the realignment of exchange rates. With those realignments largely completed, one major impetus to foreign investment has been effectively removed. Indeed, outward direct foreign investment (DFI) from Japan has slowed markedly in the last few years. Secondly, there is considerable uncertainty about the degree of access Malaysian exports will enjoy in the future to the major markets of North America and Europe. Since part of the rationale for the sizeable inflow of DFI into Malaysia has been to circumvent trade barriers against exports directly from Japan to those markets, restrictions on Malaysia's market access would clearly render it less attractive as an investment location. Thirdly, there is the lingering problem posed by Malaysia's industrial structure, in which few local firms have emerged that could serve as the nucleus of a dynamic domestically owned electronics industry. In short, the industry is still overwhelmingly dependent on DFI, so that if and when the flow should dry up it is not clear how the industry's growth momentum could be sustained. Of course, it is possible that the reinvestment of profits by the foreign firms already present in the country would be enough to sustain growth, but to depend solely on that source would be a risky strategy indeed.

What can be done to strengthen domestic electronics firms? Answering this question could appear to be the highest priority for government policy vis-à-vis the electronics industry in the next decade. Some answers make little sense and can be ruled out from the start. One line of argument starts from the observation that local firms find it difficult to compete with foreign firms that have invested in the same line of business and proceeds to argue for restrictions on such foreign investments. Even if the premise is correct, the proposed remedy is almost certainly not. One does not help local firms to compete by removing the competition. The sources of domestic firms' competitive disadvantage need to be identified and positively addressed. It would not be at all surprising to find that a major reason for local firms' failure to compete is that current government policy actually discriminates against them in favour of foreign firms. Government fiscal incentives have generally tended to favour large, well-capitalised foreign firms over small, poorly capitalised local ones. Similarly, export-oriented foreign investors have often enjoyed liberal provisions regarding equity ownership which local firms have not. Indeed, this discriminatory treatment has often encouraged local firms to remain undercapitalised, since by remaining small they could avoid having to share ownership. It would also be interesting to know how such differential treatment has affected the capital costs of foreign versus local firms – e.g. if local firms have chosen to rely more heavily on debt financing to avoid the equity-sharing issue. Of course, these drawbacks of discriminatory treatment are by now well known to policy makers, who nonetheless face a difficult task trading them off against social equity concerns. It is still worth reinforcing the point that if government policies are biased against domestic firms – or certain categories of domestic firms – then policy reform can go a long way towards helping those firms compete.

If the high cost or inaccessibility of capital is a problem, the government should consider whether subsidised credit schemes for local firms are justified. If technical competence is the problem, subsidised technical consultancy services may be called for; if weak market intelligence, then the government may need to assist smaller firms in gaining access to timely market information. More than likely, a combination of factors hampers the competitiveness of local firms. In that case, a package of financial, technical and marketing assistance may be called for. The Taiwanese model of government-supported institutes which offer a range of support services to small and medium-sized enterprises may be worth studying. One of the key institutions providing managerial and technical advice and training to Taiwanese industry is the China Productivity Centre (CPC), which in the fiscal year to June 1988 offered 1,086 classes to some 35,000 students on topics ranging from managerial techniques to automation technology, manufacturing engineering, and information technology. Furthermore, CPC has organised numerous overseas study missions for local industry to help it acquire up-to-date information about technological and market developments elsewhere in the world. The centre also provides consulting services, for a fee, to help small and medium-sized factories with automation programmes, plant rationalisation, in-plant operation improvement, and the introduction of management information systems. In addition, CPC carries on its own in-house research on improving production efficiency in order to render its consultancy services more efficacious. Where it cannot solve technical problems itself, it assists in directing firms to research institutes which can (Dahlman and Sananikone, 1990).

Malaysia has been reasonably successful in forging backward linkages from export-oriented foreign investors to local suppliers of materials, parts and components. In recent years, a number of local firms have started up or diversified into providing specialised tooling, equipment and services to foreign electronics firms. One foreign firm, which in the the 1980s set up its own precision machining and metalworking subsidiary in Penang, has contributed perhaps more than others to creating a cadre of experienced managers and engineers who have gone on to found or join independent local supplier firms. It can be expected that, in the future, a growing number of professionals working in multinationals will strike off on their own to exploit lucrative market niches supplying products or services to their former employers. Such spinoffs should be encouraged, if necessary by the injection of venture capital as a way of helping them get started. In general, the government can still do more to strengthen local supplier networks in the country. One approach is that taken by the Thai Board of Investment (BOI), which has started a new programme called BUILD (for BOI Unit for Industrial Linkage Development) to promote partnerships between foreign investors and domestic suppliers of parts and components, not only in electronics but in machinery and metalworking (*Far Eastern Economic Review*, 20 August 1992: 42).

Even if most local firms remain indirect exporters, supplying to export-oriented foreign firms, the managerial and technical skills acquired in the process should prove valuable to Malaysia's economy. In many cases, learning economies should permit the gradual introduction of more advanced process technologies and of more sophisticated products. For some products (e.g. standardised components), the large volume requirements of customers should permit the realisation of economies of scale. Some local firms which began by supplying multinationals have begun to export on their own account; more should be encouraged to do so. One important service the government can provide to smooth the way for local electronics and related exporters is to help them get their plants accredited as conforming to the ISO

9000 standard, which is becoming a widely accepted set of international quality standards. In the future, those firms with ISO 9000 accreditation can expect to enjoy far greater access to the European Community market in particular than those without it.

The normal route by which domestic electronics manufacturers have broken into the world market in Asian NICs is through original equipment manufacture (OEM). This involves contracting with a foreign customer – in some cases, a large equipment manufacturer; in other cases, a wholesale or retail distributor – to supply a particular product to the customer's specifications for sale under its brand name. The OEM supplier has considerable management discretion, including in the areas of materials procurement, plant and equipment investment, process organisation, staffing, etc. At a later stage, when the OEM relationship has matured, the customer may ask the supplier to design a product according to a general concept (original equipment design, or OED). When that point has been reached, it may be possible for the OED supplier to contemplate venturing into own brand name sales, but the costs of establishing brand name recognition can be formidable. Many firms may prefer to continue down the OED path, moving to progressively more sophisticated products.

Developing the country's human resource potential

A second key issue for the future of the electronics industry is ensuring that Malaysia produces the human resources needed to keep the industry competitive. The electronics industry worldwide is becoming less unskilled labour intensive and more human capital intensive. In Malaysia, this is reflected not merely in a rising ratio of indirect (i.e. engineering, technical, managerial) labour to direct (i.e. production worker) labour, but also in the greater education and experience required of production workers themselves. One reason for this is that the average production worker is now responsible for operating sophisticated – and expensive – automated machinery whose 'downtime' must be minimised. This implies not only that operators must be able to supervise the equipment effectively but also that they should be able to handle at least some of the routine maintenance and repair of that equipment, freeing up technicians for handling more serious problems. It also suggests that companies must be careful to select operators skilled and knowledgeable enough not to cause serious damage to equipment. As the work of operators becomes more technically demanding, so does that of technicians and engineers.

Another reason for the changing skill requirements in electronics is the growing importance of worker flexibility and, consequently, multiple skilling. To compete in the global electronics markets, firms need to be able to adapt at short notice, introducing new products and processes. Workers need to be able to learn quickly. In addition, to hold down costs in the factory, firms need to be able to shift workers to different tasks as they are needed to ensure that human resources are effectively utilised. With new methods of work organisation, inventory management and quality control, firms have also needed to broaden the responsibilities of operators. Frequently this has meant organising shopfloor personnel into work teams that manage tasks collectively. For example, rather than separating assembly from inspection, increasingly firms have assemblers inspect their own work. The integration of once discrete tasks can raise worker motivation and the assignment of responsibility to the operator for ensuring quality can strengthen incentives for 'doing it right the first time'.

Besides these innovations in work organisation, there are other factors which have tended to raise human capital requirements in the electronics industry. Malaysia's industry is becoming more sophisticated; that is, the range of new activities being performed in Malaysia is steadily growing, and with it the range of skills required. The need for process engineers able to manage the transition to a more automated production environment has been evident for some time. If, as suggested above, more consumer electronics firms perform product design in the country, hardware and circuit design engineers are likely to be in growing demand. If the products designed make use of application-specific integrated circuits, IC design engineers will be needed. As semiconductor firms in the country ship a growing share of their output directly to customers in the region, product support engineers with detailed understanding of product specifications are in growing demand. Should the country host more wafer fabrication investments, semiconductor process engineers will also be in demand. Since software is an ever more integral part of both process and product technologies, software engineers are almost certain to enjoy greater demand for their skills in the future. Finally, as automated equipment is increasingly linked and made to communicate via networks, engineers capable of designing, installing and upgrading such networks should be needed in growing numbers. This is not even considering the human resource requirements should Malaysia become a major base for research and development activities in electronics.

Strengthening Malaysia's R&D effort in electronics

Thus far, the amount of electronics R&D undertaken in Malaysia has been quite limited. This reflects in part the nature of the actors – mostly wholly foreign-owned firms – and in part the nature of the activities – mostly low-cost assembly for export. In the case of the semiconductor firms, which dominated Malaysia's electronics industry structure until recently, most R&D is closely linked to prototype fabrication of wafers and, as previously noted, Malaysia has only recently begun to develop an embryonic wafer fab capacity. Since that capacity is for simple, mature products in which there is no longer much need for R&D investment, it seems doubtful whether

Malaysia will be a major R&D centre for semiconductor process technology in the near future. Yet, as noted earlier, Malaysia has acquired considerable competence in process development for automation of 'back end' semiconductor operations – i.e. assembly and testing. It may be worth considering whether there is a justification for giving this competence an institutional expression, or whether it should be left to private firms to sustain. For example, an institute for automated manufacturing systems development could serve as a training ground for future generations of engineers and technicians; it could also provide consulting services to industries interested in automating their own operations. Of course, any decision to establish such an institute should be made in consultation and, it is hoped, cooperation with industry.

Already, there exists one government-supported R&D institute in the electronics field, the Malaysian Institute of Microelectronic Systems (MIMOS). MIMOS was founded in 1985, initially with a strong emphasis on acquiring expertise in state-of-the-art IC design techniques. This proved an unsustainable strategy, however, in view of the weak demand at the time for sophisticated IC design services. More recently, it has re-evaluated its mission and reoriented itself towards achieving less ambitious but more practical goals. For one, it has begun to use its computer-aided design system to assist local electronics firms with printed circuit board design and layout. In addition, it has begun to develop applications for microprocessor technology in different user industries. One recent success is the development of an automation system for use by a large plantation-based firm in its palm oil processing operations. It is also performing some software development and adaptation for the local market.

The experience of MIMOS is instructive, for it clearly illustrates the need for government-supported R&D institutes in developing countries to remain responsive to the needs of industry. The temptation to aim for the technological frontier has led many a research institute down a blind alley. It is the responsibility of universities to keep abreast of the latest scientific and technical developments in a given field. Even they can benefit from closer links with industry, however, since in high-technology industries like electronics, firms are often more advanced in their technical knowledge than the academic community. This is not surprising since, globally, firms devote vastly greater sums to R&D than do universities. Moreover, a powerful incentive to keep talented people within academia can be to allow them greater freedom to apply their ideas and expertise in the industrial arena, and to enjoy at least some of the potential rewards from doing so.

The government needs to weigh how to provide stronger encouragement to R&D within the private sector. It currently offers tax incentives for R&D investments, yet with relatively little apparent effect. The industrial structure is a partial explanation of the weak response. The multinational firms present in Malaysia have long-established R&D operations close to major customers, to leading universities in their home countries, or to both. At the moment, there is no compelling reason for most to perform R&D in Malaysia. It is much more likely that a large domestic firm would invest in local R&D, as no doubt some large Malaysian firms are doing. Unfortunately, however, none of those firms happens to operate in the electronics industry. Another problem with the incentives on offer is that, to qualify, a firm must apparently specify at the outset how long a particular R&D project will take and how much it will cost (*Electronic Components*, November 1989). Given the inherent uncertainties of the R&D process, this is seldom possible. Moreover, smaller firms may perform informal R&D, in the form of minor process modification or product design changes, without it being recognised as such. Effective R&D incentives must somehow be able to reward those efforts.

Fostering diffusion of information technologies

With the inexorable decline in the costs of computing power, information technology has become almost universally accessible. In this situation, what has come to matter more than how much computing power one has is how well one uses it. The policy lesson for Malaysia is that to be computerised is not enough. To derive maximum benefit from the new technologies, a society must be able to use them cleverly, to do new things or to perform old tasks in new and better ways. This suggests that the widespread availability of information technology places a premium on human creativity and innovativeness. While broad access to computing and communication technologies holds out tremendous potential for boosting productivity, increasing product variety, reducing costs and improving the quality of life – e.g. by offering the possibility of greater leisure time as well as new forms of leisure activity – to realise that potential requires a well-educated and computer-literate population. Hence, investments in human resource development matter more than ever. One small – albeit increasingly important – component of such investments must be directed towards making computer literacy almost as universal as basic literacy. At the same time it is important to recognise that computer skills need to be combined and blended with other areas of expertise if they are to be put to most effective use.

As Malaysia's economy continues to grow and mature, the role of services should grow in importance. Service industries have voracious appetites for information and, potentially at least, for information technologies. Thus, it can be expected that in the future Malaysia's electronics industry will become somewhat less hardware oriented; local demand for software and services can be expected to grow strongly. As Malaysian users of information technology acquire experience and become more demanding, this should ideally provide a stimulus to the upgrading of local supplier capabilities. Thus, the more sophisticated are domestic users, the more likely are their suppliers to acquire a competitive advantage over firms accustomed to supply markets with less demanding customer requirements. Of course, not in all market segments and applications are Malaysian information technology users going to be among the most sophisticated and demanding, but where they are, their Malaysian suppliers could find themselves richly rewarded once they have endured their trial by fire.

REFERENCES

Bank Negara Malaysia (1988) *Annual Report 1987*, Kuala Lumpur.
Dahlman, C.J. and Sananikone, O. (1990) 'Technology Strategy in the Economy of Taiwan: Exploiting Foreign Linkages and Investing in Local Capability', World Bank, Washington, DC, preliminary draft, December.
Department of Statistics (1985) *Industrial Survey*, Kuala Lumpur.
MIDA/UNIDO (1985) *Medium and Long Term Industrial Master Plan: Malaysia; 1986–1995*, Vol. II, Part 8, Electronics and Electrical Industry, Kuala Lumpur, August.
MIDA/JICA/JETRO (n.d.) *The Study on Selected Industrial Product Development in Malaysia: I. Office Electronic Equipment Industry, II. Cathode Ray Tube (CRT) Industry, III. Ceramic IC Packages/Substrates Industry*, Kuala Lumpur.
UNIDO (1990) *Policy Assessment of the Malaysian Industrial Policy Studies (MIPS) and the Industrial Master Plan (IMP), Vol. 5: Review of linkage development in the export processing manufacturing sector – particular focus on the electric/electronics and textile/garment industries*, Vienna, 15 December.
World Bank (1992) *World Development Report 1992*, Washington, DC.

9

TEXTILES AND CLOTHING: SUNRISE OR SUNSET INDUSTRY?

David O'Connor

Malaysia's textile industry[1] has come back to life. As recently as the mid-1980s, the primary textile sector was being labelled a 'sunset' industry whose days were numbered. Banks did not want to finance investments in expanding productive capacity, and firms were being cannibalised by property companies which needed some manufacturing assets to get listed on the Kuala Lumpur Stock Exchange (KLSE). The real growth rate of the textile sector in Malaysia fell from an annual average of 10.7 per cent in the period 1975–80 to an average of –1.8 per cent in 1980–5 (UNIDO, 1988). The second half of the decade witnessed a dramatic reversal in the fortunes of the industry. From 1986 to 1988, primary textile output rose by 12.4 per cent a year (Department of Statistics, 1989b). It has become fashionable (and profitable) to invest once more in the textile industry. The number of applications received by the Malaysian Industrial Development Authority (MIDA) for the establishment of textile and apparel ventures increased between 1986 and 1989 from 32 to 118. The number of projects approved in 1989 was 102, up from 70 in 1988. The average capital investment per approved project rose from M$3.35 million in 1986 to M$6.58 million in 1989. At the same time, the potential employment in approved projects also increased significantly, from 13,722 in 1988 to 20,169 in 1989 (MIDA, n.d.).

Perhaps more interesting than the question of why Malaysia's textile industry has experienced such strong growth in recent years is that of why investors had written it off (in retrospect prematurely). The textile and apparel industries have played a central role in the early stages of industrialisation of many advanced industrial economies as well as newly industrialising economies (NIEs). This is certainly the case with the 'late industrialisers' of the twentieth century, first Japan and more recently Korea, Taiwan and Hong Kong.[2] Malaysia differs from those three NIEs in one respect, namely that from an early date a relatively high-technology industry – electronics – assumed a prominent place in the country's industrial structure. While electronics also constitutes a major industry in Korea and Taiwan, its emergence as a leading sector followed upon the growth of the textile and apparel sectors. Intuitively, this would seem the logical order, since textiles and garments are both more labour intensive and less technology intensive than electronics. Still, in the early days of the electronics industries of the NIEs as well as of Malaysia, the activities performed were also highly labour intensive, consisting largely of assembly of various components, subsystems and equipment. The technologies of electronics assembly have changed more rapidly in recent years than those of textile and, especially, clothing manufacture. As a result, rising labour costs and currency values in the NIEs have affected their competitiveness in these latter activities more drastically than in the former. Pressures to transfer their textile and clothing industries to lower-wage countries have thus intensified. Malaysia has received a considerable influx of such NIE investments in the last few years, as have its neighbours Thailand and Indonesia. The recent upsurge in foreign investments has substantially changed the face of Malaysia's textile and garment industries. Taiwanese and Hong Kong capital have come to assume an especially prominent place within them.

Our primary interest is in what prospects Malaysia's industry has for continued development in the light of changes occurring in the world industry. Those changes are principally of three kinds: changes in the international trade regime governing textiles and clothing; changes in the characteristics of the major markets; changes in the technologies of textile and clothing design and production. Before we can discuss the future, however, we need to have a better understanding of the current status of Malaysia's industry. Thus, the discussion proceeds as follows. The next section is largely descriptive, providing some basic data on the industry's structure and ownership characteristics. It also pinpoints some of the competitive weaknesses of the industry. We then discuss some of the major changes occurring in the worldwide industry, focusing on issues of trade, market differentiation and technology. We point to adjustments the Malaysian industry may need to make to remain competitive, or rather to alter the basis of its competitiveness, in the light of these global changes as well as changes in its own domestic cost structure. The concluding section highlights some of the policy issues which emerge in the context of Malaysia's efforts to adjust to shifting international market conditions, intensifying competition from its low-cost neighbours, and advances in technology. Can the industry succeed in making the necessary adjustments? Will firms be able to move into higher value added activities and market segments? What support may be required, if any, from government?

THE CURRENT STATUS OF MALAYSIA'S TEXTILE AND APPAREL INDUSTRY

Malaysia's textile industry makes a relatively small contribution to manufacturing sector value added as well as to merchandise exports by comparison with the industries of many of its Asian neighbours. In 1989 for example, the textile and clothing industries contributed approximately 7 per cent of manufacturing value added (MVA) in Malaysia (see Table 9.1), compared with 38 per cent for Hong Kong, 18 per cent for Thailand, and 14 per cent for Korea and China. The contribution of textiles and clothing to total export earnings is even smaller, at 5 per cent in 1990, compared with 39 per cent for Hong Kong, 27 per cent for China, 22 per cent for Korea, and 16 per cent for Thailand. Even Indonesia, with its similarly large natural resource base, showed a much larger contribution of textiles and clothing to total merchandise exports (11 per cent).

Table 9.1 Share of manufacturing value added and merchandise exports contributed by textiles and clothing

Country	MVA Current US$m. 1970	MVA Current US$m. 1989	MVA % contribution of textiles + clothing 1970	MVA % contribution of textiles + clothing 1989	Merchandise exports Current US$m. 1990	Merchandise exports % contribution of textiles + clothing 1965	Merchandise exports % contribution of textiles + clothing 1990
USA[b]	254,115	–	8	5	371,466	3	2
Japan[b]	73,339	829,238	8	5	286,768	17	3
Italy[b]	29,093	200,937	13	13	168,523	15	13
Germany[b]	70,888	369,689	8	4	397,912	5	5
France[b]	–	204,445	10	7	209,491	10	5
Korea[b]	1,880	66,215	17	14	64,837	27	22
Hong Kong	1,013	11,034	41	38	29,002	52	39
China[b]	27,555[a]	145,646[a]	–	14	62,091	29	27
Malaysia[b]	500	–	3	7	29,409	0	5
Indonesia[b]	994	17,272	–	–	25,553	0	11
Thailand[b]	1,130	17,635	13	18	23,002	0	16
Philippines[b]	1,665	10,728	8	8	8,681	1	7
Singapore[b]	379	8,463	5	4	52,627	6	5
India	7,928	44,445	21	12	17,967	36	23
Pakistan	1,462	5,923	38	19	5,590	29	58
Sri Lanka	369	969	19	20	1,984	0	34
Bangladesh[b]	527	1,730	47	36	1,674	–	60
Brazil	10,421	120,845	13	12	31,243	1	3
Mexico[b]	8,449	51,138	15	11	26,714	3	2

Source: World Bank (1992).
Notes: [a] World Bank estimate.
[b] Value added in manufacturing data are at purchasers' values.

The last few years have witnessed an increase in the relative importance of Malaysia's textile and garment industry to its economy. For example, the contributions of textiles and garments to MVA and exports reported in Table 9.1 represent increases from 5 per cent in 1986 and 3 per cent in 1987, respectively. Indeed, 1987 marked the onset of a steep rise in textile and garment production and exports which has continued to the present. A few figures serve to illustrate the high growth of recent years and the increasing

TEXTILES

weight of the sector. The value of textile and apparel exports more than doubled between 1985 and 1988, from M$1.4 billion to M$3.0 billion (see Table 9.2).[3] From 1988 to 1989 they rose by another 30 per cent to M$3.9 billion. Over the four years 1985–9, the compound annual growth rate of exports averaged 29.2 per cent. (Electronics exports are estimated to have grown at only a slightly slower rate and still dwarf all other manufactured exports. In 1988, for example, they amounted to M$13.1 billion, or four-and-a-third times the value of textile and clothing exports, the second-largest manufactured export category.) The textile and apparel sectors are also a major source of employment. In 1988 they employed some 105,300 people, second again only to electronics. Of those, some 78,600 worked in licensed companies, while the remainder were employed in small unlicensed

Table 9.2 Exports, imports and import/export ratios for textiles and garments, 1984–8 (M$m)

	1984	1985	1986	1987	1988
Imports	1,093.7	1,057.8	1,199.2	1,576.4	2,061.5
Exports	1,154.5	1,361.5	1,700.1	2,279.3	3,044.6
Imports as % of exports		94.6	77.7	70.5	69.2	67.7

Source: MIDA, based on Department of Statistics, Kuala Lumpur, data for 1984–8 are cited in Y.H. Tan (1989).

Table 9.3 OECD imports of textiles and clothing, by region/country of origin, 1987

	Textile		Clothing	
	US$m.	%	US$m.	%
Total imports	52,921	100.0	71,996	100.0
Intra-OECD imports	39,251	(74.2)	30,875	(42.9)
Non-OECD imports	13,670	(25.8)	41,121	(57.1)
Four Asian dragons	5,987	(11.3)	25,550	(35.5)
Chaina		(4.6)		(6.5)
South Korea		(2.9)		(10.4)
Taiwan		(2.5)		(6.8)
Hong Kong		(1.3)		(11.8)
ASEAN 5	926	(1.7)	3,872	(5.4)
Thailand		(0.7)		(1.3)
Indonesia		(0.5)		(0.8)
Malaysia		(0.3)		(0.9)
Philippines		(0.1)		(1.4)
Singapore		(0.1)		(1.0)
South Asia 2	2,207	(4.2)	1,861	(2.6)
India		(2.2)		(2.0)
Pakistan		(2.0)		(0.6)

Source: OECD, *Foreign Trade by Commodities, Vol. II: Imports, 1987*, Paris, 1988.

enterprises (Tan, 1989). If all the projects approved in 1989 materialise, the number employed in licensed firms should approach 100,000 in the near future.

Malaysia's industry accounts for a tiny percentage of world textile and clothing exports, a factor which could be to its advantage inasmuch as it reduces the likelihood of serious frictions with its major trading partners. Its 1987 exports accounted for only 0.3 per cent of textile yarn and fabric imports into OECD countries and only 0.9 per cent of apparel and accessory imports (see Table 9.3). The corresponding shares of the Asian NIEs in OECD textile and apparel imports were: Hong Kong (1.3 per cent; 11.8 per cent), Korea (2.9; 10.4), and Taiwan (2.55; 6.8). For Thailand the respective figures were 0.7 per cent and 1.3 per cent; for Indonesia 0.5 and 0.8.

Industry structure

Malaysia's textile industry is weighted towards downstream activities, in particular garment assembly. The fibre sector is small, consisting of a single synthetic fibre plant (which will not be discussed here). In early 1989, Malaysia's primary textile sector consisted of 29 spinning, weaving and finishing establishments (with 100 or more employees). In addition there were 40 knitting mills (with more than 20 employees). The number of clothing factories with more than 50 employees grew from 97 in 1986 to 128 by April 1989 (Department of Statistics, 1989a). If one were to include the establishments with fewer than 50 employees, the number would be a multiple of that.

The textile industry is one in which process technology is largely embodied in the capital equipment (spinning machines, looms, knitting machines, sewing machines, etc.). One might expect foreign investment to play a limited role inasmuch as local firms should have little difficulty absorbing the technology on their own. In fact, foreigners own a larger share of the fixed assets in Malaysia's textiles industry than in industry as a whole. As of end 1987, they accounted for 54 per cent of the M$744 million in fixed assets in the textile and apparel industries; at the same time, they owned only 36 per cent of the M$20.6 billion in fixed assets in all of Malaysian industry (MIDA survey, 1988; data supplied by personal communication). In 1988 and 1989, foreign investment accounted for 77 per cent and 60 per cent, respectively, of total proposed capital investment in textile and clothing projects. (The foreign shares of total proposed investment in all sectors were 66 per cent and 55 per cent respectively.) The large foreign representation is attributable to the fact that much of the investment in Malaysia's textile and garment industries has come from firms in the 'big three' textile exporters (Hong Kong, Korea and Taiwan) seeking access to additional quotas in the major quota-restricted markets[4] as well as escaping rapidly rising production costs in their home bases.

TEXTILES

Structural weaknesses of Malaysia's textile industry

Limited marketing and design capabilities

The high degree of reliance on foreign investment is symptomatic of two weaknesses of the Malaysian industry: its limited marketing capability and limited design capability. The two limitations are interrelated in the sense that local garment firms generally rely on foreign partners and/or customers to provide them with pre-designed patterns, which they use to cut and assemble the garments to specification for marketing by the foreign counterpart. Frequently the garment maker operates on a cut–make–trim (CMT) basis, which means the foreign partner/customer provides the fabric and accessories on consignment as well. The local venture is charged with fairly limited responsibility, namely the efficient operation of a labour-intensive assembly process. After finishing, the garments are shipped either to an affiliate of the foreign partner or, in the case of locally owned firms, directly to the customer, often a large clothing retailer or the owner of a designer label in the industrialised countries. Many of the large clothing retailers maintain purchasing offices in strategic developing country locations. Within Asia, Hong Kong has become a logistical centre for the clothing industry, with major designers from the OECD countries working closely with Hong Kong firms to develop prototypes of their new collections. Once satisfactory samples have been made and supply contracts negotiated, the Hong Kong firms handle the logistics of material procurement and subcontract out the assembly to affiliates or independent subcontractors scattered throughout the region. No other country in the region has comparable expertise in the design and marketing aspects of the business to constitute a serious challenge to Hong Kong's position at the present time. This could change, however, if leading Hong Kong based clothing firms should transfer their bases to other locations in anticipation of 1997.

Underdeveloped primary textile sector

One reason for the pervasiveness of CMT arrangements is that Malaysia's primary textile sector is still relatively weak. The underdeveloped state of that sector has meant that Malaysia has had to rely heavily on imported yarns and fabrics to supply its clothing factories. This is reflected in a sizeable yarn and fabric trade deficit (M$1.48 billion in 1989, more than half as large as the garment and accessories trade surplus). Nevertheless, the import dependency of the garment sector declined for a number of years before rising again in 1989 (see Table 9.2). Whereas the ratio of textile and garment imports to exports stood at 0.78 in 1985, by 1988 it had declined to 0.68. In 1989, however, it rose again to 0.73, suggesting that domestic primary textile capacity has not been able to keep pace with the rapid growth in the clothing sector. The import dependency is high as compared with other Asian industries. In the case of Indonesia, the import/export ratio stood at 0.46 in 1988; in Thailand at 0.23 in 1987; in Korea at 0.22 in 1985; in Taiwan at only 0.06 in 1986.

There are several implications of this dependence on imports of primary textiles. First, it raises the costs to garment producers in the country, since they must cover freight and insurance charges as well as finance the shipments (except where materials are shipped on consignment). A garment industry which can rely on a local textile supply has lower transport and financing costs. Secondly, there are possible problems in ensuring timely delivery of textiles in the right quantities and with the right specifications. Firms must generally carry larger inventories to insure against possible delays in shipments. Longer supply lines also imply more inventory tied up in transit at any given time. In other words, a just-in-time inventory system becomes difficult if not impossible to implement. Thirdly, close interaction and coordination between the primary textile sector and its clothing sector customers are made more difficult when the two are not located in close proximity. The frequency and intensity of such interactions will tend to increase as the industry moves into higher value added, more fashion sensitive segments of the clothing market. Without a versatile, high-quality primary textile sector to support them, garment makers may find it more difficult to move upmarket. (These issues are dealt with in more detail in the section on the changing global environment.) In the short term, costs are likely to be the most compelling argument in favour of greater reliance on locally produced fabrics, assuming of course that local textile manufacturers are able to ship large enough volumes to reap economies of scale.

The high inventory and transport costs associated with foreign fabric sourcing have to be weighed against the potentially higher costs of local production if scale economies must be sacrificed. For certain low-volume fabric requirements, there may be no economical alternative to continued reliance on imports. Moreover, we need to consider the cost conditions in Malaysia's textile industry. Given current technologies and practices, domestic production costs for primary textiles are frequently higher than in major Asian producer countries. This is attributable primarily to the obsolete state of the industry's capital stock and the low productivity levels of many firms. For local production to be a viable substitute for imports, it must be on the basis of more efficient production methods and more advanced technologies.

Low productivity levels

Textiles remain a labour-intensive industry. Labour costs are still relatively low in Malaysia as compared with the three leading NIE exporters (see Table 9.4), but so also is labour productivity. One measure of such productivity is value added per employee. Table 9.5 contains comparative figures on value added per employee and wages per employee for Malaysia, Korea and Hong Kong. In the textile sector, Malaysia's labour productivity in 1984 was only two-thirds of Korea's while wages per employee were over four-fifths.[5] In clothing, Malaysia's labour productivity was only half Hong Kong's. (At the same time, wages per employee were only about two-fifths of Hong Kong's.)

Table 9.4 Comparison of average hourly labour costs in spinning and weaving, 1990

	Total costs US$	*Ratio to US cost* %
USA	10.02	100
Japan	13.92	139
Germany, FR	16.46	164
France	12.82	127
Taiwan	4.56	46
Korea, Rep	3.22	32
Hong Kong	3.05	30
Mexico	2.21	22
Brazil	1.97	20
Turkey	1.82	18
Malaysia	0.86	9
Philippines	0.67	7
Pakistan	0.39	4
China	0.37	4
Indonesia	0.25	2
Sri Lanka	0.24	2

Source: Werner International, in *Textile Month*, February 1991.

One factor accounting for low labour productivity is the relative scarcity of skilled labour in the textile sector. Countries with large and well-developed textile industries have built up their skill base through long experience. Malaysia's involvement in the industry has been far more limited; as a result, far fewer workers have gained exposure to textile technology. (Compare, for example, Malaysia's 30,900 textile workers in 1984 with Korea's 368,700; see Table 9.5.) Malaysia also lacks adequate institutions and programmes for training textile engineers and technicians. Thus, foreign textile investors must often bring highly skilled personnel from Taiwan or elsewhere to work in Malaysian mills. In the garment sector, there is a shortage of skilled personnel for the grading and marking operation which precedes fabric cutting. Cutting itself is a relatively skilled operation for which experienced workers are in short supply. The use of inexperienced workers for these operations can either slow down production or result in greater material wastage, or both.

A second factor making for low productivity of both labour and capital is the outmoded machinery being utilised in many firms. Malaysia has one of the lowest rates of adoption of new high-productivity textile machinery. In the spinning sector, for example, in 1985 Malaysia had only 2,000 installed

Table 9.5 Selected characteristics of the textile (321) and clothing (322) sectors, 1984

Country	Employment '000		Value added US$m.		Value added per employee US$'000		Wages per employee US$'000		Value added in output %		Wages in value added %	
	T	C	T	C	T	C	T	C	T	C	T	C
MALAYSIA	30.9	30.9	178.8	100.3	5.8	3.2	2.4	1.8	32.5	35.4	42.0	56.2
KOREA, REP.	368.7	237.3	3256.9	1378.4	8.8	5.8	2.9	2.5	37.6	41.1	33.2	43.4
HONG KONG	117.4	268.9	933.0	1684.7	7.9	6.3	4.3	4.3	25.1	31.9	53.8	69.1

Source: UNIDO (1988).
Note: T: textiles
C: clothing

open-end rotors – a far more productive technology than the older ring spinning technology.[6] This compares with 7,500 in Thailand, 13,000 in the Philippines and 29,000 in Indonesia (see Table 9.6). Assuming one open-end rotor machine is the equivalent of 4.5 short staple ring spindles, then Malaysia's installed open-end rotor capacity in 1985 was only 2.2 per cent of total spinning capacity; in Thailand it was 1.8 per cent; in the Philippines 3.8 per cent; in Indonesia 4.9 per cent. Even more seriously, Malaysia had the lowest rate of investment in new open-end rotor spinning capacity of any of the major Asian textile producers, as reflected in the ratio of cumulative shipments of open-end rotors 1977–86 to open-end rotor installed capacity in 1985. In the case of weaving, as of 1987 only 2.7 per cent of total looms installed in Malaysia were of the shuttleless variety, compared with 23.3 per cent in Taiwan, 18.3 per cent in Hong Kong and 10.8 per cent in Korea (see Table 9.7). Because of this low rate of investment in new machinery, the average age of both spinning and weaving machines in Malaysia exceeds fifteen years (see Allen H.L. Tan, 1989).

Table 9.6 Distribution of spinning capacity, by country, 1985

	Installed capacities		Cumulative shipments 1977–86			
Country	Short staple spindles (1)	Open-end rotors (2)	Short staple spindles (3)	Open-end rotors (4)	(3)/(1)	(4)/(2)
Japan	9,359,000	209,000	1,106,692	67,504	0.12	0.32
USA	13,526,000	350,000	519,009	383,338	0.04	1.10
Germany, FR	1,809,000	113,900	355,261	121,716	0.20	1.07
Italy	2,249,000	73,400	946,702	111,180	0.42	1.51
France	1,244,000	123,200	190,484	99,078	0.15	0.80
UK	839,000	45,000	72,498	19,824	0.09	0.44
Korea	3,269,000	31,500	1,294,487	30,130	0.40	0.96
Taiwan	3,841,000	95,900	1,003,426	82,070	0.26	0.86
Hong Kong	292,000	51,500	77,070	113,212	0.26	2.20
China, PR	22,500,000	125,000	213,244	97,580	0.01	0.78
Singapore	100,000	6,000		5,840		0.97
Indonesia	2,550,000	29,000	843,590	20,424	0.33	0.70
Thailand	1,800,000	7,500	306,084	12,494	0.17	1.67
Philippines	1,500,000	13,000	220,838	8,512	0.15	0.65
Malaysia	400,000	2,000	102,136	884	0.26	0.44
India	24,730,000	11,500	6,920,329	23,420	0.28	2.04
Pakistan	4,395,000	25,080	653,632	39,584	0.15	1.58
World total	149,729,000	6,582,400	22,675,873	6,276,046	0.15	0.95

Source: International Textile Manufacturers Federation, *International Textile Machinery Shipment Statistics*, Vol. 9, Zurich, 1986.

Table 9.7 Distribution of weaving capacity, by country, 1987

Country	No. of looms[a]		Shuttleless as % of total looms	New-type looms	
	With shuttle	Shuttleless		Water jet	Air jet
Japan	248,270	30,060	10.8	27,000	8,000
USA	156,770	61,760	28.3	6,200	13,400
Germany, FR	25,090	14,838	37.2	3,200	2,000
Italy	32,110	14,240	30.7	–	–
France	22,130	10,580	32.3	–	–
UK	14,360	5,000	25.8	2,700	2,500
Korea	53,793	6,500	10.8	12,000	1,000
Taiwan	62,940	19,160	23.3	11,500	6,000
Hong Kong	21,416	4,800	18.3	–	–
China, PR	630,000[b]	6,000[b]	0.1	6–7,000	100
Singapore	1,520	220	12.6	–	–
Indonesia	96,300	4,400	4.4	–	–
Thailand	70,070	620	0.1	–	–
Philippines	24,800	900	3.5	–	–
Malaysia	7,780	214	2.7	–	–
World total[c]	2,808,040	385,780	12.1	80,000	70,000

Notes:
[a] Filament weaving looms and wool weaving looms have been omitted.
[b] 1985.
[c] Includes countries not shown.
Sources: Japan Spinners' Association; Japan Chemical Fibre Association, *Textile Handbook 1988* (in Japanese), Osaka Chemical Fibre Publication Unit, 1988.

High degree of export market concentration

Malaysia's export market structure also constitutes a potential source of vulnerability. Its garment exports have always been heavily concentrated on a few major markets, in particular the United States and the EEC. In 1983, for example, the US market absorbed 28 per cent of Malaysia's textile and clothing exports and the EEC 25.5 per cent. By 1988, the share of the USA had risen steeply, to 43.1 per cent, while that of the EEC remained roughly constant (MIDA, cited in Y.H. Tan, 1989).[7] The high concentration on the US market at present makes the Malaysian industry vulnerable to any increase in protectionism there or to any significant shift in sourcing patterns of US garment importers. At least until the expiration of the bilateral agreement with the United States in 1991, access to the US market was assured, so firms had a basis for planning production. Still, there remains considerable uncertainty about how accessible the US market will be in future. The likelihood is that, at best, quotas will only be gradually phased out over a decade or more; at worst, if the current protectionist sentiment in the US Congress prevails, growth of textile and clothing imports into the USA could be drastically slowed.[8]

There is also some uncertainty about the degree of accessibility of the European market after the completion of the 'single market' in 1992. The changes occurring in Eastern Europe may create another competitive challenge to developing country exporters, since a relatively well-educated and low-paid labour force there, combined with close proximity to the EEC market, could give those countries a competitive advantage. On the other hand, the increased openness of the Eastern European economies could result in greater textile and clothing imports from developing countries, assuming those countries are able to ease their severe debt and balance-of-payments problems.

THE CHANGING GLOBAL ENVIRONMENT

The volumes of textiles and garments traded internationally are enormous. As of 1987, they were the fourth- and fifth-largest commodity groupings in terms of total imports by market economies (after crude petroleum, passenger cars, and office machinery; GATT, 1989). Together, they contributed roughly US$195 billion to world trade in 1989 (US$220 billion in 1990), divided almost evenly between textiles and clothing (see Table 9.8). The developed countries accounted for roughly 55 per cent of the US$97 billion in textile exports in 1989; developing countries accounted for only one-fourth. In clothing, developing countries have overtaken developed countries as the leading export suppliers, accounting for roughly 43 per cent of world exports in 1989.

Tables 9.9 and 9.10 provide a more detailed historical picture of textile and clothing imports into the OECD from the developing countries of Asia. In the case of textile yarn and fabrics, intra-OECD imports have remained a substantial proportion of the total: in 1975 they accounted for 81 per cent of all OECD imports; in 1987 they were just under 75 per cent. The combined share of the four leading Asian developing country exporters – China, Korea, Taiwan and Hong Kong – rose from 7 per cent in 1975 to almost 12 per cent by 1984, then tapered off to around 11 per cent in 1987. The combined ASEAN share of OECD imports was only 0.7 per cent in 1975, and by 1987 it had risen to only 1.7 per cent. In the case of clothing the picture is quite different. First, the intra-OECD trade is much smaller in relation to total imports. In addition, it has declined far more steeply, from 56 per cent in 1975 to 43 per cent in 1987. The same four leading Asian exporters have taken much of the market share lost by OECD exporters. Their combined share of OECD clothing imports rose from 28 per cent in 1975 to 40 per cent in 1984 before declining to 36 per cent in 1987. The ASEAN countries have also fared somewhat better as a group in penetrating OECD clothing markets, raising their share from 2 per cent in 1975 to over 5 per cent in 1987. Malaysia's share of OECD clothing rose from only 0.26 per cent in 1975 to 0.78 per cent by 1986.

Table 9.8   Exports of textiles and clothing, 1963–90 (US$bn)

	Developing areas	Developed countries	Eastern trading area	World
Textiles				
1963	1.10	5.35	0.60	7.05
1973	4.35	17.25	1.75	23.35
1979	10.70	35.15	4.20	50.05
1980	12.45	38.65	4.50	55.60
1981	12.95	36.60	5.35	54.90
1982	11.80	33.60	5.20	50.60
1983	12.65	33.20	5.20	51.05
1984	13.90	34.15	5.85	53.90
1985	13.55	35.70	5.70	54.95
1986	16.65	43.75	6.95	67.35
1987	22.10	51.15	9.25	82.50
1988	–	54.20	–	–
1989	24.9	53.9	–	96.7
1990	–	66.7	–	110.9
Clothing				
1963	0.30	1.50	0.40	2.20
1973	3.80	7.00	1.75	12.60
1979	13.55	17.65	4.15	35.35
1980	16.40	20.40	5.00	41.80
1981	18.45	19.00	5.25	42.70
1982	18.15	18.30	5.65	42.10
1983	18.25	18.30	5.70	42.25
1984	22.15	19.80	6.20	48.15
1985	21.75	21.05	6.00	48.80
1986	26.10	28.10	8.30	62.50
1987	35.10	34.95	10.85	80.90
1988	–	36.75	–	–
1989	42.2	37.6	–	97.3
1990	–	48.3	–	113.4

Source: GATT (1989, 1990, 1992).

The textile trade regime

Trade in textiles and clothing has been heavily regulated since the 1960s. Currently, most OECD countries (with the major exception of Japan) subject their imports from developing countries to quota restrictions. The quota levels are set via bilateral agreements between importing and exporting countries, within the broad framework of the Multi-Fibre Arrangement (MFA), whose third renewal (MFA-IV) expired in 1991. Each successive renewal of MFA has resulted in further restrictions on developing country textile and clothing exports. One of the major uncertainties in the international environment at present is what will replace the MFA. There appears to be widespread agreement in principle that trade in textiles should be

Table 9.9 Textile yarn, fabrics and related products: imports into OECD from selected countries, 1975–87 (US$m)

	1975	1976	1977	1978	1979	1980	1981	1982	1983	1984	1985	1986	1987
Total	17,323	20,262	22,034	27,139	33,857	35,857	31,779	30,201	30,095	32,900	34,618	43,624	52,921
OECD total	14,004	15,853	17,297	21,153	26,117	27,453	24,123	23,062	22,851	24,220	25,779	33,132	39,251
	(80.8)	(78.2)	(78.5)	(77.9)	(77.1)	(76.6)	(75.9)	(76.4)	(75.9)	(73.6)	(74.5)	(75.9)	(74.2)
Four Asian dragons	1,269	1,664	1,661	2,269	2,855	2,997	3,245	3,121	3,149	3,896	3,950	4,809	5,987
	(7.3)	(8.2)	(7.5)	(8.4)	(8.4)	(8.4)	(10.2)	(10.4)	(10.5)	(11.8)	(11.4)	(11.0)	(11.3)
China	360	402	428	626	880	1,073	1,182	1,170	1,198	1,551	1,578	1,927	2,543
South Korea	374	545	550	827	985	904	947	906	834	1,040	1,037	1,228	1,521
Taiwan	214	266	284	381	482	509	591	597	636	758	843	1,095	1,328
Hong Kong	321	451	399	435	508	511	525	448	481	547	492	559	685
ASEAN 5	116	248	289	320	452	453	423	428	431	539	577	679	926
	(0.7)	(1.2)	(1.3)	(1.2)	(1.3)	(1.3)	(1.3)	(1.4)	(1.4)	(1.6)	(1.7)	(1.6)	(1.7)
Thailand	45	106	114	140	209	207	184	208	201	246	272	322	390
Indonesia	3	5	6	9	19	20	18	28	59	121	122	156	265
Malaysia	28	66	91	104	111	105	109	100	88	103	113	126	160
Philippines	18	27	24	29	40	49	50	45	43	38	43	46	66
Singapore	22	44	54	65	73	72	62	47	40	31	27	29	45
South Asia 2	497	705	776	939	1,214	1,420	1,213	1,088	1,106	1,243	1,336	1,508	2,207
	(2.9)	(3.5)	(3.5)	(3.5)	(3.6)	(4.0)	(3.8)	(3.6)	(3.7)	(3.8)	(3.9)	(3.5)	(4.2)
India	328	485	584	644	802	949	755	638	623	708	731	770	1,159
Pakistan	169	220	192	295	412	471	458	450	483	535	605	738	1,048

Note: Figures in parentheses are percentages of OECD total.
Source: OECD, *Foreign Trade by Commodities, Vol II: Imports, 1987*, Paris, 1988.

Table 9.10 Apparel and clothing accessories: imports into OECD from selected countries, 1975–87 (US$m)

	1975	1976	1977	1978	1979	1980	1981	1982	1983	1984	1985	1986	1987
Total	14,230	17,639	19,957	25,213	30,993	34,676	33,504	33,195	33,734	39,350	42,152	55,674	71,996
OECD	7,929	8,972	10,374	12,729	15,848	17,641	15,259	14,844	14,680	15,822	17,614	24,596	30,874
	(55.7)	(50.9)	(52.0)	(50.5)	(51.1)	(50.9)	(46.0)	(44.7)	(43.5)	(40.2)	(41.8)	(44.2)	(42.9)
Four Asian Dragons	4,002	5,617	5,979	7,856	9,362	10,542	11,907	12,167	12,679	15,731	15,859	19,844	25,550
	(28.1)	(31.8)	(30.0)	(31.2)	(30.2)	(30.4)	(35.5)	(36.7)	(37.6)	(40.0)	(37.6)	(35.6)	(35.5)
Hong Kong	2,010	2,724	2,776	3,442	4,080	4,678	4,849	4,767	4,859	6,005	6,062	6,989	8,474
South Korea	1,041	1,686	1,839	2,478	2,788	2,810	3,454	3,472	3,473	4,369	4,287	5,418	7,487
Taiwan	801	1,027	1,134	1,630	1,907	2,118	2,407	2,534	2,737	3,405	3,366	4,069	4,915
China	150	180	230	306	587	936	1,197	1,394	1,610	1,952	2,144	3,368	4,674
ASEAN 5	278	454	569	831	1,086	1,249	1,411	1,427	1,501	2,026	2,190	2,630	3,872
	(2.0)	(2.6)	(2.9)	(3.3)	(3.5)	(3.6)	(4.2)	(4.2)	(4.4)	(5.1)	(5.2)	(4.7)	(5.4)
Philippines	97	161	226	319	417	460	524	500	516	630	651	721	1,008
Thailand	47	78	83	131	181	220	255	271	293	412	466	568	914
Singapore	95	155	175	241	308	346	352	347	346	427	435	516	726
Malaysia	37	55	76	101	136	166	176	192	213	291	347	433	620
Indonesia	2	5	9	39	44	57	104	117	133	266	291	392	604
South Asia 2	216	337	388	530	686	780	845	764	730	906	1,016	1,303	1,861
	(1.5)	(1.9)	(1.9)	(2.1)	(2.2)	(2.2)	(2.5)	(2.3)	(2.2)	(2.3)	(2.4)	(2.3)	(2.6)
India	189	298	348	488	623	697	756	667	626	748	815	1,010	1,418
Pakistan	27	39	40	42	63	83	89	97	104	158	201	293	443

Note: Figures in parentheses are percentages of OECD total.
Source: OECD, *Foreign Trade by commodities, Vol. II: Imports*, 1987, Paris, 1988.

liberalised, but there remains basic disagreement on the practical details and the timetable of such liberalisation. The International Textiles and Clothing Bureau (ITCB), which represents twenty-two exporting (mostly developing) countries, has recently advanced a proposal for the gradual phasing-out of MFA over a six-year period ending in December 1997, with the existing MFA quota allocations serving as the baseline from which liberalisation is to proceed. Australia and the European Commission (EC) have responded positively to the proposal, with the EC noting several points of similarity to its own more cautious proposal, including the list of products to be covered by (diminishing) restraints and the provision for exporting countries to manage import quotas during the transition. How strong the EC commitment to liberalisation is remains to be seen: at the end of 1989 twenty-five of the leading European textile groups formed a new organisation to lobby the Commission to promote their interests post-MFA-IV. Still, the United States and Canada are likely to create the most serious obstacles to liberalisation. They both oppose the ITCB proposal, preferring instead to replace individual country quotas with a system of global quotas in ten years, with countries not hitherto restricted by quotas – including EC exporters – having to compete within the global quota limits.[9] The US proposal would also transfer administration of the quotas during the ten-year transition from exporter countries to importer countries, thereby removing one of the few advantages developing countries derive from the existing system, namely their ability to capture and allocate the quota rents.

Intransigence on the part of the US negotiators could severely hamper liberalisation efforts. The US negotiators are facing stiff pressure from the textile lobby and its supporters in the US Congress to resist developing country pressures for more rapid liberalisation of the textile trade. The one factor working in the favour of developing country exporters is the fact that a rift has emerged in the normally solid US textile bloc. For the first time since the formation of the bloc in the mid-1980s, the apparel industry component has dissented from the protectionist legislation supported by the textile manufacturers. The American Apparel Manufacturers Association has indicated that it opposes efforts to curb imports unilaterally, preferring to have the matter resolved through multilateral trade negotiations. Lying behind this position is the increasing globalisation of the US garment industry, with many of the leading US firms relying extensively on offshore sourcing not only of fabrics but also of clothing. The firms worry that, if they do not have access to textiles produced elsewhere, their own design flexibility would be substantially reduced, since they cannot obtain all the varieties of fabric they require from US suppliers. Moreover, firms like Liz Claiborne, Inc., source a sizeable share of their garment requirements from clothing manufacturers in Hong Kong, Thailand, Philippines and other developing countries. Stiffer protection would limit their foreign sourcing options.[10]

Developing countries are far from unanimous in their evaluation of the costs (and benefits) of the MFA. Different groups of developing countries are affected to different degrees and in different ways by the quota system. There is little doubt that the transition to free trade in textiles and garments (i.e. not only an end to quotas but the elimination of tariffs) would make possible a steep increase in developing country exports to OECD countries.[11] At the same time, certain countries have been hurt more than others by the MFA, while other countries may have actually benefited. The 'big three' exporters (Hong Kong, Taiwan and Korea) face binding quotas, but since quota allocations are based on historic export performance, their absolute volume of exports (and market share) is very high by comparison with other developing countries.[12] At the same time, their textile and garment industries have been faced with steeply escalating costs in recent years as the result of a combination of currency appreciation and rising labour costs. It is quite possible that their exports would have been more adversely affected by cost increases if they did not continue to enjoy such large quota allotments. In effect, their quotas may have protected their market shares to a degree from lower-cost producers. This would be true to the extent that short-run supply in lower-cost producer countries is relatively inelastic. In the case of those countries – for example, Malaysia, Indonesia, Thailand, China, India, Bangladesh and Pakistan – which face binding quotas themselves in their major markets, supply is almost perfectly inelastic.[13] Those countries have been the main beneficiaries of quota-induced trade diversion in the past, but as their own quotas become more restrictive there is little scope for further export diversion from the 'big three' to the 'little seven'. Given their lower costs, it is reasonable to assume that a liberalisation of trade would result in a relatively greater increase in exports from the 'little seven' than from the 'big three'.[14] Those countries not restricted by binding quotas at present (including the Philippines as well as several Central American and Caribbean producers) would stand to gain the least from trade liberalisation. Nevertheless, they would still gain, at the very least from the withdrawal of the threat that, should their exports increase significantly, they could face binding quota restrictions as well. Moreover, they would stand to gain from tariff reductions on textiles and clothing.

What has been the effect of the MFA on Malaysia's textile and garment industry? The quota system has at least one potentially positive effect on developing country industries: it provides an incentive to substitute high value added for low value added items, at least within the limits of specific quota categories. For the quotas are negotiated on the basis of quantity rather than value. Thus, if a firm has a quota allocation of 100 dozen men's dress shirts, it is generally better off if it can export shirts that command a premium price at a fashionable men's boutique than if they are sold through mass merchandisers like C&A and Marks and Spencer in the UK, or Sears and K-Mart in the USA.[15] Moreover, the imposition of quotas on specific items has encouraged manufacturers to diversify into other non-restricted categories. Frequently, however, such diversification has been followed by the extension of quota coverage in the next round of negotiations. The quota system also allows for some growth (normally about 6 per cent a year on a physical quantity basis), thereby providing a reasonably stable market environment for purposes of production planning. By contrast, those items not covered by MFA face the threat of 'voluntary restrictions' or orderly marketing arrangements.[16] This injects considerable uncertainty into the trade environment and makes production planning difficult.

The data in Table 9.11 make it apparent that the MFA has not kept developing countries as a whole from improving their textile and, especially, their clothing trade balances with the developed countries. The latter's clothing trade deficits with developing countries have continued to widen, while even textile trade has edged into deficit in recent years.[17] If textile and clothing were to revert to a free trade regime, the deficits could be expected to widen further with the projected surge in developing country clothing and textile exports.[18] Of course, there would be shifts in export shares among countries, with the higher-cost producers losing out to lower-cost ones. It is not clear whether Malaysia would be a net beneficiary of such shifts. Yet Malaysia's industry would certainly be buoyed up by the general improvement in developing country export prospects. If the US-proposed global quota system were to replace the MFA, historic market share would no longer count for much and there would still be a shift in favour of low-cost producers comparable to that which might be expected under free trade. The major difference is that overall developing country exports would not expand nearly as rapidly, so competition among countries for market share would resemble more nearly a zero-sum game.

Changes in market characteristics[19]

The major OECD markets for clothing have been transformed over the last decade by a combination of demographic shifts and rising income levels. The market for standardised apparel has been sluggish, while demand has grown rapidly for more highly differentiated fashion apparel. Customer preferences have dictated more frequent style changes and greater emphasis on innovative design and styling. Fashion seasons have become shorter, hence more numerous. To accommodate themselves to these market shifts, textile and clothing firms have had to shift from mass production of a few styles to shorter production runs of a much greater variety of styles. In addition, there has been a shift towards finer yarns and lighter-weight fabrics. Quality, ability to change product mix at short notice, and reliability of delivery have become hallmarks of competitive success in the textile and garment industries. The successful OECD producers have been able to achieve these objectives through a combination of automation and the reorganisation of their internal operations as well as of their relationships with suppliers and retailers. The

Table 9.11 Net trade balances with developing countries in textiles and clothing, 1973–88 (US$bn)

	1973	1979	1980	1981	1982	1983	1984	1985	1986	1987	1988
All developed (total)	−2.06	−8.85	−9.00	−8.50	−9.60	−10.55	−15.75	−16.20	−21.10	−30.45	−33.85
Textiles	0.65	1.20	2.50	3.80	3.10	2.80	1.65	1.40	0.95	−0.90	−0.45
Clothing	−2.71	−10.05	−11.50	−12.30	−12.70	−13.35	−17.40	−17.60	−22.05	−29.55	−33.40
EEC (total)	–	–	–	–	–	–	−3.79	−3.64	−5.96	−9.94	–
Textiles	–	–	–	–	–	–	0.19	0.18	0.05	−0.90	–
Clothing	–	–	–	–	–	–	−3.98	−3.82	−6.01	−9.04	–
United States (total)	–	–	–	–	–	–	−11.86	−12.95	−14.43	−17.59	−17.70
Textiles	–	–	–	–	–	–	−0.98	−1.01	−1.25	−1.59	−1.03
Clothing	–	–	–	–	–	–	−10.88	−11.94	−13.18	−16.00	−16.67
Japan (total)	–	–	–	–	–	–	1.47	1.18	0.78	−0.74	−2.30
Textiles	–	–	–	–	–	–	2.55	2.22	2.47	2.20	1.78
Clothing	–	–	–	–	–	–	−1.08	−1.04	−1.69	−2.94	−4.08

Source: GATT (1989, 1990).

latter set of changes is known in the industry as 'quick response'; in other industries it goes by the name 'just in time' (JIT).

The changing market characteristics have altered retailers' inventory management practices. They prefer to stock small quantities of a large variety of styles at the beginning of a fashion season, then reorder the styles that sell well. This cuts their inventories to a minimum. To make such a strategy viable, however, they must be able to restock very quickly. Thus, the garment makers which supply them must have very flexible and responsive production systems. Turnaround times must be cut drastically. This has important implications for the location of garment manufacturing activities, which may negatively affect the developing countries of Asia (as will be discussed below).

The upper and upper middle segments of the market, where these realignments are most apparent, also happen to be the market segments where growth rates and profit margins are generally highest. The leading textile and garment producers of East Asia are seeking to target these market segments, since high labour costs have made them less competitive in low value added products. Malaysia is in a particularly difficult bind: it is not yet able to compete with OECD and NIE producers at the upper end of the market; at the same time, it is facing intense competition from other low-cost producers in South and Southeast Asia at the lower end. The middle and upper middle of the market are becoming more quality and fashion conscious. There is growing value added to be captured in those markets, but only for those with the necessary design and marketing know-how, quick turnaround time and other competitive advantages.

The changing nature of clothing demand in the major OECD markets has had important implications for the investment strategies of textile producers. Traditionally, OECD-based textile firms have been averse to overseas investment in their own productive capacity. They exported the output of domestic mills, reaping economies of scale in the process. At the same time, they sourced from low-cost subcontractors in developing countries for low-end fabric requirements. Seldom did they set up production facilities in their major export markets. That has changed in recent years, as relations between textile suppliers and clothing firms have been forced closer by the requirements of the market. Textile firms are becoming oriented towards 'service'. They must be accessible to and communicate closely with their major designer and clothing firm customers, given the need for quick response to changes in fashion. Thus, the last few years have witnessed a growing number of international acquisitions and associations among leading OECD textile groups (Rawsthorn, 1989). This trend would seem to suggest that close linkages between the primary textile sector and the garment sector become more important as a country moves in the direction of greater product differentiation and higher value added clothing markets. This does not necessarily imply vertical integration; a clothing firm may have to deal with a number of suppliers of specialised fabrics. What it suggests is that those supplier networks are likely to become tighter and more durable. In other words, clothing firms would be less inclined to switch fabric suppliers merely on the basis of a slight shift in relative prices, considering that considerable sunk costs may have been incurred in developing the close working relationship with a particular supplier.

Developments in textile technologies

Important developments have been occurring in textile design and production technologies which, when combined with the market changes noted above, could alter the competitive prospects for developing countries like Malaysia. Over the last two decades, the pace of technological change in textiles has accelerated. The new technologies have thus far seen fairly widespread diffusion in the spinning and weaving sectors of the OECD member countries, where open-end rotors and shuttleless looms are in general use. High degrees of automation have also been achieved in knitting, with automated knitting able to achieve substantially higher production rates than weaving (Rajah and Mukunden, 1989). Dyeing and finishing operations also make extensive use of computer controls. The one area in which diffusion of microelectronics-based automation is still far behind is clothing assembly. The difficulties of automating that process have ensured developing countries a continued cost advantage based on low-cost labour.

Spinning and weaving technologies

While automation of the primary textile sector is widespread in the OECD countries, it has progressed more slowly in most developing countries outside the East Asian NIEs (see Tables 9.6 and 9.7 for comparative statistics on installed spinning and weaving capacity by type). The OECD countries are investing in the new technologies in an effort to restore their competitiveness, while the NIEs are doing so in an effort to maintain theirs. At the same time, they are attempting to make the transition to the more quality-sensitive market segments. The high-volume producers like China, Pakistan, Indonesia and India almost certainly have a decided advantage in the low value added fabric market. Malaysia has very little basis for competing with them in standardised, low-cost fabric. It needs to position itself in the middle to upper-middle market segments but faces strong competition both from the NIEs and from other countries in the region (most notably Thailand) hoping to move upmarket. Without substantial technology upgrading, Malaysia could well find itself squeezed out. The new production technologies are generally better suited than traditional methods to the shorter production runs, greater flexibility, higher quality and quicker turnaround times characteristic of the higher value added segments of the market.

Malaysia faces a dilemma in making the necessary adjustments. For a significant proportion of its installed capacity – and of recent investment in the primary textile sector – is under the control of foreign textile firms (especially from Taiwan) which have transferred second-hand textile machinery to Malaysia to produce low-cost fabrics while investing in new machinery to produce higher value added fabrics at home. Thus, if such upgrading of production capacity is to occur, it may have to take place first within the domestically owned textile sector. Fortunately, the necessary technologies are largely embodied in capital equipment, so with adequate financial resources local firms should not face major constraints in acquiring them (although temporary backlogs in equipment orders are possible). The major constraint is likely to be the aforementioned shortage of skilled textile engineers and technicians, especially ones knowledgeable in the set-up, operation, maintenance and repair of the latest vintage of automated equipment.[20] In the short term, local firms may need to hire foreign consultants to assist them in introducing such machinery, but, with effective training and learning-by-doing, the knowledge and skills involved should be acquired by local personnel within a relatively short time. At the same time, textile engineering courses may need to be revised to incorporate more material on automated (including electronic control) technologies.

Clothing technologies

Pre-assembly

In the garment sector, technological developments are far less of a threat to the competitiveness of Malaysia's industry. The main technological development occurring in this sector is in the pre-assembly phases of design, pattern making and cutting. Computer-aided design (CAD)-based grading and marking systems are now relatively inexpensive (the cheapest costing approximately US$50,000), making them affordable to a growing number of local firms.[21] The major advantage of CAD systems is the substantial reduction in material wastage they can achieve compared with the traditional manual methods. Moreover, while the traditional methods require highly skilled labour, the computer-based system is less skill intensive, or at least the skills are of a more generic nature (i.e. familiarity with the use of computers and of CAD software). Since skilled graders and markers are in short supply in Malaysia and elsewhere in the region, the availability of CAD systems enables firms to substitute away from a scarce resource. Still, investments in such systems tend to be economic at present only for the larger garment firms.[22] With respect to automated (computer numerical control, or CNC) cutting systems, they are still not economic even for most large firms in Malaysia and elsewhere in Southeast Asia. For, while cutting is also a skilled job, it is more labour intensive. Given the prevailing labour costs in the region and the relatively high cost of the CNC equipment, few firms have been able to justify the investment. Moreover, automated cutting is still not sufficiently flexible to compete with highly flexible manual methods. Skilled technicians knowledgeable in CNC machining are also scarce. As a result, even those firms which have invested in CAD-based grading and marking have seldom invested in CNC cutters. (The situation is quite different in the OECD countries, where the two investments are frequently viewed as complementary.)

Assembly

Beyond the cutting stage, automation is even less widespread. Moreover, the prospects for significant advances in automation of garment assembly are rather small in the near to medium term. Assembly remains a one operator/one machine process. Substantial cost reductions can be (and have been) achieved in the OECD countries through the use of automated material transport systems to move pieces between workstations. Another potentially significant advance in assembly technology is the development of 'intelligent' sewing-machine workstations. These are machines with memory such that a single skilled operator can tutor them in a sequence of operations, which is then programmed into the machines and repeated automatically on command. After the initial programming, the machines can thus be tended by unskilled operators. This innovation is potentially skill saving. If low-income developing countries can generally be characterised as possessing an abundance of unskilled but a shortage of skilled labour, then the new technology could actually work to the competitive advantage of those developing countries.[23] Of course, the countries with the greatest scarcity of skills are also likely to be those with the greatest scarcity of capital to invest in these relatively expensive workstations. Whether the East and Southeast Asian countries have a shortage of skilled sewing labour at present is somewhat doubtful, so they would probably not be major beneficiaries of such an innovation in any case. Even with these innovations, there is a high probability that sewing will remain a labour-intensive process for at least another decade. This suggests that developing countries as a whole have little reason to fear a near-term loss of competitiveness in the garment sector. Even for countries with moderately high labour costs like Malaysia, the labour cost differential with the OECD countries is still of the order of 10. Productivity differentials would have to be very large indeed to offset those cost advantages.

Of more immediate concern than being priced out of the market is whether Malaysia's industry can move upmarket to higher-fashion items, so that it can capture more value per garment produced and sold. Selective automation – especially in pre-assembly – may help by adding to firms' flexibility in adapting to frequent style changes and shorter fashion seasons. Assuming the customer has the relevant design information in computer-readable form[24], it can be loaded into the garment firm's CAD system and used to generate the necessary patterns (including multiple size variations), then lay them out most efficiently on the cloth to minimise fabric wastage. All of this can be done in far less time than was possible with traditional methods. Turnaround times in grading and marking are improved by a factor of 4–6 with the introduction of CAD systems.[25] A firm with this capability is certainly in a better position to serve the fashion-sensitive segments of the market.

Implications for location of production

Such investments may not prove sufficient, however. For the advantages of shorter turnaround time in the pre-assembly phase may be negated if the retailer has to await delivery of assembled clothing from plants located on the other side of the world. Given that the major markets for Malaysia (and other Asian clothing makers) remain the United States and Western Europe, the distance to market could be a serious barrier to entry into higher value added segments in the future. The clothing firms in the major OECD markets are investing in CAD grading and marking systems as well as CNC fabric cutters to be able to make new patterns and cut new fabric for reorders on short notice. To reap the full benefits of those investments, they are sourcing a growing volume of their garments from locations closer to the market. Thus, US clothing firms are coming to rely increasingly on Caribbean and Mexican subcontractors for garment assembly, while European firms are relying increasingly on subcontractors in southern and eastern Europe as well as in north Africa.[26] Even though wages are slightly higher in many of those locations than in Asia, the cost reduction resulting from pre-assembly automation and shortened turnaround times can compensate and make such arrangements competitive. The geographic shift in sourcing patterns has certainly slowed the rate of growth of the Asian garment industries in recent years. One possible mitigating factor would be if similar principal/subcontractor relationships were to become more extensive between Japanese retailers or clothing firms and developing Asian subcontractors for purposes of supplying the Japanese market. Japanese firms are likely to cede more and more of the low end of the market to imports, but they are likely to seek to consolidate their positions in the high value added segments of the market. Given high disposable incomes in Japan and a growing fashion consciousness among consumers, that is where the growth is. Nevertheless, the lower end of the market in Japan may be somewhat more quality conscious than the lower end of other major OECD markets, though such a statement is admittedly impressionistic. This does not, in any case, imply that firms serving that market can expect to realise higher margins, since competition is also likely to be intense. To penetrate that market, greater attention would need to be given to fabric quality and workmanship, for which there should be some premium. At present far too little is known about the conditions for entry into the Japanese textile and clothing markets.

STRATEGY AND POLICY ISSUES FOR THE FUTURE OF MALAYSIA'S TEXTILE AND GARMENT INDUSTRIES

Competitive pressures on Malaysia's textile and garment producers can be expected only to become more intense in the decade to come. The industry will have to adjust or face the sunset once more. The pressures for adjustment originate from several sources, as explained above. Whatever the outcome of the current trade talks on the future of GATT and of the MFA, Malaysia can expect to face intensifying cost competition from lower-wage countries in Asia. It will therefore have to find ways to shift the balance of its production and exports into higher value added products. At the same time, the shifting market characteristics, with the increased emphasis on 'quick response' and shorter turnaround times, will bring it into closer competition in its major market, the USA, with producers in the Caribbean and Latin America. Malaysian producers must therefore devise ways to shorten cycle times, respond more quickly to shifting fashion trends, and refocus growth on regional markets, including Japan, Singapore and certain other Asian NIEs.

As an essential step towards upgrading its product range, the Malaysian industry will have to invest more heavily in new production technologies, especially within the spinning and weaving sectors. While trade-offs among the various available technologies require a measured approach to adoption, the greater flexibility made possible by new electronically controlled equipment makes it more suitable to the higher value added markets Malaysia will have to target in the future. The new skill requirements of using and maintaining that equipment will also have to be addressed. Ultimately, Malaysian firms will also have to develop stronger skills in the area of design and marketing. Continued reliance on CMT business and on foreign customers to provide the design and marketing expertise will confine the industry to assembly operations and limit the share of value added that can be captured locally.

With this broad strategic direction in view, we can identify several specific concerns which need to be addressed by firms and government policy makers if the industry is to evolve in the proposed direction.

Upgrading the primary textile sector

The first concern is how to strengthen the primary textile sector in Malaysia. The aim of strategy and policy for the primary textile sector should not be self-sufficiency.[27] A great variety of fabric types and qualities is required by the clothing sector, and there is no economic justification for local textile firms to supply all of them, especially in view of the scale economies involved in many standard fabric items. Malaysia has two neighbours – Thailand and Indonesia – which are large primary textile producers, but they remain suppliers principally of high-volume grey cloth of variable quality. Malaysia's own textile industry should not be seeking to replicate the standard bulk textile production of those countries but rather should be aiming at producing higher-quality specialised fabrics in smaller volumes. It should also be concentrating more on dyeing and finishing operations, so that it can add significant value locally to the grey cloth it imports from its neighbours. For this purpose, the new textile technologies are apt to prove essential.[28]

Financing the necessary investments is a crucial policy concern. The recent upsurge in the local clothing industry could provide sufficient inducement to local mills to invest in new capacity, but it is not assured that they will invest in the new spinning and weaving technologies. For the costs are quite high compared with those of older technologies available from countries like Taiwan and Korea. Thus, the government may need to consider how to ensure that adequate financing is made available to local mills on attractive terms to permit them to undertake the large investments required to modernise plant and equipment. One possibility apparently under consideration is a textile restructuring loan from a multilateral lending institution to make relatively long-term financing available to textile firms at competitive rates. Now that textile investments are looking more profitable than in the 'sunset' years, it may be possible for those property and other companies which diversified into textiles in the mid-1980s to raise part of the financing required for modernising their capacity through new share issues on the KLSE. Other textile firms may also be able to turn to equity markets as the KLSE continues to register strong performance. Whether new listings of independent textile firms will prove attractive to prospective investors (especially short-term ones) is uncertain. They may do better in this regard as part of diversified business groups, given the characteristic cyclicality of the textile market.

Building up the supply of skilled labour

Another critical issue the government needs to address is the supply of skilled labour to work in a modernised textile sector. Government-sponsored (or perhaps joint government–industry) textile technician training programmes, with adequate emphasis on new technologies like microelectronics, are one way to fill the skills gap. Strengthening university programmes in textile engineering and increasing the intake of students into that field is another. In the meantime, sending students abroad for degrees at institutions with strong textile engineering programmes could help fill the gap. As previously noted, there are at present many expatriate textile experts employed in Malaysian textile plants. If they are to be anything more than a stopgap, there is need to ensure that their skills are transferred effectively to local textile managers, engineers and technicians. This will require extensive and systematic in-plant training. The government needs to encourage such skills transfer, perhaps by providing fiscal incentives to firms which invest in in-house training programmes. Without skill and know-how transfer, either the expatriates are likely to become a permanent fixture, or plant productivity can be expected to drop off once they depart. Neither outcome is desirable from the point of view of developing the local industry.

Enhancing local design capabilities

To move beyond low-cost garment assembly, it is necessary to strengthen clothing (and even textile) design capabilities. To supply the necessary skills, it may be desirable to establish a specialised institute at some stage. Initially, however, it would seem more critical to foster the conditions wherein local firms face greater exposure to foreign designers. This is perhaps the most immediate opportunity for greater local learning of design skills. An intermediate step towards fostering such interactions, and one which would have positive short-term effects, is to encourage more widespread diffusion of CAD-based grading and marking systems among small and medium-sized garment firms not yet able to afford them. In the short term, this would help them become more flexible in responding to requirements for more frequent style changes and greater product diversity. In the longer term, it could facilitate closer interaction with designers, since the latter now rely quite extensively on CAD systems in the design process itself. The country already possesses certain indigenous design capabilities residing in its traditional batik textile and clothing sector. While a local design sector would have to broaden its repertoire beyond batik design, that may prove a useful starting point for establishing an international design reputation.

Building international marketing skills

To complement such design efforts, attention must be given to strengthening local firms' marketing capabilities as well. The collection and dissemination of market intelligence need not be the sole responsibility of the government. The Malaysian Textile Manufacturers Association (MTMA) can play a valuable role in this regard. Still, given that the major markets remain quota restricted, close coordination between the public and private sectors is required to ensure that quotas are effectively utilised.[29] There is no need for the government to take explicit measures to encourage a shift to higher value added items within existing quota ceilings. Private firms should have ample incentive to make such a shift in response to market forces. The government may be able to assist firms, however, with market intelligence and contacts with customers in non-quota-restricted markets. In the case of the Japanese market, independent marketing effort on the part of local firms may yield results in the future as the tight control of Japan's big trading companies over domestic distribution channels weakens.[30]

Internationalisation of Malaysian firms

To compete in the new global environment, the Malaysian textile and garment industry will have to become more aggressive not only in its international marketing activities, but most probably in international investment activities as well. Already, one of the leading Malaysian textile groups has made overseas investments in Puerto Rico and Vietnam and is reported to be seeking possible partners in the EEC.[31] Malaysian firms, like their OECD counterparts, may need to move closer to the market, in order to be able to serve the needs of their customers adequately. Thus, at least in the case of the larger firms, overseas investment in or near strategic markets can be expected to rise. Beyond foreign investment, Malaysian firms will also have to forge closer cooperative links with foreign firms. These inter-firm collaborations are of two sorts. On one side, closer links with OECD firms may ensure more secure access to markets as well as to their design know-how. It may also be required by the shift to 'quick response' product planning. On the other side, the Malaysian firm may need to establish links to subcontractors in lower-wage countries to fill out its product range on the low value added side. Of course, direct foreign investment in those countries is an alternative, at least for the larger firms. Malaysian firms are still several years behind their Hong Kong and Taiwan based counterparts in this process of globalisation. Yet, in time Malaysian firms' international networks should expand more rapidly. Such a process could well prove necessary if the industry is to adapt successfully to shifting market and competitive requirements. The critical requirement is that the internationalisation of Malaysia's industry be accompanied by a substantial upgrading in its domestic activities.[32] If offshore investment or subcontracting were to become a substitute for rather than a complement to greater domestic value addition, this would mark the beginning of the end of the textile industry's day in the sun.

APPENDIX

Table 9A.1 Hong Kong: exports, imports and trade balance for textile products, 1978–86 (US$m)

	1978	1979	1980	1981	1982	1983	1984	1985	1986	Compound Annual growth rates (1978–86)
Textile fabric:										
Exports	456	672	670	730	595	699	863	793	1,157	0.12
Imports	919	1,236	1,376	1,790	1,485	1,478	1,994	2,027	2,713	0.14
Balance	(463)	(609)	(706)	(1,060)	(890)	(779)	(1,131)	(1,234)	(1,556)	0.16
Apparel and Clothing accessories:										
Exports	3,266	4,059	4,525	5,016	4,401	4,400	5,966	5,751	6,696	0.09
Imports	270	398	673	925	987	1,093	1,483	1,692	2,525	0.32
Balance	2,996	3,661	3,852	4,091	3,414	3,307	4,483	4,059	4,171	0.04
Overall textiles:										
Exports	3,722	4,686	5,195	5,746	4,996	5,099	6,829	6,544	7,853	0.10
Imports	1,189	1,634	2,049	2,715	2,472	2,571	3,477	3,719	5,238	0.20
Balance	2,533	3,052	3,146	3,031	2,524	5,528	3,352	2,825	2,615	0.00

Source: *Hong Kong Annual Digest of Statistics,* 1987 edition, Hong Kong.

Table 9A.2 Republic of Korea: Exports, imports and trade balance for textiles (US$'000)

	1981	1982	1983	1984	1985	Compound annual growth rates (1981–85)
Textile fibres:						
Exports	55,902	50,097	53,004	91,079	90,040	0.13
Imports	856,013	769,616	809,406	927,567	847,962	0.00
Balance	(800,111)	(719,519)	(756,402)	(836,488)	(757,922)	-0.01
Textile yarn and fabrics						
Exports	2,458,911	2,250,369	2,423,040	2,614,539	2,543,715	0.01
Imports	510,312	519,587	530,756	630,818	669,657	0.07
Balance	1,948,599	1,730,782	1,892,284	1,983,721	1,874,058	-0.01
Apparel and clothing accessories:						
Exports	3,867,559	3,773,863	3,707,263	4,499,466	4,449,869	0.04
Imports	10,403	9,430	9,540	10,711	12,259	0.04
Balance	3,857,156	3,764,433	3,697,723	4,488,755	4,437,610	0.04
Total textiles:						
Exports	6,382,372	6,074,329	6,183,307	7,205,084	7,083,624	0.03
Imports	1,376,728	1,298,633	1,349,702	1,569,096	1,529,878	0.03
Balance	5,005,644	4,775,696	4,833,605	5,635,988	5,553,746	0.03

Source: Korea Statistical Yearbook, 1986, Economic Planning Board, Seoul, 1986.

Table 9A.3 Taiwan: exports, imports and trade balance for textiles (US$'000)

	1979	1980	1981	1982	1983	1984	1985	1986	Compound annual growth rates 1979–86
Textile fabrics:									
Exports	1,320,259	1,503,137	1,673,443	1,432,605	1,461,550	1,755,880	2,019,663	2,431,839	0.09
Imports	213,621	241,803	299,479	269,160	307,469	386,825	328,860	489,572	0.13
Balance	1,106,638	1,261,334	1,373,964	1,163,445	1,154,081	1,369,055	1,690,803	1,942,267	0.08
Garments:									
Exports	3,047,840	4,015,551	4,540,706	4,596,800	5,055,855	6,230,374	6,133,751	7,739,681	0.14
Imports	49,110	59,637	60,333	61,563	74,625	100,831	90,201	125,159	0.14
Balance	2,998,730	3,955,914	4,480,373	4,535,237	4,981,230	6,129,543	6,043,550	7,614,522	0.14
Total textiles:									
Exports	4,368,099	5,518,688	6,214,149	6,029,405	6,517,405	7,986,254	8,153,414	10,171,520	0.13
Imports	262,731	301,440	359,812	330,723	382,094	487,656	419,061	614,731	0.13
Balance	4,105,368	5,217,248	5,854,337	5,698,682	6,135,311	7,498,598	7,734,353	9,556,789	0.13

Note: Classification of data is based on the sectoral breakdown in the Taiwan input–output table.
Source: Taiwan Statistical Data Book, 1987, Council for Economic Planning and Development, Taipei, 1987.

Table 9A.4 Thailand: exports, imports and trade balance for textile products (US$'000)

	1984	1985	1986	1987	Compound annual growth rates 1984–87
Man-made fibres:					
Exports	7,459	11,405	6,951	9,536	0.09
Imports	46,062	39,110	33,771	57,483	0.08
Balance	(38,603)	(27,705)	(26,820)	(47,947)	0.07
Textile yarns:					
Exports	55,970	78,880	115,404	138,210	0.35
Imports	44,008	33,086	68,464	127,229	0.42
Balance	11,962	45,794	46,940	10,981	−0.03
Textile fabrics:					
Exports	234,280	243,441	306,580	351,861	0.15
Imports	156,426	128,086	167,394	249,107	0.17
Balance	77,854	115,355	139,186	102,754	0.10
Garments:					
Exports	519,647	542,521	778,099	1,413,107	0.40
Imports	2,604	1,286	2,289	3,792	0.13
Balance	517,043	541,235	775,810	1,409,315	0.40
Total textiles:					
Exports	817,356	876,247	1,207,034	1,912,714	0.33
Imports	249,100	201,568	271,918	437,611	0.21
Balance	568,256	674,679	935,116	1,475,103	0.37

Sources: *Bangkok Post Economic Review*, 1988; Thai Manufacturers Association.

Table 9A.5 Indonesia: exports, imports and trade balance for textile products (US$'000 and '000 kg)

	1983	1984	1985	1986	1987	1988	Compound annual growth rates (1983–8)
Textile fibres:							
Exports – value	–	...	...	2,159	3,399	19,090	1.97[a]
net wt		...	...	3,411	3,613	15,513	1.13[a]
Imports – value	255,172	308,172	277,925	241,678	357,802	384,138	0.26[a]
net wt	187,042	202,750	234,154	232,072	281,903	247,643	0.03[a]
Balance – value	...	...	...	(239,519)	(354,403)	(365,048)	0.23
Textile yarns + fabrics:							
Exports – value	120,511	200,475	239,832	306,802	468,702	680,384	0.41[b]
net wt	31,160	51,030	61,540	71,947	107,799	135,217	0.34[b]
Imports – value	149,254	125,587	125,772	193,047	213,006	303,657	0.15[b]
net wt	51,363	36,387	51,283	68,843	65,025	72,757	0.07[b]
Balance – value	(28,743)	74,888	114,060	113,755	255,696	376,727	0.38[b]
Made-up clothing:							
Exports – value	157,159	295,743	339,122	521,966	595,806	796,670	0.38
net wt	22,050	31,933	37,975	56,452	53,556	63,995	0.24
Imports – value	9,401	5,277	3,754	3,950	4,667	6,507	−0.07
net wt	1,741	824	710	793	922	1,131	−0.08
Balance – value	147,758	290,466	335,368	518,016	591,139	790,163	0.40

Notes:
[a] For textile fibres, the CAGR is for the period 1986–8 only.
[b] For textile yarns + fabrics, the CAGR is for the period 1984–8 only.
Sources: *Indonesia Foreign Trade Statistics, Imports and Exports*, Vol. II; *Statistical Yearbook of Indonesia, 1987*, Government of Indonesia, 1988.

TEXTILES

NOTES

1. The term 'textile industry' is used here in the broad sense, to include the whole range of sectors from fibre production through spinning and weaving to the production of finished apparel. Normally, for economy's sake, this convention will be followed throughout the paper. While in some cases we refer to the textile sector in the narrower sense – i.e. spinning of yarn and weaving of cloth – it should be clear from the context which usage is intended. Normally we employ the term 'primary textiles' when we intend this narrower usage. The terms 'apparel', 'clothing' and 'garments' are used interchangeably to refer to the sector which produces made-up wearing apparel.
2. Singapore did not rely as heavily as did the other 'little dragons' on textiles and garments to fuel its early manufactured export growth. It should also be mentioned that, while textiles and garments contributed significantly to output, export and employment growth in the other Asian NIEs, there is some controversy over how important the industry was in generating the managerial skills and technological capabilities required for rapid industrialisation. Amsden argues (1989: Ch.10), for example, that textiles played virtually no role as a base from which the Korean *chaebol* diversified into more skill- and capital-intensive industries.
3. By way of comparison, in 1988 Thailand's textile and garment exports were more than twice as large as Malaysia's; Indonesia's were about one-fourth larger. Annex Tables 9A.1–9A.5 contain textile trade data for several of Malaysia's East and Southeast Asian neighbours. They are based on Tables 5.A–5.E of O'Connor (1989a).
4. Malaysia still has unutilised quotas in several 'sensitive' categories: for example, in four out of six quota-restricted items in the European Community (EC) market, quota utilisation ranged from 75 to 83 per cent in 1988; in the case of the remaining two, utilisation was between 36 and 51 per cent (Zainal Abidin Sulong, chairman of MIDA (1989)).
5. A glance at Table 9.4 shows that the wage differential between Malaysia and Korea in the primary textile sector had widened considerably by 1990, to the point where Malaysian hourly labour costs were only about 27 per cent of Korea's. While evidence for the textile sector alone is not available, the overall increase in Korean wages in the last few years has outstripped increases in labour productivity, with the result that unit labour costs in manufacturing have risen steeply. According to one calculation, the increase from mid-1988 to mid-1989 was 43 per cent (*Financial Times*, Special Supplement on South Korea, 16 May 1990, III).
6. For example, in 1983, ring spindle technology could spin 28 metres of short staple yarn per minute, whereas open-end rotor technology could spin 98 metres per minute (Werner International, 1988). Spinning speed may not be the only performance variable affecting the choice of technique, however. One advantage of the older ring spinning technology is that it allows a greater degree of flexibility with respect to choice of product lines. Open-end rotor spinning is best suited to the coarse count yarns such as those used in weaving denim textiles (Beasley, 1989).
7. In 1987, US garment imports from Malaysia, valued at US$343 million, accounted for 53 per cent of all OECD imports (OECD, 1989).
8. According to the estimate of William Cline of the Institute for International Economics, in Washington, DC, quotas must be allowed to grow by 7 per cent a year if protection is not to tighten with the growth in the US market.
9. Rawsthorn (1990); see also, *Financial Times*, 14 June 1990, and *Far Eastern Economic Review*, 16 August 1990. It is not surprising, under the circumstances, that the EC should oppose the North American proposal.

10 See Lachica (1990) cover. For a detailed description of Liz Claiborne's international sourcing network, see Lardner (1988: 39–73).
11 This is borne out by two recent modelling exercises. The results of the first are presented in Trela and Whalley (1988). The general equilibrium effects of removing bilateral MFA quotas and tariffs in all developed countries on developing country exports are strongly positive, though more so in some countries than in others. The highest estimated export increase is 899.94 per cent in the case of Colombia, the lowest 11.45 per cent in the case of Macau. Overall, developing countries would gain by US$11.29 billion (total welfare gains, not just trade gains) from complete trade liberalisation in textiles and garments. A similar exercise, but using a somewhat different model, is performed in Goto (1990). Unlike Trela and Whalley, Goto does not assume all quotas are binding, differentiating countries according to the degree to which their exports face binding MFA restrictions in major markets. Moreover, Goto uses different elasticity parameters and focuses only on the trade effects of liberalisation. Goto's results tend to confirm those of Trela and Whalley, with a simultaneous removal of quotas and tariffs by the USA and EC resulting in a short-run increase of US$7.2 billion in developing country exports. Moreover, all groups of developing countries gain, but those which were not restricted by binding quotas under the MFA understandably gain least.
12 In 1988, those big three clothing exporters together accounted for 29 per cent of world clothing exports; all other developing countries combined accounted for only about 14 per cent of world clothing exports (GATT, 1990).
13 The binding rates are based on Tables 3 and 4 of Goto (1990). They represent the geometric mean of the MFA coverage ratio and the quota utilisation rate. Goto considers a binding rate of greater than 70 per cent to identify countries that are effectively quota restricted in their major export markets. This suggests not only that they face quotas on a large percentage of their exports but also that they utilise a high percentage of those quotas. In the case of Malaysia, while its binding rate is rather low in the EEC market, in the US market (on which it is heavily dependent) it is 76.9 percent. Of course industries facing high binding rates in the EEC market, like those of Korea, Hong Kong and Taiwan, could still benefit by setting up production capacity in Malaysia to serve the EEC market.
14 Table 5 of Trela and Whalley (1988) confirms this hypothesis. Indirect support is also provided by Dean (1990). This article contains a few interesting results: (1) For eight 'small' Asian exporters (including Malaysia), their quota restraints in the US market are binding and, as a result, their import shares have grown much more slowly than those of uncontrolled countries; (2) the tightening of restrictions on the 'big three' has benefited smaller exporters, but only in years when the latter's quotas were allowed to grow faster than the US market; (3) relative cost competitiveness remains an important determinant of US market share with regard to uncontrolled trade; the impact of cost competitiveness on import share declines as more categories of a country's exports come under restraint. By implication, an across-the-board liberalisation of imports into the US market would significantly increase the importance of relative costs as a determinant of import market share.
15 Thus far no estimates have been made of changes in value added in the Malaysian textile and garment industries on a per unit basis. In principle, given the data, this should not be overly difficult. Export value and volume data should be available by quota category, which should make it possible to determine if the unit values of specific export items are increasing (in real terms) over time.
16 This point is made in Douglas (1989) which contains a useful discussion of the costs and benefits to the Malaysian textile industry of bilateral trade restrictions under the MFA with the United States.

17 Particularly noteworthy in Table 9.11 is the surge in Japanese imports of clothing from developing countries from 1986 onwards. Also, the Japanese textile trade balance with developing countries may well be on an accelerating downward trend. Japanese textile firms – in particular, knitwear manufacturers – have exerted pressure on the government to curb imports, especially from Korea, whose knitwear exports to Japan surged in the late 1980s. At the same time, those knitting firms have invested heavily in automation to maintain their competitiveness. For example, in one major knitting district (Senshu, outside Osaka), there were only 30 computer-controlled knitting machines in 1981; by 1988 there were well over 1,000. Moreover, the operator:machine ratio has gone from 1:1 to 1:3–5. See Wagstyl (1988).

18 Refer again to Trela and Whalley (1988) and Goto (1990). These trade data must be interpreted cautiously, however, since there are important inputs – both intermediate goods like synthetic fibres and capital equipment for the textile industry – which are not captured by them. If those items were to be included in an overall 'textile-related' trade balance, the developed country deficits would certainly shrink. For example, the United States ran a trade surplus of US$1.03 billion with developing Asia in 1988 on textile fibres (SITC, rev.2, 26) (OECD, 1989).

19 This section is based in part on Hoffman (1990) of Sussex Research Associates (SRA) of the UK.

20 Amsden found, in her case study of a Korean textile firm (1989: 261), that the engineers could operate the new automated machinery, but they had difficulties repairing it, not being familiar with the electronics technologies embedded in it.

21 The estimate is based on an interview with the Bangkok affiliate of a major European supplier of CAD grading and marking systems, reported in O'Connor (1989b).

22 The results of a survey of Singaporean textile/clothing firms by Francis Chan and associates at the National University of Singapore bear this out. They interviewed 26 firms, 18 with output in 1988 of over S$10 million and 8 with output of up to S$10 million. While 38.9 per cent of the larger firms used CAD systems, none of the smaller firms reported using them. The survey was conducted as part of a study undertaken for the OECD Development Centre, Paris, 1989.

23 See Wyatt (1989) for a useful discussion of the implications of new technology for the industrial structure of the clothing sector.

24 The compatibility of software (or an appropriate conversion programme) is also necessary if customers and garment firms are to be able to interchange computerised design information. Since there are only a few suppliers of CAD-based grading and marking systems, the problem of incompatibility may not be as serious in this area as it is in many other areas of computer networking.

25 This estimate is from Hoffman (1990).

26 In the case of the United States, for example, clothing imports from developing Asia (excluding the Middle East and Oceania) rose an average of 13.2 per cent a year from 1983 to 1988. Clothing imports from Latin American and the Caribbean rose over the same period by 27.3 per cent a year. Of course, in absolute terms, imports from the former are still 6.5 times larger than imports from the latter (OECD, 1989).

27 Hong Kong is a good example of an economy with a highly competitive garment industry which runs a large trade deficit on primary textiles.

28 Given the pollution (e.g. waste water with toxic chemicals) generated by textile dyeing and finishing operations, any major expansion of this sector would have to give ample consideration to the availability of waste water treatment facilities.

29 It is also required to guard against the creation of excess production capacity in

quota-restricted product categories. The reliance of Malaysian garment makers on foreign customers for marketing and distribution in quota-restricted markets has allowed the latter to appropriate a portion of the quota rents.
30 This dependence on the *soga sosha* may make market access possible, but of course at the expense of forfeiting a certain degree of marketing responsibility (and the attendant revenues).
31 'Malaysia: Group looks abroad', *Textile Asia*, March 1988: 146.
32 While the textile and garment industries of Hong Kong and Taiwan have suffered declines in the volume of their exports due to tightening restrictions in the US market, the value has continued to rise. This reflects in part a shift to higher value added products. In part, it also reflects the increased amount of value added in those locations at the design and marketing stages. As Hong Kong, for example, has become a major regional design and logistical centre, it can 'afford' to perform less of the actual garment assembly, beyond the production of samples in small batches and on short order. Its value addition occurs increasingly in areas other than mass production of low value clothing items. This is what is suggested could happen, though perhaps not in the near term, in Malaysia. First, it needs to build up the other activities – eg., design, marketing, etc. – which could make possible such a shift in emphasis.

REFERENCES

Amsden, A.H. (1989) *Asia's Next Giant: South Korea and Late Industrialization*, Oxford University Press, New York.
Beasley, S.D. (1989) 'Textile Exports Spur Thai Economic Boost', *The Nation* (Bangkok), 30 December.
Dean, J.M. (1990) 'The Effects of the U.S. MFA on Small Exporters', *Review of Economics and Statistics*, 72, 1, February, 63–9.
Department of Statistics (1989a) *Monthly Manufacturing Statistics*, Kuala Lumpur, April.
Department of Statistics (1989b) *Monthly Manufacturing Statistics*, Kuala Lumpur, May.
Douglas, Sara U. (1989) 'The Textile Industry in Malaysia: Coping with Protectionism', *Asian Survey*, April, 416–38.
GATT (1989) *International Trade 87–88*, Vol. II, Geneva.
GATT (1990) *International Trade 88–89*, Vol. II, Geneva.
GATT (1992) *International Trade 90–91*, Vol. II, Geneva.
Goto, J. (1990) 'A Formal Estimation of the Effect of the MFA on Clothing Exports from LDCs', Working Paper WPS 455, International Economics Department, The World Bank, June.
Hoffman, K. (1990) Unpublished paper prepared for a conference sponsored by the United Nations Industrial Development Organisation (UNIDO) on 'Technology Transfer for Entrepreneurial Development', Dhaka, Bangladesh, 4–8 March.
Lachica, Eduardo (1990) 'Split Develops in U.S. Over Textile Curbs', *Asian Wall Street Journal*, 13–14 July.
Lardner, James (1988) 'Annals of Business: The Sweater Trade – I', *The New Yorker*, 11 January, 39–73.
MIDA (n.d.) *Statistics on the Manufacturing Sector 1989*, Kuala Lumpur.
O'Connor, D. (1989a) 'Trade, Technology and Textiles: Global Trends and Their Implications for Malaysia and Southeast Asia', paper presented at Malaysian Economics Association – Northern Branch Seminar on 'The Textile Industry: Challenges and Choices', Penang, 11–12 August.

O'Connor, David (1989b) 'Microelectronics-based Innovations: Strategic Implications for Selected Industries in the Second-Tier New Industrialising Countries of Southeast Asia', prepared for OECD Development Centre, Paris, November.

OECD (1988) *Foreign Trade by Commodities, Vol. II: Imports, 1987*, Paris.

OECD (1989) *Foreign Trade by Commodities 1988*, Vol. 2, Paris.

Rajah Rasiah and Mukunden Menon (1989) 'Growth and Significance of the Textile and Garment Industry in Penang', paper presented at Malaysian Economics Association – Northern Branch Seminar on 'The Textile Industry: Challenges and Choices', Penang, 11–12 August.

Rawsthorn, Alice (1989) 'Woven to Suit the Changing Market', *Financial Times*, 26 September.

Rawsthorn, Alice (1990) 'Textiles: MFA Looks Threadbare', *Financial Times*, World Industrial Review Section, 8 January.

Tan, Y.H. (1989) 'Textile Industry: Development in the Malaysian Context', paper presented at Malaysian Economics Association – Northern Branch Seminar on 'The Textile Industry: Challenges and Choices', Penang, 11–12 August.

Tan, Allen H.L. (1989) 'Textile Industry: Its Weakness and Problems', paper presented at Malaysian Economics Association – Northern Branch Seminar on 'The Textile Industry: Challenges and Choices', Penang, 11–12 August.

Trela, I. and Whalley, J. (1988) 'Do Developing Countries Lose from the MFA?' NBER Working Paper No. 2618, Cambridge, Mass., June.

UNIDO (1988) *Handbook of Industrial Statistics*, Vienna.

Wagstyl, Stefan (1988) 'Survival Strategy: Standing Together', *Financial Times*, 18 October.

Wyatt, Geoffrey (1989) 'New Technology and the Economic Organization of the Clothing Industry', *Technology Analysis and Strategic Management*, 1, 3, 299–312.

World Bank (1992) *World Development Report*, Washington, DC.

Zainal Abidin Sulong (1989) Opening remarks at the Malaysian Economics Association – Northern Branch Seminar on 'The Textile Industry: Challenges and Choices', Penang, 11 August.

10

MADE-IN-MALAYSIA: THE PROTON PROJECT

S. Jayasankaran

In October 1982, Malaysia's Prime Minister, Dr Mahathir Mohamad, announced Southeast Asia's most ambitious automotive project, the manufacture of a made-in-Malaysia automobile. Officially, the project began with the incorporation of Perusahaan Otomobil Nasional Sendirian Bhd (the National Automobile Enterprise Co Ltd) or, simply, Proton, in May 1983.

Unofficially, it began a lot earlier, almost as soon as Mahathir became PM in May 1981 *(Malaysian Business [MB]* cover story, 1 January 1986). Project Proton was conceived as the lynchpin of a broader state-led effort to propel the country into full-fledged industrialisation. Going the heavy industrial route was also seen as a way to strengthen the economic position of the indigenous Bumiputras, better to achieve the targets set by the New Economic Policy (NEP)[1].

Thus, Proton was set up as a joint venture between HICOM (the Heavy Industries Corporation of Malaysia, a state agency set up in 1978 to implement major industrial projects) and Mitsubishi. HICOM contributed 70 per cent of the total paid-up capital of M$150 million, with Mitsubishi Corporation (MC) and its subsidiary, Mitsubishi Motor Corporation (MMC), each taking up a 15 per cent stake. However, most of the funds required for construction and operation came from Japanese sources – Proton raised a total of some 33 billion yen from Mitsubishi-related banks (Shiode, 1989).

By April 1986, a year ahead of schedule, the first Sagas – as the car was named, after a nationwide contest – were rolling off the assembly line located in Shah Alam, a light industrial area some 15 km from Kuala Lumpur. At the time, the plant was running at 25 per cent of installed capacity, producing 105 cars a day. (It was initially designed for 21.3 units per hour with a volume of 40,000 units per year on a single shift, or 120,000 cars a year over three shifts.)

Proton's 'success' has been a decidedly chequered one. Certainly, its introduction has managed to shake up an industry that was in sore need of rationalisation. Nor is there any doubt about the car's quality; it is no better and no worse than its competition. The costs, however, have been high

(Chee, 1983; Jomo, 1983; Shiode, 1989). The economic burden of the Proton project in the first decade of its existence has been estimated to be at least M$1.6 billion (Chee, 1983). In 1989, the company announced its first profits ever (M$32.5 million), after four years of consecutive losses. However, it still bears some M$136 million in accumulated losses on its books. It has captured almost 70 per cent of the local passenger car market in its engine capacity range, and is likely to retain its market leader status if only because it remains exempt from the 40 per cent import duties that its competition has to bear. On the other hand, it has begun exporting, and successfully at that: in its first year of sales to the United Kingdom, the company managed to sell 10,000 units, setting a record for new entrants in the process (*Business Times* supplement, 2 December 1989).

BACKGROUND: THE AUTO INDUSTRY BEFORE PROTON

The motor industry began in the Malaysian peninsula in 1926 when Ford Motor Co. of Malaya was incorporated in Singapore. That was, however, a rudimentary operation and it was only in 1963 that the government came out with a firm policy to promote an integrated auto industry to strengthen the country's industrial base (UNCTC, 1983). Then came separation from Singapore, which upset the plans as the expected domestic market was substantially reduced.

In the late 1960s, the government began processing applications for auto assembly and components manufacture. In 1967, the first plant (Swedish Motor Assemblers) went on-stream. The government's main objectives in trying to create a viable motor industry were:

1 to promote import substitution;
2 to save foreign exchange;
3 to create employment; and
4 to nurture the evolution of a supporting auto components manufacturing industry that would enhance overall industry development through its multiplier effects.

Despite much exhortation, and numerous guidelines from the government, the local auto industry never progressed beyond the level of early import-substituting industrialisation, with a large number of makes and models, weak local linkages and poor prospects for export (UNCTC 1983). From the lone Volvo plant in 1967, the industry mushroomed to encompass 11 assemblers by 1980, which produced 25 makes of commercial and passenger vehicles, 122 models and 212 variants. This proliferation of makes and models made it very difficult for parts makers to go for economies of scale. Consequently, local parts were expensive and the local content in Malaysian-assembled cars was dismal – by 1979 local content averaged only 8 per cent and was limited largely to tyres, batteries, paint and filters (*Malaysian Business*, 1 December 1984).

Conflicting government objectives did not help. The Motor Vehicle Assemblers Committee (MVAC) – an inter-departmental agency set up under the Ministry of Trade and Industry to oversee the auto sector – had a sweeping brief. Its regulatory powers included prices, local content, import regulations and control of the number of assemblers, makes and models. But the committee's efforts ran up against the New Economic Policy; in Doner's (1988) words, 'jobs had to be created, investment was necessary and Malays had to be promoted economically'. Thus, the original MVAC decision to license only six assemblers proved meaningless. Disqualified plants were permitted to engage in subcontracting assembly work because of political influence and, in 1977, the MVAC licensed another five assemblers whose criteria for entry had been modified to accommodate the NEP's objectives.

Attempts at incorporating greater local content also met with failure. Again, this was not for lack of trying – the government successively issued directives that included protection for parts producers, mandatory local content increases (10 per cent in 1972 to 35 per cent in 1982) and other indirect measures to increase local content; those failing to meet local content requirements would pay penalties. However, such measures were abandoned for a number of reasons. First, the government felt they might conflict with an ASEAN regional scheme. There were also fears that they would cause rising auto prices, which could cause a political backlash against the government. Finally, and this was especially significant, during the 1960s and early 1970s foreign assemblers and their local partners effectively resisted localisation. The number of parts producers was small and few had influence on policy making (Chan, 1988).

The situation began changing in the late 1970s. A group of six large parts producers, led by Malaysia Sheet Glass, moved to bring some order to their industry, and in 1978 the Malaysian Automotive Component Parts Manufacturers Association (MACPMA) was formed. By the end of the year, MACMAP consisted of the 50 or so largest producers – of whom there were 200 at the time. MACPMA's strenuous lobbying efforts proved successful. In 1979, the government announced its decision to move towards an all-Malaysian car through what it called mandatory deletion of CKD (completely knocked down) vehicles. Basically, this involved the prohibition of certain components in the imported CKD kits, thereby creating market opportunities for local parts makers. These deletions were backed up by a wealth of protection – incentives, tariff protection for parts makers, duty exemptions and penalties for assemblers, etc. Local content levels increased: from 8 per cent, they rose to 18 per cent in 1982 and 30 per cent in 1986 (*Far Eastern Economic Review* [*FEER*], 24 December 1982; see also *MB*, 1 January 1986).

THE PROTON PROJECT
INDUSTRY WEAKNESSES AND MAHATHIR'S SOLUTION

By the early 1980s, it was clear that the auto industry had done nothing much towards promoting greater industrialisation. Auto sales had increased sharply; in 1984, Malaysia had a person-to-car ratio of 1 to 20.8, second only to Singapore in the ASEAN region, and much higher than either South Korea (1 to 146) or Taiwan (1 to 51). But it contributed little to the national economy. While auto sales increased from M$160 million in 1978 to M$418 million in 1983, total import values of transport equipment increased from M$484 million to M$1.2 billion during the same period. And the industry's total contribution to manufacturing output and GDP actually declined, from 2 per cent to 1.2 per cent and from 0.79 per cent to 0.62 per cent respectively (*MB*, 1 December 1984).

The costs of locally assembled vehicles remained high. One estimate put their costs as 50 per cent over their imported CBU (completely built up) equivalents. Among the reasons: extensive market fragmentation, the high price of locally made components and the 'deletion allowance' problem – the failure, or refusal, of Japanese assemblers to reduce the prices of their imported CKD packs by the same amount as the price charged by local producers of parts deleted from their packs (Chan, 1988).

Meanwhile, local assemblers charged that the state continued to be over-regulatory while lacking long-range clarity (Doner, 1988). The government wanted to rationalise the industry but also wanted to increase Bumiputra participation, so it allowed more plants to open. Then, it wanted to raise local content while simultaneously attempting to raise state revenues by levying high duties on imported raw materials essential to the manufacture of locally made parts.

In the NEP context, it was also realised that the auto sector lacked meaningful Bumiputra participation. According to figures from the Automotive Federation of Malaysia, Bumiputra equity in the auto assembly sector in 1984 comprised 30.3 per cent, still subordinate to Chinese holdings of 42.9 per cent. Meanwhile, foreigners, especially the Japanese, wielded a disproportionate influence in the sector owing to their control of technology. Bumiputra capital was considered even weaker in the auto parts sector, which was largely Chinese dominated. And the one area where Bumiputra equity seemed significant – i.e. the distribution of imported, luxury CBUs – was perceived to be riddled with 'Ali Baba' practices – the hawking of approved permits, necessary for the import of cars, to the highest Chinese bidder (*Business Times*, 25 March 1985).

The heavy industries strategy has been closely identified with Mahathir, although HICOM, the agency set up to spearhead its drive, was actually set up in 1978 during the tenure of Mahathir's predecessor, Hussein Onn. It was Mahathir, however, who initiated HICOM within the Ministry of Trade and Industry, and who moved the agency to the PM's office in 1981. It also got activated then. The heavy industrial drive – with the national car at its centre – was seen as the answer to the 'problems' of the auto sector. Rationalisation of the sector could take place. And state enterprises serve NEP targets as they are classified as Bumiputra capital. In addition, there would be opportunities for the Bumiputras to pick up managerial experience and expertise.

BEGINNINGS

If there was one person responsible for the Proton Saga, it would have to be Dr Mahathir Mohamad. The idea for a made-in-Malaysia car was apparently mooted as far back as 1980 when Mahathir, then Deputy Prime Minister and Minister of Trade and Industry, ordered the Malaysian Industrial Development Authority (MIDA) to carry out a feasibility study of the project. Aware that the country could not possibly do it alone, MIDA opened talks with Daihatsu Motors. These dragged on for two years before breaking down; apparently, Daihatsu was willing only to put up a body stamping plant and offer technical assistance. This was not the 'Malaysian' car that Mahathir envisaged.

In October 1981, Mahathir, then Prime Minister and on an official visit to Japan, had talks with Mimura, Mitsubishi Corp's president, and 'a verbal agreement was reached that Mitsubishi would come in' (*MB*, 1 January 1986). In February 1982, Dr Kubo, Mitsubishi Motor Corp's chairman, visited Malaysia and, in talks with Mahathir, reached an understanding on the type of car that was required (ibid). By all accounts, work started even before Cabinet approval had been obtained. That came in December 1982, but by then the project team – then working under HICOM – had prepared a market feasibility study and Mitsubushi had flown a clay model of the Proton prototype, prepared in its Japanese factories, to Kuala Lumpur for Mahathir's inspection (ibid).

Serious negotiations began after that. Once they began, however, the government made no attempt to improve its bargaining position by contacting other foreign firms. Mahathir thus 'accepted Mitsubishi without the company having to go through competitive bidding' (*Asian Wall Street Journal*, 1985). By all accounts, Mahathir seemed to believe that Mitsubishi was the best of the Japanese automakers when it came to understanding national ambitions. MMC not only had been the most supportive of Japanese firms when it came to regional sourcing, it had also shown an 'impressive willingness to comply with the South Korean national auto development programme through its links with Hyundai' (Doner, 1988). It had also been Mitsubishi which bothered to come up with a specific proposal; none of the other Japanese automakers apparently believed the project to be either necessary or desirable.

From Mitsubishi's perspective, the Proton project represented an opportunity to increase its share in one of Asean's most rapidly growing auto markets, from 8 per cent in 1982 to a possible 60 per cent by 1986. And, by dominating the auto market in Malaysia, Mitsubishi gained the possibility of promoting a regional production scheme in which the firm could locate various facilities for vehicle production in the ASEAN region to get economies of scale, and thus possibly dominate the much talked about ASEAN car project.

In any case, Mitsubishi was not spending very much. Initial increases in local content would be covered by the products of the newly established stamping plant largely built and run by the firm (*MB*, 1 January 1986). Nor was the firm required to come up with a completely original car – the Proton Saga was generally considered a variant of the already existing Lancer Fiore. In the words of Mitsubishi consultant Hiroshi Satoh, 'Proton took a short cut. Instead of trying to start from scratch, we opted to use existing components and make modifications to the bodyline' (ibid).

Details of the contract are unclear, but what is known is that Mitsubishi promised the following: construction of the plant, starting dates, equity shares, training of Malaysian personnel, and new design changes every two years, with model changes once every five years. Quite a few things were left vague, however. Among them: future local content levels, CKD payments, royalties, the use of non-Japanese technology, technology transfer and exports – which 'seemed to provide Mitsubishi with significant advantages' (Doner, 1988).

Given the near-total secrecy in which the negotiations were carried out, there was a dearth of information about the project. This did not stop discussion, however. Indeed, the project was almost universally criticised as not being viable; an economist was quoted as saying 'I have yet to talk to a single economist who thinks the project is viable' (*MB*, 1 December 1984). More damaging, however, was a secret report from the government-sponsored think tank, the Institute of Strategic and International Studies, which concluded that the project was 'not viable, from an economic point of view' (cited in *Asian Wall Street Journal*, 19 December 1985). A 1985 United Nations Industrial Development Organisation (UNIDO) report put it starkly. The possibilities for gain, it said, 'appeared far more secure for Japan and Mitsubishi than for Malaysia ... for the former, the sun may continue to rise, but for the latter, first light could still turn to darkness' (cited in *FEER*, 14 February 1985).

The government, however, based its optimistic projections on growing auto sales of 6 per cent a year and a feasibility report by the HICOM project group, done in collaboration with local market researchers, SGV-Kassim Chan, which concluded that the project was feasible (*MB*, 1 January 1985). According to their scenario, Proton would produce 40,000 units in 1986, 80,000 units in 1988 and 120,000 units by 1994.

However, just as Proton was cranking up its production facility, auto sales slumped. In 1985 and 1986, the country went into its worst economic recession since Independence. Total passenger car sales plunged to 38,200 in

1987 from a peak of nearly 100,000 in 1983. As a result, total Proton production for the years 1986 and 1987 hovered around 25,000 units. The weakened economy and the resulting balance of payments deficit also caused a depreciation of the Malaysian ringgit against the currencies of its major trading partners. At the same time, the steep appreciation of the Japanese yen caused the company's start-up loan of Y33 billion to increase alarmingly in ringgit terms. The ringgit costs of CKD imports also rose sharply. Thus for the year ending 31 March 1985, even before the plant had actually begun production, Proton had accumulated losses of M$11.6 million.

But Proton was privileged. The government committed itself to the project by exempting the Saga from the 40 per cent import tariff, while simultaneously raising CKD import duties for other brands three-fold, the incidence of taxes to the landed price of CKD packs for non-Sagas became almost 100 per cent (*Business Times*, 19 July 1986). As a result, it has been estimated that the Treasury lost about M$120 million in forgone import duties (Shiode, 1989). On the other hand, this meant unbeatable prices for the national car. In 1987, for instance, the price of a 1300cc Proton was around M$21,000, while its competitors retailed for between M$28,000 and M$29,000. Proton's market share increased steadily from 47 per cent in 1986 through 65 per cent in 1987 to 73 per cent in 1988. During that time, the 'rationalisation' of the Malaysian auto industry proceeded in earnest. Three assemblers – ironically including Mitsubishi – closed down. The others simply reduced output or switched to the production of vehicles that would not compete with Proton, while an estimated 3,500 people lost their jobs.

There was relatively little public opposition to the government's forced rationalisation of the industry – a great many appeals, however, were sent to the government, all of which were ignored. Most of the bigger firms, instead, jumped on the bandwagon. United Motor Works (UMW), Tan Chong Motors (Nissan) and Oriental Motors (Honda) all got into the components' manufacturing business, with the first two – the largest assemblers besides Proton – being offered stakes in Edaran Otomobil Nasional (EON), the sole distributor of the Saga; they happily accepted, much to the chagrin of some Bumiputra businessmen.[2]

The NEP objectives of the national car project were clearly reflected in its employment patterns. In 1988, the plant employed 1,300 people, 94 per cent of whom were ethnic Malays. From 1983 to 1986, a total of 323 technical people were sent for training in Japan, of whom 90 per cent were Malays, 6 per cent Chinese and 4 per cent Indians. Most Proton personnel were inexperienced, while very few experienced workers laid off from other assembly firms – who were mainly non-Malays – were hired. The chief executive of Proton at the time, Wan Nik Ismail, was quoted as saying 'if we'd wanted to employ such "veterans", we would have to get permission from the PM's Department' (*MB*, 1 January 1986).

THE PROTON PROJECT
LOCAL CONTENT

The first Proton had local content (by value) of some 36 per cent. After that, increases came slowly, mainly because of Mitsubishi's reluctance to commit itself to supposedly 'inferior quality' local components. Thus, a great many components were imported, at great cost, from Mitsubishi plants in Japan: some 55.2 per cent (by value) of the Sagas produced in July 1988 were imported from Japan (Shiode, 1989).

However, things have changed since then. Unrelenting pressure from MACPMA and the government, coupled with the high costs of importing from Japan because of the strong yen, have catalysed this change. The strong yen has led to Proton sourcing from other countries, including Taiwan, Thailand, South Korea, India, Australia and the USA. By mid-1990, according to Proton officials, the car's Japanese content would be less than 20 per cent (*Business Times* supplement, 2 December 1989). By that time, local content would reach 65 per cent (MIDA official). Proton at present manufactures 453 components, while 356 other parts are sourced from 56 local vendors. A further 133 parts are under development for local manufacturers, and, when the company finally localises its engine manufacture, local content will top 72 per cent. (The plant began engine assembly in August 1988.)

The emergence of Proton unwittingly catalysed the emergence of locals as parts exporters. Three companies – UMW, Tan Chong and Oriental Motors – have gone into parts production in a big way, with the first two reporting turnovers of M$75–100 million in parts manufacture. In 1988, 15 to 20 per cent of their production was for export to places like Australia, Japan and the Middle East (*MB*, 1 September 1989). The strong yen has also induced the relocation of Japanese parts maufacturers in Malaysia, where they produce parts mainly for export; Proton and other local assemblers also buy some of their production.

EXPORT SALES

Originally, the national car was meant purely for the domestic market, but falling domestic demand forced Proton's management to revise its plans. Export of the Proton Saga was conceived as the only way for the company to utilise excess capacity. Mahathir himself originally downplayed any possibility of export. He switched tack abruptly after sales began plummeting by demanding exports – first within five years, and then within two years of commencing vehicle production. Mitsubishi appeared reluctant at first; it did not have to be enthusiastic as the contract had left the export question vague.

Mitsubishi's reluctance stemmed mainly from two factors. First, and mainly, it did not want the Saga to compete with its own products; a Mitsubishi plant in Australia already manufactured the Lonsdale, which the company had hoped would make it big in England. If the Proton came into the picture, it would qualify for duty-free import into the UK under Britain's

Generalised System of Preferences (GSP), which would mean that the Lonsdale's price could not hope to compete with it (See Doner, 1988). The Japanese also felt that the Proton would rapidly become outdated; staying ahead in the international auto market presupposes constant changes in model design, and the Japanese were not convinced that Proton could keep up. Mitsubishi was also not convinced that EON had the marketing ability to sell the car overseas. Nor did it believe that Proton could consistently adapt technology for the different markets. EON had no experience with international marketing, and Malaysia had little, if any, international marketing channels for auto sales.

Initial efforts by Proton seemed to confirm Mitsubishi's worst fears. When the Prime Minister took ten Sagas with him to China on a trade mission, the cars went equipped with air-conditioners, instead of heaters to combat the freezing Beijing winter. The cars themselves could not be used: their engines were equipped to use high-grade Malaysian petrol, instead of the much lower grade fuels used in China.

Plans for breaking into the lucrative US market – originally a higher priority than the UK – dissolved into a welter of recrimination and lawsuits between Proton and its putative US distributor, Malcolm Bricklin. Bricklin ambitiously announced that he would sell 100,000 Sagas in his first year of operations and that his company had planned a US$10 million programme to modify the Proton to meet US standards.

Apparently, Mitsubishi was quite unsupportive. It claimed that the modification process could take up to two years, and that Proton was ill-prepared for the US market, in terms of both quality and US specifications. Presumably, it was also lukewarm to the idea of Proton competing with its own models, marketed in North America by Chrysler Corporation. As it turned out, however, Bricklin failed to get the necessary US federal and state approvals for Proton's launch and the marketing plan fizzled out, at great cost and embarrassment to Proton. If the plan to export the vehicle to the USA had not failed, it has been estimated that car export price subsidies to the USA would have been at least M$5,000 per vehicle, or over 40 per cent of the expected retail price of US$5,000. This would have been over and above the M$4,500 per vehicle capital cost subsidy believed to exist for cars produced for the local market. After the US fiasco, Proton's management seemed to resign themselves to letting Mitsubishi set the pace for export. Mitsubishi put plans for the US market on hold but otherwise said it was fully committed to Proton's export programme (*Business Times* supplement, 2 December 1989).

As of April 1990, more than 12,900 units had been exported to various countries including Bangladesh, Eire, Sri Lanka, Brunei, Singapore, Jamaica, New Zealand, Malta, Nauru and the United Kingdom. The UK shows the most promise, with a total of 10,170 units having been sold there in its first year – exceeding Proton's expectations by some 4,000 units. Quality has not turned out to be a problem. British newspaper and auto review magazines gave the Saga favourable ratings. The main problem has, in fact, been meeting demand. The first 500 Sagas sent to Singapore sold out within a week, surprising both Proton and its Singapore distributor, Cycle and Carriage. Indeed, by late 1989, even local buyers had to contend with a waiting period of two to four months.

Whether Proton makes money on its overseas sales is unclear. In parliament, Mahathir denied that the Proton was being subsidised for export, and its overseas prices do not seem significantly lower than domestic prices. When the car made the tenth spot in a London *Sunday Times* rating of economy cars, at 7,000 pounds sterling (M$30,800), it was also the most expensive, bar one. This is only a little less than its retail price in Malaysia (M$32,000), but Proton's managing director, Kanji Iwabuchi, maintained that 'export sales contribute to the company's results' (*FEER*, 3 August 1989). Indeed, Iwabuchi maintained that 'we will still make profits on Britain-bound exports even without tariff advantages under the GSP' (*MB*, 16 April 1990, cover story). Industry analysts, however, generally feel that Proton loses on overseas sales, at least in Britain, pointing to steep domestic production costs as a result of low volume and the high cost of imported Japanese components. There are also the expensive modifications made to the British-bound Sagas, required to fulfil British safety standards.

MANAGEMENT SHAKEOUT

As pointed out earlier, one of the reasons behind the national car project was to redress ethnic economic imbalances in line with the NEP. Thus, Proton's management was largely Malay. Its distributor, EON, however, was a compromise; while HICOM retained the largest shareholding (45 per cent), extensive Chinese participation was encouraged to tap their auto marketing experience and to avoid alienating Chinese car buyers. Thus, a UMW subsidiary held 35 per cent, and Tan Chong got involved as well through directorship holdings. To placate Bumiputra indignation, 15 per cent of equity was offered to UAS, a diversified Bumiputra company, and 5 per cent was allotted to Pekema, which represented the Malay Motor Traders Association. In this way, the government reasoned, it could spread the largesse from the Proton project.

EON began on an independent footing from Proton, and quickly began setting up dealerships throughout the country. It also began racking up profits from the outset, with the relatively cheap 'transfer prices' paid for the cars by EON. Besides the 'friendly' transfer prices, EON also enjoyed the high profit margins to be had from selling cars loaded with expensive options, a strategy that the distributor remorselessly used, much to the chagrin of many consumers – if consumers insisted they did not want any of EON's options, they quickly found out that they had to wait a long time for their cars.

Besides accessories, EON also derived commissions from finance companies – all Proton buyers have to go through EON's panel of thirty finance companies, which charge an interest rate of 6.9 per cent. EON's commission from each transaction is 0.9 per cent. Finally, it is estimated that a further 20 per cent of EON's profits come from servicing.

Meanwhile, Proton's losses mounted. The escalating yen, coupled with low domestic demand, led to four successive years of loss-making, culminating in losses of M$52 million and M$58 million in 1987 and 1988. In late 1987, Proton's management had asked the government for a soft loan to help ease their yen burden; the government agreed, but nothing else seemed to be working.

Embarrassed by the repeated losses, Finance Minister Daim Zainuddin fired the first salvo in June 1988. Complaining that the government was fed up with hearing excuses from managers for their poor performances, he said: 'A good management team is able to adapt the company to changes, to look for alternatives and not to make excuses one after another. If you fail, you must have the courage to resign. If you don't, you may be sacked' (*FEER*, 1 September 1989). This was exactly what happened. A day after Daim's outburst, Proton's deputy chairman, Mohammed Saufi Abdullah, resigned. On 1 August, Proton's executive director, Wan Nik Ismail, was replaced by Kenji Iwabuchi, the former managing director of MMC. Japanese management control of Proton was consolidated when another MMC manager, Kyo Fujioko, was made head of the new corporate planning division. It was a blow to Malay pride, and indicated that the government thought that only Japanese management could save the project. The US export plan got shelved, and Proton began selling its cars to EON at higher prices. Relations between Proton's and EON's managements had never really been very good. The Japanese began clamouring for participation in EON, to streamline and better coordinate production and distribution functions. Early in 1989, the government agreed. HICOM retained its 45 per cent share, but 25 per cent got assigned to a private company controlled by the Ministry of Finance, with the remaining 30 per cent going to Kuala Pura, an MMC subsidiary (*FEER*, 3 August 1989). The effect was to bring EON more firmly under Proton's control.

The immediate result was an increase in transfer pricing. Proton, apparently, sells its cars to EON almost at cost. According to the then CEO of EON, Mohd. Nazmi Mohd. Salleh, 'if we sell the car bare from Proton, we will lose money as the cost of the car from Proton compared to the price we sell to customers does not leave enough for us to be profitable. We recover our costs from accessories and hire purchase commissions' (*MB*, 16 April 1990).

THE ASEAN CAR ACCORD

Along with Mitsubishi, two other Japanese carmakers – Toyota and Nissan – are taking the lead in linking together affiliates in Thailand, the Philippines and Malaysia, aiming for economies of scale that single-country markets cannot offer. This involves ASEAN's brand-to-brand complementation scheme, whereby participating states will cut tariffs by at least 50 per cent for car components made by one of the others. The imported parts will also count towards local content rules. Given that the three countries have signed up, this makes the scheme an official ASEAN project, and marks, at least, the partial integration of the car industries of Southeast Asia (*FEER*, 15 February 1990).

Mitsubishi led the way. In 1987, it began shipping transmissions made by a Manila-based unit to MMC-Sittipol, its 49 per cent owned Thai affiliate. Sittipol has also been importing stamped metal parts and electronic components from Proton. Proton also plans to export steering systems to Mitsubishi's Philippine plant. Seeing that it was going well, Mitsubishi made a proposal to four governments, including Indonesia, which balked. Not wanting to be left out, especially with the yen appreciation, two other Japanese carmakers also sought to take advantage of the ASEAN complementation scheme. So far, the sharing of parts has been limited, and problems remain (*FEER*, 15 February 1990; see also Shiode, 1989). But the promise of an integrated car industry with economies of scale remains. Shiew Wan Shing, then head of Toyota's partner in Malaysia, was quoted as saying that 'brand complementation could benefit Proton as local car makers might want to turn to it to stamp body parts as the facility requires heavy capital investment' (*MB*, 1 September 1989).

CONCLUSION

After four years of operation, Proton finally came into the black in 1989, posting a pre-tax profit of M$32.6 million on the back of more than M$820 million in turnover. The reasons at the time included increased domestic demand, fuelled by both the economic recovery and low interest rates, and higher prices paid for the cars by EON.

Vibrant economic growth laid the foundation for Proton's listing on the Kuala Lumpur Stock Exchange in 1992. In 1990, Proton registered sales of over M$1 billion for the first time and its pre-tax profit of over M$159 million in effect wiped out its accumulated losses of M$138 million.

The company has kept improving its financials. In 1991, turnover jumped to M$1.79 billion and pre-tax profits were in the region of M$261 million. In February 1992, Proton was listed with 150 million shares, out of a possible 500 million shares, being offered to the public. The offer price was M$5 a share. At the end of the day, HICOM and the Ministry of Finance ended up as its largest shareholders with 29 per cent and 18 per cent respectively. The Japanese stake was trimmed to 17.4 per cent, while the rest is held by two Malaysian institutions and members of the public.

For the year ended 31 March 1992, Proton registered a turnover of over M$2.1 billion. Pre-tax profits were M$408 million.

Clearly the national car has been a financial success. The boom, however, is not expected to last. Auto sales in 1991 hit an all time high of 136,000 units, and no one, least of all Proton, expects the glory years to be re-created. Indeed, the national car maker expects a drop in profits for 1993 – it forecasts pre-tax profits of M$308 million, a drop of exactly M$100 million. Proton has also predicted that sales will remain flat over the next two years; it expects total sales not to exceed 101,000 units (Proton prospectus for listing, January 1992). Given relatively lacklustre prospective earnings, Proton shares have not exactly fired anyone's imagination. At the time of writing, they trade at around M$5.60.

The authorities have continued to assist the national auto maker. In early 1991, for instance, the central bank passed tough guidelines restricting financing for new cars to four years from five previously. The directive was aimed at clamping runaway consumption, but included only cars that were priced above M$40,000. Thus, Proton escaped, but all its competitors were affected.

The directive may soon affect Proton. Already its upper-end models are perilously close to the M$40,000 mark, but most observers think that the authorities will simply revise the levels upwards if Proton ever breaches them.

Proton's dependence on Mitsubishi continues unabated, although some strains are showing. In 1991, Prime Minister Mahathir announced plans for a second national car, a smaller one with an engine capacity of 660 cc. Much to the chagrin of Mitsubishi, which makes small cars as well, the Japanese partner picked was Daihatsu. The new car project is expected to start production in 1994. How much it will eat into Proton's market is anyone's guess.

Market analysts say that Mahathir may be getting increasingly peeved with Mitsubishi for several reasons. They include slow rates of technology transfer, steep technical fees and a persistently high import dependence on Mitsubishi's mother factories in Japan. That could be one reason why Proton's latest model, the Iswara, was designed by British engineers and not by Mitsubishi.

Although frosty, the profitability of Proton will ensure that the Malaysian relationship with Mitsubishi will endure. Indeed, the Japanese have become even more important to the project. Thus, technology and management dependence has actually increased, instead of the other way round.

Finally, there is the question of protection. In 1991, for the first time, Proton had a 5 per cent import duty slapped on its CKD packs; this compares with 40 per cent for all other manufacturers. Most analysts do not expect any more increases. If anything, increases could be slapped on the other manufacturers. In 1991, when vans that were price comparable with Proton were found to be getting popular with consumers, they were hit with hefty import and excise taxes.

Thus, despite calls for Proton's protection to be 'gradually reduced' – a response to the relatively high auto prices in Malaysia compared with the pre-Proton era – it is unlikely to happen. Malaysia is too small a market to afford the economies of scale demanded by modern auto manufacturers. Whether it can ever be a major exporter will depend, in large part, on Mitsubishi's willingness to cooperate.

The future health of the Malaysian car will depend on steep tariff barriers being maintained to keep its competitors at bay.

Notes

1 The New Economic Policy was born out of the racial riots of May 1989 and was expressly intended to improve the position of the economically disadvantaged indigenous Bumiputra (literally 'son of the soil'). Its twin objectives were the elimination of poverty irrespective of race and the restructuring of society to eliminate economic identification with a particular race. The second prong was to be achieved by a 30 per cent target achievement rate by the Bumiputra in 'all spheres of economic activity', including corporate equity. Overriding everything was national unity. However, the second prong has become virtually synonymous with the policy. Although the policy expired in 1990, the government remains committed to the objectives of the policy. See also Doner, 'The Dilemmas and Limits of State Autonomy in Malaysia: The Case of the National Car Project', paper presented at the Asian Studies Association annual meetings, San Francisco, March (1988).
2 For an extensive treatment on how Bumiputra car companies felt maligned over Chinese participation in EON, see Doner (1988).

REFERENCES

Asian Wall Street Journal (1985) 'Malaysia gambles for growth with car', 8 July.
Business Times (1985) 'Saga dealership issue: Common sense prevails', 25 March.
Chan, Paul (1988) 'Economics of Regulation in Malaysia with Reference to the Motor Vehicle and Components Industry', cited in Richard F. Doner, 'The Dilemmas and Limits of State Autonomy in Malaysia: The Case of the National Car Project', paper presented at the Asian Studies Association annual meeting, San Francisco, March.
Chee Peng Lim (1983) 'The Malaysian Car Industry at a crossroads', paper presented to the 7th Malaysian Economic Convention, Kuala Lumpur, 18–20 January.
Doner, Richard F. (1988) 'The Dilemmas and Limits of State Autonomy in Malaysia: The Case of the National Car Project', paper presented at the Asian Studies Association annual meeting, San Francisco, March.
Jomo K.S. (1983) 'Project Proton: Malaysian Car, Mitsubishi Profits', in Jomo K.S. (ed.), *The Sun Also Sets*, INSAN, Kuala Lumpur.
Shiode Hirokazu (1989) *Japanese Investment in Southeast Asia – Three Malaysian Case Studies*, Centre for the Progress of Peoples, Hong Kong.
UNCTC (1983) *Transnational Corporations in the International Auto Industry*, UN Centre for Transnational Corporations, New York.
UNIDO (1985) *Japan and Malaysia's Car: Rising Sun or False Dawn of Economic Cooperation?* United Nations Industrial Development Organization, Vienna.

11

PROSPECTS FOR MALAYSIAN INDUSTRIALISATION IN LIGHT OF EAST ASIAN NIC EXPERIENCES

Jomo K.S.

Since the late 1980s, and even before that, Malaysia has been touted as one of the most likely new candidates for 'NICdom', i.e. to achieve international recognition as a newly industrialising country (NIC) or economy (NIE). There is, of course, a great deal of controversy about the very criteria for NICdom, especially in Malaysia's case, because it has long been considered a middle-income country on the strength of its primary commodity exports. In recent years, there has been an ongoing contest over whether Malaysia or Thailand will be the first to qualify as the next NIC. Part of the debate is, of course, definitional. The Malaysian authorities once sought international recognition of its impressive record in terms of economic growth and industrialisation. However, after the withdrawal of import duty exemptions and other privileges under the Generalised System of Preferences (GSP) from the East Asian NICs in 1988, Malaysian Prime Minister Datuk Seri Dr Mahathir Mohamad instructed his cabinet members, government officials, university academics and the press to stop referring to Malaysia as an NIC or a potential NIC. Despite such ambiguity over Malaysia's status as a late industrialising country, there is little doubt that the manufacturing sector grew rapidly in the 1970s, early 1980s and again in the late 1980s. Since much of the growth of the 1970s and 1980s was export oriented, involving employment of relatively cheap labour, manufacturing's share of Malaysian GDP, exports and the labour force has grown rapidly over the last two decades (see Table 11.1).

However, these impressive indices of growth of the Malaysian manufacturing sector conceal important differences from the experiences of the more established Asian NICs, i.e. South Korea, Taiwan, Hong Kong and Singapore. Despite the resurgence of free market economic ideologies in the 1980s, it is now generally acknowledged (Deyo, 1987; White, 1988) that the state has been crucial to the late industrialisation of the East Asian NICs. It therefore seems useful to review these differences examining the implications of the role of the state in late industrialisation, in case any useful general-

Table 11.1 Manufacturing sector growth indices 1970 and 1990 (%)

Share of:	1970	1990
GDP	13.1	27.0
Exports	11.9	59.3[a]
Labour force	11.4	17.7

Note:
[a] preliminary.
Source: Hoffman and Tan (1980: Appendix AII.1).

isations can be meaningfully made (Gerschenkron, 1966). In this connection, it is also useful to consider the conditions for the emergence of an effective role for a developmentalist, and therefore necessarily interventionist, state. This is not to suggest that the Asian NICs' development experiences can be replicated. Even a cursory review of their records will underline the fact that there is no unilinear path to NICdom, let alone one that is relevant or available in all social and historical contexts. In sharp contrast to the claims of market economic ideology, the one thing the East Asian NICs have in common is that they are all examples of state-led development – including Hong Kong (e.g. see Castells *et al.*, 1990; Henderson, 1989b; Schiffer, 1991). While not suggesting that late industrialisation is no longer possible, there is little doubt that appropriate policy initiatives and responses to particular conjunctural factors were very important in starting off or resuming industrialisation in the Asian NICs, especially in the 1950s and 1960s.

Particular attention also needs to be focused on the character and circumstances of the developmentalist states, particularly in terms of their social bases, institutions, operations, growth and redistributive mechanisms. Recent interest in the relationship between states and markets (e.g. Deyo, 1987; White, 1988; Amsden, 1989) has advanced the debate on these issues, but without much comparison with the new candidates for NICdom. Hence, this chapter will review some of the characteristics of late industrialisation attributed to the East Asian NICs and consider how Malaysia fares in comparison.

THE RECORD

According to World Bank and Asian Development Bank (ADB) figures, Malaysia's economic growth and industrialisation records have been fairly creditable, even compared with existing Asian NICs. As Table 11.2 shows, during 1965–80, Malaysia's average GDP growth was high, but still lower than in South Korea, Hong Kong and Singapore. During 1980–8, the momentum slackened for all countries, with Malaysia averaging less than the East Asian NICs. However, it should also be noted that, besides having relatively lower economic growth compared with the Asian NICs, Malaysia

Table 11.2   Average growth rates in East Asian NICs and Malaysia, 1965–88 (%)

Economy	1965–80	1980–8
South Korea	9.6	9.9[a]
Taiwan	n.a.	8.3[b]
Hong Kong	8.6	7.3
Singapore	10.1	5.7[a]
Malaysia	7.3	4.6[a]

n.a. not available.
Notes:
[a] GDP and its components are at purchaser values.
[b] The average rate for Taiwan is for 1976–85.
Source: World Bank (1990: 181); Asian Development Bank (1986: 120).

has also had relatively higher population growth, which suggests that per capita GDP growth has risen even more slowly in Malaysia.

In terms of the contribution of manufacturing to GDP, Malaysia has also performed reasonably well. As Table 11.3 shows between 1965 and 1988, Malaysia's proportion rose from 9 per cent to 19 per cent, but still lagged considerably behind that of Taiwan, South Korea, Hong Kong and Singapore.

Table 11.3   Contribution of manufacturing to GDP in East Asian NICs and Malaysia, 1965–88

| Economy | Manufacturing | | Average growth rate | |
	1965	1988	1965–80	1980–8
South Korea	8	32	18.7	13.5
Taiwan	–	33[a]	–	–
Hong Kong	24	22	–	–
Singapore	15	30	13.2	4.8
Malaysia	9	19	–	7.3

Note:
[a] This figure is for the early 1980s (Harris, 1987: 46).
Sources: World Bank (1990: 181, 183); Harris (1987: 46).

The share of primary commodities in Malaysian exports has also declined significantly, although not as dramatically as for the other Asian NICs as Table 11.4 shows. Between 1965 and 1988, Malaysia's share dropped from 94 to 55 per cent, while South Korea's declined from 40 to 7 per cent. Conversely, Malaysia's manufactured exports rose from 6 per cent to 45 per cent over the same period; whereas South Korea's rose from 59 per cent to 93 per cent. Perhaps even more significantly, much of the South Korean increase was accounted for by a much higher proportion of machinery and transport equipment exports, which rose from 3 to 39 per cent. On the import substitution front too, South Korean industrialisation reduced the proportion of manufactured imports from 38 to 30 per cent compared with the smaller Malaysian decline from 32 to 28 per cent between 1965 and 1988.

Table 11.4 Contribution to exports and imports East Asian NICs and Malaysia, 1965–88 (%)

Economy	Primary commodities				Machinery & transport equipment				Other manufactured goods			
	1965		1988		1965		1988		1965		1988	
	X	M	X	M	X	M	X	M	X	M	X	M
South Korea	40	48	7	35	3	13	39	35	56	38	54	30
Hong Kong	13	41	8	15	6	13	25	27	81	46	66	58
Singapore	65	55	26	27	10	14	47	42	24	30	28	30
Malaysia	94	47	55	26	2	22	26	47	4	32	19	28

Source: World Bank (1990: 207, 209).

Hence, at least in aggregate terms, Malaysia seems to be progressing well on the path of industrialisation, although somewhat behind the East Asian NICs. However, these figures do not tell us very much about the actual nature and process of industrialisation, which require closer scrutiny of the manufacturing, products and processes involved.

HISTORY

Like Singapore and Hong Kong, Malaysia was colonised by the British from before the First World War, until 1957 in the case of Peninsular Malaysia, and until 1963 in the case of Sabah and Sarawak on the north-western side of the island of Borneo. There, however, the similarity ends, especially since Singapore served as the metropolis for Britain's lucrative Malayan colony. Hence, the economic activities, facilities and infrastructure which developed in Malaysia were quite different from, although very much linked to, those which developed in Singapore. Singapore developed to become a regional metropole, in fact one of the busiest ports in the world, under British colonialism. It also accommodated Britain's most important military base overseas. Much of the few manufacturing activities allowed to develop under colonialism was therefore concentrated on the island to serve its hinterland as well.

In other words, except for some raw material processing (mainly tin and rubber) and a few other industries, for which transport cost considerations were important, Malaya had little experience of manufacturing during the colonial period. Even during the first decade after Independence in 1957, when import-substituting industrialisation was encouraged by the government, the main beneficiaries were foreign (mainly British) firms seeking to perpetuate their domination of the Malaysian market after Independence behind the new protective tariff walls erected as part of the policy. In any case, many of these industries were poorly linked to the rest of the Malaysian economy and generated very little employment owing to the capital intensity of the production processes transferred from headquarters.

Both South Korea and Taiwan experienced far greater industrialisation under Japanese colonialism from the early part of the century than even Singapore. In effect, British colonialism was more stifling than Japanese as far as manufacturing growth was concerned.

Also, the British colony of Hong Kong had a head start over Singapore because of the influx of refugee capital from China after the communist victory in 1949. In any case, even Singapore's relatively retarded industrialisation under colonialism did not contribute to, but instead pre-empted and discouraged, parallel development in its Malayan hinterland.

STRATEGIC SIGNIFICANCE

Malaya was undoubtedly the most precious jewel in the crown of the British empire, contributing more foreign exchange to the sterling area than any other colony. In the immediate post-war period, Malaya's export earnings were greater than those of Britain itself. During 1948–60, the British fought a bloody and expensive counter-insurgency against a communist-led guerilla movement which sought independence from the British. Yet it was also clear soon after World War II that British hegemony had declined with the ascendance of US hegemony.

After the defeat of Japan by the Allied forces in 1945, the US-backed Kuomintang fled to Taiwan after losing on the mainland in 1949, while the South Korean government relied heavily on US – ostensibly UN – support after the communist-led forces were forced into a stalemate by foreign intervention. Hence, for the ascendant US, both South Korea and Taiwan were strategically very important for the post-war confrontation with communist forces in China and Korea. Besides military support, successive authoritarian pro-US regimes enjoyed tremendous economic support, including considerable food aid, which served to lower food prices and hence wage costs. The political and ideological confrontation also served as an important stimulus for growth and industrialisation, ostensibly to build up an economic base against the perceived 'communist threat'.

The US presence, the legacy of Japanese colonialism and the pre-eminence of refugee capital not based on landed interests facilitated crucial agrarian reforms in both Taiwan and South Korea in the early 1950s. These reforms not only served to ensure more equitable distribution of land, and hence agricultural incomes, but also raised agricultural productivity and consolidated yeoman peasantries critical to the stability of the authoritarian regimes in the then still predominantly agricultural societies. In contrast, both Hong Kong and Singapore were virtually urban societies, with small agricultural sectors and negligible rural hinterlands. Hong Kong, particularly, has long enjoyed the benefits of cheap food and other agricultural produce from China, which have reduced food, and hence labour costs. Singapore's relationship with the Southeast Asian hinterland has been similarly beneficial. Cheap food imports have been available from neighbouring Malaysia, Indonesia and Thailand as well as more distant sources. The virtual absence of a rural agricultural hinterland within the economies has also considerably reduced administrative, infrastructural and other costs normally associated with larger countries with sizeable rural/agricultural sectors.

In contrast, Malaysia has not experienced any major agrarian reform since Independence, despite considerable investments in agricultural and rural development. Although agricultural land is physically abundant, actual access has been constrained by the state since the British colonial period. Since pre-colonial cultivation practices involving access to land were virtually equivalent to usufruct, unequal access to land in the Malay peasant economy is a relatively recent and uneven phenomenon in the country caused by the nature of the colonisation process. In any case, this situation has led to considerable peasant land hunger coexisting with a widespread phenomenon of abandoned agricultural land due to the uneconomic size of farms resulting from several generations of subdivision in accordance with Islamic or customary provisions for inheritance.

The result has been a relatively inefficient peasant economy – in contrast to the situation several decades ago, when peasant farms were more productive than plantations. Although rapid growth and employment expansion outside the peasant economy and rising peasant agricultural productivity over the last two decades have contributed significantly to reducing peasant poverty, the peasant sector continues to be characterised by growing inequalities in ownership as well as in access to land, and hence in incomes. Ironically then, the largest-ever peasant demonstrations in the country occurred in 1974 and 1980, i.e. many years after Independence and under a regime which has ostensibly been committed to poverty eradication, especially among the Malay peasantry.

Malaysia's success in primary commodity or raw material production has mainly involved natural resources and crops such as rubber, oil palm and cocoa, rather than food crops. Rice production in Malaysia involves relatively high production costs, and is protected from imports and subsidised by consumers who have to pay a higher price for rice. Hence, unlike the other Asian NICs, labour costs have not been kept low in Malaysia by cheap rice prices.

RESOURCES

The resource endowment factor has been blatantly revised to conform to the facts. Some early development theories used to argue that 'a', if not 'the' crucial factor determining growth potential was an economy's resource endowment, in other words, an economy blessed with abundant natural resource endowments would be more likely to develop than one with fewer. This argument has been turned on its head to explain the Asian NIC experiences. Both Singapore and Hong Kong lack significant hinterlands under their own direct jurisdiction; at most, they can be said to have been blessed with strategic locations and deep-water natural harbours. The natural resource endowments of South Korea and Taiwan are also slight.

So the natural resource endowment argument was inverted to argue that, since they lacked significant natural resources, the East Asian NIC's were compelled to industrialise; in fact, it is argued that the imperative to industrialise was all that much greater, precisely for this reason. Conversely, it is now argued, Malaysia has lagged behind precisely because it lacked this sense of urgency owing to its rich natural endowments – a sort of Third World variant of 'Dutch disease'. In terms of minerals, this began with tin in the mid-nineteenth century, and has included petroleum and related gas especially after the mid-1970s. This has been augmented by Malaysia's forest resources, especially over the last two decades. Malaysia's success at export cash-crop agriculture in this century – beginning with rubber from the second decade, palm oil from the 1970s and cocoa more recently – has compounded this sense of self-satisfaction. The resource argument is frequently coupled with a population argument. In this regard, Malaysia's relatively low population density is another factor said to have weakened the imperative to industrialise.

In Malaysia, unlike in Saudi Arabia, for example, natural resources do not allow for a near perennial source of earnings. The virtually total absence of other resources necessary for diversified industrialisation argues against any ambitious import substitution plans in the Saudi case. Thus, the case for living off quasi-rents generated by natural resources, or for converting such quasi-rents into alternative flows of rentier income (for instance, through the purchase of real estate in Western Europe), is impossible to make for Malaysia. As such, there is no serious alternative to industrialisation (Saith, 1980).

More recently, the resource argument has shifted further to emphasise the crucial role of human resources. It is maintained that the Asian NICs have progressed precisely because their lack of natural resource endowments has been more than adequately compensated for by their wealth of human resources. Often said to be encouraged by supportive cultural values, this is usually attributed to large investments in education and appropriate educational and training facilities, programmes and commitment. In contrast, though Malaysia has invested a great deal in education, much of this has been spent on tertiary education, especially abroad, with little emphasis on skill development at intermediate levels, innovation and adaptation. These 'distortions' – largely due to the official emphasis on formal credentials, rather than actual ability, and ethnic redistribution priorities – are widely recognised not to be conducive to developing and strengthening Malaysia's own industrial capacity. By the late 1970s, Malaysian literacy and wage rates were well behind the East Asian NICs, as Table 11.5 shows.

Table 11.5 Literacy rates and real wages in East Asian NICs and Malaysia

Economy	Literacy rate 1980 (%)	Growth rate of real wages in manufacturing during 1970s (%)	Average monthly salaries of industrial workers, 1978 (US$)
South Korea	96	9.0	312
Taiwan	90	7.2	165
Hong Kong	90	2.4	254
Singapore	84	6.5	198
Malaysia	60	1.4	150

Source: Hamilton (1986: Table 5).

It has also been argued that Malaysia's delayed industrialisation, preceded by growth of per capita GNP based on natural resource exploitation, is handicapped by a high wage level on the one hand, and limited skill formation on the other. Viewed in comparative perspective, these handicaps jointly imply a loss of competitiveness to East and Southeast Asian manufacturers. Thus, because of its wage level, by the early 1980s it appears that Malaysia found it increasingly difficult to compete successfully for relatively labour-intensive export-oriented industries. On the other hand, on account of its lower skill level, Malaysia found it difficult to manufacture competitively the more advanced industrial products appropriate for its higher industrial wage level (Saith, 1990). Fortunately for Malaysia, however, the international currency realignments since 1985 and national monetary policy have considerably reduced Malaysia's handicap in this regard.

High Korean and Taiwanese educational levels, and their orientation towards economic ends, were partly products of the pre-war period, when the Japanese colonisers initiated policies for the widespread dissemination of education to the Korean and Taiwanese populations. In contrast, British education policy reflected the colonial ethnic division of labour which schooling served to perpetuate and reinforce (Jomo, 1981). Nevertheless, in 1965, both South Korea and Malaysia displayed similar educational enrolment profiles, with a marginal advantage for Korea. But by the 1980s, Korean educational performance indices clearly outstripped Malaysian. While there was universal primary educational enrolment in Korea even in 1965, in Malaysia the primary enrolment rate rose only slightly to around 96 per cent in 1982. Over the same period, the enrolment rate in Malaysian secondary schools rose from 28 per cent to 49 per cent, but jumped in South Korea to 89 per cent. The tertiary education enrolment rates were 5 per cent and 24 per cent respectively. It is often alleged that Malaysia's tolerable educational performance might make for reasonably efficient public sector administration, but contributes little to enhancing the performance of the manufacturing sector significantly. Here, lower-level entrepreneurial and industrial workforce skills, such as those derived from learning-by-doing processes, are urgently needed. In other Asian economies, such intermediate and low-level industrial skills have been partially generated by the small-scale and so-called informal sectors, which are neither as significant nor as dynamic in the Malaysian economy (Saith, 1990).

INTERNATIONAL CONDITIONS

Another conjunctural factor which is said to have contributed to the industrialisation of the Asian NICs was the favourable economic conditions in the post-war period. The post-war economic boom in the 1950s and 1960s involved a tremendous expansion in international trade creating tremendous opportunities for export-led growth. The internationalisation of manufacturing production processes from the 1960s created new opportunities for industrialisation. The General Agreement of Trade and Tariffs (GATT) also served to create an international environment conducive to such trade expansion and industrialisation. Under the Generalised System of Preferences (GSP), developing countries that found favour with the North have been exempted from import duties and other restrictions to exporting to the USA and other developed countries. Although many would maintain that economic growth has been retarded in the 1970s and especially in the 1980s, global conditions have remained generally favourable to late industrialisation. It has been argued, however, that the resurgence of protectionism and the related ideology of 'fair' – as contrasted with 'free' – trade will mean less favourable circumstances in the decade ahead for those industrialising economies with limited export competitiveness, compared with those that have achieved a greater capacity to compete internationally.

The recent interest and efforts to extend GATT's jurisdiction to foreign investments, the international trade in invisibles (services) and intellectual property issues could also strengthen transnational corporate hegemony and impose new obstacles and costs to the new late industrialisation efforts, especially if under the auspices of domestic capital (see Raghavan, 1990). However, it has also been argued that the trends are more ambiguous than they are often made out to be, especially after the collapse of the Uruguay Round of GATT negotiations in late 1990.

After the severe recession of 1985–6, Malaysia experienced a strong and remarkably sustained recovery, well into the early 1990s. Although this recovery was initially buoyed by improved primary commodity prices as well as increased logging, which eventually tapered off, there is little doubt that the marked depreciation of the Malaysian ringgit after 1985, new East Asian investor interest and the more permissive policies on foreign investments – especially in manufacturing and real property – helped ensure the unprecedented economic recovery of the late 1980s.

EAST ASIAN NIC COMPARISONS

ETHNICITY AND CULTURE

The search for a magic formula for late industrialisation has moved from economics to politics to culture. The rapid growth of the Asian NICs in particular has renewed attention to the role of cultural factors (see Berger, 1986; Berger and Hsiao, 1988; Redding, 1990). In the East Asian case, it is claimed that Confucianism has provided an important cultural advantage over other cultural traditions because of its supposed emphasis on diligence, loyalty and respect for authority. It is also argued that the relative cultural homogeneity of Japan and the East Asian NICs facilitated a supposed national consensus behind accelerated industrialisation. These simplistic cultural claims, however, do not seem to have stood up very well to counter-arguments. The East Asian NICs are hardly culturally homogeneous, let alone Confucian. Daoism and Buddhism have been influential, while the Western cultural impact has also been very significant, especially in Hong Kong and Singapore, and Christianity is the fastest-growing religion in Korea today. The recent revival of Confucianism in Singapore is blatantly government sponsored and initiated by the Western-educated, suggesting that the contribution of culture there has hardly been traditional. In any case, Confucianism has existed for centuries, which does not explain rapid East Asian industrialisation only in recent decades. However, more sophisticated and subtle analysis can obviously enhance our understanding of culture's role in late industrialisation.

Several decades ago, it was quite common for sociologists and others to explain Asian, and particularly Chinese, poverty in terms of Confucian and other ostensibly regressive values. By the 1980s, however, the situation had been reversed, with an almost naïve celebration of the ostensibly Confucian basis for the Japanese miracle and the success of the East Asian economies. Such enthusiasm, of course, has been reflected in analyses of East Asian industrialisation, especially since the superficial Confucian credentials of the four Asian NICs are not in doubt. Such culturalist explanations have also been extended to China and even North Korea, albeit more grudgingly. Some writers have even gone so far as to extend such arguments to explain Thai and Malaysian economic performance in terms of the role of the respective Chinese minorities. While not dismissing cultural factors entirely, or for that matter the undeniably important economic role of the Chinese in Southeast Asia, it might be noted that these recent enthusiasts do not seem to be bothered by either the earlier counter-arguments or contemporary counter-examples, e.g. of the Vietnamese, who also claim a revolutionary Confucian heritage.

The Confucian argument is also often invoked to explain the authoritarian nature of most East Asian NIC regimes, with colonial Hong Kong cited as the possible exception which proves the rule. Such explanations tend to give some, but not enough, attention to the historical and socio-political factors which have shaped the states and regimes which have dominated these societies and created the crucial conditions for successful late industrialisation.

The cultural factor is also invoked differently to underline the apparent cultural homogeneity of NIC societies. This is generally undisputed in the case of South Korea and Taiwan (although much of the island's elite comprises refugees from the mainland and their descendants – which is important for understanding the main divide in Taiwanese politics since the 1970s), or even Hong Kong, though it is still dominated by a British colonial elite and includes an important ethnic Indian merchant community. Although Singapore is three-quarters Chinese, there have been not insignificant tensions with the other ethnic minorities, especially the Malays, who comprise 14 per cent of the population on an island surrounded by primarily Malay neighbours. Nevertheless, the virtual absence of serious ethnic troubles in the Asian NICs stands in sharp contrast to more ethnically divided societies such as Malaysia.

This argument has been taken even further by some (e.g. Jesudason, 1989) who argue that it is precisely the ethnic nature of Malaysian society and the related character of the state that have been responsible for its limited vision and priorities in development policy generally and industrialisation in particular. This has influenced the nature and quality of state interventions and the role of the public sector in prioritising narrow ethnic goals, which have in turn undermined the ability of the Malaysian state to assume the kind of leading role played by other NIC states. It is argued that the dominant Malay ethnic bloc – in the form of the role of the United Malays National Organisation in the ruling coalition, which has ruled since Independence – has emphasised inter-ethnic wealth redistribution at the expense of other priorities. Consequently, an alternative agenda more conducive to late industrialisation efforts has been thwarted. There is certainly much merit in this argument, especially in its subtler versions, as there is little doubt that ethnic mobilisation and concerns dominate Malaysian politics and policy-making. The main problem with this neo-pluralist approach is that it prioritises the main communal divide, without sufficiently recognising the importance of other influences, including the diversity of supposedly ethnic interests, regional differences, class and history.

A crucial question to ask in the Malaysian context is whether there is or has been a strong enough national bourgeoisie – even if only among the ranks of the Chinese businessmen – to have been able to advance the agenda of late industrialisation effectively. There are several reasons why one doubts the existence of such a potential, even if it was to have been subsequently thwarted by Malay political hegemony. The very success of Malaya's open colonial economy – in contrast to South Korea and Taiwan – strengthened the development of a local comprador or dependent bourgeoisie integrated into international circuits as well as with foreign capital. Although tensions and rivalry were inevitable in a colonial context, interestingly no distinct segment of the bourgeoisie clearly committed to a nationalistic agenda has emerged, beyond those who call for greater protection against or less favours for transnational capital. Hence, not surprisingly, during the first decade after Independence, when import-substituting industrialisation was being officially encouraged, foreign, especially British, industrial capital – rather than local businessmen – took most advantage of the new opportunities. The pattern of Chinese business investments over the last two decades also suggests a greater inclination to invest in finance, real property and other speculative, but quick and high-yielding activities, rather than in industrial production. It has been argued that this pattern reflects rational responses to the investment environment, as shaped by state intervention and prevailing economic and political considerations. But this may also imply that they have not and may not be able to rise to the challenge of late industrialisation.

NATURE OF STATE INTERVENTION

Except for a few dogmatic conservative market economists with ideological blinkers, there is now widespread acknowledgement of the crucial, pro-active role of the state in East Asian late industrialisation. It is also increasingly clear that there has been considerable variation in the role, nature and extent of government intervention, and how all this has changed over time (see Lim, 1983; Jomo, 1985; Deyo, 1987; Harris, 1987; White, 1988; Amsden, 1989).

In Malaysia, too, the state has been very prominent, especially over the last two decades. However, the nature and primary purpose of Malaysian state intervention has been somewhat different, and it can be argued that these different priorities have reduced the contribution the Malaysian state might otherwise have made to late industrialisation. There is very little disagreement that the major purpose of government policy initiatives and public sector expansion in independent Malaysia, especially in the 1970s and 1980s, has been to achieve the inter-ethnic redistributive targets of Malaysia's New Economic Policy (NEP). This is believed to have weakened what might otherwise have been a greater growth effort, which might have included rapid industrialisation primarily under national auspices. It is widely believed that the ethnic Malay-dominated government has actually favoured industrialisation under foreign transnational auspices in preference to the likely alternative of domestic ethnic Chinese dominance. Thus, ethnic obsessions may have undermined the most feasible and viable options for industrialisation under domestic auspices.

In other respects, too, industrialisation policy in Malaysia has not contributed very much to the likelihood of industrialisation led by national, rather than foreign capital. As noted earlier, until Independence in 1957, the manufacturing activities developed in Britain's Malayan colony were those enjoying 'natural protection', primarily because of the prohibitive transport costs, i.e. mainly raw material processing (e.g. rubber smoking, tin smelting) and bulky and cheap mass consumption items (e.g. light beverages). Understandably, much of this was located in the port cities of Singapore and Penang.

'Imperial preference' ensured that Malaya, like other British colonies, remained a lucrative market for British manufactured exports. The import-substituting industrialisation (ISI) policy in the first decade after Independence mainly enabled these British manufacturers to set up profitable, protected processing and packaging plants, behind tariff walls, unlike some ISI policies elsewhere which favoured and enabled a domestic manufacturing community to develop and consolidate itself.

The subsequent switch to export-oriented industrialisation (EOI) reinforced, but also diversified, transnational capital's hegemony over Malaysian industrialisation. Although involving more sophisticated products and production technologies, the early years of EOI under foreign auspices mainly involved cheap, low-skilled labour. Although import-substituting and export-orientated manufacturing remained quite distinct, they were both mainly dominated by transnationals. The brief and quickly suspended 'second round of import substitution' in the early 1980s mainly involved heavy industries financed and owned by the government, largely with foreign credit, and on terms which turned out to be quite onerous. Poorly conceived, more burdensome than viable, and often poorly integrated into the rest of the national economy, these heavy industries seem to have failed to provide the boost to Malaysian industrialisation that similar projects in South Korea and Taiwan have.

The late 1980s upsurge in EOI involved greatly increased East Asian foreign investments as a result of changed international circumstances (e.g. exchange and wage rate realignments) as well as Malaysia's renewed attraction as an offshore investment location with even more attractive incentives available. It has involved some strengthening of manufacturing linkages, within the Malaysian economy, but there are still no indications of any decisive shifts in the momentum of manufacturing growth from abroad to Malaysia. This is not surprising, as post-colonial industrialisation policy has hardly given priority to domestic-led manufacturing growth.

With the benefit of hindsight and recognition of the complex factors influencing the possibilities for industrialisation, the likelihood of Malaysia achieving rapid, balanced, domestic-led industrialisation in the 1990s seems slight. Malaysia's domestic engines of industrial growth remain weak, despite the industrial restructuring since the late 1980s, which involved some development of domestic manufacturing linkages. Malaysia's recent industrial growth has largely depended on foreign investment interest. In this sense, then it would appear that Malaysia's industrialisation path is closer to Singapore's experience – insofar as it has relied heavily on foreign capital – than to that of either South Korea or Taiwan, which have witnessed the emergence and consolidation of strong domestic industrial capitalists with more than a little help from their respective governments (see Edwards, 1990). But Malaysia is no city state, and trying to emulate Singapore will have very different implications for Malaysia.

With all things considered, it seems unlikely that Malaysia will develop a dynamic domestic capitalist class capable of emulating either Taiwan or South Korea. Instead, policy-makers seem quite happy to develop Malaysia as a more sophisticated export platform for transnationals attracted by Malaysia's relatively cheap and skilled labour, good infrastructure and favourable investment climate. State intervention in Malaysia has been mainly preoccupied with inter-ethnic redistribution. Hence, the official preference for foreign investment is reinforced by policies discriminating against the non-indigenous ethnic communities in Malaysia – which has effectively frustrated the growth and consolidation of a primarily Sino-Malaysian industrial bourgeoisie. In contract, the East Asian NIC governments have all embarked on pro-active policies encouraging patterns of industrialisation desired by the authorities concerned. In South Korea and Taiwan, for instance, such efforts have included the selective subsidisation of industries to ensure exports and quality enhancement, and, hence, international competitiveness (Amsden, 1985, 1989, 1990).

FINAL REMARKS

Although Malaysia has achieved rapid economic growth and industrialisation since achieving Independence in 1957, development – especially of the manufacturing sector – has been less impressive than in the East Asian NICs. Malaysia's abundant natural resource endowments and strong agricultural exports seem to have weakened the imperative to industrialise. Unlike Japanese colonialism in South Korea and even Taiwan, British colonialism severely constrained manufacturing growth. And whereas the 'communist threat' to the former heightened their strategic significance, increased economic aid and other concessions and even encouraged land reforms which helped industrialisation, the consequences of the post-war preoccupation with counter-insurgency for Malaysia have been less 'progressive'. It is also feared that international conditions are becoming less conducive to late industrialisation (see Bello and Resenfeld, 1990; Broad and Cavanagh, 1988).

While the significance of cultural factors is acknowledged, narrow ethnic 'explanations' for Malaysia's less impressive industrialisation record are rejected. Instead, it is emphasised that judicious state intervention has been critical for late industrialisation in the Asian NICs, and has ensured domestic-led manufacturing growth in both South Korea and Taiwan – which have economies more relevant for Malaysian efforts at emulation than those of either Singapore or Hong Kong. Unfortunately, however, Malaysian policy-makers' overwhelming obsession with inter-ethnic redistribution of wealth, including the manufacturing sector, has undermined a potentially more economically and industrially progressive role for the Malaysian state, especially in support of domestic-led manufacturing growth. Lacking a developmentalist state capable of playing such a role, the prospects for rapid, sustained, balanced and domestic-led industrialisation are uncertain. This article also emphasises the significance of historical specificity in determining an economy's prospects for late industrialisation.

NOTE

An earlier version of this paper was presented at the opening keynote session on 'The Global and the Local: Space and Economic Development' for the Conference on 'States and Development in the East Asian Pacific Rim', 22–25 March, 1990, University of California, Santa Barbara. I am grateful to Rajah Rasiah and Jeff Henderson for their comments on this paper.

REFERENCES

Amsden, A.H. (1985) 'The State and Taiwan's Economic Development' in P.B. Evans, D. Rueschemeyer and T. Skocpol (eds) *Bringing The State Back In*, Cambridge University Press, Cambridge.

Amsden, A.H. (1989) *Asia's Next Giant – South Korea and Industrialization*, Oxford University Press, New York.

Amsden, A.H. (1990) 'East Asia's Challenge – to Standard Economics', *The American Prospect*, Summer.

Asian Development Bank (1986) *Asian Development Bank Annual Report*, Manila.

Bello, Walden and Rosenfeld, Stephanie (1990) *Dragons in Distress: Asia's Miracle Economies in Crisis*, Food First, San Francisco.

Berger, Peter (1986) *The Capitalist Revolution*, Basic Books, New York.

Berger, Peter and Hsiao Michael H. S. (eds) (1988), *Is there an East Asian Development Model?*, Transaction Books, New Brunswick, NJ.

Broad, Robin and Cavanagh, John (1988) 'No More Nics', *Foreign Policy*, 72, Fall.

Cardoso, F.H. and Faletto, E. (1979) *Dependency and Development in Latin America*, University of California Press, Berkeley.

Castells, Manual, Lee Goh, Kwok, R. Yin-wang (1990) *The Shek Kip Mei Syndrome: Economic Development and Public Housing in Hong Kong and Singapore*, Pion, London.

Deyo, F.C. (1987) *The Political Economy of the New Asian Industrialism*, Cornell University Press, Ithaca.

Edwards, C.B. (1990) 'Malaysia's Industrialisation: What Next?' Paper presented at the Malaysian Institute of Economic Research National Outlook Conference, Kuala Lumpur, December.

Friedrich Ebert Stiftung (1990) *Promotion of Small-Scale Industries and Strategies for Rural Industrialisation – The Malaysian Experience*, FES, Kuala Lumpur.

Gerschenkron, A. (1966) *Economic Backwardness in Historical Perspective*, Harvard University Press, Cambridge, Mass.

Hamilton, Clive (1986) *Capitalist Industrialisation in Korea*, Westview Press, Boulder, Col.

Harris, Nigel (1987) *The End of the Third World*, Penguin, Harmondsworth.

Henderson, Jeffrey (1989a) *The Globalisation of High Technology Production*, Routledge, London.

Henderson, Jeffrey (1989b), 'Labour and State Policy in the Technological Development of the Hong Kong Electronics Industry', *Labour and Society*, 14.

Hoffman, L. and Tan S.E. (1980) *Industrial Growth, Employment and Foreign Investment in Peninsular Malaysia*, Oxford University Press, Kuala Lumpur.

Jesudason, J.V. (1989) *Ethnicity and the Economy: The State, Chinese Business and Multinationals in Malaysia*, Oxford University Press, Singapore.

Jomo K.S. (1981) 'Schooling for Disunity: Education in Colonial Malaya', *Jurnal Pendidikan* (Journal of Educational Research), VIII (1978/1981).

Jomo K.S. (ed.) (1985) *The Sun Also Sets: Lessons in 'Looking East'*, 2nd edn, INSAN, Kuala Lumpur.

Lim, Linda Y.C. (1983) 'Singapore's Success: The Myth of the Free Market Economy', *Asian Survey*, 23, 6, 752–64.

Raghavan, C. (1990) *Recolonization: GATT, the Uruguay Round and the New Global Economy*, Zed Press, London, and Third World Network, Penang.

Redding, Gordon (1990) *The Spirit of Chinese Capitalism*, de Gruyter, Berlin.

Saith, Ashwani (1990) 'Location, Linkage and Leakage: Malaysian Rural Industrialisation Strategies in National Perspective', Institute of Social Studies Working Paper, The Hague.

Schiffer, Jonathan (1991) 'State Policy and Economic Growth: A Note on the Hong Kong Model', *International Journal of Urban & Regional Research*, 15.

White, G. (1988) *Developmental States in East Asia*, Macmillan, London.

World Bank (1990) *World Development Report 1990*, IBRD, Washington, DC.

12

STATE INTERVENTION AND INDUSTRIALISATION IN SOUTH KOREA
Lessons for Malaysia
Chris Edwards

At the beginning of the 1980s, the Malaysian Government, under Prime Minister Mahathir, launched a 'Look East' policy. This meant, according to Mahathir, 'emulating the rapidly developing countries of the East in the effort to develop Malaysia' (Mahathir in Jomo, 1985b). First announced in late 1981 and repeated in 1982 and 1983, Malaysia's Look East policy had a number of different strands, some of them conflicting. Some policy initiatives linked to the Look East policy included an emphasis on the development of heavy industries and a greater reliance on Japan and South Korea for technical assistance and training and for construction and industrial contracts (see Jomo 1985a: xi, 312).

Malaysia's Look East policy was formulated in the context of a crisis in the industrial (or, more particularly, the manufacturing) sector in Malaysia. From 1981, the rate of growth in manufacturing output slowed considerably. As Table 1.15 above shows, whereas the growth rate in manufacturing output had been more than 8 per cent in both 1979 and 1980, it was less than 5 per cent in both 1981 and 1982. This was the context for the Look East policy and for the promotion of the heavy industrialisation programme which was announced at about the same time. In fact, it was in 1980 that Mahathir, who was then Minister of Trade and Industry, announced his plans for the state-owned Heavy Industries Corporation of Malaysia (HICOM) to spearhead 'a move up the technology ladder to basic industries such as steelmaking' (Jomo, 1985b: 377). Mahathir realised that private investors might be slow to make such a move; hence, the government was to lead the way. And, when he became Prime Minister in July 1981, Mahathir continued to promote this, taking control of HICOM with him by 'shifting responsibility for the agency to his office from the Ministry of Trade and Industry' (Jomo, 1985a: 379).

Thus in the early 1980s, a Look East policy was formulated by the Malaysian government in the context of a slowdown in the industrial sector and a shift in industrial policy to promote heavy industrialisation. But what is a Look East policy and what is implied by Looking East? This is the question that is addressed in this chapter. Specifically, this chapter looks briefly at the lessons that might be learned by Malaysia from the South Korean experience (for a longer discussion of South Korean development in the post-war period, see Edwards, 1992). The broader question of policy alternatives is the subject of the next and final chapter.

THE DEBATE ABOUT STATE INTERVENTIONISM

In the 1960s and 1970s, a number of less developed countries (LDCs) achieved very rapid rates of growth in GDP, and a lively debate about the causes of this growth ensued. This was particularly virulent in the 1980s, with the spread of the Structural Adjustment Programmes of the World Bank and the International Monetary Fund (IMF) and the associated discussion of policy conditionality.

The 'orthodox' view of the World Bank and the IMF was that the fastest-growing LDCs owed their success to an absence of state interventionism. Indeed, in its 1983 *World Development Report* (WDR), the World Bank argued that there was an inverse relationship between price distortions and economic growth.

The World Bank argued that differences between countries in their price distortion index explained about a third of the variance in their growth performance. But even this 'third of explanation' has been strongly criticised. It has been argued that some of the distortion indices were highly subjective, that some of them did not correspond to theoretical requirements and that they were assumed to be independent of political and institutional factors (see Evans, 1989: 300, 301).

One of the countries which, the World Bank claimed, had grown rapidly owing to the adoption of the free market was South Korea. Figure 12.1 suggests that South Korea was the fourth 'least distorted' of the countries listed, and had one of the fastest rates of growth. In this orthodox view, state intervention was harmful; government was seen to be a hindrance.

But there were many economists who doubted the World Bank's version of events and the battle was joined. To advance the debate, more detailed analysis was required, and it was soon forthcoming. Studies of industrialisation in South Korea proliferated. The detailed studies of South Korea disagree on some of the details, but on one thing there has been universal agreement – namely that the history of economic policy in South Korea has been one of considerable state intervention. This is particularly true of industrial policy, where state intervention has been not only extensive but also highly selective. This has been argued by researchers not just from outside but also from inside the World Bank. For example, two World Bank 'dissidents', Yusuf and Peters, in a paper published by the World Bank in 1985, countered the view put forward in the 1983 WDR, as have other Bank

INDUSTRIALISING MALAYSIA

Figure 12.1 Price distortions and growth in the 1970s
Source: World Bank (1983: 62).
Note: In this figure, countries are listed in order of increasing degree of distortion in prices. In the first section, the colour of the squares indicates the degree of distortion in the principal categories of prices. The middle section is a composite index of price distortion for each country: as a country's distortion index increases, the colour of the circle changes from white to black. In the right hand section, the black circles show the actual annual rate of growth of GDP; the grey circles are estimates of GDP growth obtained by a regression relating growth to the distortion index.

304

SOUTH KOREAN STATE INTERVENTIONISM

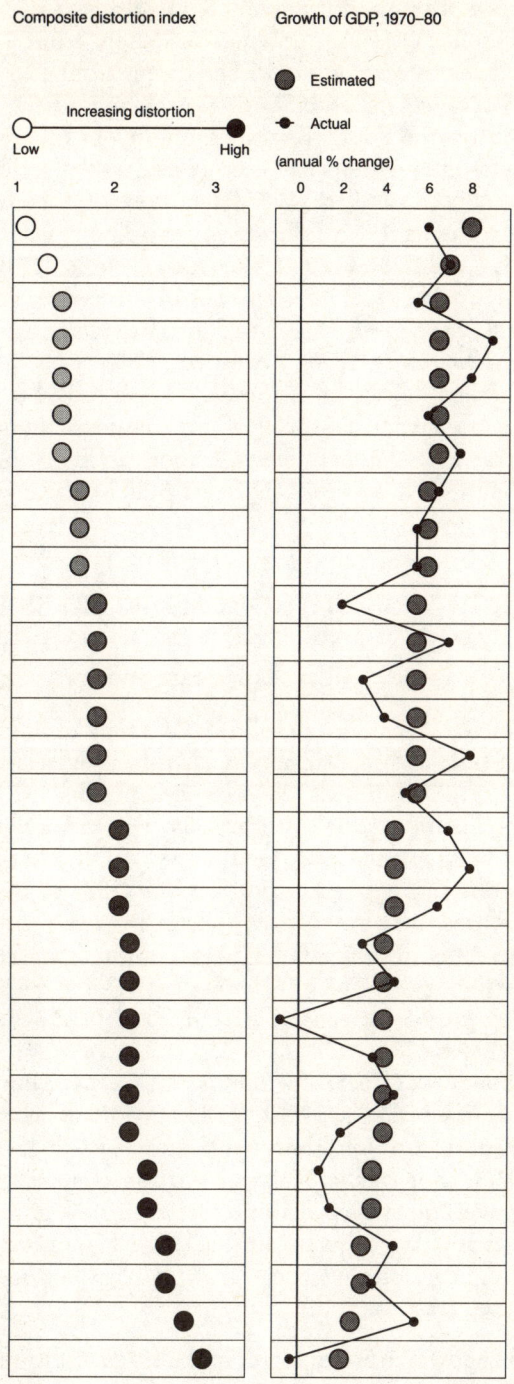

staff and advisers working specifically on South Korea (see Yusuf and Peters, 1985). But if there have been grumblings of dissent from inside the World Bank, there has been a crescendo of disagreement from outside the Bank. A large number of economists, both South Korean and others, have now done detailed research on the South Korean economy in the 1960s and 1970s, showing that state intervention has been considerable in the economy (see Deyo, 1987; Dornbusch and Park, 1987; Hamilton, 1986; Harris, 1988; Hong, 1979; IDS, 1984; Jenkins, 1989; Johnson in Scalapino *et al.* 1985; Van Liemt, 1988; Lim, 1981; Luedde-Neurath, 1986, Michell, 1988; UNIDO, 1987; and White and Wade in White, 1988). Indeed, in a recent study of industrial policy, Alice Amsden states that a key to South Korea's industrial success was that the state 'got the prices wrong' (Amsden, 1989).

Because of the significance of the South Korean model for Malaysia, it is useful to look in more detail at aspects of intervention in industrial policy by the South Korean government. Here, I look at intervention under the following headings: trade and exchange rate policies; financial policies; and other policies.

ASPECTS OF SOUTH KOREAN INTERVENTION

Trade and exchange rate policies

In the late 1950s, South Korea had followed a policy of import-substituting industrialisation (ISI) and in that period, there was extensive 'rent-seeking' (see Deyo, 1987: 110). Following the military coup in 1961, however, there were extensive reforms, especially from 1965. But this was not a period of liberalisation in the simple sense used in the 1983 WDR. There was a dramatic shift towards promoting exports as aid from the USA was reduced. But this was a state-sponsored drive for exports, and not a switch which was left to the free market. There was, in contrast to Malaysia, little emphasis in South Korea on export processing zones – manufactured exports from South Korea's EPZs accounted for less than 5 per cent of total manufactured exports in the early 1980s (see Warr, 1984: 173).

The import policy was liberal for inputs into exports, but illiberal otherwise (Schmitz in Kaplinsky, 1984: 12; Van Liemt, 1988: 32, 37, 38, 80). The effective rate of protection on import-substitutes was high in South Korea through the 1970s, as it was in Malaysia. But, in contrast to Malaysia, the South Korean government gave tariff protection for the domestic market on condition that export targets were fulfilled (see Hamilton, 1986; Luedde-Neurath, 1986, and Pack and Westphal, 1986). This policy of export targeting made sense for two reasons:

1 The purchasing power in South Korea in the 1970s was too small (even with a relatively equal income distribution) to enable the internationally com-

petitive production of many goods for which the internal economies of scale are considerable (e.g. automobile assembly and steel and petrochemical production). Even in 1986, national income in South Korea totalled less than US$100 billion, which was less than 3 per cent of the USA's, less than 7 per cent of Japan's and less than 20 per cent of the UK's. And in the 1960s, when the export drive began, South Korea's national-income was (in real terms) less than one-tenth of the 1986 figure. This meant that, if South Korea was going to be internationally competitive in industries with increasing returns to scale, then it would have to export.

2 But the risks and uncertainties facing a company thinking of exporting are considerable. Thus, it makes sense for a company newly entering the export market to be given protection for its production in the domestic market on condition that it meets export targets. If this is done, the profits from the domestic market may be used to subsidise the export sales. This is what happened in the case of South Korea. As Luedde-Neurath and Hamilton have pointed out, most manufactured exports from South Korea were unprofitable by themselves.

And so, from the 1960s, South Korean policy linked import-substituting industrialisation (ISI) with export-oriented industrialisation (EOI). Thus, it is true that the policy was outward oriented – indeed, increasingly through the 1960s, the whole of government policy was directed at stimulating exports. It had to be, for, whereas official aid inflows from 1956 to 1958 averaged 14 per cent of GNP, between 1962 and 1964 aid inflows were down to only 6 per cent (see Hamilton, 1986: 37). But the framework was not one of laissez-faire – the framework for the export drive was one of planning backed by a strong presidential commitment (see Van Liemt, 1988: 39, 40, 61).

Exchange rate policy was generally supportive of this drive (Van Liemt, 1988: 29), although the 'correctness' of exchange rate policy has been overstated. In the late 1960s, the black market premium on the South Korean won was 9 per cent, almost the same as the average for six Latin American countries at the time (see Sachs, 1985: Table 6). But the integration of import controls with exports also undoubtedly provided a major key to the export success (see Fajnzylber, 1981; Luedde-Neurath, 1986: 1). In the face of all this evidence, by the time of the 1987 *World Development Report*, the World Bank had retreated from its 1983 position by acknowledging that: 'the Republic of Korea has pursued an export-promoting strategy that combines trade liberalisation with considerable intervention' (World Bank, 1987: 100).

Financial policies

Conservative economists have spread myths not only about the trade policies but also about the financial policies followed by the South Korean government. In the early 1960s, after the fall of President Syngman Rhee, some private assets had been confiscated and the state had taken control of a large part of the commercial banking sector. Then, in the mid-1960s, real interest rates paid to depositors were raised, and it was on this Korean experience that two American economists, McKinnon and Shaw, based their 'financial deepening' theory. Their theory was that the raising of interest rates increased the quantity and improved the quality of investment. It was argued that the quantity of investment was raised because the higher real rate of interest attracted savings, and that the quality of investment was raised because the rise in interest rates attracted savings out of low-profit sectors and made it available to the high-return sectors, which had been previously 'financially-repressed'.

The McKinnon–Shaw argument can be challenged, both in terms of its theory and in terms of what happened in South Korea. Theoretically, it is difficult to see why, even if savings are raised by higher real interest rates, investment will increase: on a Keynesian view, investment is likely to be deterred by higher real interest rates.

As a description of what happened in South Korea, the McKinnon–Shaw version is highly questionable. For example, it has been questioned by Lawrence Harris, who has stated that: 'The reform contributed to growth, but that is contrary to the McKinnon–Shaw thesis, it did so because it increased the role of the state, rather than rolling it back to liberate private market forces' (Harris, 1988: 369). Harris pointed out that the state's role as an intermediary grew and its power as an intermediary also grew through its use of differential interest rates (see also Hamilton, 1986: 47; and Van Liemt, 1988: 48). Thus, in the late 1960s, when interest rates paid to depositors were high, they were not necessarily high to approved investors. In the same way as the South Korean government adopted a system of multiple exchange rates, so it adopted a system of multiple interest rates. In any case, apart from a short period in the late 1960s, interest rates were negative for most of the period 1960–1980 (see Amsden, 1989: 97; and Dornbusch and Park, 1987: Table 14). The strength of intervention in the financial markets by the South Korean state was belatedly recognised by the World Bank in its 1989 *World Development Report* when it stated: 'Korea's heavily-regulated financial system was a key instrument in the government's industrial policy in the 1960's and 1970's. Interest rates were controlled and were kept low during most of this period' (World Bank, 1989: 126).

Other policy interventions

The conclusion so far is that the South Korean government intervened extensively through the 1960s and the 1970s in trade and financial markets. But this was not all. In controlling trade and credit, the South Korean state also controlled the pattern of industrial ownership. In particular, the role of direct foreign investment (DFI) was tightly controlled – treated 'roughly', as

Van Liemt puts it (1988: 51). In general, the role of DFI has been small in South Korea, with one sectoral exception, namely electronics (Deyo, 1987: 95; and Van Liemt, 1988: 52, 55). In 1978, the share of DFI in industrial production in South Korea was low relative to that in most other LDCs (Jenkins, 1989: 17). Thus, the manufacturing sector in South Korea has been dominated by large private companies (called chaebols), and a substantial public enterprise sector (see Pack and Westphal, 1986: 97).

But the chaebols have been closely controlled, control by the state being facilitated by the high debt–equity ratios of the companies. Thus, in South Korea, the highly selective intervention by the state in promoting industry has entailed a subordination of financial to industrial capital, and of foreign to domestic capital.

Control by the state in South Korea through the 1960s and 1970s extended to every corner of the economy. Real wages in manufacturing industry in South Korea rose rapidly through the 1960s and 1970s, but from a very low base. There was little militancy in the labour force, partly because of a substantial labour surplus in the economy (particularly in the 1960s) and partly because of repression by agencies of the state (see Deyo, 1987: 150; and Hamilton, 1986: 22).

But alongside the suppression of trade unionism, the state has promoted the education of the labour force. Enrolment in schools in South Korea in the 1960s and 1970s was at a very high level given the per capita income of the country. Even among late-industrialising countries, South Korea stands out in terms of most indices of education (see Table 12.1 and Amsden, 1989: Table 9.2). But questions have been raised about the quality of this education. For example, it has been pointed out that classes in South Korea are large, that much of the learning is by repetition, that there is a heavy emphasis on moral education and discipline, and that in the field of technical education South Korea performs no better than do other late-industrialising countries (see Amsden, 1989: 219, 223). Thus, Amsden stresses, it is easy to exaggerate the role of formal education in South Korean development.

Table 12.1 Education: South Korea, Malaysia and the LDCs, 1965 and 1985

	Percentage of age group enrolled in education			
	1985			1965
	Primary	Secondary	Tertiary	Tertiary
South Korea	96	94	32	6
Malaysia	99	53	6	2
All LDCs	101	39	8	3
Industrial market economies	102	93	39	21

Source: World Bank (1989).

But the state's role in education has clearly been supportive of development, and this has been backed up by a strong interventionist role in the acquisition and development of technology. Many researchers have emphasised the positive role of the South Korean government in 'de-packaging' technology. It has promoted the overseas training of Korean managers and engineers, and it has encouraged the use of technical assistance from overseas (Amsden, 1989: 233), particularly in the form of independent consultants (ibid: 234). The state has also been closely involved in negotiations in acquiring technology licences. As numerous economists have argued, this intervention makes sense because of particularly significant imperfections in the market for technology (see Pack and Westphal, 1986: 116, 121). The imperfections stem from the lack of knowledge about the technology, and there may well be benefits to be gained if the state coordinates the acquisition of such information. Such state coordination of technology bargaining has been extensive in South Korea (see Enos in IDS, 1984, Enos and Park, 1988; and Pack and Westphal, 1986).

The experience of South Korea in the field of technology emphasises the importance of the state, not so much in promoting research and development expenditure, but rather in coordinating the acquisition and application of already existing technology. Expenditure on research and development in South Korea has been estimated at only 0.4 per cent in 1970, although by 1986 it had risen to 2.0 per cent (Amsden, 1989: 328). Again, in the field of technology, it is the selectivity of the state's role which seems to have been significant.

Thus, to sum up, it is now clear from the extensive research on the development through the 1960s and 1970s of South Korea that the state promoted industrialisation through almost every policy means at its disposal. Indeed, it has been said of South Korea that: 'No state outside the socialist bloc ever came anywhere near this measure of control over the country's investable resources' (Datta-Choudhuri in Lee, 1981: 56). But it is worth noting that this intervention was highly selective and was consistent with, and indeed promoted a high rate of profit in manufacturing (Hong, 1979: Chapter 7).

Thus, the extensive research on South Korea has exploded a number of myths about its industrial development:

- It is a myth that the free market was responsible for South Korea's success. Undoubtedly, Amsden is closer to the truth than the neo-classicists when she claims that South Korea developed because 'it got the prices wrong'.
- It is a myth that South Korea developed through direct foreign investment. Industrial output was and still is under domestic ownership.
- But it is also a myth that this domestic ownership was diffused through large numbers of small firms or plants. On the contrary, South Korea's growth was dominated by the growth of the *chaebols*, the large holding companies.

Even if it is established that there was strong and highly selective intervention in South Korea, is similar intervention feasible in Malaysia? This is the question that I look at in the next section.

LESSONS FROM SOUTH KOREA?

It is clear from the previous section that South Korea's success in terms of achieving a high rate of industrial growth over the past three to four decades has not been due simply to 'getting the prices right'. It has been the result of highly pervasive, but also highly selective, state intervention. But if this is where the analysis ends, there is a grave danger that one simple slogan – 'get the prices right' – will be replaced by another, equally simple slogan – namely 'the state must intervene'.

It is essential to analyse the political conditions in any country to understand the scope for, and the likely form and effectiveness of state intervention. In her book on South Korea, Alice Amsden states:

> it would be altogether ahistorical to think that getting relative prices 'right' requires any less strength on the state's part than getting them 'wrong'. 'Backward' countries in search of a model to guide them do not present themselves as a *tabula rasa*. They have entrenched interest groups that would be hurt if relative prices were 'freed' of distortions... Whether one attributes the acceleration of growth in Taiwan and Korea to getting relative prices right or wrong, either outcome required strong state management.
>
> (Amsden, 1989: 147, 148).

Thus, paradoxically, rolling the state back requires a strong state. But, as I have argued, the state was not rolled back in South Korea. Instead, it played an extremely strong role in forcing development.

This role can be understood only if the analysis goes beyond the mere fact of state intervention and the spheres of intervention to look at the political environment in which such policy is formulated. It is essential to look at what Evans and Alizadeh call the 'social structure of accumulation' (see Kaplinsky, 1984: 27). Once we begin to do this, an interesting question that immediately arises is: why and how did the South Korean bureaucracy manage to discipline as well as support business? For, in spite of some corruption in South Korea, the bureaucracy has been able – particularly through the 1960s and 1970s – to promote rapid industrial growth through flexible and highly selective action.

Some have attributed South Korea's success since the mid-1960s to cultural factors, to Confucianism and a respect for authority; but this is less than convincing, particularly as this was a factor which, in the early 1960s, was said to be holding back South Korean development (see Jenkins, 1989: 14, 15). Another explanation has been that put forward by Jeffrey Sachs of Harvard University, who has attributed the success of South Korea – by contrast with

Latin America – to the relative lack of urban bias in South Korea. But this seems unconvincing. Lee has described how, in South Korea in the 1960s, a substantial surplus was extracted from the agricultural sector through government procurement and pricing policies (see Lee, 1979: 511, 512). Indeed, it is precisely the lack of any strong, entrenched, class interests (rural-based or otherwise) that explains the form of state intervention in South Korea. As has been emphasised by a number of writers, especially by Amsden (1989), Hamilton (1986) and Johnson (in Deyo, 1987), the South Korean state has not been 'captured' by particular interest groups or classes. Hamilton has argued that: 'Clearly the Korean state cannot be thought of as the instrument of big business – it has maintained a large degree of autonomy from the power of capital' (Hamilton, 1986: 46).

Amsden, Hamilton and Johnson all emphasise that:

- the landlord class was weakened by the land reform programme undertaken soon after the end of Japanese colonialism;
- the domestic, merchant capitalist class, which was in any case quite small in the 1950s since much of the Japanese capital had been taken over by the state, was weakened further by the campaign against illicit wealth and by the nationalisation of much of financial capital at the beginning of the 1960s; and
- the growth of a labour aristocracy was impossible because of the repression of organised labour and a substantial labour surplus through the 1960s and early 1970s.

As a result, the bureaucracy, which had been established under Japanese colonialism and which had been further strengthened by the large aid programmes of the 1950s, found itself, especially from the second half of the 1960s, with a large 'space' in which to work. Industrial policy, which was increasingly centralised through the Economic Planning Board after the Park coup in 1961, could be, and was, highly selective and effective. Thus, with the subordination of financial to industrial capital as represented by the state, the stage was set for a period of rapid industrial accumulation facilitated by wages which were low, owing to anti-trade union pressure, low food prices and a labour surplus.

As soon as the industrial policy problem is set within a socio-political and historical context, contrasts between South Korea and Malaysia become evident. Here, it is useful to highlight three contrasts:

1 the colonial experiences were quite different:
  - under Japanese colonialism, industry was developed in Korea, whereas under British colonialism in Malaysia, it was the plantation sector which was rapidly developed;
  - South Korea gained its political independence a decade or so before Malaysia;

2 the geo-political situation of South Korea differed considerably from that of Malaysia, with important implications for industrialisation, land reform, aid, rural-urban and agriculture-industry relations;
3 Malaysia is ethnically divided, whereas South Korea is ethnically homogeneous, and Malaysia's ethnic divisions have coincided with economic roles.

These factors have meant not only that the initial conditions of the two countries differed at independence, but that the political conditions for further development differed. Thus, the manufacturing sector in Korea was more highly developed in 1945, at the end of Japanese colonialism, than it was in Malaysia. Most of this industry was located in the North, but the textile industry was well developed in the South. Furthermore, import-substituting industry was encouraged in South Korea through the 1950s, whereas over the same period there was no attempt to encourage manufacturing industry in Malaysia. As a result, in 1965, even though the gross domestic products of the two countries were about equal, the manufacturing sector's share in South Korea (at 18 per cent) was double that in Malaysia (9 per cent) (see Table 12.2). Thus, South Korea's experience of manufacturing industry has been longer than that of Malaysia.

The defeat of Japanese colonialism combined with the geo-political situation of South Korea produced pressures for an extensive land reform, which took place in the 1940s and 1950s. There was huge popular backing for land reform following the defeat of the Japanese and the example of North Korea

Table 12.2 GDP, population and manufacturing industry, South Korea and Malaysia, 1965 and 1987

	South Korea	Malaysia
GNP per capita (US$'000)		
1987	2.7	1.8
Population (mn)		
1987	42.1	16.5
GDP (US$ bn)		
1965	3.0	3.1
1987	121.3	31.2
Value added in manufacturing as % of GDP		
1965	18	9
1987	30	22
% p.a. growth in manufacturing output		
1965–80	18.7	–
1980–87	10.6	6.3

Source: World Bank (1989: 165, 167, 169).

(see Amsden, 1989: 37). But land reform in South Korea brought little dislocation to production since there was little change in the size of land holdings. Ownership replaced tenancy, and partial compensation to landlords meant that finance was transferred into commerce and industry. Thus, the land reform served to redistribute income without dislocating agricultural production, while at the same time promoting accumulation in trade and industry.

The geo-political situation of South Korea led to substantial aid from the US government. In the periods 1956–8, 1959–61, 1962–4 and 1965–7, aid to South Korea averaged 14, 8, 6 and 2 per cent of GDP respectively (see Hamilton, 1986: 37). Thus, aid was substantial in the late 1950s and early 1960s and facilitated accumulation in industry, particularly as the proportion of food aid in the total rose in the 1960s and kept the real industrial wage low (see Hamilton 1986: 37). But as aid as a whole declined in the 1960s, South Korea was forced to export.

Unlike Malaysia, it could not rely on primary products to finance its imports. But, also unlike Malaysia, after the first 'easy' phase of import-substituting industrialisation in the 1950s, South Korea did not rely on export processing zones for promoting its manufactured exports. Instead, as I have emphasised, exports from South Korea were built up from a base of producing for a protected domestic market. Export targeting was the name of the game in South Korea, whereas a dualism developed within the Malaysian manufacturing sector, with an ISI sector quite separate from the EOI sector based in the EPZs.

The growth of manufactured exports from South Korea was essential because, as aid declined, there was no other source of foreign exchange to finance imports. But, as I have emphasised, the state was able to play an active role in the promotion of exports through targeting because of the peculiar strength of the bureaucracy vis-à-vis other groups.

In contrast, the bureaucracy in Malaysia has implemented – relative to that in South Korea – an inefficient industrial policy. Under British colonialism, there was a reluctance to provide incentives for the development of manufacturing industry for fear of harming colonial plantation interests as well as British manufactured exports. But, in the 1960s, manufacturing industry was promoted by being given protection in the domestic market. This was the 'easy' stage of ISI, equivalent to that in South Korea about a decade earlier. Whereas, however, after the 'easy' stage, South Korea promoted manufactured exports on the basis of a protected home market, Malaysian policy switched tack to the promotion of exports from export processing zones.

REFERENCES

Amsden, A. (1989) *Asia's Next Giant: South Korea and Late Industrialization*, Oxford University Press, New York.

Deyo, F. (ed.) (1987) *The Political Economy of the New Asian Industrialism*, Cornell University Press, Ithaca.

Dornbusch, R. and Yung Chul Park (1987) 'Korean Growth Policy', *Brookings Papers on Economic Activity*, 2.
Edwards, C.B (1992) 'Industrialization in South Korea' in T. Hewitt, H. Johnson and D. Wield (eds), *Industrialization and Development*, Open University,
Enos, J. and Park, W. (1988) *The Adoption and Diffusion of Imported Technology; The Case of Korea*, Croom Helm, London.
Evans, D. (1989) *Comparative Advantage Growth*, Harvester Wheatsheaf, Brighton.
Fajnzylber, F. (1981) 'Some Reflections on South-east Asian Export Industrialization' *CEPAL Review*, December.
Hamilton, C. (1986) *Capitalist Industrialisation in Korea*, Westview Press, Boulder, Colo.
Harris, L. (1988) 'Financial Reform and Economic Growth: A New Interpretation of South Korea's Experience', in L. Harris, *et al.*, *New Perspectives on the Financial System*, Croom Helm, London.
Hong, W. (1979) *Trade, Distortions and Employment Growth in Korea*, Korean Development Institute, Seoul.
IDS (1984) 'Development States in East Asia', *IDS Bulletin*, 15, 2, April.
Jenkins, R. (1989) 'The Political Economy of Industrialisation: A Comparison of Latin American and East Asian NICs', mimeo, University of East Anglia, Norwich, UK.
Jomo K. S. (ed.) (1985a) *Malaysia's New Economic Policies*, Malaysian Economic Association, Kuala Lumpur.
Jomo K. S. (ed.) (1985b) *The Sun Also Sets*, INSAN, Kuala Lumpur.
Kaplinsky, R. (ed.) (1984) *Third World Industrialisation in the 1980's*, Cass, London (also *Journal of Development Studies*, 21, 1).
Lee, E. (1979) 'Egalitarian Peasant Farming and Rural Development: The Case of South Korea', *World Development*, 7, 493–517.
Lee, E. (ed.) (1981) *Export-Led Industrialisation and Development*, ILO, Geneva.
Lim Youngil (1981) *Government Policy and Private Enterprise: Korean Experience in Industrialisation*, Korean Research Monograph 6, Institute of East Asian Studies, University of California, Berkeley.
Luedde-Neurath, R. (1986) *Import Controls and Export-Oriented Development: A Reassessment of the South Korean Case*, Westview Press, Boulder, Colo.
Michell, T. (1988) *From a Developing to a Newly-Industrialised Country: The Republic of Korea, 1961–82*, ILO, Geneva.
Pack, H. and Westphal, L (1986): 'Industrial Strategy and Technological Change', *Journal of Development Economics*, 22, 87–128.
Sachs, J. (1985) 'External Debt and Macroeconomic Performance in Latin America and East Asia', *Brookings Papers*, No.2.
Scalapino, R. *et al.* (eds) (1985) *Asian Economic Development Present and Future*, Institute of East Asian Studies, University of California, Berkeley.
UNIDO (1987) *The Republic of Korea*, Industrial Development Review Series, UNIDO, Vienna, 30 March.
Van Liemt, G. (1988) *Bridging the Gap: 4 NICS and the Changing International Division of Labour*, ILO, Geneva.
Warr, P. (1984) 'Korea's Masan Free Export Zone: Benefits and Costs', *Developing Economies*, 22.
White, G. (ed). (1988) *Developmental States in East Asia*, Macmillan, London.
World Bank (1983) *World Development Report 1983*, World Bank, Washington DC.
World Bank (1987) *World Development Report 1987*, World Bank, Washington DC.
World Bank (1989) *World Development Report 1989*, World Bank, Washington DC.
Yusuf, S. and Peters, R. (1985) *Capital Accumulation and Economic Growth: the Korean Paradigm*, World Bank Staff Working Paper No. 712, Washington DC.

13
POLICY OPTIONS FOR MALAYSIAN INDUSTRIALISATION

Chris Edwards and Jomo K.S.

What should Malaysian government industrial policy be in the 1990s? To address this issue, we propose briefly to review Malaysia's industrialisation experience thus far (as we have done in the first chapter) and the existing discussion on industrial policy options.

MALAYSIA'S INDUSTRIALISATION EXPERIENCE

One may distinguish five phases in Malaysian industrialisation with fairly distinct characteristics. The first phase during the colonial period was largely limited to export and import processing and packaging of food and simple consumer items, especially when encouraged by transport cost considerations. Much of this manufacturing activity was located in Singapore, Malaya's commercial centre during the British colonial period, which was dominated by British and, to a lesser extent, local Chinese interests.

The second phase after Independence in 1957 saw the growth of import-substituting industrialisation (ISI) on industrial estates protected by high tariffs. Generally quite capital intensive, often British-owned and usually poorly linked to the rest of the national economy, such industrialisation generated relatively little new employment and soon reached its limits in the small domestic market.

The transition to the third phase of export-oriented industrialisation (EOI) began in the late 1960s as the limits of import substitution became apparent and a new international division of labour emerged, particularly involving manufacturing. Legal and policy reforms paved the way for accelerated industrialisation involving electronic components, electrical goods, textiles and other manufactured exports. Though also poorly linked to the rest of the national economy, the new labour-intensive industries generated much new employment, though initially at generally lower wage levels. However, as unemployment declined and productivity rose, wage levels also rose, at least until the early 1980s.

The fourth phase from the early 1980s is less distinct because it involved not the explicit abandonment of export-oriented industrialisation, but only the government's promotion of selected heavy industries, which took the form of a second round of import substitution. The global economic crisis of this period and its ramifications for Malaysia, e.g. through the electronics industry product cycles, had a major impact on the national economy as a whole. Meanwhile, new private investments in manufacturing fell, compounding problems related to fiscal and debt crises, slow growth and rising unemployment culminating in the mid-1980s. Hence, the early and mid-1980s saw an unplanned, but nonetheless severe, shaking-out of the Malaysian manufacturing sector.

The fifth and current phase of industrialisation since 1987 has seen a dramatic recovery in the fortunes of Malaysia's manufacturing sector. This is partly attributable to international currency realignments after 1985, resulting in the massive depreciation in effect of the ringgit (even against the US dollar), which has lowered production, especially labour, costs. Deregulation and new investment incentives may also have contributed to the resurgence in manufacturing investment, growth, exports and employment, though past experience suggests that the recent recovery may be unsustainable and quite vulnerable.

MIPS AND IMP: CONTRASTING STUDIES ON MALAYSIAN INDUSTRIAL POLICY

We discuss the industrial policy options of the Malaysian government through the 1990s in the context of a fundamental question, namely should the government adopt a laissez-faire or free market strategy, or should it intervene extensively and, if so, what forms should such intervention take? The strategic question about the roles of the market and of government intervention was raised by two major studies of industrial policy carried out for the Malaysian Government in the mid-1980s. These studies, some details of which are given in Table 13.1, were:

(a) the Malaysian Industrial Policy Study (MIPS); and
(b) the Industrial Master Plan (IMP).

The IMP pointed out that Malaysia has been a relative latecomer to industrialisation because successful primary export growth adequately financed previous import needs, weakening the urgency to industrialise – a sort of Third World strain of 'Dutch disease'. Other more profitable alternative investment opportunities (e.g. in real property and finance) have also discouraged manufacturing investments.

Malaysia's economy is said to be characterised by various imbalances, with the manufacturing sector narrowly based upon a few labour-intensive and resource-based industries. However, the relative share of resource-based products has been declining, accounting for less than 20 per cent of all

Table 13.1 Studies of industrial policy in Malaysia in the 1980s

	Malaysia Industrial Policy Study (MIPS)	Industrial Master Plan (IMP)
Date started	August 1983	July 1983
Date completed	December 1984	February 1986
Cost (US$'000)	320	2,025
External financing/ executing agencies	UNDP/World Bank	UNDP/UNIDO
Study carried out by	IMG Consultants, Australia	Individual experts under Dr Seongjae Yu
Volumes of report	8	22
Volumes publicly available (as of May 1990)	1 (Final Report, 8th volume)	14 (plus Executive Highlights)

Sources: Chee Peng Lim (1987); MIPS (1984).

manufactured exports in 1983 (IMP, 1986: 13). Export-oriented industrialisation since the late 1960s has mainly generated low-skilled labour-intensive exports requiring relatively simple final assembly work.

While acknowledging the impressive growth of the electronics industry, the IMP also recognised the limited and lopsided nature of its development to date:

> structurally, it has a heavy dependence on production of components, accounting for 80 to 85 per cent of the industry's total output; and within this sector, semiconductors assembly and testing activities have predominated, contributing 83 to 92 per cent of total component output. The consumer and industrial electronics, which normally account for more than 55 to 70 per cent of total output in other NICs and advanced countries, only contribute 15 to 20 per cent in Malaysia. This lopsided structure makes the Malaysian electronics industry very precarious, particularly because components manufacturing is limited to relatively simple assembly and testing activities based on imported materials, and is dominated by foreign transnational corporations whose main motivations to operate in Malaysia are low wages and attractive tax incentives which are available in the country. The side effect of this extreme structural skewness is the lack of linkages within the industry, especially between the companies in FTZs and non-FTZs.
>
> (IMP, 1985: 49)

While claiming that foreign investment has made a positive contribution to manufacturing growth, the IMP acknowledged that the heavy and sustained dependence on foreign investment in some important industries in the key areas of technology, marketing, management and components supply jeopardises the development of an indigenous industrial base (IMP, 1985: 13). The plan further recognised that the manufacturing sector is dominated by large, often foreign-controlled firms, though it failed to mention the consequent massive outflow of economic surplus in various forms.

The IMP acknowledged that the Malaysian manufacturing sector's technological dependence is excessive. Such dependence has resulted in the outflow of royalty payments, fees and other charges to the parent transnationals, ostensibly for technology transfer. As many transnational corporations actually prefer joint ventures with local firms, especially in manufacturing and services, such outflows have increased in significance compared with simple profit or dividend repatriation. It has been found that most joint ventures with local majority holdings have actually been controlled by the foreign partners, especially in technology-related matters (Abdul Razak, 1984).

There is very little evidence of any significant and meaningful transfer of technology. This should not be surprising since, in the present context, technology is transferred only insofar as it is necessary and desirable for the foreign firm's profit maximisation, though of course this could be quite considerable in certain circumstances. Obviously, transnationals will not transfer technology such that the recipients eventually threaten their profits. In their study of electronics and electrical firms in Malaysia in 1980, Cheong and Lim (1981) found that the transnationals retained research and development activities with the parent firm in the home country and controlled equipment and parts supply, key personnel and marketing. Production mainly involved assembly, processing and testing, activities requiring little skill and training, and which were generally irrelevant to other manufacturing sector production in any case. With weak linkages to the rest of the economy, other industries could hardly benefit from whatever technology transfer might have taken place.

In summary, the IMP identified five major problems that have adversely affected Malaysian industrialisation:

1. technological dependence and lack of an indigenous industrial technology capacity;
2. shortages of engineers and technicians;
3. deficiencies in existing industrial incentive schemes including:
   - ad hoc and excessive domestic market protection;
   - large-firm and capital-intensive biases associated with the pioneer status incentive;
   - neglect of small-industry problems and requirements;
   - rigidities and inflexibility in the existing incentive scheme;
   - biases in export incentives;
   - few incentives for technological development;

- some major incentives not automatically available;
4 lack of private sector initiative;
5 constraints imposed by NEP restructuring efforts.

In both the IMP and the MIPS studies, there was an emphasis on the anti-export bias of the protection given to the domestic market, but, whereas the IMP saw the potential for linking these, the MIPS saw them as quite separate activities. At present, the Malaysian ISI and EOI sectors are quite separate. The Malaysian manufacturing sector has developed along 'dualistic' lines, with a protected ISI sector producing almost entirely for the domestic market and to a large extent insulated from the world economy, and an EOI sector, equally insulated from the domestic market (see Table 17 in Chapter 1).

We believe that it is important to recognise this dualism, because it is, as we pointed out in Chapter 1, an obstacle to the efficient development of Malaysian manufacturing. Indeed, we identify this 'dualism' as one of the greatest problems of the Malaysian manufacturing sector. Superimposed upon a resource-based manufacturing sector, there is a dual industrial economy of two segregated sectors, the ISI and the EOI. The IMP and MIPS contained different policy prescriptions in this regard. The emphasis of the MIPS was on a reduction in the protective structure and a move towards uniformity and 'neutrality' of the tariff and non-tariff structure, whereas the emphasis of the IMP was more on export targeting and on the formulation of an industry-by-industry policy strategy.

However, both studies agreed that the structure of industrial incentives in Malaysia needed to be subjected to systematic and detailed cost–benefit analysis. But there was a difference in the assumptions of the two studies. These two studies diagnosed the industrial 'problem' in Malaysia from quite different assumptions and, not surprisingly, came up with different policy prescriptions. We find it easiest to summarise their differences in the context of a discussion on the third page of the IMP's Executive Highlights. The IMP contrasted three philosophical assumptions on which a Malaysian industrial development plan could be based. These were:

1 the *market rationale* assumption 'which is presented by America' and for which 'the premise is that the market is rational in allocating resources and motivating innovative decisions and, therefore, it is not necessary to have any explicit industrial development planning';
2 the *state rationale* assumption 'which is adopted by the centrally planned economy, and for which the premise is that decisions made by the state are always rational';
3 the *plan rationale* assumption which is identified with Japan and many other newly industrialised countries and for which the 'premise is that while the competitive market mechanism is indispensable, rational planning is fundamentally important in achieving industrial development objectives'.

Thus, the IMP focused on three industrial policy alternatives, namely free market, central planning and state coordination. In planning for Malaysia, the IMP opted for state coordination whereas the MIPS placed much more emphasis on the free market model. Hence, whereas the IMP 'Looked East' towards the model of Japan, South Korea and state direction, the MIPS 'looked West' towards the USA and the market.

Perhaps these differences are not surprising when you consider that the chief consultant for the IMP was a South Korean economist (Dr Seongjae Yu) and the sponsoring agency for the IMP was the pro-State-interventionist United Nations Industrial Development Organisation (UNIDO). By contrast, the MIPS was carried out by a firm of Australian economists with the sponsoring agency being the 'free market'-oriented World Bank.

It is fair to say that the IMP has had more publicity and been more influential institutionally than the MIPS. There are three reasons for this:

1. the IMP was more comprehensive than the MIPS. The budget for the IMP was more than six times that of the MIPS and it studied some particular industries as well as more general policy issues;
2. chronologically, the IMP started at about the same time, but then continued after and tended to 'absorb' the MIPS; and
3. the IMP was more in tune with the policy emphasis of the Malaysian government.

But even if the IMP has had more influence than the MIPS, should it continue to do so? And how much influence has the IMP had? Has Malaysia followed the 'plan rationale' assumption and, if not, should it? To what extent has it 'looked East' and copied the South Korean model? If it has, should it continue to do so? If it hasn't, should it?

THE MYTH OF FREE MARKET DEVELOPMENT IN THE EAST ASIAN NICs

The IMP has advocated that Malaysia should adopt an interventionist industrial strategy similar to that of South Korea. One major criticism of the MIPS study is that it failed to see industrial development as a question of strategy and bargaining as well as a function of state planning. This was the main contrast between the MIPS and the IMP. However, while the IMP also endorsed the need for the rationalisation of industrial incentives, it emphasised the strategic role of the state in industrial development. The IMP emphasis is much more in line with industrial policy in the East Asian NICs than is that of the MIPS. For, the belief that South Korea's industrial growth had been promoted by free trade policies and that state intervention had been neutral from the 1960s and into the 1980s has been shown to be quite false.

In the early 1980s, a number of economists were arguing that the spectacular growth in the East Asian NICs since the 1960s had been due to the free market, and that there had been little or no state intervention in the economy. In the 1980s, it was commonly alleged that South Korea, Taiwan, Hong Kong, and Singapore – the so-called 'Gang of Four' countries – had grown rapidly because they had 'got the prices right'. A typically orthodox view was that of Tsiang and Wu, who argued in 1985 that 'the experience of rapid economic growth in Taiwan, Korea, Hong Kong and Singapore during the past two or three decades was achieved not by economic tricks, but by sensible policies based on sound neo-classical principles' (Tsiang and Wu, 1985: 329). This was at the height of the neo-classical counter-revolution, coinciding with the coming to power of Margaret Thatcher in the UK and Ronald Reagan in the USA. This was the period of strong attacks on the state – a common joke in Brazil at the time was 'The economy grows only at night when the government is sleeping'; the state-interventionist UNCTAD was said to stand for 'Under No Circumstances Take A Decision'. In 1983 the *World Development Report* of the World Bank presented an analysis of development which attempted to show that there was an inverse relationship between 'market distortions' and economic growth; that is, the greater the degree of state intervention, the slower the rate of economic growth.

But subsequent careful, detailed research carried out by numerous economists and political scientists has shown the 1983 *World Development Report* to be wrong. A substantial body of research now exists to refute the World Bank's claim. The evidence is that, since the 1960s, the South Korean, Taiwanese and Singaporean governments have intervened extensively in almost every conceivable part of the economy.

Thus, to implement a free market strategy as recommended by the MIPS requires as 'strong' a state as is required to implement a selective interventionist strategy as emphasised in the IMP. To see whether either can be implemented requires an analysis of the Malaysian political structure. It seems that the bureaucracy in Malaysia has not been as independent of vested interests – both before and after the New Economic Policy (since the early 1970s) – as were the South Korean, Taiwanese or Singaporean bureaucracies in the 1960s and 1970s. State intervention has been widespread in Malaysia, particularly in promoting parity of share ownership between Malays and non-Malays, but it is doubtful whether this has been either as growth-promoting or even as equity-promoting as has been the selective intervention by the South Korean state. Given this, what are the implications for industrial policy?

POLICY OPTIONS FOR THE FUTURE

Certainly, it seems desirable that a detailed analysis of the industrial incentive structure be publicised, that is, that the structure of industrial incentives be more transparent. In this respect, both the IMP and MIPS are in agreement. A detailed public analysis of rents might weaken the rentier elements and strengthen the bureaucracy. Even if this is possible, what changes should be made to the incentive structure and industrial policy more generally? More specifically, how can such state intervention deal with the problems of dualism in the Malaysian manufacturing sector? What can be done to force the ISI sector into the world market and how can the benefits from the EPZ sector be increased? What should be done to encourage the development of resource-based industries? This is what the next three sections briefly look at.

The import-competing sector

As far as the ISI sector is concerned, the primary thrust of the MIPS recommendations is 'to reduce the overall level and wide dispersion of protection in the import-competing sector and, in particular, to reduce the severe cost disadvantages confronting the majority of exporters and potential exporters compared with import-competing manufacturers' (MIPS, 1984, Executive Summary: 1). Following this, the MIPS recommended that the level of effective protection be approximately halved to about 13 per cent (MIPS, 1984: recommendation 10), and that export subsidies be provided equivalent to the protection for the import-competing sector (MIPS, 1984: xvi). But there are two problems associated with the proposal for export subsidies: one is that the subsidies would impose an additional burden on government expenditure; and, the second is that such subsidies might contravene the rules of the General Agreement on Tariffs and Trade (GATT), as Appendix VII of the MIPS Final Report recognised

The IMP, backed the MIPS recommendation that the average level of protection should be lowered to around 13 per cent (IMP, 1985, Executive Highlights: 87) and, like the MIPS, argued that the current incentive system has a strong bias against exports (IMP, 1985: 15). But although it recommended the remission of duties on imports which went into exports, it did not recommend export subsidies (see IMP, 1986: 88). But it did recommend export targeting, and held out the possibility that such export targets could be linked with incentives (IMP, 1985: 98).

Such a linking between export targets and incentives seems to be worth pursuing. It is worth pursuing, not just because it is a policy that South Korea pursued with some success, but also because it has sound economic logic behind it. It is likely that, for many industries, protection in the domestic market will facilitate sales in the export market at much lower prices. As Paul Krugman pointed out in an article published in 1984, this cross-subsidisation will apply where production is subject to economies of scale over the relevant range of output. Krugman argued that: 'By giving a domestic firm a privileged position in some one market [sic], a country gives it an advantage in scale over foreign rivals' (Krugman in Kierzkowski, 1984: 181). This advantage will arise in the cases of both static and dynamic economies of scale. It will also apply to investment in research and development. That is, the assured profits in the domestic market spread the research and development costs over a (potentially) larger output. But the cost advantage may remain only a potential and may not be exploited unless the state intervenes to push the producer into transforming the potential advantage in the export market into an actual one. Thus, there is a case for what may be called 'EPconEP' – 'effective protection conditional on export performance'.

As emphasised by detailed research on South Korea and Taiwan, 'EPconEP' played an important role in building up manufactured exports alongside production for a protected domestic market. This made sense given uncertainties in the export market and the small size of the domestic market. This meant that, if South Korea and Taiwan were going to be internationally competitive in the 1960s and 1970s in industries with increasing returns to scale, then it would have to export, and such exporting was made much easier if done on the back of a protected domestic market. Thus, EPconEP made sense for South Korea, as it did for Taiwan (see Wade in White, 1988: 48–53). And if such an argument makes sense for South Korea, it is likely to apply with equal force to Malaysia, since Malaysia's GDP is only about a quarter of that of South Korea (see Table 12.2).

If economies of scale apply widely, then there is little scope for small-scale firms to be internationally competitive. And, even if production itself is not subjected to economies of scale, it seems likely that export marketing is. In an interesting study of small firms, Ian Little states, in referring to East Asia, that 'Big firms have economies of scale in export marketing, and it is generally true that most small units export little or nothing' (Little, 1987: 230). It is, perhaps, not surprising that the most rapid growth in South Korea and Taiwan has been among medium-sized and large enterprises (see Little, 1987: 207, 227). In an export-oriented economy, the prospects for small-scale firms which are independent of larger firms are dismal and they must be content to be subcontracted to the larger foreign or domestic companies. But even becoming subcontractees may not be easy – thus, in Malaysia, the government has attempted to promote small industries through a Sub-contract Exchange Network – introduced in 1986 – but without much success (see Malaysia, 1989: 193, 196).

If the prospects for small firms are weak, this may not necessarily be a cause for regret, if Little is correct when he says: 'Analyses based on disaggregated data found that small firms are not reliably more labour-intensive than their larger counterparts; nor are they consistently more technically efficient in their use of resources' (Little, 1987: 203). Thus, in manufacturing industry at least, small is not necessarily beautiful, and, not surprisingly then, 'overall the IMP is not very impressed with the potential role of small industry' (Chee, 1987: 90).

Malaysia's rather shallow industrial structure and high import propensities suggest possibilities for more import substitution, though of a different type. While considerable industrial development has taken place, the potential for import substitution remains far from exhausted. The size of the domestic market has grown with the population and has been accompanied, more importantly, with rapid economic growth and higher incomes. In the long term, making the ISI sector world competitive is the only efficient way of integrating the sector into both the world economy and the large export processing zone sector in Malaysia.

One useful aid to making industry internationally competitive is for a continuation of selective state intervention, but with a change of direction to force the companies at present producing for a protected domestic market into the export market. Such a policy of EPconEP would not add to government expenditure, since the cost of subsidies would continue to be borne by the final domestic consumers, nor would such an incentive structure contravene the rules of GATT.

In addition to this intervention in trade, supplementary intervention is desirable in the areas of:

- *finance* – this needs to be subordinated to the needs of industry as it was in South Korea and Japan;
- *technology* – the state needs to be actively involved in the negotiations for technology transfer;
- *infrastructure* – given the economies of scale in the provision of infrastructure, it is probably desirable for the state to be directly responsible for such provision but, failing that, it is important to establish an efficient regulatory structure and/or to promote competition to minimise the undesirable effects of private monopolies;
- *the training of labour* – this is particularly important and is discussed in more detail below.

The export processing zones

In looking at industrial policy for the EPZs, two questions immediately arise: first, how can the benefits to Malaysia be increased from the existing pattern of production? Second, can benefits be increased by improving the links between the EPZ producers and the rest of the economy?

As far as the first is concerned, there are three possible avenues for increasing the retained value added:

(a) by increasing direct taxation;
(b) by increasing local sourcing; and
(c) by inducing the production of goods with a higher value added content.

The first of these avenues seems an obvious path to increasing the retained value added. It was one which was favoured by the MIPS, which stated that 'these benefits [from EPZs] could be increased considerably by policies aimed at increasing taxation of company income in the FTZs and LMWs' (MIPS, 1984: 146). But this solution may not be effective as it seems likely that in a major EPZ industry, namely electronics, transfer pricing is practised. That is, it seems that companies transfer profits into Malaysia. The MIPS stated that the high apparent rate of profit reported by the electronics industry (46 per cent per annum – see also Table 1.9 above) suggests that the companies were transfer pricing into Malaysia. Increased taxation on profits seems to be an obvious policy to pursue, given the high rate of profit in the EPZs and given the existence of double taxation agreements (DTAs). The existence of DTAs between the Malaysian and other governments would seem to mean that, even if Malaysia offers tax concessions to companies operating in Malaysia but headquartered in foreign countries, the benefits of those concessions will accrue not to the companies, but to the foreign governments. If this is the case, then tax concessions would not be an incentive to locate in Malaysia. In fact, however, the DTAs generally treat the tax exempted under tax holidays as if the tax had been paid. This is done through so-called 'tax-sparing' clauses. Even without such clauses, companies based in EPZs and paying little or nothing in taxes can and do avoid paying taxes by, for example, remitting profits through offshore zones. In these circumstances, tax concessions may constitute a real incentive to locate in Malaysia. In any case, even if the tax concessions were to be withdrawn, it is quite likely that the profits would be transferred out of Malaysia by the companies rearranging transfer prices.

Even if the taxes could not be evaded in this way, it is possible that the companies would move their operations out of Malaysia, in which case Malaysia would lose even the small amount of retained value added represented by the wage bill and the surplus on local purchases. On the issue of whether the companies are footloose, there may be considerable differences between industries. Thus, those companies which are exporting items of clothing under the Multi-Fibre Arrangement (MFA) quotas granted to Malaysia may well be less footloose than others, in the sense that they are tied by the quotas. But in 1982, only a small proportion (less than 11 per cent) of the value added in Malaysian EPZs came from the textiles and clothing sector. Clearly, what is needed is an analysis of the profits of companies based in the EPZs and the extent to which these companies can avoid taxes or are footloose and likely to be driven away by higher taxes.

The second avenue for increasing retained value added is by increasing local sourcing. Here, there is a likely role for the State Economic Development Corporations as well as the Trade Associations in supporting potential local suppliers and in bringing them into contact with the big companies in the EPZs. These linkages will be easier to forge if the local suppliers are internationally competitive or have some immediate prospect of becoming so. In this respect, local content regulations may play a role, but more selective action (for example, through research or process development grants) may be more effective. Here, there may be a case for favouring locally owned local suppliers rather than subsidiaries of multinationals because of the greater tendency for reinvestment and the transfer of skills by locally owned companies. Export-oriented industrial production – especially of electronics

– has begun to develop some backward linkages as changing international conditions, especially the ringgit's depreciation, have encouraged greater local sourcing of manufactured inputs.

The third avenue is likely to be the most effective one in the longer term, even though at first sight it seems the least attractive. The government's obvious role here is to encourage skill development in the Malaysian labour force at the intermediate level through such bodies as the Penang Skills Development Centre and the Industrial Training Institutes and, at the more advanced level, through universities and polytechnics. Without this, the shortages of skilled labour which were becoming evident at the end of the 1980s will be truly acute by the mid-1990s.

How can the linkages of the EPZs with the rest of the Malaysian economy be improved? The MIPS Final Report highlighted the extreme import dependence of the EPZ companies (MIPS, 1984: 145), and recommended that restrictions on sales to the domestic economy should be lifted and that incentives should be given for higher research and development expenditure by Malaysian companies (MIPS, 1984: 203, 204). In the section of its Executive Highlights report dealing with the electronics industry, the IMP bemoaned the lack of linkages and stated that: 'Of the many problems, two deserve attention, lack of entrepreneurial ventures and low technology capability' (IMP, 1985: 49). It argued that the local companies in this field are too small to develop the appropriate technology and welcomed the establishment of the Malaysian Institute of Micro-electronic Systems (MIMOS).

It is probable that it will be more difficult to develop backward linkages from the EPZs to the domestic economy than it will be to induce the import-competing sector into exports. But both will be impossible unless the government recognises that industrial policy has to be based not only on detailed analysis but also on a readiness to bargain with the companies (both public and private) involved in the manufacturing sector. An area of industrial policy where detailed analysis is particularly required is that of the resource-based industries.

Resource-based industries

The need for industrial policy to be based on detailed economic analysis is particularly illustrated by the resource-based industries. One example is the rubber-products industry. Just because Malaysia exports more natural rubber than any other country, it is commonly argued that Malaysia should produce and export more rubber products than any other country. At present, Malaysia produces almost 40 per cent of the world's natural rubber, and yet processes less than 6 per cent of this into the production of rubber goods. By contrast, South Korea, which produces no natural rubber, processes more than twice as much natural rubber as Malaysia, and, in 1987, produced more than three times as many tyres as Malaysia.

A number of factors explain this relative backwardness of the Malaysian rubber tyre industry:

(a) Tyres, especially passenger car tyres, contain a high proportion of synthetic rubber and the cost of synthetic rubber to Malaysia is higher than the cost to its competitors (see Boston Consulting Group, 1989: xxvii).
(b) The tyre-producing plants in Malaysia are operating on a small scale in an industry which is characterised by large plants and large firms.
(c) Tariffs in, and shipping freight rates to, overseas markets escalate according to the stage of processing so that any cost advantage of proximity to natural rubber supplies for Malaysia is offset or outweighed by the escalating tariffs and freight rates.

The first and the third reasons suggest that Malaysia will have to continue to offer incentives to offset these disadvantages. In this respect, the MIPS recommendation of abolishing export duties (see MIPS, 1984: xiii), including those on rubber, would be counter-productive inasmuch as the export duties give protection to industrial consumers of natural rubber. Indeed, in a report on tyre production in Malaysia, the US-based Boston Consulting Group has recommended a larger subsidy on natural rubber purchased by exporters of tyres, the size of the subsidy to be conditional on the proportion of exports in total sales (Boston Consulting Group, 1989: xviii). Like the IMP, the BCG report favours conditional export targets, since it argues that the current policy is one of 'protecting an "infant industry", which has so far only matured into a structurally uncompetitive industry unable to operate profitably outside its protected domestic market' (Boston Consulting Group, 1989: xxix, 85).

Such industrialisation has further integrated Malaysia into the world economy. Import substitution has also remained dependent on foreign technology, machinery and inputs under the auspices of foreign manufacturers trying to consolidate virtual monopolies in the protected domestic market. Despite some improvement of this situation, both import-substituting and export-oriented manufacturing remain heavily import dependent. In 1989, 33 per cent of the import bill comprised intermediate manufacturing inputs, which amounted to M$20.0 billion, compared with manufacturing GDP of about M$25.5 billion. Since exports of manufacturers came to M$36.7 billion, manufactured exports accounted for about 81 per cent of total manufacturing value of M$45.5 billion, if we ignore the accounting problems involved. Manufacturing grew by 12.0 per cent in 1989, with the recovery in domestic demand, and continued growth of external demand and investments. Rubber products, electronics and electrical products grew most rapidly during 1987–9.

More generally, manufacturing has recovered sharply after being in the doldrums in the mid-1980s. Capacity utilisation has picked up after falling sharply in earlier years. Production of electronic and electrical products particularly has bounced back after falling by 23 per cent in 1985 as a result of excess world supply and stiff competition. After similar reductions in the production of integrated circuits and semiconductors in 1985, production has picked up steadily since.

Thus, for all areas of industrial policy – applying to the import-competing, export-processing and resource-based manufacturing sectors – a detailed analysis is a prerequisite for the formulation of an efficient and effective industrial policy. Both the MIPS and IMP studies recommend detailed cost–benefit analyses of industrial incentives. What is needed is studies not just of effective protection levels but of what goes on behind the protective barriers in terms of costs and profits. Detailed analysis is essential because the general lesson that comes from looking at the experience of the East Asian NICs is that state intervention is a necessary, but not sufficient, condition for rapid industrial growth. The need is not just for state intervention, but for intervention which promotes efficient growth and re-investment. The need is for a set of industrial policies that actively create and promote comparative advantages.

For a stronger industrial policy, we have argued that:

(a) in general, an interventionist industrial policy is desirable because of inherent market imperfections;
(b) in the particular case of South Korea, an efficient interventionist policy was practised from the early 1960s.

It is also clear that Malaysia has been following an interventionist policy in the development of the industrial sector. It has used tariff protection in developing the ISI sector and it has offered tax concessions and FTZ/LMW status to promote the EOI sector. However, Malaysian intervention could be made more efficient. In this respect, Malaysia should copy South Korea and Taiwan in practising pro-active interventionist policy based on a more detailed and coordinated knowledge of industries, and one which disciplines companies as well as supports them.

From the experience of Japan, South Korea and Taiwan and from theories about the limitations of markets, intervention is most likely to be needed in the areas of:

1 *Technology*. Because of information imperfections in the market, there is a strong chance that the cost of gaining information about technology will be high relative to the probable benefits. Thus, there may be a gain to society by the state underwriting the company against that risk by meeting some of the cost of getting the information. This gain is likely to be particularly large because there are likely to be economies of scale in the acquisition of information (see Pack and Westphal, 1986).
2 *Finance*. Because of imperfections in the market stemming from risk and

uncertainty, companies may underinvest in long-term production facilities since the rate of profit or surplus required by the companies is likely to be higher than that required by society. As a result long-term investment is likely to be smaller than the social optimum unless the state underwrites it.

3 *Training labour.* Because of externalities in the market, companies which spend money on training are not assured of being able to recoup that cost. As a result, training is likely to be under-funded without state coordination.

4 *Trade.* Because of imperfections in the market arising from economies of scale, uncertainty or both, although companies may find it easier to compete in international markets from the platform of highly profitable domestic sales, a company's profit-maximising output may be less than the level of output that gives a lower (but nevertheless satisfactory) level of profit. Thus, it may be socially beneficial for the state to step in and impose export targets in return for protection in the domestic market.

The lesson is that, just as there are many different types of markets, so there are also many types of imperfections. The lesson from the experience of Japan, South Korea and Taiwan is somewhat paradoxical, namely that state intervention may create the correct market signals by changing the market – in this sense, Alice Amsden is correct when she says that the South Korean state was right 'to get the prices wrong'.

The crucial question is: can Malaysia adopt a more pro-active industrial policy? One argument might be that the government already imposes conditions on industry through the New Economic Policy (NEP). Can it go beyond these? And even if state intervention is considered desirable to correct market imperfections, are the political conditions appropriate for pro-active state intervention?

IS A MORE PRO-ACTIVE POLICY POSSIBLE?

In Malaysia, with the success of its primary product exports, the pressures to export manufactured goods have not compared with the situation in the East Asian NICs. And, by contrast with the situation in South Korea and Taiwan, the Malaysian state has not exercised the 'autonomy' it enjoys to promote industrialisation under national auspices. The political structure in Malaysia has consisted of an uneasy alliance between Malay and Chinese elites, with much of the recent wealth of the Malays derived from political privilege, and that of the Chinese being derived from trade, manufacturing, construction and services.

Industrial development in Malaysia through the 1960s and 1970s was dominated by foreign investment. This was particularly true of production in the export processing zones, but it was also true of the ISI sector – in 1970, foreign investors controlled more than half of the import-competing manufacturing sector (see Edwards, 1975: 122). At the same time, many of the foreign subsidiaries have had local directors so that there has been a 'comprador' element in the ownership (see Edwards, 1975: 326). It is this element of 'rentier politics' combined with an ethnically preoccupied bureaucracy that has determined the form of state intervention in Malaysia. Thus, the executive of the Malaysian state has been reluctant to impose export targeting and other similar measures along South Korean lines, in spite of this being advocated by the IMP.

Hence, the bureaucracy in Malaysia – relative to that in South Korea and Taiwan, for example – has implemented an inefficient industrial policy. Under British colonialism, there was a reluctance to provide incentives for the development of manufacturing industry for fear of harming plantation interests. In the 1960s, manufacturing industry was promoted by being given protection in the domestic market. This was the 'easy' stage of ISI, equivalent to that in South Korea and Taiwan about a decade earlier. But whereas, after the 'easy' stage, South Korea and Taiwan promoted manufactured exports on the basis of a protected home market, Malaysian policy switched back to the promotion of exports from export processing zones.

It is a difficult task to trace the links between these industrial policies and the political structure in Malaysia. While the bureaucracy in Malaysia had 'autonomy' from vested interests, as did the bureaucracy in South Korea, its interventionist measures largely reflect a strong preoccupation with inter-ethnic redistribution. There has been intervention in Malaysia, but it has led to an industrial dualism. The overriding strategy has been the implementation of the New Economic Policy objectives. There has been a number of objectives of the NEP. One has been to reduce the incidence of poverty, regardless of ethnic group, to about 17 per cent; the second has been to restructure society so as to: (a) produce an employment pattern that reflects the racial composition of the population; and (b) increase to at least 30 per cent the share of Malays in the ownership and control of corporate wealth.

The NEP was instituted in 1971 and the targets were to be achieved by 1990. A variety of policy instruments has been used in the attempt to achieve the NEP objectives, including scholarship and other educational preferences, preferences in employment, especially in the public sector, and licensing and other restrictions imposed on companies, particularly under the Industrial Coordination Act of 1976. In the early 1980s, non-financial public enterprises (NFPEs) proliferated. The Promotion of Investments Act (1986) further relaxed some of the restrictions on foreign equity participation, while an assurance was given to the private sector that the public sector – which had grown in the 1970s and early 1980s – would be reduced (*Malaysian Management Review (MMR*, 1989: 93)

There has been considerable debate in Malaysia about:

(a) whether the NEP targets have been achieved;
(b) how the NEP policies have affected economic growth; and,

(c) whether NEP-type targets will be renewed in the 1990s.

Although there is considerable disagreement about definitions and the reliability of some of the statistics, there is some agreement that the poverty reduction target has been reached, though there was little change in income inequality over the NEP period (see Jomo, 1989).

Much progress has been made on employment restructuring, but the pattern of employment in the upper echelons is still far from reflecting the racial composition of the population (*MMR*, 1989: 35–7). Over the years, the target for the restructuring of wealth to Malays has been interpreted in terms of 30 per cent ownership of share capital in limited companies in Malaysia. It seems that confirmed ownership by Malays has risen from about 4 per cent in 1971 to about 19 per cent in 1990 (see *MMR*, 1989: 38), although the degree of actual Malay ownership and control is generally thought to be greater. Malay control is greatest in finance, plantations and mining, and smallest in manufacturing, construction and commerce (*MMR*, 1989: 38, 39). Foreign ownership in general is estimated to have fallen from 62 per cent in 1972 to 25 per cent in 1988 (see *MMR*, 1989: 38), although this is underestimated owing to the 21 per cent of unidentified share owners. Also, it should be noted that these proportions are derived from the par (or issued) and not the market values of shares. Even at par values, foreign ownership in manufacturing is almost certainly much higher than the 23 per cent average for the corporate sector as a whole.

In general, then, the NEP targets are likely to have been reached by 1990. However, there is very little agreement about the effect of the NEP on growth. This is hardly surprising since there are a number of policies under the NEP heading, and each will have had different effects. It appears as if there was a less efficient use of new capital in the mid-1980s with the proliferation of heavy industries; the incremental capital–output ratio (ICOR) rose, and this seems to be particularly true of the public sector. This has been associated with the expansion of the non-financial public enterprises (NFPEs) in the 1980s, and, since some of the NFPEs were used to achieve the NEP objectives, part of their poor performance has been attributed to the NEP (see *MMR*, 1989: 22).

In the same way as there is little agreement about the effects of the NEP, so there is little agreement about whether or not similar policies to those of the NEP should be continued after 1990. In January 1989, the National Economic Consultative Council was formed to discuss the NEP and post-1990 policy. It met through 1989 and 1990, by which time the government announced that it would go ahead with formulating post-1990 economic policy, ostensibly because of the considerable debate and disagreement about the form that national economic policy should take in the 1990s.

There has been some particularly strong criticism of the ownership restructuring policy. It is argued that this policy has fostered the growth of a rentier class (see *MMR*, 1989: 44) and of 'money politics'. The policy has been accused of aiming at a 'parity of millionaires', with there being little incentive for the growing Bumiputra rentier class to become efficient entrepreneurs. An argument which is widely echoed in Malaysia (among Malays as well as non-Malays) is: 'restructuring the ownership of share capital does not add very much to raising the income of the average Bumiputera household and putting more and more financial resources to acquire companies would be misplaced' (*MMR*, 1989: 59).

Thus, the weakness of a non-specialised bureaucracy subordinated to vested 'political' interests has combined with a strong rentier class based in the dominant Malay political group to prevent the emergence of an efficient, 'deepening' industrial policy. But such advocacy is likely to fall on deaf ears. Some variation of the NEP is likely to be continued in the 1990s. Given this, it is all the more essential that Malaysia should try to emulate South Korea and Taiwan in strengthening the 'rational bureaucratic' basis of industrial policy in the government. Malaysia must, in this respect, learn from the experiences of the East Asian NICs despite the political, economic, social and cultural differences. What is needed is an industrial policy that will break down the dualism that has developed in Malaysian manufacturing industry. On this, both the MIPS and IMP agreed. Where they differed is on the steps that need to be taken to achieve this.

It is not clear whether the more powerful body (or bodies) for industrial policy-making should be the Ministry of International Trade and Industry (MITI), the Malaysian Industrial Development Authority (MIDA), the Economic Planning Unit (EPU) in the Prime Minister's Department or some other. One thing is certain, however. If Malaysia is to overcome the legacy of industrial dualism and to deepen and integrate the industrial structure, and if it is to strengthen the base of skilled labour, while at the same time handling the environmental problems which will become more acute in the next five to ten years, then a powerful Industrial Policy Unit (IPU) is required.

To sum up, the lessons from the East Asian NIC experience are:

1 state intervention is a necessary, but not a sufficient condition for a growth-oriented industrial policy;
2 such state intervention requires a detailed specification of the policy objectives, an analysis of the instruments to be used to achieve those objectives and the imposition of discipline and performance requirements on the private and state sectors;
3 such intervention requires that the bureaucracy be strong enough and open enough to minimise 'rentier politics'. The 'social structure of accumulation' has to be permissive.

It is important to emphasise, however, that a strong bureaucracy with the required level of 'relative autonomy' – of independence from vested interests – is a pre-condition not only for 'successful' state intervention, but also for the imposition of so-called free markets on the World Bank/IMF model. The question confronting Malaysia in the 1990s is not whether the bureaucracy is technically capable of formulating a growth-oriented industrial policy; rather it is whether the bureaucracy is sufficiently above rentier and ethnic politics to be able to implement such an industrial policy.

REFERENCES

Abdul Razak Abdul (1984) 'Joint Ventures between Malaysian Public Corporations and Foreign Enterprise: An Evaluation', in Lim Lin Lean and Chee Peng Lim (eds) *The Malaysian Economy at the Crossroads: Policy Adjustment or Structural Transformation*, Malaysian Economic Association, Kuala Lumpur.

Boston Consulting Group (1989) 'Report by the Boston Consulting Group on Tyre Production in Malaysia', unpublished consultancy report.

Chee, P.L. (1987) *Industrial Development: An Introduction to the Malaysian Industrial Master Plan*, Pelanduk Publications, Kuala Lumpur.

Cheong Kee Cheok and Lim Kok Cheong (1981) 'Implications for the Transfer of Technology and Primary Ancillary Linkages: A Case Study of the Electronics and Electrical Industries in Malaysia', in H. Osman Rani, Ishak Shari and Jomo K.S. (eds) *Development in the Eighties, with Emphasis on Malaysia*, Universiti Kebangsaan Malaysia, Bangi, a special issue of *Jurnal Ekonomi Malaysia*, 3 & 4.

Edwards, C.B. (1975) 'Protection, Profits and Policy: An Analysis of Industrialisation in Malaysia', PhD thesis, University of East Anglia, Norwich, UK.

IMP (1985) *Medium and Long Term Industrial Master Plan: Malaysia, 1986–1995*, UNIDO, Vienna, August.

Jomo K.S. (1989) *Beyond 1990: Considerations for a New National Development Strategy*, Institute of Advanced Studies, University of Malaya, Kuala Lumpur.

Krugman, P. (1984) 'Import Protection as Export Promotion: International Competition in the Presence of Oligopoly and Economies of Scale', in H. Kierzkowski (ed.) *Monopolistic Competition and International Trade*, Clarendon Press, Oxford.

Little, I.M.D. (1987) 'Small Manufacturing Enterprises in Developing Countries', *World Bank Economic Review*, 1, 2, 203–35.

Malaysia (1989) *Mid-Term Review of the Fifth Malaysia Plan 1986–1990*, Government Printer, Kuala Lumpur.

Malaysian Management Review (1989) Special issue on the New Economic Policy, 24, 2, August, Kuala Lumpur.

MIPS (1984) *Final Report of the Malaysian Industrial Policies Studies (MIPS) Project*, IMG Consultants Pty Ltd, Sydney, Australia (restricted circulation).

Pack, H. and Westphal, L. (1986) 'Industrial Strategy and Technological Change', *Journal of Development Economics*, 22, 87–128.

Tsiang, S. and Wu Rong-I (1985) 'Foreign Trade and Investment as Boosters of Take-off: The Experience of the Four Asian NICs', in W. Galenson (ed.) *Foreign Trade and Investment: Economic Development in the Newly-Industrialising Asian Countries*, University of Wisconsin Press, Madison.

White, G. (ed.) (1988) *Developmental States in East Asia*, Macmillan, London.

STATISTICAL APPENDIX

Table S.1 Gross domestic product, by industry of origin, 1970–2000
(M$m in 1978 prices)

Sector	1970	1980	1990	2000	Average growth rate (%) Achieved 1971–90	Target 1991–2000
Agriculture & forestry	6,254	10,190	14,892	20,820	4.4	3.5
Mining & quarrying	2,962	4,487	7,688	8,910	4.9	1.5
Manufacturing	2,995	8,742	21,381	58,010	10.3	10.5
Construction	811	2,066	2,788	5,470	6.4	7.0
Electricity, gas & water	238	640	1,511	3,910	9.7	10.0
Transport, storage & communication	785	2,542	5,489	14,200	10.2	10.0
Wholesale & retail trade, hotels & restaurants	2,469	5,383	8,700	19,640	6.5	8.5
Financial, real estate & business services	1,854	3,686	7,650	16,490	7.3	8.0
Government services	2,005	4,563	8,459	13,080	7.5	4.5
Other services	445	1,020	1,656	3,400	6.8	7.5
(−) Imputed bank service charges	225	854	4,020	13,710	15.5	13.0
(+) Import duties	955	2,046	2,972	5,560	5.8	6.5
GDP at purchasers' values	21,548	44,511	79,103	155,780	6.7	7.0

Source: *New Straits Times*, 22 August 1992.

STATISTICAL APPENDIX

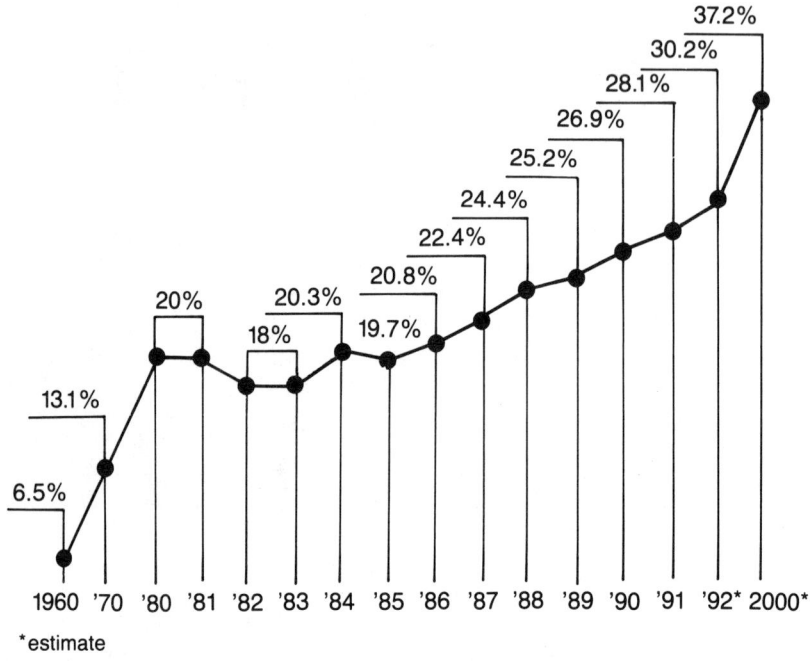

Figure S.1 Manufacturing sector: contribution to GDP, 1960–2000
Source: *New Straits Times*, 22 August 1992.

Table S.2   Unemployment and employment, 1985–2000

Year	Unemployment rate (%)	Jobless	Employed
1985	6.9	414,500	5,624,600
1986	8.3	515,700	5,706,500
1987	8.2	525,500	5,883,400
1988	8.1	534,700	6,087,500
1989	7.1	539,800	6,287,700
1990	5.8	536,800*	6,621,000
1991	4.3	450,000*	7,040,000
2000	4.0	378,200	9,364,500

Note: * estimate by Manpower Department, Human Resources Ministry.
Source: *New Straits Times*, 22 August 1992.

Table S.3 Foreign participation by selected countries in approved projects, 1985–91 (M$bn)

Country	1985	1986	1987	1988	1989	1990	1991
Japan	0.264	0.116	0.715	1.222	2.690	4.213	3.158
Taiwan	0.032	0.011	0.243	0.830	2.160	6.339	3.548
United States	0.112	0.054	0.163	0.535	0.321	0.567	1.724
Singapore	0.100	0.184	0.259	0.420	0.915	0.895	1.027
United Kingdom	0.027	0.050	0.077	0.197	0.765	0.867	0.538
South Korea	0.025	0.004	0.004	0.042	0.189	0.650	1.669
Indonesia	0.013		0.002	0.023	0.105	1.083	1.234
Australia	0.026	0.035	0.126	0.026	0.030	0.054	0.411
Total	0.959	1.688	2.060	4.878	8.653	17.629	15.956

Source: New Straits Times, 22 August 1992.

Table S.4 Investments approved by MIDA in manufacturing projects, 1987–91

Year	Domestic Investments			Foreign Investments			Total	
	M$m	% of total investments	Change	M$m	% of total investments	Change	M$m	%
1987	1,873.90	47.6	–	2,060.00	52.4	–	3,933.90	100
1988	4,215.90	46.4	124.98	4,878.01	53.6	136.80	9,093.91	100
1989	3,540.10	29.2	–16.03	8,568.06	70.8	75.65	12,108.16	100
1990	10,538.99	37.4	197.70	17,629.14	62.6	105.75	28,168.13	100
1991	12,175.59	43.3	15.53	15,956.26	56.7	–9.49	28,131.85	100

Source: New Straits Times, 22 August 1992.

Table S.5 Approved projects by ownership, 1987–91

Ownership	No of projects					Capital investments (M$m)					% share of total investment				
	1987	1988	1989	1990	1991	1987	1988	1989	1990	1991	1987	1988	1989	1990	1991
Wholly Malaysian-owned	105	262	184	235	211	912.0	2,341.0	960.2	1,473.2	3,225.4	23.2	25.7	7.9	5.2	11.4
Wholly foreign-owned	82	169	276	582	221	1,401.3	2,696.7	5,910.3	6,817.4	7,214.9	35.6	29.7	48.8	24.2	25.6
Joint ventures:															
• Malaysian majority	87	141	148	184	155	1,043.4	1,499.5	2,843.8	13,044.4	7,755.7	26.5	16.5	23.5	46.4	27.6
• Equal ownership	49	132	156	230	121	481.6	1,391.4	2,174.2	6,429.7	9,270.8	12.2	15.3	18.5	22.8	33.0
• Foreign majority	10	28	20	33	21	95.6	1,165.3	219.6	403.4	665.0	2.4	12.8	1.8	1.4	2.4
Total	333	732	784	1,264	729	3,933.9	9,093.9	12,108.1	28,168.1	28,131.8	99.9	100	100	100	100

Source: *New Straits Times*, 22 August 1992.

Table S.6 Distribution of industrial estates by state, as at 1 January 1992

States	No of industrial estates Proposed	No of industrial estates Existing	Total planned area (hectares) excluding housing Proposed	Total planned area (hectares) excluding housing Existing	Total (hectares) developed Proposed	Total (hectares) developed Existing	Industrial Land Total (hectares) saleable Proposed	Industrial Land Total (hectares) saleable Existing	Total (hectares) allocated Proposed	Total (hectares) allocated Existing	Total hectares still available Proposed	Total hectares still available Existing
Johore	–	22	–	2,958.48	–	2,922.05	–	2,254.37	–	1,438.18	–	830.55
Malacca	6	8	815.61	630.18	725.66	630.16	625.50	518.44	–	501.47	652.50	15.17
Negri Sembilan	4	7	76.07	477.27	–	458.92	–	334.97	–	311.84	–	23.13
Selangor	16	22	n.a.	2,732.49	n.a.	2,090.78	n.a.	2,036.24	n.a.	1,953.33	n.a.	100.91
Labuan	–	2	–	214.23	–	206.23	–	198.81	–	198.81	–	–
Perak	5	26	907.37	2,066.25	40.90	1,487.36	40.90	1,206.04	26.21	923.18	14.69	286.68
Penang	2	10	1,650.00	1,953.98	n.a.	1,658.95	n.a.	1,316.89	n.a.	1,301.23	n.a.	219.11
Kedah	2	16	1,594.26	889.22	–	839.29	–	714.79	–	688.62	–	29.42
Perlis	1	4	47.00	153.84	–	76.94	–	63.09	–	38.79	–	24.30
Pahang	5	10	519.08	2,536.06	–	934.48	–	1,466.08	–	564.84	–	884.85
Kelantan	–	7	–	737.63	–	458.99	–	360.49	–	295.46	–	65.03
Trengganu	4	14	1,630.46	2,380.65	–	2,084.96	–	1,453.92	–	1,029.80	–	424.15
Sabah	5	8	711.08	230.10	–	230.10	–	143.98	–	121.57	–	22.41
Sarawak	5	10	1,706.02	2,179.83	–	1,168.57	–	719.86	–	814.46	–	155.60
Total	55	166	8,274.93	20,140.29	766.56	15,249.78	693.40	12,787.97	26.21	10,163.58	667.19	3,081.30

n.a. = not available
Source: *New Straits Times*, 22 August 1992.

Table S.7 Free Trade Zones (FTZs) by state, as at 1 January 1992

State/Name of FTZs	Number of FTZs	FTZs Total hectares still available	Number of FTZs fully occupied
Johore Johore Port Authority Industrial Land FTZ	1	– –	1
Malacca Batu Port Authority Tanjung Kling FTZ	2	– –	– 2
Selangor Sg. Way FTZ Ampang hulu Kelang FTZ Telok Panglima Garang FTZ	3	– – –	– – 3
Perak Jelapang II FTZ Kinta FTZ	2	– 26.3	26.23	1
Penang Prai FTZ Prai Wharf FTZ Bayan Lepas FTZ	3	11.78 – –	11.78	2
Sarawak Muara Tabuan Free Trade Industrial Zone	1	14.17	14.17	–
Total	12		52.18	9

Proposed FTZs:
(1) Sarawak: Sejingkat Free Trade Zone
(2) Perlis: Padang Besar FTZ
Source: *New Straits Times*, 22 August 1992.

BIBLIOGRAPHY OF UNPUBLISHED OFFICIAL SOURCES

Malaysian Industrial Development Authority (MIDA)

Directory of approved companies in production
Annual survey of approved companies in production
Annual survey of progress of implementation of approved manufacturing projects
Half-yearly industrial trend survey
Annual statistics on projects granted approval

Ministry of International Trade and Industry (MITI) – formerly Ministry of Trade and Industry – (Industry Division)

Application form for manufacturing licence under the (ICA) 1975 and/or for incentives under the Promotion of Investment Act 1986
Annual survey of manufacturing companies in production
Progress report of approved projects
Application form for exemption from import duty and/or surtax on raw materials/component parts for manufacturing finished products for the domestic market
Ministry file on ICA/incentive-related applications and correspondence

Department of Statistics (DS)

Annual survey of manufacturing industries (Census of Manufacturing Industries for 1959, 1963, 1968, 1973, 1981)
Financial survey of limited companies (annual)
Company registration statistics (reported in annual *Statistical Bulletin*)

Registrar of Companies

Annual reports of individual companies

Malaysian International Chamber of Commerce and Industry (MICCI)

Membership directory
Annual Business Assessment Survey
Various ad hoc short surveys

BIBLIOGRAPHY

Kuala Lumpur Stock Exchange (KLSE)

KLSE Handbook

Bank Negara Malaysia (BNM)

Short-term/long-term capital flow estimates (net private DFI inflow, net investment income outflow)
Estimates of royalty/rental payments abroad

Japanese External Trade Organisation (JETRO)

Statistics on Japanese DFI in Malaysia

INDEX

American Federation of Labor and Congress of Industrial Organisations (AFL-CIO) 10; petition for withdrawal of duty-free privileges under GSP from Malaysia 130
Anti-poaching measures 69
Apparel firms: microelectronic technology (CAD) introduction 124–5; wages 132
ASEAN Car Accord 282–3; ASEAN's brand to brand complementation scheme 283; economies of scale 283; Mitsubishi 283; MMC-Sittipol 283; Nissan 282; Toyota 282
Asian NICs 217
Auto industry: 'Ali-Baba' practices 25; auto assembly 273; Bumiputra equity 275; components manufacture 273, 278; contribution to national economy 275; cost of locally assembled vehicles 275; emergence of locals as parts exporters 279; government's objectives 273; increase in CKD import duties to protect the Proton Saga 278; local content 273, 274; MACPMA lobbying 274; mandatory deletion of CKD vehicles 274; Motor Vehicle Assemblers Committee (MVAC), 274; second national car 284; See also Proton Car Project

Bank Negara 201, 202
Buddhism 295
Business Assessment Survey 114

Capital Issues Committee (CIC), 109

Census of Manufacturing for 1981 169–170
China Productivity Centre (CPC) 227–8
Christianity 295
Competition: stimulus to change in production process 132
Competitiveness 46, 71
Confucianism 295; authoritarian nature of East Asian NIC regimes 295; emphasis on diligence, loyalty and respect for authority 295; reason for poverty 295; revival in Singapore 295
Consumer electronics firms and electrical firms: automation 125; horizontal integration of work tasks 125; wages in consumer electronics firms 133; working conditions in consumer electronics firms 133; see also electronics industry
Cultural factor in industrialisation 295–6; cultural homogeneity of NIC societies 296; racial tension in Singapore 296; state intervention in Malaysia 296; see also Buddhism, Christianity, Confucianism, Daoism

Daoism 295
Deregulation: capital market 43; labour 43
Development potential: consumer goods 151–2; consumer non-durables in local market 152
Development strategy 45, 98
Domestic Resource Cost (DRC) 22
Direct Foreign Investment (DFI): component within overall development framework 99;

cumulative stock 81; in electronics industry 226; in industrialisation strategies of second-tier NICs 147; local equity participation conditions and inflow of DFI 108; long-term implications 147; sectoral pattern 84, 85; sectoral pattern of stock composition 88–9, 90; sources 10, 84, 86–7; trend of approvals 77, 78, 79, 80

Discrimination against women in internal labour market 70

Dynamic efficiency 51

East Asian NICs 10; examples of state-led development 287; governments' pro-active policies for industrialisation 299; lessons from experiences 333–4; role of state in late industrialisation 286

East Asian NIC comparisons: ethnicity and culture 295–7, 299; history 289–90; international conditions 294; nature of state intervention 297–8; resources 291–4, human resources 292–4; strategic significance 290–1

East Asian 'tigers', 11

Economic instability 65

Economic liberalisation 2, 10

Economic Planning Unit (EPU) 333

Edaran Otomobil Nasional (EON) 278; cheap transfer price from Proton 281; commission from finance companies 282; equity participation 281; profit margins from options 281; restructuring of ownership 282; rise in transfer pricing 282; servicing 282

Education 52; qualifications 69

Effective Rate of Protection (EPR): in Malaysian manufacturing 19, 20, 21, 23; on import-substitutes in South Korea 306

Electrical components and electronics sector: expansion 46

Electrical Industry Workers' Union (EIWU) 130

Electronics components industry: introduction of JIT and falling levels of employment 135; wages 132–3; working conditions 132

Electronics industry 9; absence of independent unions 122, 130, 131; access of Malaysian exports to markets in North America and Europe 226; accreditation to ISO 9000 Standard 228–9; assembly and selling of semiconductor devices 211; assembly investment in component industry 221; automation 126, 214, effect on wages 214, manpower needs 214; backward linkages 9, 228; change in image 214; computer peripheral assembly operations 223, disk drive assembly and sub-assembly 223, hard disk drives (HDD) 223; consequences of growing capital intensity 214; consumer electronics industry 9, 220; development of human resource potential 229–230, 232; discrimination against domestic firms by current government policy 227; diversification 219, case for building up consumer electronics sector 219; dominance in industrial sector growth 211; employment 212, female 35; financial, technical and marketing package 227–8; firms in FTZs 122; gross output 211–12; growing sophistication 229, 230; growth of component industry 222; growth of consumer electronics 219, 222; hardware manufacture 9; high volume component manufacturing 222; implications 212, labour costs 214, skilled labour 214, specialised tooling 214; in-house machine shop 215; in-house unions 130; increase in level of automation 107; machinery 122; major investments wholly foreign-owned companies 221–3; major investors 220; market links 214; office automation equipment 223; output structure 212, 213; ownership pattern 213; research and development 230, demand-driven 231, diffusion of information technology 232, in consumer electronics 220–21, multinational firms' operations 232, role of universities 231; response to growing number of assembly investments in component industry 221; semiconductor operations performance as share of total electronics industry 212; skills 126–7,

INDEX

214; software development 224–6, industry in Malaysia 225, shifting emphasis 224–5; Taiwanese component and material suppliers 222; tax incentives 214; telecommunication sector 224, mobile cellular telephony 224, switching and multiplexing systems 224; tight government control over workers' organisations 214; *see also* consumer electronic firms and electrical firms, electrical components and electronics sector, electronics compnonents industry

Employment: casualisation of labour contracts 4; changes 64; contracting out employment 67; during first phase of industrialisation in Malaysia 24; factors influencing firms' policy 4; female participation in manufacturing employment 24, 35, 70; growth 61; in FTZs 134–7; in manufacturing sector 3, 27, 36, 54; Malay participation in manufacturing employment 34–5; part-time workers 67; policy 68; private sector employment 47–8; public sector employment 47–8; relationship with sales 4; relationship with wages 3; security 4; skill polarisation 69; transaction costs 51; *see also* labour force, workforce and Female labour

Employment Act 68

Employment exchange service 69

Employment mobility 60; drift 'southwards' 60

Export processing zones (EPZs): mean permanent employment in FTZ firms 135

Export processing zones (EPZs) 26; avenues for increasing retained value added 325; double taxation agreements (DTAs) 326; increasing local sourcing 325, 326; linkages to rest of economy 28, 329; little technology transfer 28; SEDCs and linkages 326; Trade Associations and linkages 326; transfer pricing in electronics industry 326; skill development 327; *see also* free trade zones

External debt 29, 30

Electrical and electronics industry 152; gross exports 212; import-leakage propensity 177; links at input and output ends of electrical industry 152–3; links in electronics industry 153; value added 212; *see also* electronics industry, electrical components and electronics sector, electronics components industry

Environmental consequences of industrial action 2

Family policy 70

Federal Industrial Development Authority (FIDA), 7, 24; *see also* Malaysian Industrial Development Authority (MIDA)

Federal Land Development Authority (FELDA), 169, 185; land development schemes 185

Female labour: salary 123; *see also* electronics industry, labour force, workforce

Fifth Malaysia Plan 1986–90 8, 167, 185

'Financial deepening' theory (McKinnon-Shaw) 308; questioned by Lawrence Harris 308

Financial Survey of Limited Companies 81

Fiscal incentives in industrialisation 6, 41

Food subsidies 45

Foreign equity restrictions 42

Foreign Exchange Control Act 201

Foreign investment 42; *see also* direct foreign investment

Foreign-majority-controlled firms: direct contribution to economy 84; employment generation 83; export propensity 91, 94; import propensity 94, 95; indirect contribution to economy 84; outflow of investment income 95, 96; output 83; pre-tax profitability as return on equity capital 98; profitability trend 91, 92, 93; propensity to receive investment incentives 96; tax revenue contribution 96, 97

Foreign-owned ventures 77, 79, 81; Bumiputra equity 82, 83

Foreign sourcing of loans 81

Free market strategy 322

Free Trade Zones (FTZs) 6–7, 25, 118, 119–121, 175, 177; control 127–8, 129; day-to-day operation control

INDEX

130; development 7; domination by foreign capital 7, 127, 128–9, 142; employment 134–7, 142; exemption from mandatory collective bargaining obligation 180; export performance 137, 142; exports 7; health of workers 123; inducement for workers to retire early 123; industrial linkages 7; labour 7, 177; local management control 127; Malaysian manufacturing equity 142; material purchases 171; ownership of firms 129; preference for female labour 125; role in spread of transnational capital 118; size 177; technological transfer 7; telecommunications, telecommunications equipment production 229, unions 130–31; trade benefits 142; vicissitudes of world economic environment 142; wages 131–5, 177; working conditions 123
Free Trade Zones Act 1971, 6, 119
Freedom of association 45
Fringe benefits 70

Gang of Four countries 322
General Agreement on Tariffs and Trade (GATT), 142; export subsidies and contravention of rules 323; late industrialization 294; talks on future 258; Uruguay Round of negotiations 294
General System of Preferences (GSP) 70; industrialisation in developing countries 294; privileges 10; relocation of industries from East Asian NICs 129; withdrawal of privileges from East Asian NICs 286

Heavy industrialisation 28–33; annual public sector investment 29, 30; cost of production and management 38; international competition 29; low capacity utilisation of plants 32; NEP targets 276; protection 29; public foreign borrowing 29; seen as answer to auto sector's problems 276; strategy associated with Dr Mahathir Mohamad 275; *see also* Proton car project
Heavy Industries Corporation of Malaysia (HICOM) 29, 272; equity in Proton 272, 282; plans for agency to spearhead move up technological ladder 302; *see also* Proton car project
Hong Kong: absence of agricultural sector 290; cheap food and agricultural produce 290; education levels 293; influx of refugee capital from China 290; logistics centre for garment industry 239; strategic location 292
Human Resource Development strategy 72
Human-resource-oriented enterprises (HRE) 1

In-house unions 130; in Japanese firms 131; *see also* 'Quality of Company Life' Committees
In-the-job retraining 69
Income distribution 24
Income irregularity 90
Income security 51
Industrial Coordination Act (ICA) 1975, 77, 202, 331
Industrial Development; dominated by foreign investment 330; issues 98–99
Industrial dualism 43
Industrial estates 6; economic linkages with rural industries 177–8; economic profitability 178–9; failure 6; industrial estate programme 6; linkages 179–80, employment 179–80, household income 179, output value 179; phases in development 6; sectoral linkages 180–81, indirect employment effect 187; sectoral profile 178–9, rural industrial estates (RIEs) 178, semi-urban industrial estates (SIEs) 178, urban industrial estates (UIEs) 178; sourcing of raw materials 181; spatial distribution 6
Industrial incentives 322–3; link with export targets 323; strong bias against exports 323
Industrial Master Plan 42, 99, 206, 317; abandonment of industrial dispersal policy 6; assumptions on which industrial development plan can be based 320; critique of manufacturing sector 10; development strategy for electronics industry 213, 219, 318;

346

INDEX

dominance of foreign controlled firms in manufacturing sector 319; emphasis in line with East Asian industrial policy 321; export targeting 323; foreign investment 318–19; influence and publicity 321; key sector-specific 213; 'Look East', 321; Malaysia a relative latecomer to industrialisation 317; narrow base of manufacturing sector 317; policy alternatives 321; problems 319–20; rate of protection 323; response to dualism in manufacturing sector 320; signal of government's resolve to address structural weaknesses hampering broad-based industrialisation 213; state coordination 320; targets 212

Industrial policy 8, 297; detailed analysis a prerequisite to formulation 329; discrimination against non-indigenous ethnic communities 299; industrial dualism 331; inefficient compared to that of South Korea 314, 331; links with political structures 331; NEP objectives overriding strategy 331; obsession with inter-ethnic redistribution of wealth 297, 331; priority to domestic-led manufacturing growth 298; 'rational bureaucratic' basis of industrial policy 333

Industrial Policy Unit (IPU) 333
Industrial Relations Act 1967 130
Industrial relocation 60; drift 'southwards' 60
Industrial work environment: problems 12
Industrialisation: association with economic progress and development 1; comprador element in ownership 331; dependence on foreign investment 298; domestic-led industrialisation 298, 299; EOI strategy 211; export-oriented industrial growth 2, 25, 36, 316, 317, East Asian investments 298, effects 26–8, 'footloose' 36, reinforcement and diversification of transnational capital's hegemony 298; export-oriented production 3; heavy industries 2, 26; import-substituing industrialisation (ISI) 2, 18–25, 36, 289, 298, 316, 317, poor linkage to rest of economy 289, problems 21–2; in colonial Malaya 1, 18, 289, 316; phases 18, 316–17; pluralism 320; protection 19–20, 22, nominal rates of protection 20; reappraisal of direction of EOI 211; role of domestic capital in industrialisation process 13; role of state in East Asian NICs 286; see also heavy industrialisation, late industrialisation, rural industrialisation

Industrialisation strategies: 'second-tier NICs' reliant on inputs of foreign capital 147

Input-competing sector 323–5; 'cross-subsidisation' 323; current incentive system strongly biased against exports 323; economies of scale 324; EPconEP (effective protection conditional on export performance 234; export subsidy 323, and GATT 323; export targeting 323; ISI world competitive 325; potential for import-substitution 325; reduction of effective protection 323; state intervention 325

Insecure states 68
Insider allies 111
International competition 65
International competitiveness 3
International division of labour 25
International environment 11; and late industrialisation 299
International Monetary Fund: Special Drawing Rights 34
International Textiles and Clothing Bureau (ITCB) 249
Internationalisation of industrial production 119
Investment Coordination Act 34
Investment Incentives Act 1968 19, 24, 41, 119, 202
Investment Promotion Act 1986 77

Jabatan Telekom Malaysia (JTM) 224
Johore: expansion of employment 60; development strategy 60; economic twinning with Singapore 60; next industrial growth centre 60
Just-in-time (JIT) production: in consumer electronics production 218;

347

incorporation of JIT techniques and increase in technical staff 132; integrated tail-end production in electronics components firms 136; systems 7, 16, 125–6, 138–9

Kedah Development Authority (KEDA) 187, 188

Labour: absorption in manufacturing 54–65; contracting 4; control methods 132; costs 71; laws 4, 65; mobility 69; policy 4; regulations 49; rights, violation 10; shedding 4; shortage 57; turnover 69
Labour flexibility 3, 7, 44, 72; external 65; flexibilisation process 43; internal 69; international labour market flexibility 4, 69; Malaysian manufacturing sector 40, 54
Labour force: rural 8
Labour market 40, 41; dualism 49; fragmentation 49; policy 44
Labour (market) adjustment 48; external (mid-career), 48; inter-generational 48; internal 48; redeployment 48
Labour security 4; protection 45
Labour Utilisation Relief 1971 41
Late industrialisation: cultural factor 295, 296; economic conditions in the post-war period 294; ethnicity factor 295; historical specificity and prospects 300; history 289–90; inter-ethnic wealth redistribution in Malaysia 296; international conditions 294, 271; internationalisation of manufacturing 294; natural resources endowment factor 291–3; neo-pluralist approach 296; strategic significance 290–91
Leakages 182
Licensed Manufacturing Warehouses (LMWs), 6, 119, 177; material purchases 177; size 177; wages 177
Linkage approach 164
Linkages: backward 118; chemical industry 152; electronics and electrical industry 152–3, 319; food and beverages industry 151; FTZ firms and domestic economy 139; industry and size and formation of linkages with local economy 160;
limited capacity of industry to generate linkages 151; locally owned and controlled company and national economy 159; main mineral and metal industries 154; marketing policies and practices 159–160; strengthening of manufacturing linkages 298; through raw material or component inputs in manufacturing industry 157; with national economy via outputs in manufacturing industry 157–8
Locally controlled firms: export propensity 91, 94; import propensity 94, 95; outflow of investment income 95, 96; reinvestment as a proportion of profit 96; tax revenue contribution 96, 97
Locational approach 163–4
Look East policy 9, 302; context of formulation 303

Mahathir Mohamad 9, 28; and heavy industries strategy 275; and Proton Saga 276
Malacca 60; FTZ development 7, 119
Malaya: contribution of foreign exchange to sterling area 290; counter-insurgency 290
Malaysia: agrarian reform 291; attractive place for DFI 98; bureaucracy not independent of comprador bourgeoisie 296; constraints to access to land 291; economy at Independence 18; export platform for transnationals 299; disadvantage compared to Asian NICs 217; domestic market 24; economic growth and industrialisation record 287, 297; education distribution 292; education levels 293; effect of policy adjustments of industrial countries 98; human resources 292; impact on economy of external changes 98; income distribution 24; industrial strategy 72; infrastructural facilities and services 114; labour supply 72; limited skill formation 293; loss of competitiveness 292; national bourgeoisie 296; national monetary policy 293; natural resource endowments 292; natural resource endowments and agricultural exports

INDEX

and imperative to industrialise 299; offshore investment location 298; peasant demonstrations 291; peasant economy 291; politics and policy-making dominated by ethnic mobilisation and concerns 296; population 292; private sector investment 98; promotion of industrialisation under national auspices 330; quasi-rents 292; recession and recovery 294; rice production 291; transformation of economy 210

Malaysia Automotive Component Parts Manufacturers Association (MACPMA) 274; pressure on Proton 279

Malaysia Inc. 42

Malaysia Industrial Development Authority (MIDA) 115–16, 119; applications received for establishment of textiles and apparel activities 234; feasibility study for made-in-Malaysia car 276; negotiations with Daihatusu Motors 276

Malaysia Manufacturing Future Survey 116

Malaysian Industrial Policy Study (MIPS) 20; criticism 321; effective protection 323; estimate of rate of profit in Malaysian manufacturing 23; export subsidies 323; free market model 321; increasing direct taxation 325; looked West 321; primary thrust 323; response to dualism in manufacturing sector 320

Malaysian Institute of Microelectronic Systems (MIMOS) 208, 231

Malaysian Textile Manufacturers Association (MTMA) 260

Manufacturing Labour Feasibility Survey (MLFS) 1988, 40, 55, 56, 70, 73

Manufacturing sector 37; as foreign exchange earner 15; contribution to economy 11, 37, 148, 288; consumption goods 149, 150; dependence of Malaysian manufacturers on finished and unfinished inputs from abroad 149; dependence on DFI 210; dependency on inputs of production equipment 155–6; domestic investment 77; dominance of electronics 211; domination by transnationals 298; dualism 38, 320; efforts at diversification of Malaysian industrial base 211; elements 148; employment 14, 15, 17, 41; EOI strategy 211; exports 15, 16, 41, 210, 288, growth rate 15, high import content of 15; foreign equity participation 81–3; foreign ownership 147; growth expansion 149, 286; growth in employment 24; growth rate of manufacturing output 14–15; in colonial Malaya 17–18, 297; investment goods 149, 150; local content in production equipment 156–7; net output 14, 19, 36, 41, 151; pattern of dependency and independence 151–4; recovery after recession 328; size and pattern of ownership 151; structure and composition 11; types of product and process technology 148; underdevelopment of 17

Market access: FTZ 4; TNC 113

Market liberalisation 42, 43

Market uncertainty 64

Materials Requirement Planning (MRP) 125–6

Mid-Term Review of the Fifth Malaysia Plan 32

Migration 8

Mineral and metal industries 153–4; forward and backward linkages 154

Ministry of International Trade and Industry (Japanese) 10

Ministry of International Trade and Industry (MITI) 116, 383

Ministry of Trade and Industry 202, 203, 204, 205, 207

Mitsubishi 272

Mitsubishi Corporation (MC) 272

Mitsubishi Motor Corporation (MMC) 272

Muda Agricultural Development Authority (MADA) 187, 188

Multi-Fibre Arrangement (MFA) 9, 122, 246; developing countries' textile and clothing trade balance 251; evaluation of costs and benefits to developing countries 250

INDEX

National Union of Rubber Products Workers 130
Neo-classical counter-revolution 320
New Economic Policy (NEP) 2, 11, 25, 42, 118; auto industry 275; conformity of manufacturing sector to requirements 158; debate on success of implementation; employment pattern in national car project 278; equity restructuring requirement 108; heavy industry route to achieve target 272; industrial growth dependent on objectives 41; labour market in context of 41; MVAC efforts 275; objectives 2, 25; objectives overriding strategy in industrial policy 331; ownership restructuring policy and money politics 332–3; policy instruments to achieve objectives 331; purpose of government policy initiatives and public sector expansion conditions in industry 320; regulations 83
NIC status 10; Malaysia touted as likely new candidate 286; Prime Minister's instruction to stop reference to Malaysia as a NIC or potential NIC 286
Non-farm activities (NFA), 8, 167: diversification 170; food manufacturing sector 170; government assistance 171; inequality of non-farm income distribution 168; institutional entrepreneurs 169; labour force 169; origins of rural entrepreneurs 170; performance of entrepreneurs 170; rural NPA Bumiputra entrepreneurs 169; rural poverty 167–8
Non-farm sector 167
Non-financial public enterprises (NFPE) 331
Non-wage labour costs 57

OECD countries 157, 245, 246, 250, 253, 254
Outline Perspective Plan (OPP) 11
Ownership of firms: association with control or decision-making 147; tendency towards greater foreign capital investment in capital goods sector 158

Penang, FTZ development 7, 119
Person-to-machine ratio 174
Perusahaan Otomobil Nasional Sendirian Bhd (Proton) 272
Perwaja Steel plant 32
Pioneer Industries Ordinance 41
Plantation rubber agriculture 18
Plaza II international currency realignment agreement 10
Plaza Accord 1985 210
Policy initiatives 98
Policy options 12, 322–30
Post-election riots, May 1969 24
Poverty 45
Price 45
Price distortion 303, 304–5
Price support systems 45
Primary commodities 18, 288, 291
Private expenditure 45
Privatisation 42
Probation 68
Profit-sharing pay systems 71
Promotion of Investments Act 1986, 34, 331
Protection: anti-export bias protection given to domestic market 320
Proton car project 9, 32; change in management 282; cheap transfer prices to EON 281; consolidation of Japanese management 282; contract 277; discussion 277; economic costs 273; employment pattern and NEP objectives 278; exemption from import tariff 278; export 279, destinations 280, price subsidy 280, profitability of sales 281; export sales 279, Mitsubishi's reluctance 279–80, plans, to US 280, to China 280, to UK 280–81; feasibility study 276; funding 272; government assistance 284; government projection 177; in the black 283; listing on KLSE 283; local content 277, 279; losses 282; Mitsubishi's view of project 276–7; negotiations with Daihatsu Motors 276; perception of Mitsubishi as the best partner for project 276; production of Saga 272; Proton Saga Iswara 284, protection 284–5; recession and car sales 277–8; strains between Mitsubishi and Proton 284; strategy for reaching NEP objectives 281; talks between Dr. Mahathir

INDEX

Mohamad and Mitsubishi 276; *see also* Auto industry
Public expenditure 45

'Quality of Company Life' Committees 131

Raja Mohar Committee 24
Rationalisation (productivity-raising) 51; and relocation of end-of-line processes 138; of auto industry 278; of labour process in semiconductor firms 127
Real exchange rate 30; fall in the wake of economic crisis 34
Realignment of currencies 10, 226, 293; and auto industry 278
Recession 33, 42, 294; effect on workforce 135; reduction of workforce 134
Regulatory framework 72
'Rent-seeking' in Malaysia 21
Rentier politics 331
Research and Development (R&D): activities retained with parent firm 319; in large MNCs 191, 194; need for centralised agency 142
Resource-based industries 26, 36, 327; Boston Consulting Group 328; conditional export targets 328; integration of Malaysia into world economy 330; Malaysian tyre industry 328; obstacles to 36; rubber products industry 329
Resource endowment factor 291; early development theories 291; inversion 292
Retrenchment of workers following equity restructuring 135
Rigidities 65
Ringgit, depreciation of 3, 10
Rural Development Authorities (RDAs) 169
Rural development strategies 8
Rural industrialisation 8, 163–5; agricultural development 187; agricultural processing industry 187, conditions necessary 165; approaches 163–5, linkage approach 164, locational approach 163–4; development strategy 8; employment generation 166; group farming solutions 186; growth 166; income generation 166; indirect employment effect 181; infrastructural provision 186; linkages: capital equipment expenditure 164, domestic 177, economic 175–8, employment 179–80, household income 179, output value 179, rural 164, 166, sectoral 180–81; migration 174, 175; outmigration of local resources 186; restructuring of Malaysian society 181–2, direct employment generation 182, indirect employment effects 182, ownership 182; rural urbanisation 174–5; spatial strategy 172–5, indirect location 173–4, Western Industrial Corridor 74; target group 166; villagisation 186; worker welfare levels 166; workforce 177

Selangor, FTZ development 7, 119
Semiconductor and telecommunications firms 123; changes in product and production technology 123; incorporation of more efficient production techniques 125; miniaturisation process 125; precision in manufacture 125; wages 132; *see also* semiconductor industry, electronics industry
Semiconductor industry: automation 211; cyclical market 211; dynamic random access memories (DRAMs) 217; features 213; footloose 214; IC design services 218; introduction of JIT inventory methods 215; Japanese metalworking firms in lead frame supply 215; lead frames 215; local firms in area of supply direct direct materials 215; Malaysia as a possible site for wafer fabrication 217–18; non-standard (i.e. application specific) ICs (ASICs) 218–19; printed circuit board (PCB) design 219; supporting industries 216–17; wafer fabrication 216, demands on infrastructure 216, specialised supporting industries 216; *see also* electronics industry, semiconductor and telecommunications firms
Singapore 60; absence of agricultural sector 291; cheap food imports 290–91; natural resource endowment

351

292; strategic location 292
Small industries 5
Small-scale establishments, and manufacturing employment 63
Social adjustment 43, 44, 45
Social distortion 45
Social efficiency 22; of industries 22–3
Social structure of accomodation 311
South Korea: acquisition and development of technology 310; agrarian reforms 290; attribution of success 311–12; bureaucracy 312; chaebols 309; control of industrial ownership pattern 308; contrasts with Malaysia 312–13; economic aid 290; Economic Planning Board 312; economic policy 303; education policy 293; export processing zones 306; exchange rate policy 307; foreign exchange sources 314; geo-political situation 313, 314; high rate of profit in manufacturing 310; import policy 306; industrial policy 306; industrialisation under Japanese colony 290; ISI policy 306; integration of import controls with exports 307; labour force 307; lack of entrenched class interests 312; land reform 313–14; manufacturing sector 309; McKinnon-Shaw's 'financial deepening' theory 308; myth about South Korean industrial development 310; natural resources endowment 292; official aid inflows 307, 312, 314; policy of export targeting 306–7; promotion of education 309; R&D 310; reforms 306; role of DFI 308–9; selective intervention in promoting industry 309; state confiscation of private assets 308; state control of commercial banking sector 308; state coordination of technology bargaining 310; state intervention in economic policy 303; state intervention in financial market 308, World Bank recognition 308; state-sponsored drive for exports 306, 307; strategically important for post-war US confrontation with communist forces in Korea and China 290; structures for growth and industrialisation 290; suppression of trade unionism 309
Stabilisation 45
Standards and Industrial Research Institute of Malaysia (SIRIM) 208
State: conditions for emergence of role for developmentalist state 287; in late industrialisation of East Asian NICs 286, 297, 299
State intervention: belief that intervention has favoured industrialisation under foreign transnational auspices 297; creation of correct market signals by changing market 330; extensive in East Asian NIC economies 322; preoccupation with inter-ethnic redistribution of wealth in Malaysia 299; purpose 297; rentier politics and ethnically preoccupied bureaucracy determined form in Malaysia 331; World Bank's view on relationship between state interventionism and LDC growth 303, criticism of World Bank view 303, 306
Structural adjustment 2, 10, 11
Structural Adjustment Programmes of the World Bank and the International Monetary Fund 303
Supply-side 43, 44, 45
Syarikat Telekom Malaysia (STM) 224

Taiwan: agrarian reform 290; economic aid from US 290; education 293; industrialisation under Japanese colonial rule 290; natural resource endowment 292; stimulus for growth of industrialisation 290; strategic importance for post-war US confrontation with communist forces 290
Tariff Advisory Board 19, 41
Tax concessions 2
Taylorist management 50
Technological gap 191
Technology control 7
Technology pricing 8
Technology transfer 8; agreements 8; bargaining position of LDC firms 192–3; benefit to local ancillary firms 138; changing bases of Malaysia's comparative advantage 207–8; Committee to Formulate a Plan of Action for Industrial Technological

Development 207; comprehensive rationalisation programme 208; contractual agreements between private firms 194; definition 190; DFI and context and nature of technological transfer 195; existing policy on remuneration 204–6, considerations 204, lump-sum payment 204–5, running royalty payments 205–6; government's role 208–9; imperfect market conditions 191–2; international technology transfer to Malaysia 195–201, by industry groupings 198, 199, pattern to manufacturing sector 195, royalties 199, sources 195, 197; limited choices 190, 191; limited to production technology 139; manpower training 200–201; methods 194, data 194, 196, 199; modernisation programme 208; need for more aggressive approaches to raising technological level of production 206; no pressure in first phase of Malaysian industrialisation 24; objectives of studies 207; policy guidelines 202–4; priorities in developing technological base and upgrading science and technology levels 208–9; problems 8; product adaptation 193; profit maximisation 319; R&D 194, 201, need for universities and R&D institutions to have linkages with MNCs 201; royalty payments 204–6, overview of existing policy framework 201–2; technical aid programmes 194; terms and conditions 193; transfer pricing mechanism 192; upgrading domestic industrial technology 208

Technology Transfer Unit (TTU) 202, 205, 206

Textile and garment industry 9; accident rate 122; additional quota in quota-restricted markets sought by foreigners 238; capital-intensive 122; changes in market characteristics 251–4; changing clothing demand and implications for investment strategy 253; circumscribed unions 123; clothing technologies 255–7; current status 235–6; data on ventures 234; dependence on imports of primary textiles 239–40; development of textile technologies 254–5; diversification into non-restricted categories 250–1; effect of MFA on Malaysian industry 250; enhancing local design capabilities 260; export market concentration 244–5, challenge of Eastern Europe 245, vulnerability to protectionism 244; female employment 35; financing necessary investments 259; global quota system 249, 251; growth rate 234; import-leakage propensity 177; international investment activities 261; international marketing skills 260; international trade 245, exports into OECD 245, 247, 248; linkages between primary textile sector and garment sector 253–4; location of production 257; low productivity levels 240–4; machinery 241, 243; market characteristic changes and location 253; primary textile sector 237; process technology 239; proposed liberation of trade 249; quick response 253, 258; quota restrictions 122, 247; regulation of trade 246; relative importance to economy 236–7; relocation 122; service-orientation 253; skilled personnel 241, 255, 258, 259–60; strategy for future 258–61; textile restructuring loan 259; turnaround time 253, 258; underdevelopment of primary textile sector 239–40; upgrading primary textile sector 258–9, specialised fabrics 259; upgrading product range 258; weaknesses 239, limited design capability 239, limited marketing capability 239; weighted towards downstream activities 237; working conditions and environment 122; *see also* textile firms

Textile firms: air-jet looms 124; automation 124; capital-intensive 124; knitting 124; wages 132; weaving 124

Textile Workers' Union (TWU) 130

Tin-mining 18

Trade Union Ordinance of 1959 130

Trade Unions: absence in early phase of FTZs 130; efficacy 131; female membership 35; gradually allowed in several FTZ industries 130; little room for manoeuvre 130; opposition by American firms 130, 131; *see also* in-house unions and 'Quality Of Company Life' Committees

Training 52–3; 'in-plant' training 53; job structure 53; job training 53; need for skilled labour training programmes 142; off-the-job training 69; specialised training within firms 136–7; vocational (or craft) training 53

Transnational capital 11

Transnational Corporations (TNCs), 5; allowable price at which equity can be divested 109; Bumiputra equity participation 5, 109; decision-making 5, investment decisions 111, marketing channels and policies 112–13, raw materials, components and intermediate inputs 113, technology sourcing 112; differences in behaviour of domestic market-oriented and export-oriented TNCs 108; domestic linkages 5; domestic-oriented TNCs 5; effective contribution towards industrial development 99; employment creation 107; equity restructuring of domestic-market-oriented firms 108; export-oriented firms 5; indigenisation of management 109; inter-industry linkages 109; management 5; management control 109; NEP ownership requirements 5; non-ability to reinvest 114; perception and assessment of Malaysian investment climate 114–15; profitability and performance 113–14; propensity to import raw materials 91

Unemployment during economic crisis 34

United Nations Industrial Development Organization (UNIDO), 6, 321; sponsored studies for IMP 10

Upstream and downstream integration 110

Wage costs 57
Wage flexibility 51
Wages: FTZ firms 131–3; levels in mid-1980s 10; manufacturing sector 3, 27; minimum wage protection machinery 45; minimum wages 46; public sector wages 47–8; reason for casualisation of labour 66

West Coast manufacturing corridor 6; *see also* rural industrialisation

Worker security 50, 72

Workforce: availability 123; blue-collar workers 4, 71; feminisation 4, 69–70; increase in technical personnel following restructuring of production process 139; legislative and administrative protection 66; management 4, *see also* electronics industry and labour force; minimal protection 66; multiskilling 139; retraining 139; stability 57; white-collar workers 4, 71

World Development Report 303